MW00652255

HEAD OF THE MOSSAD

SHABTAI SHAVIT

HEAD OF THE
MOSSAD

In Pursuit of a Safe and Secure Israel

University of Notre Dame Press
Notre Dame, Indiana

University of Notre Dame Press
Notre Dame, Indiana 46556
undpress.nd.edu

Published in the United States of America
Printed in Canada

Library of Congress Cataloging-in-Publication Data

Names: Shavit, Shabtai, 1939- author. | Ṭal, Rami, editor. | Rodal-Spieler,
Ariel, translator.
Title: Head of the Mossad : in pursuit of a safe and secure Israel / Shabtai
Shavit ; [edited by Rami Tal ; translated by Ariel Rodal-Spieler].
Other titles: Rosh ha-Mosad. English
Description: Notre Dame, Indiana : University of Notre Dame Press, [2020] |
Includes bibliographical references and index.
Identifiers: LCCN 2020018392 (print) | LCCN 2020018393 (ebook) |
ISBN 9780268108335 (hardback) | ISBN 9780268108366 (adobe pdf) |
ISBN 9780268108359 (epub)
Subjects: LCSH: Shavit, Shabtai, 1939– | Israel. Mosad le-modiʻin
ve-tafḳidim meyuḥadim. | Intelligence service—Israel. | National
security—Israel. | Intelligence officers—Israel—Biography.
Classification: LCC UB251.I78 S5313 2020 (print) | LCC UB251.I78
(ebook) | DDC 327.1256940092 [B]—dc23
LC record available at https://lccn.loc.gov/2020018392
LC ebook record available at https://lccn.loc.gov/2020018393

CONTENTS

ACKNOWLEDGMENTS

I began learning Arabic in kindergarten, when the Arabs of Balad-a-Sheikh, which later became Tel Hanan, would come to pick olives from the trees in the yard of our cabin in Nesher every year during the harvest season. Perhaps this is the reason that in tenth grade I chose to specialize in Middle Eastern studies and was a graduate of the first class of this track in Israel. When I started university following my military service, it was only natural for me to study Arabic language and literature and Middle Eastern history. From there to the Mossad the road was short. The path to becoming the director of the Mossad was much longer.

Preceded by six Mossad heads—Reuven Shiloah, Isser Harel, Meir Amit, Zvi Zamir, Yitzhak ("Haka") Hofi, and Nahum Admoni—I was the first Mossad director that was not a member of the 1948 generation. I never knew Reuven Shiloah. I met Isser Harel only once I had already become director of the Mossad; and I worked with the other four directors quite closely throughout my years in the Mossad. They were role models and mentors to me, and I am grateful to them for everything they taught me. I am especially grateful to Nahum Admoni, to whom I owe, to a great extent, my appointment to the position.

Among the events that took place during my tenure as head of the Mossad (1989–96) were the collapse of the Soviet Union and the end of the Cold War era; the First Gulf War and Prime Minister Yitzhak Shamir's navigation of the state and the Israel Defense Forces through it; the peace agreement with Jordan, in which the Mossad played a central role; and the assassination of Prime Minister Yitzhak Rabin.

I had the great privilege of working for the Mossad for thirty-two years, seven of them as director. The Mossad has always been a sanctuary within the beleaguered State of Israel, from the War of Independence until today. It would be impossible to cover all of the organization's achievements, but there is no doubt that every one was made possible by the human factor—combatants, operations people, intelligence analysts, operations supporters, technologists, and administrative personnel. This is another opportunity for me to thank all of these people from the bottom of my heart, and to say that it was a pleasure to command people like them and that my achievements are their achievements.

There are several more people whom I would like to thank. Itzik Barzilai's experience and deep knowledge of Iran has been of great help to me. Shmuel Bar's expertise in intelligence analysis and understanding of the Middle East, global powers, and radical terrorism are no less than phenomenal. Shlomo Doron was my right-hand man in everything related to our struggle against the nonconventional aspirations of our enemies and the nuclearization of the Middle East. Dr. Hagai Tsoref, the director of the State Documents and Commemoration Department of the Israel State Archives, was an enormous help to me on two issues—one was the Yom Kippur War, and the other was the Palestinian refugee problem and the United Nations Relief and Works Agency (UNRWA).

Rami Tal, who edited the book, was for me much more than an editor. The man is bursting with knowledge. My conversations with him, which sometimes turned into arguments, gave me a lot of food for thought throughout the writing of the book. The production team, especially Kuti Tepper, Mimi Baram, Keren Sitbon-Hemo, and Shlomit Partok, brought forth a fine and meticulous product. Dana Dagan, who for years worked as my assistant in my company

("Athena," part of the Mer Group), typed up the manuscript with boundless dedication and speed. Dov Eichenwald, editor in chief and CEO of Yedioth Books, went out of his way to make sure this book was published. And Ariel Rodal-Spieler translated this book with professionalism and dedication.

Prof. Uriel Reichman, president and founder of the Interdisciplinary Center (IDC) Herzliya, has provided me with an academic home that combines academic expertise with public and national commitment. My collaborative activities with Prof. Boaz Ganor, dean of the Lauder School of Government, Diplomacy and Strategy and executive director of the Institute for Counter-Terrorism (ICT) at the IDC Herzliya, within the framework of the institute yielded fruits that are expressed in the pages of this book. And a special thanks is due to Stevie Weinberg, the ICT's deputy executive director, who helped me, in his efficient manner, with anything I needed throughout my writing.

Finally, I thank my loved ones, my family, my wife Yael, and my children and grandchildren, who have stood by me, supported me, and helped me understand the true meaning of life.

Shabtai Shavit

INTRODUCTION

The ceremony marking the change of command of the Mossad, during which I received my letter of appointment, took place on April 19, 1989, at the Prime Minister's Office in Jerusalem. Among those present were Prime Minister Yitzhak Shamir, who had chosen me to serve as director of the Mossad; minister of defense and former prime minister Yitzhak Rabin; Israel Defense Forces (IDF) chief of staff Dan Shomron; former Mossad directors; the Mossad Division Heads' Forum (Rasha); the Heads of Services Committee (Varash); the military secretary to the prime minister; the prime minister's veteran stenographer Mitka Yaffe; the outgoing Mossad director Nahum Admoni and his family; and my own family, with the exception of my youngest son, who was off skiing in Switzerland.

The ceremony was modest and conducted with an air of understatement characteristic of Prime Minister Shamir. The prime minister read out Nahum's letter marking the end of his tenure and thanked him briefly for his service and for his long-standing contribution to Israel's national security. Nahum delivered some parting words. The prime minister read out my letter of appointment and wished me good luck in the new position. I then gave my prepared remarks, to which I had given a great deal of thought.

I began by mentioning my twenty-five years of service in the Mossad, which I believed had trained me for the esteemed role that I was taking on. Even so, I accepted the role with apprehension, veneration, and trepidation. I thanked the prime minister for choosing me, and Nahum for warmly recommending me for the job. I thanked my family and especially my wife, who at the beginning of my career had partaken in covert activities along with me. I emphasized the great sacrifice required of the family members of Mossad operatives.

I praised the Rasha forum, which constitutes the management of the Mossad. These are people who have accumulated hundreds of years of experience among them, and because covert affairs are learned in the field rather than in academia, their combined experience is priceless. They are people who are tough, who tend to say little and keep their feelings hidden. I also commended the Varash forum, stressing that the cooperation among Military Intelligence, the Shin Bet, and the Mossad, through which each body contributes its unique abilities, creates a force multiplier that brings about results that no one body could produce alone. Finally, I expressed my support and best wishes to the Mossad's employees and operatives scattered across the globe, including in enemy countries, whose actions guarantee the security of the people and the State of Israel.

I thought that the occasion of my acceptance of the position, in the presence of the prime minister and others, merited the expression of my thoughts, and my remarks lasted a few minutes. I remember that while I was speaking the prime minister leaned over to the person standing next to him and whispered, "I never knew that Shabtai could speak!" I had met with Prime Minister Shamir several times before that ceremony, in various meetings and contexts, but I had never said, whether in response to a question or at my own initiative, more than the minimum required to express my opinion on the issue at hand. I had always felt that the prime minister's time was a precious commodity and that his status required reverence both in speech and in behavior. Thus to him I appeared to be "the silent type"—which incidentally, could have described him as well—and, as the saying goes, I have never regretted the things I did not say.

The ceremony ended with a toast and a tasting of Jerusalem's famous *burekas* (savory stuffed pastries) served in the prime minister's bureau, and then everyone went on their way. I drove from Jerusalem toward the coastal plain, and, with a feeling of awe, I entered the office of the director of the Mossad and took my seat on the chair that I had gazed upon for so many years.

The late 1980s and early 1990s, during which I served as director of the Mossad, were a historic crossroads in the world order. The geopolitical and geostrategic transformations that took place during this period were of a magnitude and weight the likes of which had not been seen since the end of World War II. During these years, the State of Israel witnessed the following milestones:

- In December 1987, the First Intifada (a Palestinian uprising against the Israeli occupation) broke out and the Hamas organization was established, adding a religious aspect to political terrorism.
- In November 1988, the Palestinian National Council (PNC) declared Palestinian independence in Algiers, thereby implying its acceptance of the principle of the division of the land into two states.
- In December 1988, the UN General Assembly acknowledged the declaration of the establishment of a Palestinian state, and the Palestine Liberation Organization (PLO) received UN observer status.
- In November 1989, the fall of the Berlin Wall symbolized the end of the Cold War and the collapse of the Soviet Union. From that point and throughout the 1990s, approximately one million Jews immigrated to Israel from the Soviet Union, a development that, in my humble opinion, was the best thing to happen to the State of Israel since its independence in 1948.

- In June 1992, Yitzhak Rabin was elected prime minister. Following fifteen years of Likud rule, the Labor Party returned to power, though it was not to last for long.
- In September 1993, the Oslo Accords between Israel and the PLO were signed in Washington, D.C., and were approved by the Knesset (the Israeli parliament).
- In July 1994, the exiled Palestinian leadership in Tunis, headed by Yasser Arafat, returned to the West Bank and the Gaza Strip and established the Palestinian Authority.
- In October 1994, a peace agreement was signed between Israel and Jordan, the second Arab state to make peace with Israel.
- In November 1995, Israeli prime minister Yitzhak Rabin was assassinated by a despicable evildoer.
- In May 1996, the Likud, headed by Benjamin Netanyahu, returned to power. In May 1999, the Labor Party, led by Ehud Barak, took back the reins, but only until February 2001, when Ariel Sharon brought rule back to the Right. As of this writing (2018) the Right has remained in power.

The Middle East also experienced dramatic changes during this period (the end of the 1980s and early 1990s). The Iran-Iraq War, which had lasted nearly a decade, came to an end with the Iraqis having the upper hand, though the war did not end with the Iranians' total surrender. Iraqi supremacy was achieved through the combination of chemical weapons and surface-to-surface rockets/missiles on the battlefield. The Iranians did not have a response to the chemical weapons used against them, or to the missiles and rockets that penetrated deep into Iran, including the capital, Tehran. Iran, under the rule of mullahs (educated Shiite Muslims who were trained in religious law), learned its lesson from the war and decided to build up comprehensive nonconventional strategic capabilities, including chemical, biological, and nuclear capabilities and the ability to launch strategic surface-to-surface missiles.

The First Gulf War, which broke out in 1991, was a formative event from both a regional and a global perspective. The following steps led up to it. First came the waiting period and intelligence preparations, during which the question was raised regarding whether Saddam Hussein, so soon after the conclusion of his war against Iran, would embark on another escapade. Then came the Iraqi invasion of Kuwait, followed by President George H. W. Bush's building of an impressive and broad coalition that included Saudi Arabia, Egypt, and Syria. The fact that these countries joined the coalition against Iraq, which was supported by Jordan and the Palestinians, was the last nail in the coffin of the notion of pan-Arabism in the history of the Middle East. Another step was the Israeli-American dialogue on the issue of Israel's participation in the war. President Bush urged Prime Minister Shamir not to intervene, and in exchange he promised that the US military would make taking out Iraq's surface-to-surface missile batteries a top priority. Shamir was under tremendous pressure from some of his cabinet ministers and from the IDF to take military action, but he refused, even though there were those who claimed that Saddam Hussein's apparent possession of surface-to-surface missiles armed with chemical warheads was another reason for the IDF to intervene.

Iraq launched thirty-nine surface-to-surface "Scud" missiles into Israeli territory. The US Army was unable to destroy even part of the Iraqi surface-to-surface missile system, but Prime Minister Shamir gritted his teeth and stuck to his position of nonintervention. Government ministers and IDF brass found it difficult to comprehend how Shamir, a former underground commander and an adherent of Ze'ev Jabotinsky's vision of the Iron Wall (outlined in 1923 in an essay arguing that peace between Jews and Arabs in Palestine would be achieved if and only if the Jews were strong enough to convince the Arabs that they could not vanquish them), a commander of a special operations unit in the Mossad and a man of the political Right, could refuse to involve the IDF in the war against Saddam Hussein.

At that time, only a few people knew that a week before the Iraqi invasion of Kuwait, a secret meeting had taken place between Prime Minister Shamir and King Hussein of Jordan, during which the two had shaken hands on an agreement that the Iraqi threat to Israel (with the exception of missiles) would be eliminated (more about this is written in a separate chapter). This pact helped Shamir to maintain his stubborn stance against Israeli intervention in the war.[1]

Turkey, after over a decade (the 1980s) of maintaining a lukewarm relationship with Israel, began to respond to its courting. Relations between the two countries, including between their security and intelligence apparatuses, rapidly improved and resulted in strategic cooperation and understandings.

The nature of terrorism during this period also changed beyond recognition. In the past, terrorism had been local, that is, nationalistic and secular, its perpetrator groups struggling to achieve self-determination, autonomy, or independence. The impact of this terrorism was usually minor and localized. The terrorism of today, manifested in Israel with the establishment of Hamas in 1987 and Islamic Jihad, is a religious Islamic terrorism whose extremism is increasing with time and whose reach has become global. It is imperialist terrorism in the sense that it expresses Allah's command to fight the infidels, by either converting them to Islam or annihilating them, and to establish a global Muslim caliphate. It is a terrorism that, according to the principles of its belief (mainly Shiite but also found among marginal Sunni groups) does not recognize coexistence with the other. Its war against the infidels is considered a holy war—jihad. The act of suicide in the war against the infidels is considered a religious commandment and grants the perpetrator the title of *shahid* (martyr). It is a terrorism in which the end sanctifies the means and in which the single attacker is able to target many more infidels. It is a terrorism with a global distribution of individuals and small groups of citizens, connected via the internet, and unlike military bodies it is not formed around territory, hierarchy, uniform, infrastructure, a chain of command, and so forth. The media impact made by global jihadi organizations is global, costs them nothing, and plays out in real time. The historical father of this type of terrorism is Sheikh Hassan al-Banna, who founded the Muslim Brotherhood movement in Egypt in the 1920s. The Muslim Brotherhood's violent activity since its establishment has been limited to Egypt itself, but its religious ideology of the rule of sharia (Islamic law) has fed most of the fundamentalist Islamic terrorist organizations that we know today. The bin Laden school of global jihad—al-Qaeda—first appeared on the radar of intelligence bodies in Israel and the West in the early nineties, and its outgrowths—ISIS and their ilk—developed toward the end of the United States and its allies' war in Iraq and the "Arab Spring."

ISIS took terrorism to an extreme that human history had not seen since the Hun invasion of the West. The organization displays a combination of nihilism and suicide bomber culture. Unlike al-Qaeda, ISIS has already begun working, with each territory that it conquers, toward the establishment of a global Islamic caliphate. Terrorist groups around the world (Boko Haram in Nigeria, the Houthis in Yemen, Wilayat Sina in Sinai, Al-Shabab in Somalia, and more) have announced their allegiance to the caliphate.

The domestic and regional events that characterized the late 1980s and early 1990s, during which I served as director of the Mossad, pale in comparison to the changes that took place on the global stage during this period. I am referring, of course, to the end of the Cold War and the collapse of the Soviet Union.

Although World War II ended with a crushing victory for the United States, its allies, and the Soviet Union over Nazi Germany and Japan, the ink on the surrender documents had not yet dried when the world had to accept a new world order. The main feature of this new order was the Cold War between the two superpowers, the United States and the Soviet Union, who for fifty-five years competed with each other over the expansion of their areas of influence in the world, beyond the borders that were determined at the end of World War II. Today, in retrospect, it can be argued that the world during the period of the Cold War (1945–90), with a few exceptions, was infinitely more stable than the world in which we live today. These exceptions were the fight for control of Czechoslovakia, won by the Soviets, and the struggle for influence in Greece, which concluded with an American victory, as well as the Berlin Crisis and the Korean War. The global stability that prevailed was the result of a geostrategic balance of power, which saw the confrontation between the two superpowers continuously teetering toward brinkmanship, and when they reached the point of Mutual Assured Destruction (MAD), the world, absurdly, became more stable. This point was reached at the beginning of the 1960s, following the Cuban Missile Crisis. The fear of the annihilation of humankind in a nuclear event was what brought about the global stability that lasted many years, until 1990. Because the leaders of the two superpowers were rational actors, they made sure to create a mechanism to be used in times of crisis, in the form of a direct telephone line between the Kremlin and the White House. I reference this fact in order to imply that the finger liable to press the Iranian nuclear button would be influenced, at least potentially, by considerations that are not rational but messianic. Moreover, no emergency hotline for the prevention of crises would be present in this case. In a world with the capability of MAD, the nations saw fit to align themselves with one of the two superpowers in accordance with their own interests and worldview. This added another layer of security to global stability in the shadow of the nuclear threat. Nations asserting themselves to be "nonaligned" constituted a third bloc. In this context, one must mention Pakistan and India, which developed nuclear weapons in the 1970s, and the rivalry between the two, which undermined stability, certainly in that region. China, which finally came out of hibernation during the Cold War period, must of course also be mentioned. But in spite of all this, it can be said that the influence of the nonaligned bloc on the global order was marginal.

The Soviet Union collapsed and the United States became the only superpower from 1991 to 2000. However, the United States failed to take advantage of this decade during which it was, for all intents and purposes, "the only sheriff in town" to establish a new world order, with stability based on shared interests and the desire of the world's citizens to live in a better place (as portrayed in Francis Fukuyama's "The End of History"). Instead, the United States' contribution to the world in the last decade of the twentieth century accelerated the transition from a bipolar world to a multipolar world whose main feature at the time of this writing (2018) is instability, the likes of which the world has not seen since World War II.

The Mossad's Essential Elements of Information (EEI), as well as those of other agencies in the post–Cold War era, focused on a series of issues, the principal of these being the proliferation of nonconventional weapons and local, regional, and global terrorism, with an emphasis on religious (jihadist) terrorism. The Mossad, by definition, is tasked with seeking out responses to the EEI everywhere in the world outside the borders of the State of Israel. The responses to these two issues have been found not only in the Middle East and western Europe, which were the Mossad's traditional arenas from its inception until the end of the Cold War, but also in eastern Europe and the former Soviet Union, Southeast Asia and the Far East, South America, and even Africa and Australia.

All of these changes required the Mossad to adapt accordingly with regard to human resources, budgets and means, and deployment and combat doctrine.

This book is intended to share the writer's insights, impressions, experiences, and thoughts of his time as director of the Mossad (1989–96) against the backdrop of the events described above, as well as other experiences. The book does not purport to present scientific research; rather, it conveys the author's personal opinions.

CHAPTER ONE

INTELLIGENCE

On Research and Intelligence Assessment

The Mossad Division Head's Forum (Rasha) is the equivalent of the IDF's General Staff. In addition to its weekly meetings for the purposes of reporting and decision-making, the Mossad director convenes Rasha at his discretion for nonroutine purposes. Not long after I took office in April 1989, I convened the group to bid farewell to those members who were retiring and to welcome the new members. I believe that some of the things that I said during that meeting in 1989 deserve to be repeated today.

The people who were present at that meeting reflected the history of the Mossad, its generational changes and its continuity. I was the first Mossad director who did not belong to the generation that had fought in the War of Independence, but during the meeting I made a point of emphasizing that despite the changes the Mossad had undergone since its establishment—in its missions, arenas of action, tools and capabilities, priorities, and scale—one thing that never changed and that must never change was what I called the

1

"human spirit." It was especially important for me to say this in light of the processes that were affecting Israeli society—the culture of materialism, the disintegration of values, and the dissipation of Zionism.

I thought it appropriate to use that event, as I began my term as director of the Mossad, to emphasize my "credo" regarding the preservation of secrecy in our organization. Even then, in 1989, this was a serious challenge in light of the fact that Israeli society was deeply entrenched in the era of modern communication, in which the principle of "the public's right to know" had become "the public's duty to know." But I told those present that we could not hold anyone responsible but ourselves and that in the interest of sanctifying and nurturing the value of leading by example we, as commanders and senior managers of the organization, had to take the lead in that responsibility.

Meir Amit, who had joined the Mossad in 1964, remodeled the director's office in a style that was functional, simple, and modest. When the Mossad moved to its current location, all of the furniture moved with it.

The Mossad director's desk and the chairs that sat around it served five Mossad chiefs for thirty-two years, until the end of my term. These table and chairs, around which countless decisions had been made, had become something of a symbol over the years, one that many among us did not wish to tinker with. The arrangement in which people sat around the table was also fixed. The deputy director's place was at the narrow edge of the desk, to the right of the director. The others sat opposite him. This seating arrangement was symbolic to a degree, conveying to those present that the director of the Mossad was the one making the decisions. The role of the deputy sitting at his side was only to advise and make recommendations. I take pains to describe the interior of the office in great detail to emphasize the fact that during the many hours I sat at the side of that table over two-and-a-half years, first as a vice-director and later as a deputy, I had a lot of time to think. Following each discussion with the Mossad director I wrote down my reflections in a small notebook. My thought was that the contents of this notebook would become part of my work plan should I one day be appointed director myself.

And indeed, upon entering office, I already had a blueprint for the next half decade, entitled "Effecting Change while Maintaining Continuity." I presented it during my first few days on the job, to the prime minister, to the Knesset Foreign Affairs and Defense Committee's Subcommittee on Intelligence and Secret Services, and to the Rasha Forum. For reasons that are clear, I cannot divulge the plan here, aside from some morsels that I believe do not constitute a violation of secrecy today.

At the end of the first quarter of 1989, I was aware that the next five years would bear witness to far-reaching changes, the beginnings of which could already be discerned. I judged that Iraq would become the most threatening force in the Middle East and would approach nuclear capability. I assessed that nonconventional warfare, including cyberwarfare and nuclear, chemical, and biological weapons and their means of delivery, would be central to both our intelligence gathering and our prevention efforts. I predicted the possibility of a renewed "eastern front," which, if realized, would become a major threat to the State of Israel. I anticipated that terrorist activity would become a central priority for us. I recognized that western Europe, our main arena of activity, would become more difficult and complicated to operate in because of our political situation and our eroding popularity in the court of public opinion, which would adversely affect western Europe's willingness to "tolerate" our independent activity on their territory. I foresaw the reduced cooperation with European intelligence agencies with regard to the terrorist organizations operating under the umbrella of the PLO. Even back then I saw that the computer would become a main target of attack on our part and that innovative technologies with composite materials would play an important role in the development of our future tools.

I argued that these changes, which would become the future challenges of the Mossad, would require us to make structural changes, divert efforts, and break new ground toward new goals, using innovative and sophisticated means. This would be quite a jolt to the organization, but it would be carried out gradually and would develop out of the sense of continuity that characterized the Mossad.

All of my predictions were correct, but I could not have foreseen the extent of their force and scope. In January 1994, I delivered a lecture at the National Defense College on the role of the Mossad in light of the changes taking place in the international and regional order. If in the past I had presented my predictions for the future, in this lecture I summed up the past. Specifically, what took place between 1989 and early 1994?

- The Soviet Union collapsed, and the Cold War that had begun in 1945 ended with a crushing victory for the United States and Western democracies.
- The bipolar world became unipolar and was on its way to becoming multipolar.
- This new world's multipolarity was not only military; it was also reflected in economic blocs:
  — NAFTA (North American Free Trade Agreement—the United States, Canada, and Mexico), a bloc of 360 million people with a GDP of $6 trillion
  — APEC (Asia-Pacific Economic Cooperation), the Pacific bloc
  — the EC (European Community), the Common Market, a bloc of 360 million people
- China slowly and surely rose to become a superpower that would skip over Russia and compete with the United States.
- The world experienced both a consolidation into various blocs and a fragmentation into ethnic and tribal units.
- The world became one of regional conflicts.
- The UN, which had succeeded in the enacting of sanctions, failed in the resolution of conflicts.
- The Gulf War accelerated some far-reaching changes:
  — A vast international coalition was created.

- — In this coalition, Arabs fought against other Arabs, thereby putting an end to the vision of pan-Arabism.
- — Only one global superpower took part in the Gulf War.
- — It was a war in which Western weapons had absolute superiority.
- — It was a war that proved that strategic depth was no match for strategic weapons.
- The fall of the Soviet Union and the Gulf War spurred the Middle East peace process. Over the course of 1993, there were three parallel Israeli diplomatic initiatives vis-à-vis two Arab states—Jordan and Syria—and the PLO (the Oslo process).
- The Iran-Iraq War that ended in 1988 and the First Gulf War in 1991 convinced Iran to enter the race toward nonconventional weapons, making the issue of proliferation and the danger of a nuclear Iran the central priority of our Essential Elements of Information (EEI), as well as those of other intelligence services.
- The phenomenon of Muslim fundamentalism, which expressed the Arab dream to return to the glory days of Islam, was on the rise.

In January 1991, following Military Intelligence's presentation of its annual intelligence assessment to the government, we were asked by the prime minister to address, in the Mossad's presentation, not only our assessment for the year but also our evaluation from a multi-year perspective. This was an unexpected assignment. MI's assessment was presented on a Friday, and our assessment was due to be presented the following Sunday. We had only the weekend to prepare. I made two decisions: I would put aside the assessment that had been put together by the research department, and I myself would present the product that we would prepare over the weekend. But before I get to that, here is a bit of background on how the idea to establish a strategic research team within the Mossad's research department, whose task it is to deal with central issues on Israel's national security agenda from a long-term (five to ten years) perspective, came about.

The Yom Kippur War was a defining event in the short history of the State of Israel. The shock waves caused by this war have not yet subsided. The IDF and the Israeli intelligence community were among the first victims of the war; the Agranat Commission, which investigated the period preceding the outbreak of the war and its first three days (October 6–8, 1973), made several decisions that had a significant influence on the intelligence community.

The first main decision was the addition of a new dimension to the concept of authority and responsibility that had not existed until then—sanctions. The head of Military Intelligence, who had erred in his assessments, was fired from his post, and it was determined that sanctions would be the law going forward and the new norm in the intelligence community.

The second main decision was that the method that had been adopted, according to which there was only one body conducting national assessments—Military Intelligence—would be amended to become a pluralistic system of assessment, whereby the Mossad would establish its first research department. This meant that the Mossad would go from being an intelligence-gathering and special operations agency to an intelligence-gathering, special operations, and research and assessment agency—a dramatic change. The Foreign Ministry would upgrade its research body, and the Shin Bet would also establish its own research department that would cover its areas of responsibility.

Between the years 1973 and 1976, I served as the head of the Mossad's operations department. During the period immediately following the Yom Kippur War, I was closely involved, along with Zvi Zamir, director of the Mossad at the time, in everything related to the Agranat Commission and the establishment of the Mossad's research division following the commission's decision. I point this out because I believe that this very intense preoccupation with the issues of intelligence and assessment developed my ability to identify all kinds of nuances in the patterns of behavior and decision-making among our colleagues in Military Intelligence in the post-Agranat Commission era. I identified two things, one measurable and the other more psychological.

The first was that early warning of a war with Syria took first priority in MI's EEI during the second half of the 1970s and throughout the 1980s, at the expense of other issues, such as Iraq and Egypt. The second was that, as a general rule, MI's research refrained from dealing with assessments beyond the annual report. And the reason I use the term *psychological* to describe this is that when you have the threat of sanctions hovering over your head, it is only human to minimize the risk you take upon yourself. All of this was the background and the catalyst for the establishment of the strategic team in the Mossad's research department.

The strategic team was established at the beginning of 1989. Its mandate was to investigate key issues related to Israel's national security for a five-year and a ten-year time line. The team was composed of external experts who came from academia, the defense industries, and other bodies in the country engaged in intelligence research. The team was multidisciplinary and comprised no more than ten people. Its composition was not fixed—it changed according to the research topic. Only the best people in their respective fields were selected. The research topics were chosen by a team that included the Mossad director, the head of the research department, and the head of the team itself, the late Dr. Ilan Amit, who served in the role for many years, starting from the team's establishment. I would like to take this opportunity to express my gratitude to and admiration of this man, who in my humble opinion was one of the greatest Israeli thinkers, certainly among the people I knew. The team relied on the assistance of the research department personnel, who served as the team members' research assistants in every respect.

Prime Minister Shamir, who had instructed us to present a longer-term intelligence assessment, beyond the yearly one, did so with the knowledge that the strategic team existed and that he was to be its first "client." Here, too, for security reasons, I will reveal only some of what our presentation included. I began my remarks with a recommendation regarding a country that was seemingly not a formally defined threat to Israel. Pakistan is not included in our definition of the Middle East, unlike the American (both the CIA's and the State Department's) definition of the region, which does include this state. Many observers view Pakistan, a Muslim country with a large arsenal of nuclear weapons and means of delivery, as the world's least responsible country with regard to nuclear proliferation—and it is assisting Iran in its own efforts to develop nuclear weapons whose goal is to threaten us. In our view, I said, it was important and even urgent to include Pakistan in our definition of the Middle East, with all of the implications that this involves.

The following were the threats I presented in January 1991:

- The greatest danger was the combination of Islamic fundamentalism and nuclear capability. A nuclear Iran run by a group of fanatical ayatollahs with their finger on a nuclear trigger would be an imminent threat to the State of Israel and to the stability of the Middle East and the world at large.
- By the end of the decade, it would be impossible to exclude the possibility that another country in the Middle East would undergo a process of Islamization. In this context, we specifically mentioned Turkey and Egypt.
- The Islamization of another state in the Middle East would be a blow to the diplomatic process, and if it were a state belonging to our innermost circle, we had to prepare for the possibility that this country would withdraw from a peace agreement and pursue confrontation.
- We estimated that within the range of our assessment, that is, ten years at most, the Arab countries would not be prepared to pay "the price of peace" required of them, even with the economic prosperity they would receive in return.
- Regarding Iraq, which was the number one destabilizing factor in the Middle East, we asked in January 1991: Where was it heading? Would it try to return in one way or another to the family of

enlightened nations? Or was Saddam Hussein planning another "wild card" for us and the world, which, at the time of this assessment, could not be predicted?

- Whether Egypt would play a positive or negative role in the context of the peace process was not clear. At the time of this evaluation, Egypt had put quite a few spokes in the wheels of the process, and it was difficult to know what else awaited us with regard to this matter. Therefore this was an important issue to continue monitoring.
- We could expect that terrorist organizations would use nonconventional weapons. This assessment was validated in 1995 when a Japanese terrorist organization crossed the line regarding the use of chemical weapons for the first time in modern history. The "Engineer," Yahya Ayyash, who had studied chemistry, chose to apply his knowledge to the development of conventional explosive devices for suicide bombers. One could not rule out the possibility that somewhere along the way, another chemistry student would choose the path of chemical terror.
- The final threat was that in future military confrontations there was a risk of attacks on Israeli population centers using surface-to-surface missiles with chemical warheads.
- Alongside the chances of peace within the range of the assessment—by the year 2000—we emphasized that true peace could be realized only if it was based on three essential factors: true reconciliation, economic and social prosperity, and democratization in the Arab world. I said then, in January 1991, that if I had to assess where we would be at the end of the twentieth century in terms of each of these three conditions, all I was willing to predict was that I was not sure we would achieve true reconciliation but that there was a chance of achieving coexistence with some degree of compromise. I was not sure that our neighbors would gain prosperity, but there was a good chance of achieving economic growth in the region. I was sure, I said, that we would not achieve democratization, but it was possible that by the end

of the century the beginnings of political liberalism in the Middle East would be glimpsed.

It is important to draw attention to the geostrategic rift that had begun to develop around the time of this assessment in January 1991. From 1992, the year in which Yitzhak Rabin was elected to his second term as prime minister, the peace process became a cornerstone of government policy. As I mentioned above, in 1993 there were three parallel diplomatic processes—with Jordan, Syria, and the Palestinians. The 1996 elections brought the Likud back to power, this time with Benjamin Netanyahu at its helm. The 1991 intelligence assessment did not take into account a change of government in Israel. This is not unusual, however—assessments presented by the Israeli intelligence community never include analyses and forecasts regarding the variable of Israel itself. In contrast, net assessments take Israel's capabilities, intentions, and actions into account, but generally these assessments are made by the political leader with his senior aides, while taking the intelligence assessments into consideration and usually even after consulting with the heads of the various intelligence agencies.

In 1995 I established a team called Forum 2000, whose function was to discuss the threats and opportunities that the Mossad might face leading up to the end of the twentieth century and the beginning of the twenty-first. Because this was an internal organizational analysis, the team's mandate covered the following topics: (1) the international-strategic arena; (2) technology; (3) Israeli society; (4) the Israeli intelligence community.

At the outset, I outlined the work required of the team. I noted that the Mossad's mission consisted of several layers:

1. The Mossad needed to gather intelligence that addresses the threat perception. The intelligence had to be of the highest quality and also to be able to provide a response to the task of prevention and/or preemption with which the Mossad was charged.

2. The Mossad had to have research and assessment capabilities:
    (a) It had to enable the pluralism of research in the community.
    (b) The Mossad's research had to be at a level that gave it the ability to critique the intelligence output of other research bodies in the community.
    (c) The Mossad's research needed to expand to include EEI issues of a civilian nature, such as the maintenance of a strong economic sector.
3. The Mossad would continue to contribute to the development of the connection between Israel and the Jews of the Diaspora. This task would continue to be relevant in the era of the 2000s.
4. The Mossad would contribute to Israel's economic strength according to a designated economic EEI.
5. The Mossad would continue to maintain and expand its ties with intelligence services around the world in order to support Israel's diplomatic relations.

In the global and regional spheres, the team came up with the following insights:

1. The bipolar world (of the United States and the Soviet Union) had become unipolar (the United States), but alongside it other centers of power were developing, leading toward a multipolar world.
2. Economic competition was replacing military conflict or military balance of power as the key to influence and control in the world.
3. The importance of Middle Eastern oil would rise in light of the increase in global consumption, with an emphasis on East Asian countries and the Pacific. Therefore, international involvement in the Middle East, including American military, economic, and political input, would continue and even intensify.
4. The Middle East would continue to be unstable. Economic gaps between countries and between competing groups within them would continue to trigger military violence and subversion between states, as well as civil unrest, including violence, within states, particularly by Islamist opposition organizations.

5. The processes of Islamization in Arab societies would continue, as the demographic and economic conditions of the growth of Islamic fundamentalism would continue to exist. Islamist movements might take control of Arab countries, and even in countries where these movements did not seize power, the influence of Islamic ideology on the population would persist. Israel would continue to be a target of Islamists' hostility.

6. The current leaders of the important Middle Eastern countries, and of the countries connected with the peace process, were autocratic rulers who were nearing the end of their lives. In some countries there were obvious succession issues (Syria, the Palestinian Authority, Morocco, Saudi Arabia, Egypt, and Jordan). Thus, within the next five to ten years, upheavals in the regimes of the region, including the countries involved in the peace process, could be expected, and these might have either a positive or a negative impact on the process.

7. The Arab world would continue to be fragmented, and Israel would be able to act vis-à-vis individual states. There was no threat on the eastern front.

8. The peace process between Israel and its neighbors would continue: Peace would be maintained with Egypt and Jordan; the Syrian process might lead to a cold peace; relations between Israel and Saudi Arabia would be calm; and to Israel's east there would be an independent Palestinian entity with some connection to Jordan.

9. The threats against Israel would come from countries in its outer circle. Among these countries, Iran would be the main adversary because of its potential (population, territory, and military and economic capabilities), its ideological hostility (the premise being that the regime would not change in the period under discussion), and its plans to develop nonconventional weapons.

10. Regarding the meaning and timetable of the Iranian nuclear threat: the assessments from the Forum 2000 discussions were that by the middle of the first decade of the twenty-first century

(i.e., 2006) the Iranians would have a certain degree of operational capability (some launchers and some nuclear missiles) that would constitute an existential threat to the State of Israel. In retrospect, this assessment was not realized thanks to successful Israeli covert operations, and international cooperation, to stop or slow down Iran's progress. The realization of the threat would also be accompanied by a new situation—a nuclear "balance of terror"—which would mean restricted room for strategic maneuvering in the war on terror, in reprisals and punitive measures, and, primarily, in the manner in which conventional forces were used in war (for example, attacks in the depth of the enemy's territory or threats to a capital city). These scenarios would become apparent if a nuclear Iran were to extend its patronage over countries that were in conflict with Israel.

11. Iraq would resume oil exports and undergo economic recovery. It was likely that close monitoring of its nonconventional weapons capabilities would continue. Keeping Iraq outside of the peace process would require the investment of intelligence inputs but, to our understanding, less than what was invested in Iran. It should be mentioned that the Forum 2000 predictions completely missed the outbreak of the Second Gulf War (2003).

An entire section of Forum 2000's work was devoted to the implications of the peace agreements. This section dealt with changes in our EEI and in the manner in which we gathered intelligence, cutbacks in resources and the need to refocus, terrorism, intelligence, economics, and Israel's relations with the United States and the Jewish people. There is no point in going into detail about this section, as the change of government in 1996 led to a halt to the peace process.

Forum 2000 was concerned with identifying changes in Israeli society that would affect the future and nature of the Mossad. The team recognized correctly that the Mossad would be affected not only by the changes taking place in Israeli society but also by those taking place in the international arena, but it was difficult to predict the extent to which this would be the case. It could be determined with a high degree of certainty that Israeli society was changing rapidly and moving from a worldview that focused on the collective to one that was influenced by a culture of individualism. These changes were not coincidental but rather the result of a prolonged process of "Westernization," alongside economic prosperity and fatigue from the concept of "the mobilized society." The Israeli sees his family as being his first priority. Second is his workplace, where he assigns the greatest importance to his financial reward. Only then come his personal satisfaction, his social connections, and the status and prestige of his job, and at the very bottom of the ladder is the contribution his workplace makes to society as a whole. Israeli society is much less provincial than in the past. Its citizens travel the world and are exposed to global media. Therefore, the Israeli is more skeptical, more critical, and often more cynical. The changes affecting the global order, such as the dissolution of the patterns that dictated awareness of security threats and the atmosphere of a "farewell to arms," led to a process by which security bodies appeared redundant, and in the Middle East led to the peace process. In Israel, these processes shook the foundations of the consensus over the question of national security. How would all of this affect the Mossad? There was no doubt that, in the foreseeable future, security bodies would continue to be perceived as central and necessary institutions, perhaps even the most important in Israeli society, but in 1996 we saw the following trends as likely to emerge:

1. A more critical public view of the security bodies, a growing demand for their transparency, aggressive media scrutiny, and decreased willingness to approve budgets
2. A growing devaluation of the field of security in its previous form and as a "national mission"
3. A view of the Mossad as "just another place of work" rather than as a "way of life"

4. The need for security services, including the Mossad, to compete with other employers in the labor market, though the material rewards they had to offer were smaller
5. Relocation abroad, a regular part of the Mossad's work, being seen as a burden and as something forced

Twenty years after these predictions, one can marvel at the accuracy with which Forum 2000 identified future trends. Even more striking were the Forum's 1996 predictions with regard to the challenges and future development of technology:

1. The dominance of technological means and capabilities in the Mossad would increase.
2. Many more significant pieces of intelligence would be collected using sophisticated technological means.
3. Visual intelligence (VISINT) would become an important collection tool.
4. Global and regional databases in computer networks would be commonplace and widely available.
5. Access to communication systems and databases would require dealing with complex protocols as well as encryption mechanisms.
6. Access to large quantities of information would require the use of smart filters. The filtering of textual material will not suffice; the filtering of audiovisual material would also be necessary.
7. Intelligence would need to be used to crack technological systems. The formulation of the EEI and the processing of such intelligence would require a very high level of expertise.
8. The Mossad's cumulative database would be very large and would require the development of tools for the retrieval and pushing of relevant material within the organization.
9. Personal communications would be global, and the multimedia involved would be readily available in large volumes. It would become necessary to deal with global personal communications.

10. Smart cards would be commonplace and would include a lot of data (personal and commercial information, contacts, and more).
11. Nanotechnology and microelectronics would develop significantly.
12. Global command and control would be available to us, as well as to the actors we were dealing with.

The Forum 2000 team also examined the future of the relationships, allocations of responsibility, boundaries, and so on within the intelligence community. Without going into detail, for obvious reasons, it can be said that the team was successful in 1996 in predicting the reality in the community today (2017).

Issues in the Israeli Intelligence Community

The Arab-Israeli conflict is characterized by a number of elements that distinguish it from most other conflicts in the world:

- It has lasted longer than all of the other conflicts that exist today.
- The numerical disparity between the two sides is greater than in any other conflict.
- On one side is one country, and on the other side are more than twenty countries and an entity with many characteristics of a state.
- Many on both sides claim total entitlement to the disputed territory and are unwilling to compromise.
- On one side is a democratic state, and on the other are authoritarian regimes.

In the past, these differences have had an impact on the role of intelligence in the conflict, they continue to do so today, and it is safe to assume that they will continue to have an influence in the future.

The main feature of the role of intelligence in this conflict is its heterogeneity and pluralism.

The Israeli-Arab conflict is a complex and convoluted matrix. The first and most basic variable in this matrix is territory. We customarily refer to the concentric territorial circles of the conflict (one inside the other, with Israel as their common center). In the first, innermost circle, the adversary is the Palestinians. In the second circle are the countries bordering Israel—Lebanon, Syria, Jordan, Saudi Arabia, and Egypt—some of which have official peace treaties with Israel. Others generally maintain hostile policies toward Israel, though there is sometimes a convergence of interests with Israel on a certain level. Even so, all of them have claims against Israel regarding its treatment of the Palestinians, control over the holy places, and more. In the third outer circle are countries that do not border Israel but view themselves as part of the Arab world and are therefore involved on some level in the Israeli-Arab conflict; these include Iraq, the Persian Gulf states, Yemen, Sudan, and North Africa. And in the fourth circle are Iran and Pakistan, Muslim powers that, despite their distance from Israel, show an interest and involvement in the conflict (with Iran's involvement being far greater than Pakistan's).

Military theory asserts that intelligence must be collected on the enemy's capabilities and intentions and that an appropriate response must be prepared based on an assessment of these capabilities and intentions. In applying this principle to the Middle East conflict, we see asymmetry both in the intentions and in the capabilities of the various actors in the Arab coalition against Israel.

The sum of the enemy's capabilities include all elements of the enemy's power (in the case of the Israeli-Arab conflict, the enemy consists of more than twenty countries and a Palestinian entity)—that is, its military, economic, social, diplomatic, internal security, scientific, and technological power and its general national resilience.

The sum of the enemy's intentions refers to the intentions of each of the actors in the coalition against Israel. This is where intelligence encounters a problem, because these are adversaries with authoritarian regimes. Whereas in the open societies of democratic countries it is not difficult for a professional intelligence body to uncover the leadership's intentions, this is not the case in countries with authoritarian regimes, in which only a tiny number of people are exposed to the leader's intentions and in which sometimes intentions can be found only inside the head of the ruler. For example, Egyptian president Anwar Sadat informed senior Egyptian military commanders of the exact date of the launch of the attack against Israel in October 1973 only a few days prior to that date. This does not contradict the contention (in the chapter on the Yom Kippur War) that Sadat's intention to go to war against Israel began to crystallize in 1971.

The intensity of the hostility toward Israel, the level of involvement, and the degree of commitment of each member of the Arab coalition have changed over the years, and this has made it even more difficult to expose and identify Arab intentions vis-à-vis Israel, as well as to accurately assess threat perception (the threat to Israel attributed to one factor or another).

In a war of intelligence, each side strives to preserve its secrets, as it defines them. In this respect, the models of the United States and the Soviet Union during the Cold War (1945–90) make an interesting case study of completely different perceptions of operations security. This difference in perception was a direct function of the United States being an open society with a democratic regime and the Soviet Union being a state with a dictatorial regime.

The Soviet regime made a decision that all information about itself—100 percent of it, nothing less—and anything related to it was considered confidential. The result was that all information was inserted, figuratively speaking, into a black and opaque box that was guarded zealously. In contrast, the Americans decided to include only about 5 percent of all information in the "black box," the tiny portion that it believed that, if exposed, would severely damage the main components of American power. There was not even an effort to guard the other 95 percent.

It is not difficult to understand that the Soviet model could be successful only if the box was well and truly sealed. One break-in would reveal all of the information inside to the adversary.

The American model was based on the assumption that protecting 100 percent of the information was an impossible task and that it was therefore better to protect only 5 percent. As for everything else, the assumption was that it would be very difficult for the enemy to pick out the real, significant signal from the vast cacophony of information that was open to all. If one were to project this Cold War scenario onto the Israeli-Arab conflict, it can be assumed that the amount of noise in the communications emanating from Israel makes it difficult for the enemy to properly understand its intentions.

Anti-Jewish, anti-Zionist, and anti-Israeli terrorism has accompanied the Zionist presence in the Land of Israel since the arrival of the Bilu pioneers in the late nineteenth century. It has taken on various forms, but throughout the period since the Bilus' arrival—more than one hundred years—it has been one of the main features of the conflict. At first the terrorism was local, but over the course of time it became global. Initially it was secular and tribal, but it became increasingly nationalist and religious. Originally it was political in nature, expressing aspirations of self-determination and independence, but it later became theological with the aspiration of establishing a "sharia" state in the world of "the kingdom of Allah."

Intelligence activity vis-à-vis the phenomenon of terrorism is exempt from one important task that it must fulfill in other fields: speculation regarding the issue of intentions. There is no question that Arab terrorism, since it reared its head and in all its forms, was intended to prevent the fulfillment of the Zionist ideal, that is, the return of the Jews to the Land of Israel and the establishment of a sovereign Jewish entity there. Since the establishment of the state, its goal has been clear—the destruction of the Israeli political entity.

Intelligence efforts against terrorism, like efforts against regular armies and sovereign states, focus on alerts (of intended attacks) and on the assessment of the enemy's capabilities. These efforts require broad territorial deployment and the ability to produce high-resolution, detailed intelligence images continuously, so as not to miss any changes occurring in the highly dynamic environment.

The intelligence efforts are carried out using a variety of methods and means. With all due respect to SIGINT, ELINT, and COMINT, disciplines of intelligence that consist mainly of listening to, receiving, and deciphering signals between communications devices, telephones, or computers, I believe that the pinnacle of the art of intelligence is HUMINT (human intelligence). Why do I say this? Because HUMINT is the only intelligence discipline that enables us to ask questions of the source and receive answers. As a direct result of this dialogue between the handler and the source, HUMINT is the more promising discipline in terms of its potential to delve deep into the enemy's true intentions. This point deserves to be emphasized especially given today's reality, in which there is an almost religious worship of technology and a tendency to devote the lion's share of the intelligence budget to it.

A long-standing tradition in the intelligence world is the exchange of information and assessments between friendly intelligence agencies. Such exchanges will always be made between allied countries, but there is not necessarily always total symmetry between the two states' political interests and the interests of these countries' intelligence agencies.

The deeper and more intimate the cooperation, the more likely it is to result in joint operations. However, it is rare for one intelligence agency to share with another, friendly as the two may be, its top secrets—unless there is a "quid pro quo," in which the giving party receives a suitable reward in return. There is also an (unofficial, of course) intelligence "stock exchange," with buyers and sellers, and as in any stock exchange, the buyers try to buy cheap and sellers try to get top dollar. Typically, this "stock exchange" operates on the basis of a single seller versus a single buyer, but sometimes there is an "intelligence deal" involving more than two sides.

An ironclad rule of the global intelligence stock exchange is the "third-party principle," which states that the party that has acquired intelligence may not sell the "merchandise" that he has bought to a third party unless he has received the consent of the seller. It is difficult to ensure that this rule is always observed, but if and when those who breach it are exposed—and this does sometimes happen—their reputation is damaged, and the stock exchange members either refrain from selling them information or demand exorbitant prices for the information they need.

Intelligence stock exchange members should be very sensitive to the possibility that other members may try to sell them inaccurate information aimed at leading them to draw erroneous conclusions that serve the seller's goals—in other words, fraud. This has happened before and will happen in the future; information from sources controlled by foreign intelligence services must be treated with extreme caution.

The concept of information sharing is very general and broad. It can be examined through many different prisms:

1. The security prism of the need-to-know principle
2. The types of information shared with others—raw intelligence or intelligence that has been processed in some form
3. The distinction between bona fide intelligence bodies and bodies that do not belong to the intelligence community
4. Information that is relevant to or needed by the law enforcement system, as opposed to information that is not
5. Hierarchical criteria—in the United States, for example, which information is transferred at the federal level and which at the state or municipal levels; also, which information goes to which branches of government, executive, legislative, and/or judicial
6. The types of information shared with allied or friendly countries and with foreign intelligence services

Sometimes the political-strategic reality creates strange bedfellows. In the Middle East, some of these odd partnerships were created at the initiative, or with the involvement, of the UN. One of the positive differences between the UN and its predecessor, the League of Nations, is the military force that the UN can employ in order to quell conflicts between states. These forces can act as a buffer between combat forces or as a liaison between the parties. In the Middle East conflict, these forces often served as an intermediary to establish ties between Israeli intelligence and security forces and their counterparts in neighboring Arab countries; the degree of intensity of these ties reflected the magnitude of the two sides' common interests. The lowest level of cooperation occurred when the parties' mutual desire was simply to preserve calm on both sides of the border. The highest level of cooperation was achieved when both sides found themselves facing a common enemy, whose potential to cause harm to both sides was greater than the potential for hostilities between the two. An example of the first case is the arrangement made to maintain quiet on Israel's borders with Syria and Lebanon. An example of the second case is the cooperation between Israeli security and intelligence bodies with their counterparts in the Palestinian Authority in the face of the threat of Hamas and Islamic Jihad (though it is difficult to know whether this cooperation will last if there is a real agreement to put an end to the rivalry between the PLO, which still controls the Palestinian Authority, and Hamas, which controls Gaza). Another example in this category is Jordan, which, decades before the signing of its official peace treaty with Israel in 1994, maintained extensive ties with Israel.

The so-called "third-party principle" in the relationship between Israel and its great ally, the United States, merits a brief discussion. During the period of the Cold War (1945–90), the limits of the intelligence cooperation between the United States and Israel were clear-cut. It was a bipolar world in which each of the two superpowers had a camp of allies. It was clear that the United States would not share intelligence with us about Saudi Arabia, or the Gulf States, or Egypt in the post–Yom Kippur War period, when Egypt became an important ally of the United States in the Middle East, and certainly not about Turkey, which was an official NATO member state and was considered a major American ally because of its proximity to the Soviet Union and its control over the straits leading from the Black Sea to the Mediterranean Sea and from it to the Atlantic Ocean and the Suez Canal.

The British foreign intelligence service (MI6), one of the oldest in the world, enjoys great prestige and esteem in the intelligence world. Unlike in most Western democracies, this agency reports to the foreign minister and not to the prime minister. This structure has always dictated complete symmetry between the principles of British foreign policy, including in the Middle East, and intelligence cooperation between Britain and other countries. It is therefore not difficult to understand that British foreign policy, which prioritized its relations with the Arab states over its relations with Israel, also directly affected the intelligence ties between the two countries. Things changed for the better with the end of the Cold War and the collapse of the Soviet Union, when Britain and Israel found themselves facing more and more common threats, in particular radical Islamic terrorism and the proliferation of nonconventional weapons. This will be expanded upon below.

The end of the Cold War era in 1990 was an important milestone for the Israeli intelligence community as a whole, and for the Mossad, whose role has an international character, in particular. Throughout the Cold War era, the intelligence community maintained a regional system that covered the Middle East and Europe. Here and there, according to unique and ad hoc needs, it spread its wings to cover other parts of the world but always made a point of returning to its home system.

The geostrategic changes that accompanied the end of the Cold War generated a sharp and relatively quick transition from a bipolar world to a multipolar world. The coherent blocs that had formed around the two superpowers were dismantled. At the same time, the main EEI were narrowed—whereas during the Cold War era, the EEI were largely superpower-dependent (that is, the intelligence agency determined its EEI in accordance with the superpower that headed the bloc to which it belonged), in the post–Cold War era the EEI became dependent on the subjects that concerned most of the world's actors—radical Islam and the proliferation of nonconventional weapons. This change required the Mossad to expand its deployment and activities to parts of the world in which it had not previously operated, or at least in which its activities had been marginal and temporary. Iran's development of nonconventional weapons has always been dependent on suppliers of knowledge, technology, advice, and raw materials from all over the world, and since this matter has become the focus of Israeli EEI, it is no wonder that Israeli intelligence has spread across the globe. At the same time, radical Islam and terrorism have become global threats that cut across borders, states, and regimes, threatening not only the United States and western Europe but also Russia, China, India, Indonesia, Australia, Egypt, Jordan, and more. The spread of radical Islam has become global, and this requires an appropriate response, not only in terms of improved means and capabilities, but also in terms of deployment. As a result, the post–Cold War era has witnessed intelligence coalitions that would have been difficult to imagine in the past: for example, ties between the Israeli Mossad and the Russian or Chinese intelligence services.

In the old world, which consisted mainly of independent nation-states and blocs with political-strategic characteristics rather than legal characteristics, intelligence systems and law enforcement generally operated in parallel, and practically the only encounter between them was in cases of espionage or subversive activities of one state by another. More and more, the new world is trying to regulate its system of ties and relations on the basis of bilateral and multilateral agreements and treaties. This trend has inevitably led to a greater interface between the intelligence and legal systems.

In the old world, international conflicts were characterized by the delineations of the global strategic order and were usually resolved through wars. In this reality, intelligence and law enforcement systems had no reason to meet. The new world's demarcations are between coalitions of political, democratic, liberal blocs that value free economies and human rights and other blocs, the most dangerous of which is that of radical Islam, a politically amorphous, antidemocratic, anti–human rights bloc that has waged a holy war against all of the values of the free world. The battlefield in this conflict encompasses the whole world, and especially its civilian home front. The laws of war that befit the old world do not apply to this new conflict, and there is therefore an urgent need to rewrite the laws of war.

The intelligence EEI of the old world during the Cold War era were simple and clear; the role of intelligence was to shed light on the capabilities and intentions of the enemy, which was either a state or a bloc of several states. The essence of the EEI was the ability to issue alerts in the case of war. In the post–Cold War era, the EEI became increasingly obscure. Terrorism took on a more central role, the proliferation of nonconventional weapons and materials became an important issue, and organized crime, drugs, and ecology—three issues that had been marginal in the past—came to occupy an important spot in the EEI. Recently, other subjects such as megaterrorism and nonconventional terrorism, including cyberterrorism, have also been added to the list. When we connect all of these new EEI to the issue of terrorism, the threat suddenly becomes defined, immediate, and strategic. In the strategic environment dominated by these EEI, cooperation between intelligence communities and law enforcement agencies becomes inevitable and must be both intimate and ongoing.

I will devote a few sentences to the system of connections between the Israeli intelligence community and the law enforcement authorities. The Mossad's full name is "the Institute for Intelligence and Special Operations." It is primarily an intelligence collection agency. The elements of research and assessment were added only following the Agranat Commission's conclusions in the wake of the Yom Kippur War in 1973. In addition, the Mossad is expected to carry out any task that the government imposes on it, as well as tasks that no other body in the country has the capability or authorization to carry out. The Mossad operates exclusively outside of the country's borders. The interface between the Mossad and the law enforcement authorities is minimal, and it therefore does not operate an interrogations branch. In cases in which interrogation is required, the Mossad employs the assistance of the Shin Bet. The Shin Bet operates mainly within the country's borders and functions as an intelligence collection agency responsible for counterespionage, subversion, and counterterrorism. It has a very strong interrogations branch that works closely with the law enforcement agencies. Military Intelligence operates as an intelligence collection agency and as the research body responsible for the national assessment of war; in those cases where it is required to enforce the law, it is assisted by the IDF's Information Security Department (formerly Operations Security), which is subordinate to the head of MI and the Military Advocate General's Office. These two bodies work with the state prosecutor. The work of the Israel Police is generally intertwined with the law enforcement system. Their relationship is very tight, though not without tension.

The difference between the concept of "intelligence as proof" and the concept of legal proof has always been obvious to those engaged in intelligence gathering in the Shin Bet and the Israel Police, and less so for Military Intelligence and the Mossad, because the latter two's contacts with the law enforcement system are minimal and loose by nature. For the Mossad, this situation changed after the First Gulf War, when it became heavily involved in the issue of nuclear proliferation and was also given responsibility for prevention. When you are engaged in the area of prevention, law enforcement agents become your partners. As an intelligence officer, you have the job of providing intelligence that proves that someone—a person or company—is indeed providing the enemy with prohibited knowledge and technologies. The job of law enforcement agencies is to bring the person or company to court and convict them. In many cases, their demands of you as the provider of intelligence are extremely rigorous because the intelligence must stand the test of criminal law—proof beyond any reasonable doubt—in order to obtain a conviction. This tension between the two bodies requires you as an intelligence collection agency to take additional risks, often endangering human lives, and to invest even more human resources and money only to meet the requirements of the law and to prove what to you seems completely obvious. In the war in which the free world finds itself today, a war in which there exists an absolute asymmetry between a moral society and a society devoid of values, there is certainly an argument to be made regarding the lowering of the bar of legal requirements on issues related to the war on terror.

At this point I will play the role of Cato the Elder (the Roman senator who used to finish all his speeches with the words, "And, additionally, Carthage should be destroyed") and raise a subject that appears to me one that is convenient for the Western world to avoid dealing with. This issue is the defining of terrorism. In a world where the community of free nations has established an international war crimes tribunal, one would think that a first priority would be to redefine the laws of war (as I discussed earlier); this would involve defining terrorism, which is the main feature of this new era of war. It seems to me that the Europeans have quite a few reasons—not necessarily professional ones—to sidestep this obstacle, but I am surprised that the American system has refrained so far from "grabbing the bull by the horns" and defining terrorism.

Another significant change that emerged from the post–Cold War geostrategic environment was the substantial upgrade in cooperation between friendly intelligence services. If in the past this cooperation was characterized mainly by the exchange of intelligence material and joint research meetings, in the new era it has been propelled to the point of operational cooperation. This step was inevitable—the countries of the world understood that in order to successfully confront global terrorism, operational cooperation between their intelligence services was essential.

Nonconventional weapons, by definition, pose a threat to global stability, and therefore all countries facing the threat, whether potentially or imminently, must cooperate in order to deal with it. Another factor that spurred cooperation was the realization by the various intelligence services, the Western ones in particular, that in the course of their activities against the threat of nonconventional weapons they were actually interfering with each other; the correct way to prevent this and to streamline their activities was through operational cooperation, which enabled coordination and the division of labor.

The most striking case of changes in the characteristics of the conflict over time is that of Iran. Iran was a country friendly to Israel since the latter's early years, and from the late 1950s it became one of Israel's most important strategic allies. This of course was until the Khomeini revolution of 1979, which turned Iran into Israel's greatest threat—a real existential threat.

It should be recalled that until the Khomeini revolution Iran was a cornerstone of Israel's national security doctrine and formed an integral part of Israel's regional alliances, with Iran and Turkey on the northern front and with Ethiopia and Sudan (and later Morocco) to the south.[1] Among other things, Iran was Israel's main oil supplier.

If we had to define the essence of the Iranian nonconventional threat to Israel in one sentence, it would come down to the following question: *If and when Iran obtains military nuclear capability, will the decisions of its leadership be rational or messianic?*

The amount of attention and intelligence resources that Israel has invested in dealing with the threat of nonconventional weapons since its establishment is unprecedented, and incomparable with any other issue in the EEI. The buildup of nonconventional weapons in the Middle East has always been under constant surveillance by Israeli intelligence and security bodies, though the subject has gotten the attention of the public only at certain "breaking points." Among these have been the Egyptian use of chemical weapons against the rebels in Yemen in the early 1960s; the activities of German rocket scientists in Egypt during the same period; Iraq's efforts to build up and use all kinds of nonconventional weapons under Saddam Hussein's rule, including the use of chemical weapons against the Kurds and especially its nuclear efforts, including the building of the Osirak reactor, which was bombed by the Israeli air force in 1981; the Egyptian ground-to-ground missile project "Condor" in the 1980s; and the assistance of Pakistan, North Korea, China, and the Soviet Union to certain Arab countries in various areas of nonconventional weaponry. In light of all this, it is fair to say that the State of Israel, since its establishment and to the present day, has coped successfully with the threat of nonconventional weapons, both on the operational, defensive, and offensive level and on the diplomatic, international, and public diplomacy level. The temptation to use nonconventional weapons, whether as a threat or in actual practice, is too great and therefore requires constant counteractions.

As global technology progresses—and it is making giant leaps forward—every variable relating to nonconventional weapons becomes more lethal. Their range increases, their accuracy improves, their miniaturization develops, their carrying capacity increases, warning time decreases, and so on. *For the foreseeable future, I do not see the possibility of Israel being able to reduce the amount of resources it allocates to facing the threat of nonconventional weapons.*

Whereas the State of Israel should be commended for the manner in which it has dealt with various threats involving nonconventional weapons over a long period of time, unfortunately the same cannot be said for the way the state has dealt with the Israeli-Palestinian conflict. However, and at the risk of being suspected of lacking objectivity, I would exempt Israeli intelligence from this assertion; I believe that it has done its job well, from the prestate period until today, and I refer here to all branches of Israeli intelligence.

I consider myself qualified to discuss the period prior to the establishment of the state, as the work I did while studying at the Hebrew University concerned the activities of the Shai, the intelligence arm of the Haganah, the forerunner of the IDF. I see myself as authorized to determine, in all modesty, that the Shai files to which I was exposed were the model of vigorous and methodical intelligence work. They gave a comprehensive picture of the Arabs in the Land of Israel in the 1940s, according to a number of indices, the principal of these being the village index (about a thousand villages on the territory of the British Mandate).

The main tool at Shai's disposal was HUMINT—the operation of agents. OSCINT—the monitoring and analysis of the Arab press—played a secondary role.

Shai succeeded in building a database of village files, in each of which the relevant intelligence officer could find his intelligence "dream come true." Each case contained what was needed to enable the intelligence officer to provide decision makers with policy and strategic recommendations and to give to the planners of the operations the material they needed to plan any type of action vis-à-vis the village. Shai's regional commanders certainly deserve kudos for carrying out professional work at the highest level within the field of intelligence.

I, along with other intelligence officials, have often encountered the cynical expression "Intelligence exists to make mistakes." My opinion, which is based on decades of intelligence work both in the field and at headquarters, at all levels and in many positions, is that intelligence is an essential tool for decision makers, enabling them to make decisions in a rational and orderly process that is not based solely on "gut feelings." Having said that, any decision, whether strategic or tactical, made in connection with the Israeli-Palestinian conflict is a function of the decision maker's political outlook. Therefore, proper groundwork in decision-making consists of the definition of a goal, the gathering of intelligence and analysis of the findings, the laying out of possible courses of action, the analysis of each course's pros and cons, and the selection of the preferred course of action. The decision itself does not apply in this case, because it cannot be isolated from the decision maker's political worldview.

When attempting to translate the Israeli Right and Left's political worldview and vision into the language of someone who is not a politician but rather a practitioner—someone who approaches problems from a pragmatic rather than an ideological perspective—one must ask, "What is the degree of risk that each of these parties is willing to undertake in order to ensure the existence of Israel as a Jewish and democratic state, while simultaneously providing an appropriate response to the demands of the Palestinians?" Risk assessment should propel us to choose a preferred course of action with regard to most of the issues on the table, but there will remain "soft" issues anchored in the world of values and in the historical memory of each side, and these cannot be dealt with through some kind of compromised partition.

Nonetheless, over time, from the First World War until today, the progress graph of the Zionist movement and later of the State of Israel shows steady and continuous advancement—with regard to territory, demography, the economy, science and technology, the military, and international standing. It is important that we be aware of this, because the stronger side has greater safety margins and the options available to it are more varied.

In its routine role, intelligence focuses on providing advance warnings of the enemy's intentions to wage war, and on gathering and assessing information about its capabilities. However, another important role of intelligence, which the general public is not always aware of, is to identify and encourage reconciliatory trends and intentions among our enemies that signal a possible willingness to accept our existence here and enter into peace negotiations with us. In the cases of Egypt and Jordan, intelligence identified their willingness to negotiate peace, succeeded in persuading then-leaders Begin and Rabin, and even served as a matchmaker at the beginning of the process in the case of Egypt and as an active participant in the negotiations right up to the signing of the peace treaty in the case of Jordan.

Regarding Israel's intelligence relations with other countries, the Mossad has a clear advantage over other branches of intelligence by virtue of its function and because of its direct subordination to the political leader, the prime minister (as opposed to Military Intelligence, which is subordinate to the chief of staff). In theory, there is a very clear division of roles and authority between the Foreign Ministry, which deals with diplomatic relations between states, and the

Mossad, one of whose jobs is to maintain intelligence relations between Israel and other countries. In practice, however, the boundaries between intelligence issues and diplomatic issues are blurred. For various reasons, decision makers sometimes prefer to relay messages to each other via intelligence services and not through the foreign ministry. Moreover, to this day there are quite a few countries in the world that for various reasons do not want to have open diplomatic relations with Israel but maintain contact—sometimes intensive contact—through the intelligence channels.

In such cases, the Mossad representative responsible for this connection is a representative of the State of Israel for all intents and purposes, and not only regarding intelligence matters. The Mossad representative's presence in the foreign country, his or her dialogue with senior people and sometimes even with the country's ruler, gives the Mossad a real advantage in assessing these countries' intentions, the ability to warn of changes before any other party, and the ability to use the ties created in order to advance Israeli interests.

What are the decision makers' basic working assumptions when designing a system of intelligence? The *first working assumption* should be that intelligence sources are the most important asset and resource in the entire sphere of intelligence. The preservation of the sources' secrecy must be sacrosanct. The establishment of intelligence sources is the most difficult, time-consuming, and expensive aspect in the entire field of intelligence work. The damage caused from the exposing of sources has dire consequences for the system and the state. I believe that the principle of protecting sources must take precedence over any other consideration. In order to reassure those with whom you are providing the intelligence that it is indeed reliable, various mechanisms should be put in place to protect the identity of sources.

In the Yom Kippur War of 1973 we had a colossal failure of intelligence. After the war, a state commission of inquiry was established, headed by the president of the Supreme Court and comprising another Supreme Court justice, two former IDF chiefs of staff, and the state comptroller. I was serving as the Mossad operations officer at the time. I prepared the intelligence material for then-director of the Mossad Major General (reserve) Zvi Zamir's appearance before the commission. I attached two indexes to the material. The first gave full identification of all of the sources mentioned in the material, which we used in our testimony before the commission of inquiry. The second described the sources without actually identifying them. As we arrived at our first appearance before the committee, we deposited all of the intelligence material into the hands of the secretary of the committee. One of the committee members asked us to leave the list of sources with the secretary as well. The director of the Mossad then turned to the group and warned them that those names were among the most important and compartmentalized sources of the Mossad and that most of them continued to provide intelligence. Half-joking, he added, "Look, I have no choice but to know who these sources are, and I assure you that that's why I sleep very badly at night." At that point, the committee members held a brief consultation, after which they decided to make do with the index containing only the description of the sources, with our understanding that if they asked for a source to be identified during the hearings we would provide them with the information. We kept the first index with us at all times.

The second working assumption is that the "need to know" principle must be strictly observed within the system. There are two aspects to this principle. On the one hand, it is intended to ensure that anyone who does not need to receive a piece of intelligence will not do so, thereby increasing the protection of the source. But what is more important is to ensure that the piece of intelligence does reach everyone who needs to see it. This is perhaps the most difficult problem in information sharing—how to ensure that every bit of intelligence reaches the people who need it in order to carry out their job. Of course, the story of the Saudi students, al-Qaeda men who learned how to fly and later carried out the attacks of September 11, 2001, illustrates this point. A few months before the attacks, CIA director George Tenet and national coordinator for counterterrorism Richard

Clarke were convinced of an impending "spectacular attack," and in July a warning was received from a credible source that al-Qaeda was planning a large-scale operation in the United States. Though the names of some of the Saudis who were training to be pilots were known to some of the intelligence agencies, the terrorists succeeded in carrying out their plan. With hindsight analysis, it was argued that if all of the US intelligence agencies had shared their information with each other, the attacks would have been avoided. However, a 1995 Justice Department order severely limited the ability of these agencies to share information obtained by listening in on telephone conversations. In his 2004 testimony to the national commission investigating the September 11 terrorist attacks, Attorney General John Ashcroft said, "The single greatest structural cause for the September 11th problem was the wall that segregated or separated criminal investigators and intelligence agents."

The *third working assumption* is that an intelligence system cannot function effectively only on the basis of procedures and "authority charts." An intelligence system that is not based on discretion, along with procedures, is doomed to fail. A good intelligence organization knows how to distinguish between having tunnel vision and having gumption. Someone with tunnel vision works only according to procedures and is afraid to exercise discretion. Someone with gumption is not afraid to exercise discretion even if it involves potential risks. The dynamics of intelligence systems are so rapid that no mechanism or updating of procedures can catch up with them. In my opinion, we must encourage more gumption in our system, for people with this quality have an added value without which the danger that the organization will stagnate increases.

In the course of the Agranat Commission's investigations, it emerged that Lieutenant Benjamin Siman-Tov, an officer in a relatively junior position in the Southern Command's intelligence unit, wrote an assessment that deviated completely from the intelligence assessment of the Southern Command and of the Intelligence Directorate at IDF headquarters. The prevailing assessment interpreted the movements of the Egyptian army in the days preceding the war as part of an exercise, and any information that indicated that Egypt was preparing for war was deciphered as a deception intended to confuse Israel and cause it to put its army in a state of alert in vain. The young lieutenant, on the other hand, understood the information he had received and the Egyptian army movements to be signs indicating an intention of war. However, his assessment remained stuck in the Southern Command's intelligence unit because of the rigid military hierarchy: his commander, the Southern Command's intelligence officer, refused to pass it on to his superiors. The commission of inquiry established a precedent when it recommended that the Intelligence Corps allow for the breaking of the hierarchy in similar cases in the future so that atypical intelligence assessments could bypass the regular chain of command and go directly to headquarters. The IDF adopted this principle and has adhered to it to this day.

The *fourth working assumption* is that the command channels within the system should be as short as possible, from the "production floor" of the agent in the field up to the political decision maker. This ensures that the agent in the field understands not only the literal orders and instructions but also the "spirit of the commander." It also allows the commander to develop an intimate familiarity with the people in the field and to better understand and judge the information that they pass on. In general, the organizational culture of bodies with a relatively short command channel is better than those with a long channel. In "flat" organizations, the individual's sense of partnership, and hence his or her sense of responsibility, are more developed, and the organizational culture is generally characterized by an aspiration for excellence.

An intelligence organization needs money, and a lot of it. In systems like ours, which deal with life-and-death, existential issues, the norm in the past was to see intelligence as having no price. Over the years, tools for the production of intelligence have become more sophisticated, and their cost has reached a level that is prohibitive, even to a country under threat. The organization then finds itself in a situation in which it must act within a given budget and decide which priorities take precedence in apportioning it. This was not my favorite task when I was head of the organization, and I assume that others serving in similar positions also did not take great pleasure in it. Regardless, it is a vital task and requires the attention and discretion of the organization's highest echelons.

Trust and support between the appointed heads of the professional bodies and the political echelon are an imperative condition for the ability of the various bodies to fulfill their tasks. The intelligence system operates in the context of existential threats to the people and to the state. The potential damage that could arise from a mistake could be critical. Every person in this system is required to have a very high threshold for taking huge risks. Trust and support between the professional directors and those in charge at the political level are a crucial condition for success. Once trust is broken, support follows suit and there is almost no way to fix the situation. In such a case, the best thing is for the professional chief to resign.

I headed the Mossad for seven years and served under three prime ministers from two different parties. When I am asked about my greatest achievement, I respond, with a smile that reflects a lot of truth, that it is the fact that I completed seven years of service without a state commission of inquiry, in a country that is inundated with them.

The CIA—Our Big Sister

The red light of the intercom on my desk lit up. It was the director of the Mossad, Nahum Admoni, on the line. "Do you have a few minutes?" he asked, and when I answered yes, he said, "Come down to my office."

The year was 1987. I was deputy director of the Mossad and head of the Headquarters Division. I was in my office, two floors above the director's bureau. I went down the stairs, and the secretary opened the door for me.

Had I been given ten chances to guess which people I was about to meet, I still would not have been able to guess. Sitting in the office with Nahum were four men whom I easily identified as Americans. Nahum introduced me to them, giving my full name and title. Then-CIA director and former federal judge William Webster and his deputy director of operations, Clair George, introduced themselves.

It was my first meeting with the CIA. The rumor, which may or may not have been true, was that when they returned to the United States a CIA officer was appointed to investigate why the Central Intelligence Agency of the United States had not known about me, the number two man in the Mossad, until the meeting I described above. The Americans should indeed have known about me, but apparently there is no perfect intelligence organization.

In 1979, the Revolutionary Guards took over the US embassy in Tehran, seized hostages, and got hold of the embassy's information archive. Later, and in a roundabout way, we received a document from the archives of the CIA office in Tehran that had been released by the Iranians as part of a smear campaign against the Americans in general and the CIA in particular. The document we received was a report by a CIA agent in Tehran from late January 1966 describing a young Israeli couple that had arrived in Tehran in mid-January and would drive around the city in a little Triumph. The couple in question was my wife Yael and myself. In those days, sophisticated "link analysis" software did not yet exist, and apparently the CIA did not cross-check the information.

My first direct acquaintance with America was in the early 1980s, on the eve of my first appointment as a Mossad division head. It was a one-time opportunity to take my family on a three-week vacation to the United States. We went to New York and Washington on the East Coast, traveled cross-country, stopping at the famous parks, and visited Los Angeles and San Francisco on the West Coast.

What insights do I have from that time?

During our first few days, we stayed at a friend's apartment in Queens. On the first day of our arrival, we went out to walk the streets of Manhattan, and we couldn't get enough of the sights. It was obvious to us that the next morning we were going back to Manhattan, but our son Ariel, then ten years old, announced that he preferred to stay in the apartment. When we raised our eyebrows, he explained: "It bugs me that every time I look up from the street, I can't see the sky—the tops of the buildings hide it!" I think the English word for this feeling is *awe*, and in this case, it was in the sense not of admiration but of fear. Since then, whenever I recall this story, I also recall the verse: "Out of the mouth of babes and sucklings hast thou ordained strength" (Psalm 8:2). This was the first experience etched in my mind during my first encounter with America.

In some godforsaken town in the Midwest, our youngest son broke out in cold sores all over his face. We drove through the town until we spotted a sign for the hospital. A conversation developed while our child was being treated. As soon as we said that we were from Jerusalem, the atmosphere in the room became electrified and some of the people in the room approached us and reached out their hands to touch us. In a flash we realized that Jerusalem, for these Americans, was a spiritual rather than a physical concept. Their reaching out their hands to touch us stemmed from a deep-seated belief that if we came from Jerusalem we must be humans of another kind, perhaps angels.

This scene did not take place in the church but in a very modest hospital, while our son was undergoing medical treatment. We Israelis had to take some time to recover from the incident. Later, I'm not sure why, I asked the people in the room if they had ever been to New York. Not one of them had been, ever! This was a wake-up call to us that New York is not America.

A third experience: Traveling through the endless expanse of farmland, occasionally you would pass a sign next to the road saying "Pick & Pay." You would slow down and pull into a small makeshift parking lot. Next to the sign would be a box in which to leave money, and paper or plastic bags for collecting the fruit. You would pick the fruit and leave the money in the box. Throughout this whole process, you would not find one person with any connection to a field or orchard.

And the final insight that really hit home for me that America was a land of processors, a country run by regulations and standards, was related to the fact that in New York, San Francisco, and everywhere in between, the electric socket was exactly the same! I had been used to Europe, with its jungle of electrical outlets.

In January 1985, it was decided with then-director of the Mossad Nahum Admoni that that summer I would go to the United States to study for one year and that the following summer I would be appointed as head of the Headquarters Division, a role that was considered, for all intents and purposes, to be that of deputy. This arrangement was a godsend for me from every perspective.

First of all, my formal appointment, a year and a half in advance, as the Mossad's number two man was no small matter. Likewise, a year of study at an American university was an opportunity for me to deepen my acquaintance with the United States and understand how this superpower thought, made decisions, and planned and implemented policy. In other words, this year was supposed to prepare me for being the future director of the Mossad.

I greatly appreciated the willingness of the "people of Israel" to fund a year of study for me in the United States, and I saw it as my duty to make the most of this year. I chose the best—Harvard University in Cambridge, Massachusetts. The application process was long and exhausting—interviews, tests, essay writing, and so on. For obvious reasons, throughout the entire acceptance process I had to find the right balance between what to reveal and what to hide. Only one person, the dean of Harvard Kennedy School of Government, had to be let in on the fact that I belonged to the Mossad.

Into that one calendar year I crammed two academic years. The curriculum I built converged, to the extent possible within the existing constraints, everything that could have contributed to a better and deeper understanding of what made America a world power. Through lectures, seminars, independent study, position papers, presentations, and tests, I studied topics including international relations and public policy; US foreign policy; how federal policy works; lessons from historical events as input into decision-making; American media and society; the battle among powers for technological supremacy; communication and information in foreign policy; the interaction between intelligence and public policy; how the US defense budget was built and approved; the C4I environment (Command, Control, Communication, Computers, and Intelligence) in integrated military and civilian management, and more.

In addition to my formal studies, my wife and I made every effort to establish social ties with the students, all of whom were people in the midst of their careers (the program was a midcareer master's in public administration). The great majority of the students were Americans from a wide variety of geographical regions and professions; and then there were a few students like me who came from all over the world. It was a very intense year, a kind of laboratory in which I was sated with information, insights, ways of thinking, history, strategy, and tactics. For me, as someone who had returned to university after twenty-one years of work at the Mossad, it was pure pleasure and a recharging of my batteries before my next step.

Individual comfort and personal well-being are sacred values in American society. This was certainly true for the period in which we lived there—1985 to 1986. The citizen expects minimal intervention by the sovereign in his private affairs, while the sovereign must provide the citizen full compensation for the tax dollars he pays. In the American market economy, the customer is king, and he or she is always right. This principle explains the efficient and polite manner in which the seller—every seller—treats the customer. Within a few days of arriving in Boston, we rented an apartment, furnished it, bought a car, installed a telephone in the apartment ("How many lines would you like, sir?" the telephone operator asked, an unimaginable wonder for an Israeli at that time), opened a bank account, registered our son for high school, and of course completed all the admission and registration procedures at the university. All this, without any stress or elevated blood pressure. Everyone smiled at us and was happy to serve us, because as paying customers for the services we would receive we were kings. Our experience of establishing ourselves in Boston is one we still talk about today, comparing it amusingly with our culture, in which the customer serves the seller.

We had barely had time to breathe in our new apartment when I was quickly reminded where I had come from. Phone call from Israel. It was from a colleague with whom I was used to speaking on the phone in code so that no one could possibly understand what we were talking about. In this secret language he relayed to me the news of the arrest of Jonathan Pollard; I, of course, had no idea who he was and what he had done. The phone call was basically a heads-up; a person suspected of spying for Israel had been arrested around the same time that I arrived in the United States, and there was no way of knowing whether this would at some point raise a red flag, so it was important for me to be forewarned. I was not told to do anything differently or to change my daily routine; I should just lie low and not lose my cool should the doorbell ring one day and a stranger begin asking me intrusive questions. This never happened, and after a day or two we went back to being regular students.

Just as a new Israeli prime minister tends to hold his or her first meeting abroad with the president of the United States, I held my first visit abroad as director of the Mossad at the CIA headquarters in Langley, in the suburbs of Washington, D.C., in May 1989. Over the next seven years I would visit there many times. I did my best to establish a relationship based on "win-win" calculations, despite the vast differences in size, resources, and deployment between the CIA and us.

The relationship between the Mossad and the CIA has been and always will be in large part derived from the state of Israel-US relations. These relations are based not only on common interests but also on shared Judeo-Christian values. When David Ben-Gurion formulated the components of Israel's national security during the state's early days, he included the support of a world power as a necessary condition for the continued existence of the State of Israel. Throughout most of Israel's existence, the United States has, and still does, fulfill this role. The United States has been a guarantor of Israel's survival since its establishment. This guarantee has not always been de jure (official or legally binding), but even when it has been de facto (fulfilled in practice) it has carried great significance because Israel's enemies and potential enemies have understood that the United States would never allow Israel to be destroyed.

This principle was also reflected in the field of intelligence, though it had limitations. For example, the CIA and other US intelligence agencies generally did not share their intelligence with us if it was related to a country that was hostile to us but friendly with the United States.

Throughout almost the entire Cold War, there was symmetry between the two countries' political and intelligence relations. The Soviet Union was a fierce opponent of both the United States and Israel, as were all of the Arab countries that were aligned with the Soviet Union. However, information on countries such as Saudi Arabia and the Gulf States (and Egypt from 1974), who were allied with the United States, was not included in the intelligence cooperation between the CIA and us.

During the golden years of the 1960s and '70s, in which Israel was the source of much admiration among Third World countries, especially in Africa, the Israeli intelligence community and the IDF had a unique added value that served American interests in these parts of the world. These Third World countries saw the United States as a capitalist, imperialist, and colonialist power. They themselves were undergoing the process of liberation from colonialism and the adoption of socialist concepts. Israel, newly liberated from the colonialist power of Britain, having won its independence in a war of liberation against Arab states, who were not popular among black Africans (many of the slave traders in Africa were Arabs), a young country with a strong army, an agricultural wonder that had developed interesting forms of settlement, was much more attractive to the Third World countries than the United States. Our presence in these places served American interests.

Israel's wars in 1967 and 1973 were a live combat laboratory for the United States, allowing it to examine its weapons systems over many years and take steps to ensure their supremacy over those of the Soviets and the Eastern Bloc. Operation Diamond in 1966—the defection of an Iraqi MiG 21 pilot along with his aircraft—was a strategic achievement that enabled American fighter pilots to fly a plane of this type for the first time, and American experts to study all of the aircraft's systems.

Our presence in the Middle East has made us first-rate experts on the history, culture, language, traditions, and ways of thinking of Arabs in the Middle East. It would not be an exaggeration to say that our intelligence and security services have taken the discipline of HUMINT to a level nearing perfection. In my opinion, to this day HUMINT is the "aircraft carrier" on which all other intelligence disciplines rely. It is the only discipline in which you can ask sources questions, interrogate them, and get a complete picture of intelligence, rather than the partial or occasional pictures provided by the other intelligence disciplines. Because of this advantage, it is through HUMINT that you can get the best understanding of the intentions of the enemy's decision makers. The CIA generally enjoyed the fruits of our HUMINT intelligence, whereas we usually enjoyed the fruits of American intelligence that came from technological sources (COMINT, SIGINT, VISINT, and so on).

During the Cold War, the CIA, as well as other American intelligence agencies, was a global intelligence service whose EEI encompassed the entire world. The Mossad, on the other hand, was a regional intelligence organization whose EEI focused almost entirely on the Middle East. But with the end of the Cold War in 1991, an interesting phenomenon began to occur: the EEI of the Western democracies underwent a process of fusion, focusing on two main threats—the proliferation of nonconventional weapons and global terrorism. This development required the Mossad to expand its activity—both in intelligence gathering and in prevention—to any place in which the threats of nonconventional weapons and terrorism existed—in other words, to the entire world. As a result, since the end of the Cold War, greater symmetry has developed between the EEI of the CIA and the Mossad.

One of the disciplines of the intelligence world is "info sharing" between friendly intelligence services. At an even higher level of cooperation are discussions regarding research and assessments between experts belonging to the two intelligence services. These have taken place between the Mossad and the CIA since the dawn of their relationship. A ground rule that any self-respecting intelligence service sticks to, and a point on which the CIA was obsessive, is to never reveal "sources and capabilities" to a friendly agency, but only intelligence products; these too are often veiled, in order to conceal not only the source but also the tools used for gathering the intelligence.

From the moment I took over as director of the Mossad in April 1989, I set myself a goal: to convince the CIA director to provide us with operational technologies that would allow us to dramatically improve our activities. The Americans agreed to limited cooperation, whereby we would propose an objective that the CIA would be interested in, and after they agreed we would carry out all of the preparatory work; at the stage at which the technology needed to be installed, they would provide it. The technology was indeed supplied and installed by an American technician. In this way, they guaranteed themselves control over the operation while we invested in the preparations. However, the benefit to us must not be underestimated—namely, the intelligence product from the operation, in which they took part together with us. The lesson that I took away from this arrangement was that we should invest more in developing our own technologies.

As I have already mentioned, with the end of the Cold War in 1991, the old EEI became irrelevant; it was replaced by the new EEI, which focused on the threats of nonconventional weapons and global terrorism. It was not long before the (mainly, but not exclusively) Western intelligence services realized that the new EEI required them to make significant changes in their definition of objectives and methods of conduct, especially with regard to cooperation with other services at a much higher level than in the past. It was clear that without cooperation the various agencies often got in each other's way, with damage sometimes being caused as a result. And most importantly, the potential of the intelligence and operations that could have been produced via cooperation was far from being fully exploited.

In the Mossad, this situation was felt intensely. As mentioned, the new EEI required the Mossad to expand its operational range far beyond the Middle East. I noticed that the Mossad was working increasingly on the same goals and objectives as the CIA, and sometimes as other intelligence services in Europe. My conclusion was that the era of cooperation in its old format had also ended. In addition to cooperation on intelligence, research, and evaluation, there was now a need for operational cooperation. Our people had begun to recognize and even encounter CIA operatives, among others, in the same theaters of action and near the same targets we had been working on around the world. The optimal solution was, of course, to agree on a division of labor and then share the results. However, when we proposed this to the CIA, our suggestion was not warmly received. There were several reasons for this, in my view. One was the American obsession with concealing sources and capabilities. Another was the fact that the CIA collaborated with countless intelligence services around the world, and a division of labor with the Mossad alone might raise some eyebrows. Finally, the CIA had clearly defined levels of cooperation with friendly agencies—it was quite possible that our proposal for a division of labor would have involved elevating the level of our relationship.

However, since the preemption component in both nonconventional weapons and global terrorism continued to develop beyond the component of intelligence gathering, the heads of Western intelligence agencies, including the CIA director, understood that operational cooperation could not be avoided. Such cooperation began to grow, on a bilateral and even a multilateral basis, when agency heads accepted that on these issues no intelligence agency could triumph by itself and that interservice cooperation was a necessary condition for success. At this point, and to increase the chances of success, the agency heads agreed to divulge their respective sources and capabilities.

Latin America—that is, Central and South America, from Mexico and southward—was a great concern of mine, as I saw it as a major potential target for terrorist attacks in general, and for attacks on Jewish targets in particular. Unfortunately, I was right to be concerned. In 1992 the Israeli embassy in Buenos Aires was blown up by a car bomb, and two years later the city's Jewish community center, AMIA, was attacked. The two attacks were carried out by Hezbollah with Iranian assistance.

My concern over this region had its genesis back in 1988, when, as deputy director of the Mossad, I conducted a study tour of the continent. The general intelligence picture established in the late 1980s and early 1990s, both through regular monitoring and via specific intelligence activities, was not encouraging. Our first important insight from the study of the continent was that the Arab communities in South America were integrated in all aspects of life, society, and politics, unlike in the rest of the world, where the Arab communities generally centered almost exclusively on economics and business. Obviously, this is the full right of Arab citizens in these countries, but it had political, security, and intelligence implications for Israel. Demographically speaking, it is important to mention that the largest Palestinian community in the world outside of the Middle East is in Chile.

There is no lack of Arab politicians in South America, including the Argentinean president of Syrian descent Carlos Menem, during whose term in office the attacks on the embassy and the AMIA building were carried out. Rumor had it that during that period Arabic was the spoken language in the presidential palace. There are many governors, members of parliament, and ministers of Arab origin as well as Arab journalists and owners of newspapers and radio and television stations. Many citizens of Arab origin work in South America's security services.

The triborder area between Brazil, Argentina, and Paraguay, called Foz do Iguacu, is reminiscent of a typical large town in Lebanon. Arabic is the second most common language there, after Spanish. Traders of Lebanese origin dominate the huge local market. Five times a day, the muezzin calls out from the minarets of the town's many mosques, inviting the faithful to come to pray. Tens of thousands of people and cars pass freely between the three countries each day. In the 1980s and 1990s, Foz do Iguacu served as a convalescent home for Hezbollah fighters who were wounded or simply tired after months of fighting in southern Lebanon and were sent to the town to rest, with the help of Iranian elements. The area became an unusual point of intersection between Arab terrorist organizations and South American organized crime groups and drug cartels. The only difference between these two types of organizations was that the terrorist organizations fought for political or religious goals, while the criminal organizations fought for money and power for its own sake. But their doctrines and methods of action were almost identical, and their growing cooperation was based on the comparative advantages each party brought to the table.

There was a massive Iranian presence on the South American continent, established through Iran's diplomatic missions.

In hindsight, it can be said with certainty that in Argentina Hezbollah created the ideal conditions to plan and carry out attacks of the kind they did. The terrorists for such operations could enter the country under the cover of tourism and could easily hide among the large Arab communities throughout the country. Passports, if necessary, could be obtained from the Iranian embassy. Documentation of any other kind could be obtained for a fee, without registration and with no questions asked, in Foz do Iguacu. Weapons, explosives, and caches could be obtained in the Paraguayan city of Ciudad del Este, which was controlled for all intents and purposes by the cartels.

When Buenos Aires was the target, it was preferable for the operatives to prepare for and embark on the attack from a different point. In the case of the embassy attack, the starting point was most probably Ciudad del Este. Cars could be bought there without any trace of purchase, with the help of local collaborators. Operational apartments could be easily obtained, without registration or tracks. One could assume that the Iranian embassy used its capabilities to bring into the country anything that was difficult or unwise to bring in through the ordinary border crossings. The Iranian embassy could also provide other forms of assistance. Couriers and "cutoff" (personnel who disrupt the conveying of messages and/or materials) were copious and could blend in easily without being identified. Retreats were also very easy to plan in such an arena.

On one of my first visits to Langley, the director of the CIA hosted me for lunch in his private dining room with his deputies and other senior CIA officials. Over the meal, during a general conversation about terrorism, I asked them if they were aware of what was going on in Foz do Iguacu. From the looks that were exchanged around the table I realized that they had no idea what I was talking about. I described to them in detail the situation there and the potential risks involved. At the end of the meal, the director instructed his people to begin looking into the subject. And indeed, the CIA began to invest resources into it, including through cooperation with some of the intelligence and security services in South America. Unfortunately, we were unable to prevent the terrorist attacks on the embassy and community center in Buenos Aires, which, with the wisdom of hindsight, were written on the wall.

My first visits to Langley were in 1989, at the end of the Cold War, when the Soviet Union was at the top of the CIA's EEI. During each of these visits I had the opportunity to meet with both operations and research people. The meetings were informal, and when the subject of discussion was the Middle East they took the form of a dialogue, whereas when the subject was the Soviet bloc they were for the most part briefings for me. The researchers were real experts, each in his or her own field of expertise, yet curious to hear every word uttered by a visitor from the Middle East.

I will never forget the last briefing I received on the Soviet bloc, at a time when one could already sense the impending collapse of the Soviet Union. The researchers who briefed me bombarded me with data on the volume of Soviet agricultural production and coal and steel output over the previous year and their forecasts for the following year, and endless other statistics, all of which were seen as indicators of the strength of the Soviet Union. It was implied, though not explicitly stated, that the bottom line of this briefing was that in terms of its capabilities the Soviet Union still constituted a real threat to the United States.

I did not feel like a great expert on the Soviet Union in that setting, and I did not want to pester the researchers with questions, but I was reminded of a seminar I had taken at Harvard in 1985 about the methodology used to build the US defense budget. To an observer, the seminar seemed more like a math lesson than an in-depth discussion that took into account all nonquantifiable variables in assessing the enemy's power. And to those who might respond that a university seminar is no more than an academic exercise, I would point out that William Kaufmann, the professor who taught the seminar, was considered the guru of the Pentagon, with no defense budget proposal being submitted to Congress before he had reviewed it and given his input.

Here is another story about CIA intelligence research. It was the early 1990s, and the head of the CIA's research division was visiting Israel. We were having dinner together at a Tel Aviv restaurant and conducting a comprehensive review—a *tour d'horizon*—of the state of the world. At that time, the issue of nuclear proliferation was already very high on the Mossad's EEI. Over the course of the conversation, I raised the issue of the nuclear cooperation between Pakistan and Iran, and as an aside I made the pseudophilosophical comment that if the human race was to experience another nuclear event, it would probably be between India and Pakistan.

My dinner companion straightened up in his chair and fired half a dozen questions at me, the essence of which were "On what basis are you saying this?" I replied that I was not drawing on any credible intelligence source, but rather on simple logic, based on three truths. The first was the deep hostility between India and Pakistan, which, since Pakistan's separation from India in 1947, had resulted in war or the brink of war. The second was that both countries had nuclear arsenals with means of weapons delivery, and the third truth was that in both countries there existed a fatalistic culture that saw human life as worthless, in contrast to almost all of the other countries of the world.

The CIA official accepted my explanation, but it was evident that he was not satisfied; it was as if he wanted to say that he found it difficult to believe that the director of the Mossad would express himself in such a way without having some very weighty evidence to back himself up. It later came to my attention that the man had taken my words so seriously that as soon as he returned to the United States an American team was sent to Pakistan to investigate my assessment, in case my words had not been a simple observation but rather had immanent operational significance. Since that incident, I have been more careful in expressing my assessments about the fate of the world, especially at intimate dinners after a glass of wine.

Things were easier with CIA operations officers, with whom I had mutual chemistry right off the bat. They knew that my background was also in the world of operations. During this period of the end of the Cold War, my colleagues saw the world as black and white, with the Soviet bloc as the dark side and us as the "protectors of the light." Of course, I did not meet all of these officers, but I regarded those whom I befriended and who were at the top levels of command as "cold warriors." They radiated warmth and extraordinary appreciation for Israel and the Israelis for the miracle they had created in the Middle East, their courage, their creativity and craftiness, and their manning of one of the more important outposts for American interests.

The sense of solidarity and intimacy that they felt with us sometimes made for some awkward situations. For example, in casual conversation over a few beers, they would tell jokes with just a hint of anti-Semitism; when I said to them, "Hey, guys, you're crossing the line!" they would answer, smiling, "You're Israelis, it's not like you're typical Jews." They had to be told that Israelis and Jews were one and the same. It wasn't that they didn't understand this per se, but in their world the overlaps and nuances between Israeli and Jewish identity were not so clear.

Throughout my tenure as director of the Mossad (1989–96), I made every effort to preserve the Mossad's role as an asset for the CIA. In the overall balance, it was very difficult to maintain equality between the benefits that each side reaped from the other. The gap between a world power with almost unlimited capabilities and a "minipower" like Israel made this kind of balance impossible. However, and in all modesty, I would like to mention that then-deputy director (later director) of the CIA George Tenet came to Israel specifically to bid me farewell and to grant me a medal on behalf of the CIA. For me, this was proof that I had met expectations—first of all my own, but also those of our closest friend.

Cyber Warfare—A New Definition for an Old Profession

The term *cyber* burst into our lives two decades ago and brought about profound changes in the world. The discipline of cyber intelligence had actually existed in the Israeli intelligence community since the state's early years, under other names, and with much less potential for harm to the enemy than today. The envelope that defines the threat and the response was always dependent on the technologies' limitations. From the outset, the Israeli intelligence community has generally been able to maximize its range of operational capabilities within the limits of technology. As technology developed over the years, so did the scope of capabilities and operations. Today the world is at a point where the potential cyber threat rivals, and perhaps even surpasses, the potential threat of other nonconventional weapons. Let's take a look at how it all began and how it evolved.

Prior to the establishment of the State of Israel, the Shai, the Haganah's intelligence service, was active in cyber intelligence. Among other things, the Shai succeeded in tapping into the British Mandate's central telephone switchboard in Jaffa. According to Shai sources, "Tapping the telephone lines allowed us to listen to the conversations of British government officials and Arab leaders day and night."[2]

In the 1940s and '50s, the peak of the intelligence war between Israel and the Arab countries was the recruitment and operation of agents (HUMINT), immediately followed by "tongue catching," operations not using technology, but whose intelligence product was of very high quality. The objective of these operations was to capture a military officer beyond Israel's border with an Arab country, bring him to Israel, and reap the intelligence that was stored inside his head.

The first cyber operation to which the Israeli public was exposed (because of a mishap) took place in 1954. The mission was to service a warning device on the Syrian Golan Heights, near the international border. The team consisted of five soldiers, who were captured by the Syrians when they crossed the border. One of them, Uri Ilan, committed suicide during his captivity, leaving a note attached to his foot with the words "I did not betray."[3]

Alongside the cyber intelligence technique of tapping communication lines, additional technologies were developed in the field of electronics.

What we know about the capabilities of the superpowers in this area during the Cold War is no less interesting and highlights the gap between the capabilities of the superpowers and those of the "regular" developed countries. The superpowers were able to drop tiny, camouflaged audio-surveillance systems from reconnaissance aircraft, flying at high altitudes near enemy installations, that would intercept information and transmit it to intelligence satellites. The superpowers also knew how to physically connect to communications cables deep in the ocean or at the points at which they met land.

In the 1990s, the cyber world took things up a notch. Technological capabilities developed that could achieve all of these things but control them remotely, at a standoff distance, and without physical contact.

Cyber warfare is a constant war between the attacker and the defender, with each side developing capabilities in both areas—defense and attack—in parallel. The war is between those whose job it is to protect national databases and infrastructures and those whose job it is to circumvent or break down the defenses of the enemy in order to expose, sabotage, destroy, and silence them. This duality exists not only at the political and military level but also in other sectors of society—the economy, banking, science, the high-tech sector, and so on.

At the end of the 1990s, cyber warfare in the United States was classified as an additional weapon in the nonconventional weapons arsenal. This meant that cyber warfare joined the club of chemical, biological, and nuclear weapons capabilities. Decision makers and shapers of public opinion around the world classify cyber warfare as a weapon that, while seemingly "clean" or "dry"—that is, it does not kill people directly—has the potential to cause no less damage to a particular country and to humankind in general than that caused by other nonconventional weapons.

The transformation that took place in the realm of information and communications between the mid-1970s and the twenty-first century propelled cyberspace, and its destructive potential, to a level that no one could have imagined. In the past, the most common wireless communication systems were HF and UHF, their transmission was usually via Morse code, and the encryption was manual or mechanical. The world of that era was bipolar and stable. Today's world is multipolar and much less stable. Back then, the world was large, scattered, and decentralized. Now it is a global village. Today's world is characterized by the following:

- Online communication from any point on earth to any other point on earth
- Complete transparency among all the inhabitants of the world
- Meaningless international borders
- The convergence of global terrorism and global criminal organizations
- The primacy of real time—information that is not used in real time is irrelevant
- Intelligence from open sources (OSINT) being top priority
- A reality in which, if you have identified a weak link in the global IT network, you can easily penetrate the sea of global data, extract and plant information, plant bugs, and cause disruption and destruction, either in real time or whenever you choose

Deterrence in cyberspace is particularly problematic. The concept of deterrence is central to the nonconventional arena, as deterrence is the real force that prevents the use of nonconventional weapons, the result of which is disastrous. With nuclear weapons, deterrence is based on Mutually Assured Destruction (MAD), which means that when each side has second-strike capability, a regime of deterrence is in place.

The question is whether deterrence can be achieved in cyber warfare, given the fundamental difference between cyber warfare and other types of nonconventional warfare. The difference lies in the difficulty or inability to unambiguously identify the aggressor, combined with the inability to maintain deterrence based on second-strike capability.

Traditional deterrence is based on the fact that actors on both sides are identifiable. Moreover, they take care to identify themselves and enhance their capabilities in order to bolster deterrence (this applies more to nuclear capability and less to chemical and biological capabilities, though Saddam Hussein, for example, did declare his capabilities in this area publicly). When a party in a given conflict is the victim of a cyberattack and must respond, a key question it will face is that of the "smoking gun," meaning that the party is required to prove the identity of the attacker unequivocally before responding. Often the assailant may be an eighteen-year-old hacker in jeans and a T-shirt, carrying out the attack from his basement, which could be located literally anywhere on earth. And even if it is possible to pinpoint him, it is not always possible to know with certainty whether he is acting on his own behalf or at the request of a client, which could be a business, a criminal organization, a terrorist group, or a state.

The operational significance of this dialectic is that cyberspace, as an arena of military action, has a built-in tendency toward offense. It is possible that the strengthening of offensive capabilities and their disclosure will actually contribute to the establishment of a deterrence regime. True deterrence is possible only when one of the players has the proven ability to paralyze an entire country. In current reality, this is still hypothetical. Should it turn out that there is truth to the allegations that Russian hackers, acting in concert with the Russian authorities, carried out a cyberattack on the Democratic Party headquarters during the 2016 US presidential election campaign, we can imagine that this will serve as "raw material" to Americans planners formulating an entirely new kind of deterrence strategy, one that the world has not needed until now. It is not unreasonable to assume that this strategy will include means of defense against a similar attack in the future, as well as offensive plans for an attack. One can also assess that Russia's success, if the attack did indeed take place, will encourage it and other countries to use cyber warfare in the future.

In 2007, a team of IBM hackers conducted a test called the "X-Force Experiment," which demonstrated that it was possible to penetrate a civilian nuclear facility in the United States. The hackers showed that the command-and-control systems could be secretly manipulated, including the reactor's cooling system. In other words, the experiment proved that a cyberattack could wreak havoc on a nuclear power reactor and, even more frightening, could cause a meltdown of the reactor core and massive radioactive contamination, as happened in Chernobyl in 1986 (from faulty engineering).

The cyberattack on Iran's nuclear facilities through the Stuxnet computer worm has already been dubbed "Hiroshima of the cyber war." The ability to attack industrial control systems was a "crossing of a threshold" in cyber warfare. The Stuxnet operation marked the birth of a new dimension in cyber warfare—the nonconventional cyberattack (NCCA).[4]

Looking to the future, we can assume that following or in parallel to the American establishment of a deterrence doctrine in cyberspace, we will also see international initiatives to regulate the issue that will attempt to define what is permissible and what is prohibited in a manner that is acceptable to all.

For the sake of clarity, table 1 compares types of nonconventional weapons according to different variables. The weapon of EMP (electromagnetic pulse), which paralyzes the target of an attack, is included in the table.

Table 1. Nonconventional Weapons

	Use	*User*	*Damage*	*Deterrence*	*Legislation and Regulation*
Chemical weapons	Regular	States/organizations	Containable Evaporates	In kind; upgraded response	International conventions
Biological weapons	Minimal	States	Deadly Contaminated areas Lasting effects	In kind; upgraded response	International conventions
Nuclear weapons	One-time	States		MAD	International conventions
Cyber warfare	Daily	Anyone	"White damage"	None	None
Electromagnetic pulse (EMP)	Unknown	States	Local or territorial paralysis	None	None

Some see the new technology of quantum communication, which has developed in recent years, as the ultimate response to cyberattacks. The theoretical basis for this technology was developed by Chinese mathematician Andrew Chi-Chih Yao, dean of the Institute for Interdisciplinary Information Sciences at Tsinghua University in Beijing, one of the top nine universities in China. The technology is based on a combination of quantum mechanics, a branch of physics, and theoretical computer models. Its great advantage lies in the fact that while with all other types of communications it is possible to eavesdrop on one or more connections in the communications network, in quantum communication it is not. Any attempt to intercept information that passes through quantum communication will be immediately exposed, because the very attempt causes the information to change in a way that alerts the network's members. China is considered the world leader in quantum communication technology, and recently an experimental network was launched there that transmits information between various institutions in Beijing and Shanghai. According to foreign publications, the United States and Israel have also made efforts to develop quantum communication.[5]

The Snowden Affair and Its Implications

If the Stuxnet operation was the "Hiroshima of cyber war," then the Snowden affair was an "intellectual earthquake," in the sense that it illuminated for the first time the normative questions related to cyber warfare. The main question that arose was: What is the right balance between a state's security needs and individual freedoms, in particular freedom of speech? Although there were rumors that the National Security Agency (NSA), which deals with electronic intelligence, had been secretly accessing the databases of Google, Yahoo, and others, it was only on October 30, 2013, that real evidence was produced. The immediate response of the organizations that had been penetrated by the NSA was to encrypt all of the data flowing between the company's data centers. The companies' spokespeople also issued unequivocal denials, maintaining that they had not cooperated with the government. These revelations showed that cyber infiltration concerns not only national security and diplomacy but also the economy, especially when it comes to financial data about internet technologies.

The European Union and most of its member states reacted immediately by announcing their intention to reexamine their cooperation with the United States on these issues, in light of the disclosure that the United States was giving priority to its intelligence agencies, which they believed created an unfair advantage for American bodies competing with European bodies. The American internet industry, which usually cooperates to some extent with the administration when it comes to national security, was astonished at the extent of NSA infiltration into friendly countries as well as hostile countries. Internet financial companies (databases for use in advertising) have also begun to use encryption. Notably, NSA operations in the United States are subject to far more legal and regulatory restrictions than those outside of the United States.

Some voices in the United States suggest that the Snowden affair was an intelligence operation carried out by either Russia or China, or by a joint operation between the two. There is quite a bit of circumstantial evidence to support this theory (Snowden fled from the United States to Hong Kong and from there went on to Russia, where he obtained political asylum that was extended in January 2017 for another two years). A book published in the United States in early 2017 suggested that the moral dilemma Snowden supposedly found himself in was simply a cover story for his actions. And there you have another interesting aspect of the cyber world.

Normative Dilemmas Created by Cyber Warfare

The revelation that the NSA had eavesdropped on German chancellor Angela Merkel's iPhone raised the following question: Is the information that can be obtained by spying on friends more important than the damage caused if and when such actions are discovered?

In this regard President Barack Obama said, "Could technology interfere with our common sense?" On the face of it, it seems that this is a condemnation of the manner in which the NSA used technology. But a more in-depth analysis of his statement suggests that his approach to the issue was not one-sided and that he was aware of the dilemmas involved.

Snowden and those behind WikiLeaks claim that their disclosure of the practice of wiretapping and other methods used by the NSA and similar agencies contributed to the transparency and values of an open society. These values—liberty, transparency, civil rights, equality before the law, privacy, and more—make up the foundation of societies in Western democracies. But the question is, Will total transparency contribute to a better world? Is maintaining the security of the state not a value? Is protecting the lives of agents/spies not a value? Is the struggle against global terrorism not a value?

Western society has succeeded in creating mechanisms whose function is to protect the citizen from abuses of power or arbitrary rule, and these mechanisms must be exercised when necessary. However, full transparency will not contribute to a better world; rather, it will lead to anarchy.

Among the thinkers who examine these kinds of "cyber dilemmas" are those who interpret the phenomenon as a new type of colonialism. They refer to cyber capabilities as a new type of weapon designed to enable the "cyber superpowers" to expand their influence over, and perhaps even control, "weaker" countries, not by causing destruction but by paralyzing and disabling their infrastructures.

On the NSA's Capabilities as Published by Snowden

For years, the NSA's policy was that surveillance and hacking, anywhere around the world and for any purpose that it saw as serving the interests of the United States, was legitimate.

The NSA is an organization of thirty-five thousand employees with an annual budget of $11 billion. It dwarfs all of its counterparts in the world, except perhaps those in Russia and China.

In general, citizens of the world buy their e-mail and internet services from US companies that cooperate—some more than others—with the NSA. This means that citizens and bodies from other countries are less influential in international markets than their US competitors.

Even the encrypted traffic of global telecommunications networks is not immune to the NSA's enormous power. The advent of computers, including personal computers, the internet, and cell phones, has made the NSA the world's largest spy agency. The NSA can intercept all of the traffic that passes through fiber-optic cables; it can connect to any telephone system or website in the world; it can digitally "rob" any laptop and can plant bugs on smartphones anywhere in the world.

Among Snowden's leaks was the revelation that ahead of President Obama's meeting with UN secretary-general Ban Ki-moon in April 2013, the NSA had eavesdropped on the secretary-general and provided Obama with the talking points he had prepared for their meeting.[6]

The NSA operates surveillance aircraft over territories defined as being "of interest" (Colombia); it maintains surveillance bases aboard US Navy ships near other places of interest (China) and transmits the results via satellite in real time to the organization's headquarters in Fort Meade, Maryland, about thirty kilometers from Washington, D.C. The NSA runs surveillance bases at eighty US embassies and consulates around the world and oversees all financial and banking traffic worldwide. The NSA can organize itself to deal with events around the world on short notice by immediately concentrating and pooling the various resources at its disposal.

The United States has sixteen different intelligence agencies, but at the president's daily intelligence briefing more than half of the information comes from NSA sources. The NSA has an intelligence alliance with services from England, Canada, Australia, and New Zealand, called the "Five Eyes." There is a division of labor among them and they share data with each other. Other intelligence alliances are the Nine Eyes, the Fourteen Eyes, and the NATO Special Committee, made up of the heads of the security services of NATO's member countries.

The NSA cooperates with Israel, while at the same time collecting information on Israeli targets.[7]

The NSA is the largest employer of mathematicians in the United States, for the purpose of breaking codes.

The NSA is the biggest employer of hackers.

"Tech Has Outrun Politics." Nobody has assessed the risks and benefits involved in using new technologies against allies and friends. There is a need for new leadership, top-down reform, and legislation. If this is not done, the NSA could turn the United States into a totalitarian regime.

Do we want to live in a world where at any given moment we can become transparent and exposed to both enemies and friends? Where technological capabilities are operated by technocrats and robots, before any proper staff work has been carried out by political decision makers? Where the threat of annihilation hangs over our heads, and if and when it happens, heaven forbid, we won't even be able to identify the enemy that pulled the virtual trigger?

I, for one, do not want to live in a world like this. I am told that the "next big thing" is quantum communication, which has already passed the stage of practicability. I am told that this technology is the antidote to cyberattacks. My hope is that this type of communication will not add transparency to our world but will bring it back to what it was—a world in which our privacy is preserved.

CHAPTER TWO

INTELLIGENCE AND THE INTERNATIONAL ARENA

How to Confront Fundamentalist International Terrorism

It is next to impossible for someone from a Western culture to truly understand radical Muslims' frustration with and hatred for anyone who is not a Muslim. In order to help try to clarify the origins of this abhorrence, I refer to the words of three renowned professors who have explained them as well as I ever could.

Prof. Yehuda Bauer, an expert on the subject of the Holocaust and an Israel Prize laureate, describes the radical Islam of the school of Osama bin Laden, who led al-Qaeda, and ISIS leader Abu Bakr al-Baghdadi, as a colossal disaster and threat to the West that is similar in scope and intensity only to the communist threat of the Soviet Union and the Nazi threat of Hitler's Germany. The common denominator between these three threats is their declared aspiration to change the global order and take over the world, eliminating all those who stand in opposition to them.

Prof. Yehezkel Dror, a leading authority on governance and international relations, describes global terrorism as a reality in which fewer and fewer people can kill more and more people. This ability, which will continue to grow, stems, inter alia, from terrorists' willingness to commit suicide and from the danger of terrorist groups getting control of weapons of mass destruction.

Prof. Irwin Cotler, a prominent legal expert from McGill University in Montreal and a former Canadian member of parliament and justice minister, has discussed the anti-Semitic aspect of fundamentalist Islam, emphasizing that the extent of Islamic hatred for Judaism and Jews has reached the dimension of calls for genocide. He has proposed replacing the word *anti-Semitism* in this context, as there is an internal contradiction in the definition of Muslim hatred of Judaism as anti-Semitism, and the intensity of the detestation requires a new definition of the phenomenon.

It is customary to mark September 11, 2001, as the point in time when fundamentalist Islam's global ambitions made their debut, although their flag bearers at the time, Osama bin Laden and al-Qaeda, had been around for several years prior to this historic date. The first question that comes to mind when we think of the heinous attack on the World Trade Center in New York and the Pentagon in Washington, D.C., concerns the root of the hatred that could bring people— some of them graduates of universities in the United States and western Europe—to commit such acts. I recommend searching for the answer to this question in the explanations of Bernard Lewis, a professor emeritus at Princeton University, who was considered the greatest historian of his generation on the Muslim world. Lewis, a London-born Jew, was known as the "doyen of the Orientalists."

Exploring the "roots of Muslim rage"—the name of an article he published several years ago—Lewis stated that the entire Muslim world today is experiencing a sense of frustration and crisis. Everything has gone wrong. For more than a thousand years, Muslims were accustomed to the notion that they were the most advanced people in the world and that they had set the gold standard in politics, economics, and science. With the new age, the Muslims realized that their power had faded and that even the adoption of Western technology could not revive it. The imported Western ideas of socialism and capitalism did not stem the economic and cultural decline of the Islamic world. Then came the thought that salvation perhaps lay in the adoption of the model of the Western democratic regime. Unfortunately, the only Western model that succeeded in taking root in the Muslim world was that of the one-party dictatorship. The political independence won by Arab and Muslim states during the twentieth century did not give rise to freedom.

The reaction to these disappointments was opposition to all ideas imported from the West, and the blaming of the West for all of the evils resulting from the failed attempts to imitate its culture. Muslims now had two options. Some felt that the failure had stemmed from the abandonment of ancient traditions, of authentic Islamic civilization. The two main trends that emerged from this perception were Wahhabi fundamentalism, as disseminated by the Saudis, and Iranian-inspired Shiite fundamentalism. The other option was supported by embracers of modernity, who maintained that the failure had resulted from the fact that the Muslims had adopted only the superficial layers of Western civilization and not its deeper contents, and that consequently efforts should be made to implant Western values more fully. Throughout the Muslim world there are people who believe this, but the despotic regimes make it difficult for them to express their opinions openly.

Osama bin Laden represented an extreme expression of the first option. However—and here Lewis added a very interesting point—we cannot underestimate the importance of Arab oil. The huge profits accumulated by the Saudi rulers enabled them to develop extensive networks of schools that nurtured Wahhabi fundamentalism. It may be that had it not been for oil, this movement would have remained an insignificant phenomenon in a marginal country. According to this view, oil has been the Arabs' downfall, because it allowed the regimes to amass enormous amounts of money that strengthened their political and military power and to suppress any efforts toward democracy and freedom. It is no coincidence that the only Arab countries in which a civil society has developed are Morocco and Jordan, neither of which has any oil.

Responding to the question of whether America is hated in the Muslim world because of its support for Israel, Lewis pointed out that while its affinity with Israel obviously does not help America's popularity, the Middle East is not the only region in the world in which this great and rich empire is detested. It is hated mainly because it is so successful, and this resentment is exploited by local elements for their own purposes. For bin Laden, for example, the main problem was his country, Saudi Arabia, which he wanted to purge of the presence and influence of the infidels.

Westerners tend to ask the wrong question: "Why don't they love us?" The simple answer is that you cannot be wealthy, powerful, and successful and expect to be loved, especially when you haven't lost a fight in hundreds of years. The correct question to ask is: "Why have they stopped respecting us, or at least being afraid of us?" Muslim culture espouses the notion of the benevolence of the victor. The winner does not rub the loser's face in the mud. But the outcome of the struggle must be clear to both sides. A battle whose result is ambiguous is an invitation for trouble. The Ottomans provided many examples of this behavior: they crushed the rebels with a strong hand but did not humiliate them. They showed generosity toward them and even helped them to rehabilitate themselves. If the powerful party does not exhaust its ability to achieve such a victory, its behavior is interpreted as cowardice.

Is it an exaggeration to call this a clash of civilizations? According to Lewis, these differences are of great significance. The Christian world and the Muslim world have been at odds and fought against each other on many fronts for more than a thousand years. In the late eighteenth century, there were dozens of Oriental studies departments in Western universities, and hundreds of translations of Arabic, Persian, and Turkish works were printed. The Western world longed to understand its historical adversary. But this curiosity did not go both ways. In the Muslim world, scholars did not learn the languages of the West, were not interested in Western history and thought, and did not often translate Western literature into Arabic. Things changed a little once they realized the force of the Western threat, but curiosity about the "other" is a distinctly Western phenomenon. In Muslim society, this interest arises only in the face of a threat. This cultural phenomenon may not last forever, but it is more deeply rooted than many people tend to think.

What will the long-term effects of the war in Afghanistan be? People like bin Laden and some Palestinians thought that the West and Israel had "gone soft" and wouldn't have the stomach to wage a war. The Afghanistan war, as well as Israel's response to the al-Aqsa Intifada, proved that the West is determined to fight when its civilization is attacked. Now there are two possibilities: either the people of Muslim world, especially the Arabs, decide that in order to establish a better society they must choose the path of peace and cooperation with the West, or they choose to believe that their defeat was simply an unfortunate episode and that they must continue along their current path. For now, they seem to have chosen the latter option of continued struggle, and their means is international terrorism. When I say *they*, I do not mean all Arabs or all Muslims. The use of the word *they* is qualitative, not quantitative or statistical. "They" in this case are those who determine the agenda and implement their apocalyptic vision.

It is commonly said that terrorism is the weapon of the weak, and the weak in this context are the occupied, the poor, the hungry, the desperate, and the hopeless. This classic definition of terrorism does not apply to the al-Qaeda and ISIS schools of fundamentalist terrorism; these are very rich terrorist organizations that acquired permanent residency first in Sudan, a few years later in Afghanistan, and finally in Iraq and Syria. The leaders of these organizations are extremely wealthy, and their businesses finance the organizations' activities throughout the world. Many of these terrorist groups' members come from social classes that can be defined as middle class. These facts demonstrate that the root of the conflict is not socioeconomic but cultural.

The late 1970s were watershed years that saw the transition from the terrorism (for the sake of convenience we will refer to it as classical terrorism) of the first half of the twentieth century to the modern terrorism of the last quarter of the twentieth century and into the twenty-first century. Before we delve into the distinctions between these two types of terrorism, let us say a few words about the definition of the term *terrorism*.

First, there is no universal consensus on the definition of terrorism. The reasons for this lie in the political and international complexity of all the considerations and interests of states in their attempt to give the phenomenon a definition that would have universal legal validity. Because of this complexity, it is easier for the countries of the world to deal with the phenomenon of terrorism without defining it at all, or alternatively to define it "privately," in a way that can be reconciled with the laws of the state. For the purposes of this book, I will use the definition formulated by the International Institute for Counter-Terrorism (ICT) at the Interdisciplinary Center Herzliya (IDC), soon after it was established in 1996. Full disclosure: at the time of this writing, I serve as the chairman of ICT. This definition states that *terrorism is the use of violence against civilians to achieve political ends.*

ICT's definition was intended to be short and simple, in an effort to encourage broad international consensus—an attempt that has as yet been unsuccessful. It includes three necessary conditions for the definition of a phenomenon or behavior as terrorism: (1) violence as the means; (2) civilians as the target; and (3) political objectives.

The line between war and terrorism is crude. In order to refine it, we thought it appropriate to define another type of conflict—guerrilla warfare. Now let us compare the three types of conflicts.

In *war*, the sides use the entire arsenal at their disposal, with the goal of conquering or liberating territory. Conventional wars are on the decline, and alongside them a new type of conflict has developed called "low-intensity warfare" or "asymmetric warfare" (though these two things are not necessarily exactly the same).

In *terrorism*, the use of weapons is very limited but extremely lethal. The goal of terrorism is to change a regime, to liberate a nation, or, in the case of international jihadist terrorism, to establish a global Islamic caliphate. The phenomenon of terrorism of all kinds is constantly on the rise.

In *guerrilla warfare*, the use of weapons is limited. The goal is to liberate occupied territory and change the regime, and the top civilian echelons of the state, alongside all uniformed people, are viewed as legitimate targets. Guerrilla warfare has also been on the increase along the time line of history.

A comparison between classical terrorism and its modern incarnation reveals the following significant distinctions.

- First of all, classical terrorism was *local*, covering the territory of a particular region or country, but not more. Modern terrorism is *global*.
- Classical terrorism was *secular*; although in the Middle East today there are still some traces of terrorist groups whose leaders were or are Christian Arabs, modern terrorism is *religious-Muslim-fundamentalist*.
- Classical terrorism was *nationalistic*, striving to achieve self-determination, whereas contemporary terrorism can be defined as *imperialistic* in the sense that it aspires to create a Muslim world that lives according to the laws of sharia (Islamic law).
- Solidarity in the era of classical terrorism existed between secular territorial groups. Solidarity today is a function of the global religious common denominator. The classical terrorist organizations had *socialist or Marxist* political tendencies, as opposed to today's groups, which follow *Islamic theology*.
- Classical terrorism had a *weak, mostly local, resonance*. Contemporary terrorism has a strong, real-time *global resonance*, and it gets it for free.

A few insights help us assess the potential of the threat of modern terrorism. The basic premise, which must be clear to anyone dealing with this subject, is related to the historical development of Islam. Many aspects of the religion of Islam are drawn from Judaism and Christianity. It originated in the desert of the Arabian Peninsula in the seventh century and succeeded in rising up and conquering half of the world and establishing an empire that was an Arab caliphate. The Muslim conquerors succeeded in spreading the new religion, whether by persuasion or by coercion, throughout the caliphate. Islam prospered economically, culturally, and scientifically and made a significant contribution to humanity at that time. The empire of Islam continued to survive in the form of the Ottoman Empire until the First World War, when it suffered a humiliating defeat; after approximately 1,300 years of power and splendor, it was shattered to pieces by the Western colonial powers. Against this background one can and must understand the depth and intensity of the longing to restore Islam to its former status and realize that the strongest glue that connects people is neither politics nor society nor economic status but religious solidarity.

In discussing the potential of the threat of modern terrorism, we must understand the implications of the ultimate goal of establishing a global Muslim caliphate. In order to establish such a caliphate it is first necessary to conquer the world and Islamize its inhabitants; there must be a war of "Gog and Magog" following the resurrection of the *Mahdi* (a motif that is analogous to the Messiah in Judaism). Here we can highlight a fundamental difference between the followers of al-Qaeda and those of ISIS, despite the fact that the latter organization is an outgrowth of the former. Al-Qaeda members adhere to the scenario described above, as it appears in the canon of Shiite Islam, while ISIS followers believe that the issue can be forced—that it is necessary and possible to establish the world caliphate alongside the struggle against the infidels. And indeed, the leader of ISIS declared the conquest of the city of Raqqa in Syria as the beginning of the establishment of the caliphate; any additional territory occupied by ISIS—with no need for territorial contiguity—would declare its inclusion in the caliphate (for example, the Sinai Province in the Sinai Peninsula or Boko Haram in Nigeria).

Because the establishment of the Islamic caliphate is a divine commandment, so is everything that is derived from it. When a person acts according to a divine commandment, human reason (*ratio*) does not come into play. Thus the concept of "coexistence" is fundamentally unacceptable—there is only a divinely commanded war against the infidels. Moreover, there is no need for provocation by the infidels as a justification to fight them. The divine command alone places believers into a mode of constant war, whose end will come only when the desired global caliphate is established.

The concept of jihad in Islam has many meanings and interpretations, ranging from spiritual explanations similar to the concept of spiritual strengthening in Orthodox Judaism, to the willingness to commit suicide for the sake of spreading Islam. In the world of jihadist global terrorism, suicide by self-sacrifice is considered a holy commandment; he who martyrs himself for Allah becomes a saint (*shahid*), and his family enjoys financial support and respect from the community. The phenomenon of the individual suicide bomber greatly increases the overall threat potential of jihadist terrorism and reinforces the statement that "fewer and fewer people are killing more and more people." The suicide attack on the World Trade Center in New York and the Pentagon in Washington proves this more than any other instance: nineteen suicide bombers killed thousands of civilians.

The individual suicide bomber, assuming that he complies with the basic rules of clandestine activity, can fly under the radar of intelligence and achieve the element of surprise without his opponent being able to detect anything and thus take action to thwart the attack. Another factor that augments the potential threat relates to the fact that in the suicide bomber's plan of action there is no need to plan an escape route following the execution of the attack. This makes it even more difficult to uncover any clues that may help expose the planned attack before it occurs or to analyze it after it has already been carried out. When we are dealing with an enemy with a religious ideology and with an end that sanctifies the means, we cannot and must not exclude the possibility that they will use chemical, biological, or nuclear weapons. The line of the use of chemical weapons by states and nonstate actors in the Middle East was crossed many years ago (by Egypt in Yemen, by Iraq against the Kurds and Iran, by the Syrian regime against the rebels, and by ISIS against its enemies). Biological weapons, which have deadlier potential than chemical weapons, can also be found in the Middle East, as can nuclear weapons; these can easily fall into the hands of a terrorist organization, potentially making it even more true that fewer and fewer people are able to kill more and more people.

The world's radical Islamic organizations, such as al-Qaeda and ISIS, have confronted the Western democracies with a variable that did not exist during the time of the conventional wars or during the era of classical terrorism. These terrorist organizations are amorphous, without headquarters or a clear hierarchy, and their virtual deployment is global. Their means of communication is the internet, through which they communicate with their members, coconspirators, supporters, and adherents from around the world. They use the internet to spread their message through their propaganda networks, as well as to recruit, to train, and to produce various types of weapons. Since without holding at least a minimal amount of territory they cannot exist, they are constantly looking for areas to live—places where there is political instability or where they can find allies. These could be, for example, the Palestinian territories, from which the Palestinian terrorist organizations operate, or areas in southern Lebanon that have been taken over by Hezbollah, to the chagrin of the Lebanese government but with the support of Syria and Iran. They could include Sudan, where bin Laden found an ally in Hassan al-Turabi, who provided bin Laden and his people with a territorial base from which to operate not only out of sympathy but also in exchange for financial payment. They could include Afghanistan, where bin Laden essentially bought the Taliban government that was in control, with part of the deal being the right of residence and a base for al-Qaeda operations. And they could span the entire planet, throughout which the members of the organizations and their infrastructure are scattered, as is the case today, following the US military operations in Afghanistan after 9/11.

The policy of the Israeli government has always been that the countries from which the terrorists operate bear the burden of responsibility, as they do not prevent the terrorist organizations from using their territory. Israel therefore sees as its right to fight the terrorist organizations in the territory of the countries that harbor them. More than once, the Israeli government has been condemned for this policy by the enlightened nations of the world. The American war against al-Qaeda around the world reflected a policy similar to that of Israel, as did the CIA's targeting of a car carrying al-Qaeda commanders in Yemen, not to mention the dozens of operations aimed at thwarting radical Islamic activity that have been carried out throughout the world.

The next territory that the Islamic terrorist organizations set their sights on was Iraq, which had been torn between the Shiites and the Sunnis after the US occupation. The Arab Spring was a dream come true for the radical Islamic terrorist groups. In Egypt, the Muslim Brotherhood came to power for the first time since their inception in the 1920s. In Tunisia, Ghannouchi, who established the Islamist *Ennahdha* party and was a political exile in England for decades, is currently in power. Syria has descended into an era of extreme instability that has involved almost the whole world. The Sunni territory that connects Iraq and Syria has become the cradle of ISIS, which is an offshoot of al-Qaeda. Today (2018), when we can assess that ISIS's presence in Syria and Iraq is declining, we can also identify the next area from which al-Qaeda and ISIS will seek to base themselves, and that is Africa. From North Africa to sub-Saharan Africa, these groups are establishing themselves all over the continent, beginning in Libya and going all the way down to South Africa.

The conflict between al-Qaeda and Israel is only about a decade old. Al-Qaeda's hostility toward Israel has nothing to do with any provocation on Israel's part but has its roots in radical Islamic ideology, according to which Jews have no right to exist and their elimination is a religious obligation. In some of his earlier remarks, bin Laden mentioned Israel as being only his third priority. In one of his speeches, he called Israel "a miserable polity," indicating that it was of no real importance. In an interview he gave a few years before the 9/11 attacks, he even said that if the Americans were to leave Saudi Arabia, he would be willing to sign a peace agreement with Israel!

The first real connections between bin Laden and Palestinian terrorists, members of Islamic Jihad and Hamas, were apparently established while he was living in Sudan during the first half of the 1990s; Palestinian terrorists found their way to al-Qaeda's training camps in Afghanistan. Some of them returned to Israel with the mission of setting up secret al-Qaeda cells. However, this did not lead to any real terrorist activity until the 2002 Mombasa attack on an Israeli-owned hotel and the attempted firing of missiles at an Israeli plane that had just taken off from Mombasa. The Mombasa attacks were a historic milestone in Israel's struggle against terrorism. In general, Israel's war on terror had been limited to the borders of the Middle East. It had occasionally extended to other places in the world, but only for specific one-time missions. The attacks in Mombasa forced Israel to join the club of countries, headed by the United States, that were fighting terrorism internationally.

This new reality of terrorism is different from anything we have ever known. This is global terrorism without borders, headquarters, or conventional military units. The new terrorist organization is light and agile and knows how to adjust quickly and cheaply to any change it detects in the enemy. It cannot be attacked by traditional methods of combat. It is, to a large extent, a virtual enemy. The closest historical analogy that I can think of is the communist Comintern between the 1920s and the 1940s. The Comintern was a beast with several heads and several arms that spread out across the globe, operating without a clear hierarchy, chain of command, or orderly system of making decisions, issuing orders, and receiving reports. Anyone who felt a sense of solidarity with the organization's vision and goals saw it as their duty to take action to realize the vision, even without a clear organizational and hierarchical framework. The same can be said about al-Qaeda and ISIS today, with one difference: the common denominator of those who identified with the Comintern was communism and secularism, whereas the common denominator of those who identify with al-Qaeda and ISIS is radical Islam. ISIS inherited from al-Qaeda the view that Israel and the Jews are an enemy that must be destroyed, and today (2018), its forces are situated in Syria near the Israeli border and in Sinai.

Statistically, Israel suffers from fewer al-Qaeda and ISIS attacks than moderate Muslim and Western countries, which does not necessarily mean that they see Israel as a secondary target. There are two explanations for this fact. One is that the radical Islamic organizations are seeking to first "impose order" at home, within the Muslim world, and only in parallel or afterwards to continue the fight against the infidel West. In the meantime, tiny Israel may well disappear on its own. A second explanation is that at this stage the extremist terrorist organizations do not want Israel to direct all of its military strength against them.

The global media contribute to the amplification of radical Islam's threat potential. In a world that is a completely transparent global village, with real-time communication from every point and to every point on earth, terrorist attacks around the world take over television screens and radio stations as the number one topic of interest. In other words, the global Islamic terrorist organizations receive a free platform for the transmission of their messages and propaganda, as well as their threats, thus sowing fear and terror and adding to the instability and uncertainty that already exist in the world.

An important question that concerns all those dealing with the phenomenon of terrorism is whether it is indeed a threat to the state's national security (Israel included). In the past, terrorism was a local problem—its objectives were local, and therefore so was its influence. Today it affects the entire world. And since the world is a global village, terrorism in one place may have an effect on the entire world order. In the past, terrorists used relatively simple weapons and combat doctrines, which also led to their influence remaining local. Today, we do not rule out the possibility that global terrorist groups will use nonconventional weapons, including cyber warfare. Plainly, nonconventional weapons threaten the national security of states. These threats, if they materialize, will certainly have strategic significance. These are "hardware" threats. Then there is the question of whether global terrorism can have a strategic effect in the area of "software": in other words, whether terrorism can attain strategic goals by harming the national resilience of a people or a state.

One of terrorism's main goals is to sow fear and terror among the civilian population in order to ultimately damage national resilience. A concrete example of how this may harm national security is if the vulnerable public puts pressure on its leaders to make decisions that clearly conflict with the interests of the state but do serve the interests of the terrorists. If a terrorist organization succeeds in creating such a process and outcome, there is no doubt it will thereby be achieving a strategic triumph. This scenario may sound purely theoretical, but it is not: it is palpably relevant to the Jewish population of Israel, which has been dealing with the phenomenon of terrorism since the establishment of the state seventy years ago, as well as during the eighty years preceding the state, with the beginning of Zionist settlement in Israel. I am touching on this issue only cursorily, but decision makers must take it in hand and monitor it over time so that they or their successors aren't surprised to find themselves one day suddenly facing a desperate situation. This insight is based on the assumption that a continued terrorist campaign against an entire population over a period of many years may well influence its national resilience.

The attack on the World Trade Center in Manhattan on September 11, 2001, was a milestone in the history of global jihadist terrorism, as it provoked the United States, the world's leading power, to begin thinking, planning, and building the tools and capabilities to contend with the threat in all aspects—how to defend against it by developing new technologies and combat doctrines, how to attack it using new weapons, how to deal with the legal and moral challenges to Western democracies, and more. The US government understood the depth and dimensions of the threat and established the Department of Homeland Security (DHS) to help cope with it. This was the largest organizational change to be made in the US government since the end of World War II. However, building an overarching strategy and implementing it, both within the security forces and in public consciousness, requires a process that can take years. European countries such as France and Belgium truly understood the extent of the threat only fifteen years after the United States, after they suffered terrible blows by radical Islamic terrorism in their capital cities. Even an optimistic forecast suggests that it will be quite a few more years before western Europe is properly equipped to contend with the threat.

Israel was the first country that was forced to deal with radical Islamic terrorism. It preceded the Western countries in learning about the threat and building up the capabilities to deal with it, and it shared its experience and insights with its allies around the world. The problem with such insights is that they are not properly absorbed until these allies experience the threat for themselves. And this is natural and predictable, especially if we remind ourselves that the 9/11 attacks were the first assault by a foreign enemy on American territory since Pearl Harbor, sixty years earlier!

Below are some of the key insights that the State of Israel, through the IDF, the Shin Bet, the Mossad, and the police, has shared with its friends around the world since the early 1980s. Israel shared its experiences on the basis of the working assumption that the only way to deal with global terrorism effectively is through international cooperation, in which each member contributes its comparative advantage to the joint effort, thereby creating a force multiplier. We called on the world to learn from our experience and to legitimize aspects of the strategy we developed over years of trial and error.

This strategy is based on the following principles:

- In the context of an ongoing violent conflict in which the enemy is looking for every opportunity and any soft underbelly to attack, the right to self-defense justifies preemptive strikes.
- In the context of an ongoing conflict in which victory cannot be achieved by the occupation of territory, the right to self-defense justifies the use of targeted killings of members of the enemy's top level of command.
- Heads of state that support terrorism by harboring and aiding terrorist organizations, are, in my view, legitimate targets.
- Radical Islamic terrorist groups, unlike secular organizations, have a three-tier hierarchy: the military layer, the political/civilian layer, and the organization's spiritual leadership. Secular military organizations are made up of only two tiers of command—military and civilian. The spiritual leadership of the Islamic terrorist groups are involved in every minor detail of their operational activity. All leaders of radical Islamic terrorist organizations are legitimate targets, including political leaders, military commanders, and religious leaders.
- The conflict is driven not by diplomatic, political, or economic motivations but by religious ones, and the element of provocation is meaningless. Therefore, the transfer of the war to the territory of a state sponsor of terrorism must have international legitimacy.

The second half of the twentieth century witnessed the decline of classical, or conventional, wars, in which mighty armies fought against each other and tried to wear each other down until one side completely surrendered. Alongside these wars, there was an increase in guerrilla warfare and terrorism, which later became known as low-intensity wars or conflicts. These new wars have completely different characteristics from the classical wars of the past.

During the last two hundred years of the classical wars (from 1750 to the post–World War II years), the international community was able to agree on the legislation on the laws of war and definitions of war crimes, and international moral norms and a normative yardstick were established to determine what was permissible and what was prohibited in conventional warfare. The international community has not yet succeeded in creating a legal and normative system for international terrorism. There is still not even an international consensus regarding the definition of terrorism. But, ironically, proponents of moral wars (especially those in western Europe) insist on judging those fighting terrorism according to archaic laws and norms belonging to another era of warfare.

The characteristics of modern international terrorism present and create new problems, for which the legal and normative framework of past wars is not at all applicable or capable of dealing with.

- What is the law for terrorists acting under divine orders, without any provocation?
- What is the law for terrorists who attack civilians?
- What is the law regarding countries that support terrorism in various ways (with money, weapons, training, exit bases, shelter, and so on)?
- What is the law for suicide bombers?
- What is the law for suicide terrorists using weapons of mass destruction?
- Is the legal test in the era of international terrorism the test of action or the test of intent?

I would like to expand a little on two areas in order to illustrate the enormous difference in the basic premises of the era of the old wars and the era of terrorism: the strategy of prevention as opposed to a response strategy, and the issue of targeted killings. After Pearl Harbor and the Iraqi invasion of Kuwait, US presidents asked for congressional approval in order to take action. After the terrorist attacks of September 11, 2001, President George W. Bush asked Congress to approve a preemptive strike. Why?

After half a century of response-based strategy, the Bush administration believed that a purely defensive policy was obsolete and irrelevant. In an environment of international terrorism, state sponsors of terrorism, and the combination of terrorism and weapons of mass destruction, the perception of responsive warfare is no longer fitting. If we believe that the enemy is preparing for an aggression at some point in the future, we must stop it by taking preventive actions. In the Cold War era, a preemptive strategy was impossible. The strategic environment today is one of terrorism without the borders of nation-states. Terrorists plan deadly attacks without any provocation from the other side. Terrorism has no political territory, infrastructure, or financial resources that can be threatened; it has no ideology that is formulated precisely and is an expression of nihilism with a culture of suicide. In such an environment, the cost of victory with a strategy that relies only on response to attack is unacceptably high, so a strategy of prevention is the only answer. A similar logic is also applied in the context of targeted killings. The environment is, as mentioned above, one of ongoing terrorism in the name of God, characterized by methods of action that allow fewer and fewer people to kill more and more people. Thus the side defending itself must focus more and more on the few that are causing the terror. The perpetrators of terrorism are civilians who hide in populated areas. The defenders' methods of action consist of specific, real-time intelligence and the ability to target the individual terrorist who has sought refuge within a community, without harming innocents. In other words, targeted killings are a logical consequence with a moral aspect, since they save innocent lives.

Another reason that a strategy of prevention is justified is the distinct religious—radical Islamist fundamentalist—component that has typified terrorism in recent years. This element makes it impossible to reach a compromise or even to negotiate with the perpetrators of terror, because they aspire to total world domination and see anyone who is not one of them as an enemy to be destroyed by any means necessary. Therefore, there is both a moral and an operational justification to strike the ideologists, messengers, planners, and perpetrators of this terror, and not to wait for them to attack.

(In the case of the Second Gulf War, George W. Bush was apparently also motivated by the desire to take revenge on Saddam Hussein for his intention to assassinate his father while he was visiting Kuwait in 1993 after the end of his term. The administration of Bush's successor, President Clinton, revealed the Iraqi leader's intention, but there were always doubts about the story's accuracy, as there was no real evidence to support it, and over the years the opinion that the story was baseless grew more prevalent. Even so, in September 2002, about six months before the United States launched the Second Gulf War, Bush Junior called Saddam Hussein "the guy who tried to kill my dad.")

Despite the inherent logic in both the preemptive strike theory and targeted killings, the international community has not yet adopted these models in international agreements. Even countries that support these actions use them selectively. In the case of the United States, the war in Afghanistan was a war of response, and the war in Iraq, though perceived as a preventive war, was seen by decision makers in the administration as a "last resort." Many issues in this context are still under discussion:

- What degree of "imminence" has to be present in order to justify a preemptive strike?
- Should the preemptive strike be used as a primary instrument in the war on terror?
- What is the source of the authority that proposes and approves a preemptive strike?
- What is the role of external allies in the decision-making process of a preemptive strike?

- What is the role of the UN and the Security Council?
- Regarding the use of nuclear weapons in the framework of this strategy—is it a yes or a no?

With regard to targeted killings, they developed and reached operational maturation in Israel, through trial and error and on the basis of moral considerations according to which there is complete justification in targeting the terrorist and trying to avoid causing collateral damage as much as possible. However, in order to prevent the proliferation of the use of this measure, it is permitted to be used only against targets defined as "ticking bombs," in the sense that the anticipated attack is imminent and the terrorist is on his or her way to carrying it out. Even in these cases, the approval of the prime minister is required.

The million-dollar question that the average citizen of the world today wants to know with regard to terrorism is: How do we defeat and eliminate it? We must be courageous and respond truthfully— there is no magical solution that can put an end, once and for all, to the phenomenon of terrorism. Having said that, terrorism can certainly be contained and reduced to a level that human society can live with, as it does with disease or road accidents. To this end, the international community must take a large number of steps at the strategic, tactical-operational, and ideological levels.

In the struggle against jihadist terrorism at the operational-tactical level, and given the international nature of terrorism, insights must be properly absorbed and then converted into tools.

- The means of intelligence gathering must be improved and refined to the point that reconnaissance can be conducted under all weather conditions.
- The tools used to collect samples and materials from the air must be improved.
- Sophisticated information-gathering capabilities must be developed that can track the flow of terrorist funds.

- Cyber capabilities—both defensive and offensive—must be developed, with the aim of maintaining a one-and-a-half-generation lead on the enemy and the private market.
- "Intelligence incrimination" must be improved and brought to the level of "legal incrimination": that is, we must strive for information from intelligence to provide sufficient evidence to prosecute and convict the terrorist.
- Intelligence cooperation between countries and friendly agencies should be improved and enhanced to the point of real-time collaboration.
- It is vital to develop operational cooperation between friendly intelligence services around the world, despite their inherent inhibitions with regard to keeping their tools and methods of action classified.
- It is important to expand the combat doctrine to include the integration of intelligence, the ability to mark targets, and the use of precision weapons in real time in order to focus our efforts on terrorist leaders and prevent harm being caused to innocent people.
- It is essential to maximize cooperation in the field of HUMINT in a way that incorporates the comparative advantages of each agency in order to maximize intelligence output for the community of free nations.

Since global Islamic terrorism threatens the world not only with violent means but also through religious ideology, which is almost impossible to suppress by force, an ideological dimension must also be added to the war on terror. For this purpose we must work toward creating a few conditions, which today seem utopian.

The West must make efforts to develop cultural cooperation with leaders and prominent figures representing moderate Islam. The flag bearers of international Islamic terrorism constitute a minority of the 1.3 billion Muslims in the world. The West should establish a dialogue with moderate Islamic leaders and persuade them to take a stand against radical Islam and its terrorist envoys. They must be convinced that terrorism is futile and will only lead to the continued deterioration of the Muslim world. It is better to live in coexistence with the Western world, which will ensure that the two cultures live side by side, developing and blossoming.

At the same time, a series of steps must be taken in the area of economic cooperation. It should be borne in mind that since the end of the First World War the Muslim world has been in political, economic, cultural, and scientific decline, which means that in addition to the religious and cultural dimensions of the conflict there are nationalistic, economic, and other aspects. The Muslim world suffers a great deal from poverty, hunger, and despair. These are elements that feed terror. A population that is satiated, even if it is under occupation, will choose negotiations as a path to achieving national liberation over armed struggle. The implication of this reality is that it is necessary to help these backward economies before even attempting to educate Muslim nations about democratization. Developed market economies will stimulate the growth of the middle class in Muslim society, which is a condition for processes of democratization.

As has been said, global Islamic terror cannot operate without a territorial basis. Therefore, action must be taken against countries that support terrorism. The United Nations would be the natural roof under which an international coalition to fight these countries might be formed, but for obvious reasons—the fact that there is an automatic majority in the UN that would thwart any such initiative—it cannot serve this role. Therefore, the alternative is to establish a body called the League of Nations against Terrorism or some similar such name.

The first function of this body would be to agree on a universal definition of the term *terrorism*. My suggestion for the definition is "any use of violence against civilian populations to achieve political ends." This definition would serve as the basis for future legislation and for the required regulation. The organization's source of authority would be a convention agreed upon by its founders. The body would include international experts in a variety of fields and would examine the involvement of both countries and organizations in terrorism. A "scale of involvement" would be established to define the type and extent of a country's involvement, and an updated list of countries involved in terrorism, according to these indices, would be published periodically. The body would support the need and the obligation to punish countries for their involvement in terrorism, and a clear and fixed "price scale" would define the penalty to be paid by the country in question. This price scale would be adapted to the various types of involvement, with the aim of changing these countries' balance of interests and convincing them of the futility of supporting terrorism. A secondary boycott would be imposed on states and economic bodies that continued to maintain economic and other ties, whether secretly or openly, with countries that had been boycotted for their involvement in terrorism. Finally, a permanent international counterterrorism mechanism would be established, one of whose objectives would be to supervise the implementation of punitive measures against the countries involved in terrorism and to warn of any deviations on their part.

Israel was the first to propose, years ago, from international platforms, the idea of establishing such a body. President Chaim Herzog spoke about this at the UN, and Prime Minister Yitzhak Rabin not only expressed support for the idea but actually delved into the structure, objectives, and tools such an organization would have.

So, if I am asked whether it is possible to eliminate terrorism, my answer would be that if all or most of the steps I have listed above are taken, there is definitely a high probability that the community of free nations will succeed in reducing international terrorism to a level that is tolerable.

Iran: A Personal Perspective

My acquaintance with Iran and the Iranians began in mid-1965, about a year and a half after I had begun my service in the Mossad. One morning, I was unexpectedly summoned to the bureau of Mossad director Meir Amit. This caught me completely off guard. I was a junior officer, new to the world of intelligence—why would the director of the Mossad for the past year, someone who had served as the head of Military Intelligence and fought in all of Israel's wars, want to see me? As I left the room that I shared with several other employees, I decided to take the stairs rather than use the elevator so I would have a few extra minutes to organize my thoughts before the meeting.

When I reached the Mossad director's office, one of the secretaries informed him that I had arrived and then immediately accompanied me into his room. Meir invited me to sit next to him at his T-shaped desk. It was the first time I had ever visited the office of the director. At the time, I never could have imagined that in twenty-four years I would be the one sitting at that desk, in another office but with the exact same set of furniture that fitted it out in 1965. There were two or three other people sitting in the office whose identity I cannot recall, probably because of my nerves and excitement.

Meir got straight to the point. He spent half an hour describing the entire span of Israel's relations with Iran, including their security relations and intelligence cooperation, which was led by the Mossad. Turning to me, Meir informed me that after considering several candidates, he had found me to be the most suitable replacement for an officer who had been "on loan from the Shin Bet" and was about to complete his two-year service in Iran. I should perhaps point out that at that time the Mossad was for all intents and purposes a hierarchical body that was run like the military, with the exception of uniforms and a jurisdiction of military law—that is to say, a decision was actually an order. Meir added, as an aside, that our service would not be in Tehran but rather in a place defined as a "hardship post"—hence the length of service being only two years. He also mentioned that we would be living undercover there but with a "concession": our local partners, and they alone, would be aware of our true identity. He announced that the date of our departure for Iran was set for January 1966 and that we were to undergo an intensive and multidisciplinary training period. I write *we* because everything that Meir said to me also applied to my wife Yael, whom I had already assumed would be joining me. At the end of the meeting, as I stood up and started heading toward the door, Meir stopped me and told me the following: "We will meet more than once before you depart, but I already want you to write down what I'm about to say to you: the Persians do not like our presence there. They believe they have already learned all they can from us and that they can do their work now without our help. They are looking for a reason or an excuse to get us out of there. As for you, I want you to note that even if you don't succeed in adding any particular value, I forbid you to come back from there with the key." By the word *key*, he meant, of course, our presence in the territory: I could not permit any developments that might lead to the withdrawal of Israeli intelligence personnel from Iran.

My heart skipped a beat and I left the office.

I later understood why Meir attached such importance to the "key." The first reason was related to Israel's national security doctrine, as defined by its founding father David Ben-Gurion. One of the cornerstones of this doctrine was the "triangle theory." Ben-Gurion believed that Israel, surrounded by enemies, needed regional allies in its outer circle, so in a relatively short time the two triangles—the northern and the southern—were formed. The "northern triangle" consisted of Jerusalem, Ankara, and Tehran. The "southern triangle" was made up of Jerusalem, Khartoum, and Addis Ababa. (After the coup in Sudan in 1969, Khartoum withdrew from the triangle and was replaced by the Moroccan capital of Rabat.) These triangles, which operated for years with countries that did not have diplomatic relations with Israel and which, except for Ethiopia, were mostly Arab and Muslim, dealt not only with security and intelligence matters but with all the issues that exist between countries with diplomatic relations and that are usually handled by the countries' foreign ministries. From its inception, the Mossad was trusted to represent Israel in countries with which it had no diplomatic relations, and in all matters, not only in intelligence. The presence of our agency was one of the most important anchors in the northern triangle, and its existence was in danger, which explained Meir Amit's instructions that I must under no circumstances return home with the key!

The second reason for the "key's" importance lay in the extraordinary value of the intelligence product that our "foreign outposts" provided the State of Israel. The tripartite alliances allowed Israel, surrounded by enemies on all sides, close contact with the enemy states. In the Cold War era, the two superpowers competed for influence in the Middle East. The Soviet Union's first successful military penetration was in Iraq, whose army gradually adopted the Soviet doctrine. The practical significance of this change was the Soviet supply, over many years, of land, naval, and air weapons systems to Iraq. This was of great interest to Israel. Some of this intelligence made its way to Israel even before Egypt and Syria received the Soviet weapons systems supplied to Iraq. And this was another good reason for the Mossad chief's concern that I might return to Israel from my mission to Iran with the key of our foreign outpost there.

The six months following my meeting with Meir Amit were dedicated to training for the mission. Every day, several hours were devoted to the study and practice of the theory of clandestine activity. I took daily Persian lessons with a tutor and studied Iraqi Arabic intensively under the guidance of Ibn al-Rafidain, the legendary broadcaster who broadcast from the Voice of Israel to Iraq in their colloquial tongue each week. For two months, I was assigned to the southern base of Military Intelligence's HUMINT unit, in order to study their activities. The list went on. Separately, Yael studied photography, the development and management of a secret photo lab, and a lot of clandestine activity.

My training continued for two more months in Tehran, where my daily agenda consisted of one or two Persian lessons and a few hours of wandering through Tehran's bazaar to practice the language, strengthen my cover story, and get to know the city, its commerce, and its residents.

For two and a half years, we lived in Iran's southwestern province, whose southern border is the Persian Gulf and whose western border is shared with Iraq. This border was not marked, as it lay inside the huge delta created by flow of the Euphrates and the Tigris from northern to southern Iraq. The delta stretched out over hundreds of square kilometers of water, some of it flowing but most of it standing and forming huge swamps that were full of life. The swamps were surrounded by dense and impenetrable wild vegetation, most of it reeds, and groves of trees that rose high above the swamp into which their roots were sunk. Small villages were scattered around the perimeter of the swamp; the raw material for their houses were reeds that were woven to create outer walls, rounded roofs, and interior rooms. All of the houses stood on stilts that were sunken into the swamp water, and the only vehicles were primitive boats of various sizes, most of which were used for transport though others were used for fishing, which provided most of the villagers' food.

All of the delta's inhabitants were Iraqi tribesmen. East of the delta's borders was an expanse of desert that basically extended to Pakistan and Afghanistan. There were three urban centers in the "dry" area of the province. The first was the city of Abadan on the shores of the Persian Gulf, where the oil industry was concentrated at the time, run by a very large community of energy experts of different nationalities. The second was Khorramshahr, about a half hour's drive north of Abadan. This city served as the commercial port and Iran's southwestern point of departure to the Persian Gulf and from there to the Indian Ocean. The third city was Ahwaz, about two and a half hours north of Abadan. This city was the administrative center of the province and was referred to by the Arabic speakers as "Arabistan" and by the Iranians as "Khuzestan." The province's demographics were mixed, consisting of both Iraqi Arabs and Iranians.

Throughout history, the province was inhabited only by Arabs. The Iranian government, aiming to solidify its sovereignty in the province, initiated a campaign using financial and other incentives to encourage Iranians from other provinces in the enormous country to relocate to Khuzestan. The province of Khuzestan and the Iran-Iraq border were sources of contention between the two countries that lasted for many years and were often catalysts for crises and military action.

In order to properly complete my description, I must add that the weather in this desert province was extreme. Summer temperatures approached 122 degrees Fahrenheit with 100 percent humidity. You could crack an egg on the roof of a car and it would turn into an omelet within two minutes. The desert coolers in the house would become blocked from the humidity and stop working. Market vendors would stand in barrels full of water behind their stands. The daily routine would begin at five in the morning. At 10:30 the city would "shut down" and anyone who didn't need to wouldn't go out into the street. The city would wake up again only at four in the afternoon. This is where we lived for two and a half years; it's where we raised our eldest daughter and where we learned about Persia and the Persians.

And what did we learn? It would be impossible to recount everything. Therefore, I will try to summarize the most important insights we gained, those that helped me consolidate my worldview and opinions and assisted me throughout my career—especially in my role as director of the Mossad—in making decisions regarding Iran and in making recommendations to the decision makers and the prime ministers I served.

The first insight came with being exposed to the size and diversity of this huge country. This is a country whose territory is larger than that of all of the countries of western Europe put together. It is a country whose south has an extreme desert climate and whose north has a central European climate. A resident of Tehran could decide on any given day to drive an hour and a half north to ski or to drive an hour and a half south and take a swim in a large lake.

The population of Iran is made up of a huge mix of races and some thirty-six ethnic groups. Looking at a map of the countries bordering Iran on all its sides, one will find that each of them is represented among the various ethnic groups, who over time have become citizens or residents of Iran—from the Slavs on the Caspian coast in the north, to the Kurds and Azeris in the northwest and west, to the Iraqi Arabs in the west and south, and the combination of Baloches, Afghans, Kazakhs, and others in the east and northeast.

The insight I derived from Iran's ethnic structure and size is that only an authoritarian, centralized regime, with powerful and intimidating governing systems, could control a country of this magnitude and a huge population of innumerable races and ethnic groups with no common denominator between them. Moreover, the country's lengthy land borders crossed demographic and ethnic boundaries. These borders had been set in wartime and advanced irredentist aspirations (the aspirations of a cultural or ethnic group to free themselves from the yoke of the political entity under which they are subjects), which led to unrest, instability, and conflict.

During the imperial period, Iran was ruled by various dynasties, each taking power in turn following the destruction of the previous dynasty. The source of Iranian pride can be found in two historical periods: the era of Cyrus the Great, who built a huge empire in the sixth century BCE, and the period of dynasties that ruled from the seventh century until the Khomeini revolution in 1979.

The first Arab conquest of Iran was by the Sassanid kingdom; it began in 637 CE and was completed by 642 CE. Over the years, countless dynasties, some led by Arab rulers and others by Iranian rulers, rose and fell. In the eleventh and twelfth centuries, kingdoms of foreign invaders, such as the Seljuks and the Mongols, ruled. Later, in 1502, the Safavid dynasty rose to power, ruling until 1736. The Zand dynasty followed, and in 1779 the Qajar dynasty, which ruled until 1925, took over until the ascension of the Pahlavi dynasty.

The next insight we gained and processed over time was the hatred, contempt, and loathing that most Iranians feel toward Arab Muslims and other ethnic groups who adhere to the religion of Islam. This hatred originated in the second half of the eighth century, when the Muslims completed their conquest of Iran, destroying Iranian culture, eradicating the Zoroastrian religion that prevailed in Iran and forcibly converting the country's inhabitants to Islam, imposing the

Arabic script while burning down Iranian libraries throughout the country, and "contaminating" the Iranian language with countless words from the Arabic language. The only ones to protest were the Iranian poets, who insisted on preserving the language and expressed their dissent through antiphrasis in their works. The poet Rudaki, who died in the year 941, was famous during the Samanid dynasty (819–1000), a period distinguished by an Iranian cultural renaissance. The poet Firdusi, who wrote the national epic work *Shahnameh* (Book of Kings), was the most prominent of that generation of poets; he died between 1020 and 1026.

Iran was Sunni until the early sixteenth century, when the founder of the Safavid dynasty, Ismail, decided to make Shia Islam the state religion. The reason for the change was the desire to distinguish Iran from its enemies, the Sunni Ottoman Empire and Uzbekistan in Central Asia.

The Iranians are proud of their Aryan origins. The shah's official title was "the Light of the Aryans." The syntax of the Persian language is very similar to that of German, and the language survived despite the Muslim conquest imposing the Arabic script. The Iranians consider themselves racially superior to the Muslims of the "inferior" Semitic race. The Iranian attitude toward the Arabs is one of contempt and racial superiority, as well as resentment over the Arab conquest and all that came with it.

An interesting question is: What preceded what in the Iranian experience? Did race precede religion or vice versa? Are Iranians' Aryan roots more significant for them than the religion of Islam in Iranians' sense of identity, or is it the other way around?

Historically speaking, the Muslim occupation of Iran led to the suppression and decline of the influence of the Zoroastrian religion that had prevailed in the territory of Persia but was ultimately unsuccessful in imposing Arabism on the territory and its citizens. I think it would be correct to say that Iranian identity—at least until Khomeini's revolution in 1979—was ethnic first and foremost, rather than religious. In fact, even since the 1979 coup, it is very difficult to say that there is true religious solidarity between the Iranians and the Muslim world, especially since Iran is Shiite—even if there is some degree of solidarity, it is with Islam's Shiite minority.

A close look at Iran since the revolution leads me to conclude that the religious establishment that currently dominates Iran attributes more importance to Muslim religious identity than to ethnic identity. Had ethnic identity been of supreme importance, it is doubtful whether a man like Khamenei, whose ethnic origin is Azeri and not Persian, would have attained the status of the all-powerful spiritual leader. The Khomeini revolution symbolized, more than anything, the hatred of those who flew the banner of religion toward the secular regime of the shah, who encouraged Western modernity.

There is no doubt that one of the roots, and perhaps the biggest factor, of the profound hatred of Israel is the fact that the shah, who had exiled Khomeini from his country, was a very close ally of Israel.

During the 1960s, the period that we served in Iran, within the consciousness of the Iranian intelligentsia, the world was divided into Germany and all the rest. An Iranian traveling abroad would try to begin his journey in Germany; there was a very large German presence in Iran, a big embassy, a Goethe-Institut for the study of the German language, German restaurants, German investments, and strong economic and commercial ties. There is no doubt that all of this can be explained by the sense of shared ethnic identity between the Iranians and the Germans. There were, however, also common geostrategic interests between them.

This is the place to mention that Reza Shah, the father of the last shah of the Pahlavi dynasty, who ruled Iran from 1925 to 1941, was so pro-Nazi that the Allies exiled him to South Africa and crowned his son Muhammad Reza in his stead. A few years later, in 1951, Dr. Mohammad Mossadegh was elected prime minister of Iran and nationalized Iran's oil industry. The Western powers refused to relinquish their influence in a country as important as Iran, and the CIA orchestrated a military coup against Mossadegh, which failed and forced the shah to flee his country. In 1953 the CIA organized a second, this time successful, military coup, which was followed by the shah's return. All of this took place around the same time as the Nasser revolutions in Egypt, the many military coups in Syria, and finally the coup d'état in Iraq in 1958. The shah began the second chapter of his reign concerned about the possible consequences of these revolutions, and with a hatred and fear of the Arabs. This is certainly one of the explanations as to why the shah sought intelligence, military, and economic cooperation with Israel. Moreover, Iran found itself in a dilemma: it had been a powerful empire but was currently weak, and it was looking for a way to restore its former glory. It knew that in order to fulfill this ambition it had to emulate the West, certainly in terms of technological advancement.

A further insight: throughout Iran's history, there has been a constant tension between religion—the religion of Shiism—and secularism. In modern times, during the years of the shah's reign, secularism and modernity ruled the roost. However, the shah was able to maintain a controlled "exhaust pipe" that allowed believers to express their faith in the public sphere, especially during Ashura, the days of remembrance of the prophets Ali and Hussein, central figures in the Shiite religion. On these memorial days, huge processions of believers would walk through the streets dressed in black, flagellating themselves with chains and cutting themselves with knives to the point of streaming blood, while reading verses from the Koran that put the marchers into a state of uncontrolled ecstasy. Each year, ahead of Ashura, the government would use the various media in order to warn foreigners in the country about the expected events and would recommend that they remain in their homes and refrain from going out to public places. I, living there as a local, was able to experience these horrifying rituals firsthand.

The "White Revolution" in the early 1960s was a formative event in the history of Iran. This revolution, initiated by the shah, turned the country's peasant farmers from serfs and vassals into independent landowners. This change affected the status of the country's feudalists, among whom were many clerics, which exacerbated the relationship between the secular shah and the ayatollahs, the religious leaders. The reform was made possible only after the dissolution of the Majlis, the Iranian parliament, which enabled the passage of the land reform law.

Muhammad Reza Pahlavi, the dynasty's last shah, succeeded his father Reza Shah, who was exiled to South Africa in 1941. It took him some twenty years to stabilize the kingdom. During World War II, Iran was occupied. After the war, the shah had to contend with the landowners who controlled the Majlis. Immediately following the war, the Soviet Union was on the verge of establishing a communist state in the Azeri region. From 1951 to 1953, Prime Minister Mossadegh, who had nationalized the oil company, threatened the shah's rule. Beginning in 1961, the shah took initiative and launched a series of reforms in an ambitious attempt to establish a strong and modern Iran. After the passing of the land reform law, the shah advanced legislation according to which profits in the industry would be distributed among the workers. Cooperatives were established in agricultural areas, which financed irrigation and maintenance projects instead of landowners. The shah pushed through educational reforms aimed at reducing illiteracy in the country. As a result of the reforms, the level of income in 1969 increased by 50 percent (compared to 1962). Oil revenues increased and enabled the construction of seven dams for electricity generation and irrigation. Throughout his rule, the shah maintained a pro-Western policy; he was a member of pro-Western regional alliances such as CENTO, also known as the "Baghdad Pact," which was founded in 1955, when Britain still played a central role in the Middle East. Its members included Iran, Turkey, Iraq, Pakistan, and the UK. This alliance broke up after the 1958 military coup in Iraq and was replaced by the American-influenced RCD (Regional Cooperation for Development) pact that was established in 1964 and included Turkey, Pakistan, and Iran. The RCD encouraged a secular, modern, and Western Iran.

A helpful way to understand the Persians in a nutshell is to read the book *The Adventures of Hajji Baba of Ispahan*, which constitutes a kind of encyclopedia of the Persians as a race, as a people, and as individuals. The archetypal Persian character is proud of his imperial heritage and of his Aryan race and denies the claim that the religion of Shia Islam binds him to the Arab world. The typical Persian respects the other and will take great pains not to insult him. But even if a Persian can demonstrate boundless cruelty and wickedness in his actions, his speech will be gentle. He may be extremely self-effacing in encounters with authority figures, for example bowing down, never turning his back on the authority figure, and peppering his speech with profuse expressions of humbleness and exaltation. The typical Persian puts on facades and speaks half truths. This tendency is connected to the Shiite religion, which, as a minority in the Muslim world, permits its believers, as part of *Taqiya* (the duty of prudence) to deviate from the truth in order to survive. The Persians invented the art of negotiation and bargaining, which is inherent in the bazaar culture. The beaming seller will extol the virtues of his wares and praise the buyer's good taste, proclaiming what a perfect choice he has made in the product he is about to buy; at the outset of the negotiations he will declare that for this particular buyer he is willing to sell at a loss, and he will offer the buyer hot tea until he has steam coming out of his ears. He will wear the buyer out and sell him the goods at an exorbitant price, even after all the discounts he offered over the course of the negotiations.

Patience is a profound and fundamental characteristic of the Iranians. The Persian will tell you that patience is the source of all victories in negotiations, whether it is bargaining in the bazaar or political negotiations. Patience, according to the Persians, increases your chances of achieving your goals. And when you ask where this patience is supposed to come from, you will be offered the metaphor that a carpet takes years to weave! And carpet weaving is a uniquely Iranian art.

Of course, these are all generalizations, and they do not apply to all Persians everywhere. However, I would say that anyone who has been to Iran, and perhaps the Iranians themselves, will confirm that the things I have described are characteristic of many, if not most, of the Persian people.

Much similarity can be found between the period of the shah and the era of the sharia (Islamic religious law) state with regard to the characteristics of the regime. During the shah's rule, he was called "the Light of the Aryans," and his subjects regarded him as a divine manifestation on earth. The security services he established, SAVAK, which included the domestic security service and the military intelligence service, as well as police and gendarmerie bodies, terrorized citizens and used any means necessary to suppress any expression of opposition to the shah's regime.

In today's sharia state, the spiritual leader Khamenei and Khomeini before him are considered the spokesmen of Allah, and therefore the citizens accept everything that comes out of their mouths as the word of Allah. This belief gives the spiritual leader veto power and the authority to make the final decision on every matter. In other words, the spiritual leader has ultimate authoritarian power. The equivalent of the shah's security services in the era of the sharia state is the Islamic Revolutionary Guard Corps (IRGC), which controls all of the security services and their own military, which operates parallel to the regular army. The IRGC also controls the state's range of nonconventional capabilities, as well as in the Basij militias, fringe groups of ruthless hoodlums who, for a minimal fee, are prepared to serve the government in any mission; they are often used to suppress any signs of opposition to it.

There is an inherent contradiction between Iranian pride based on Iran's Aryan origins and imperial past, and the pride of a Shiite sharia state that believes in the vision of the world caliphate. As I have already mentioned, I tend to believe that the Khomeini revolution in 1979 gave primacy to Shiite Islam as an Iranian value but at the same time was motivated by the imperial legacy of the past. The refined Iranian vision is, therefore, to bring back the glory days of the empire in the form of the future Islamic caliphate.

The Iranian Conundrum

This section begins with a picture of the "nuclearizing" Iran of 2010 and updates it through events leading up to 2018, the time of this book's writing. I thought it useful to include earlier assessments in order to provide the reader with a window into the thinking and analysis of senior intelligence officials whose job it is to advise the political leaders, in whose hands lies the responsibility of making fateful decisions.

Anyone hoping for a lecture according to linear logic is likely to be disappointed. I have written a collection of insights, working assumptions, rumors, and, most of all, dilemmas and ponderings; at the time of writing, I had not yet formulated a clear and consistent opinion. What is more, things were, and remain to this day, in a constant state of fluidity.

The section is laid out as follows:

1. A description of Iran's domestic situation as of 2010.
2. A description of what was happening in the halls of government in Washington during Obama's administration. In my assessment, the bottom line was that the United States would not attack Iran and would accept a one- to two-year breakout time.
3. A description of what, in my opinion, was happening in the halls of government in Tehran. In my final analysis, I expressed the opinion that their intention was to reach military nuclear capability and that they were more determined than ever. I also emphasized the changes in the country's power structure, which was on its way to becoming a "praetorian" regime of the IRGC, to which the clerics would be held hostage.
4. An analysis of what was happening in the corridors of government in Moscow; I came to the conclusion that Iran was a bargaining chip between Russia and the United States, with the former agreeing to join an American coalition against Iran only if

the United States recognized Russia as a world power of equal standing and influence.

5. An analysis of the possible courses of action against the Iranian nuclear threat, a list of priorities, and what would happen "the day after" if any action would be taken.

Iran: The Domestic Picture

In 2010 the Iranian regime was a multilayered hybrid creature with so many duplications in its system that it was difficult to discern who held the authority, not only formally, but de facto. The Iranian regime was neither a democracy nor a totalitarian regime but rather a strange combination of both. An Iranian scholar who was once asked who controlled Iran answered, "Everyone and no one!" On the surface, it appeared that the government was completely subordinate to the clerics. This was true immediately following the Khomeini revolution in 1979, but since then the situation had changed, in light of the erosion of the clerics' power and the rise of militant elites fighting for power and influence and navigating between religious orders, political laws, personal ties, and bureaucratic directives.

At the center of all the circles of influence was the Supreme Leader Khamenei. However, he was surrounded by the clerics, the government, and senior military officials, a total of about 10 percent of the country's population—close to seventy-five million citizens. Obviously, in the presence of such a large and diverse group of elites, even the supreme spiritual leader found himself facing challenges and dilemmas in exercising his authority. "Our people"—*Khoudi* in the Persian language—were those belonging to elites. Anyone who was not a member of the *Khoudi* had no right to express criticism of any kind. The Supreme National Security Council was made up of Khamenei's chief consultants and was the channel through which the supreme leader's decisions were communicated to all state apparatuses. There was also the Assembly of Experts and the Council for the Preservation of Interests. The former appointed the supreme leader, and the latter approved or rejected the decisions of the Majlis (the Iranian parliament). The two councils had a majority of clerics, and their job was to preserve the supreme status of religion in the state.

In another circle were the commanders of the IRGC and the armed forces, who were appointed by the supreme leader and senior clerics from the holy city of Qom. President (from 2005 to 2013) Ahmadinejad was acting prime minister, drawing his authority from the supreme leader. However, he supported and advanced the IRGC, and they in return supported him. The media were also subject to the authority of the supreme leader.

The Iranian population was young. In 2010, about 70 percent of Iranians were under the age of thirty-five. There were at least thirty-six different ethnic groups, each with its own language, culture, and customs. The rule of the mullahs—Islamic clerics—had caused unrest among these groups, although there were no signs of coordination between them. Still, all of them, and especially the largest ones—the Azeris in the northwest, the Arabs in Khuzestan in the south, the Kurds, and the Baloch—demanded some degree of self-determination, ranging from autonomy to full independence. This struggle was expressed by demonstrations, strikes, and sometimes even acts of terrorism. But at that point (and at the time of writing this book, in 2018) these groups did not pose a serious threat to the government.

In the years leading up to 2018, the power structure of the ruling elite was changing. The IRGC were gaining more and more power and influence. The number of senior officers who had been released after a lengthy service in the IRGC was increasing, and now they were taking the places of members of the first generation of the revolution. In 2010 former IRGC members made up about half of government ministers and about a third of the members of the Majlis. At least twenty of Iran's thirty provinces were controlled by former IRGC members, and Iran's most important embassies around the world were staffed by ambassadors who were ex-IRGC. The balance of economic power was tipped in favor of the IRGC, to the detriment of the bazaars, which had traditionally constituted the basis of economic power in Iran. The IRGC held approximately one hundred economic enterprises in the field of national infrastructure and about five hundred companies in the fields of industry, banking, seaports, communications, insurance, and recreation. Today (in 2018) it is estimated that the IRGC is the third-largest economic body in Iran, after the National Iranian Oil Company and the Imam Reza Foundation, located in the city of Mashhad. There is a concern that the IRGC's increasing control of the main centers of power and the destabilization of Iran's domestic situation may, given certain conditions, lead to the forceful takeover of Iran by the IRGC and to its official transition into a military dictatorship in the name of Islam, with control over a nuclear weapons arsenal and long-range ballistic missiles.

The wave of demonstrations that swept Iran in June 2009 was not necessarily the result of presidential election fraud. The fraud was just an excuse. The deeper motive for the outbreak of the protests was the economic, social, and political situation. The "man on the street" had realized that the regime had taken from him the few political rights he thought he still had. The masses threw their support to Mir-Hossein Mousavi and Mehdi Karroubi, who gave them the courage to take to the streets and release their long pent-up frustrations. In the fiery demonstrations that took place on December 7, 2009, students shouted: "Mousavi is the excuse, the entire regime is the target!" The regime, which had feared a defeat in the elections, had always planned on rigging the results. To deter popular resistance in advance, before the elections the regime held a series of extensive maneuvers and demonstrations to suppress any riots, using the Basij militias.

The illegitimacy of the regime, which was exacerbated by the rigging of the elections, and the internal rift within the regime's leadership—between the conservatives and the ultraconservatives, between Ayatollah Rafsanjani and President Ahmadinejad, and among other factions and bodies—further underscored the struggle over the future of the regime and its character, looking ahead to the day after Khamenei. The supreme leader's status and strength was significantly impaired, and his ability to find compromises that would satisfy everyone diminished. Nevertheless, no signs or developments have been identified that really threaten the continuation of his rule.

The United States: The Attempt to Decipher the True Signal

From the end of the Second World War in 1945 until the collapse of the Soviet Union, the Cold War was the main instrument that shaped and stabilized the global order. Since the Soviet Union's collapse in 1991, it had been a virtual cold war, in which the United States served as the only "policeman" of a unipolar world for a decade, until 2000.

The election of President Barack Obama in 2008 marked a major strategic change in US foreign policy. Obama changed the strategy from one of confrontation to one of engagement. Presumably, President Obama truly believed that the engagement strategy would be successful. But when the global reality appeared more and more to be a battleground between a Muslim culture that was not interested in compromise and a culture of liberal democracy, whose leader was emerging from an economic crisis at home and who was embroiled in two wars with no end in sight, and whose main ally, Europe, was grappling unsuccessfully with Islam on its own soil, there was no doubt that the strategy of engagement was going to be interpreted by the Muslim world as weakness, with the understanding that all it needed to do was to continue to erode the power and influence of the United States.

Below I will present an assortment of opinions that were heard in Washington in 2015, from government officials, members of Congress, and people in security, intelligence, and academia.

The US administration was preoccupied with the deterioration in Afghanistan and Pakistan and the situation in Iraq, so it treated Iran as a lower priority, even though that country was geographically located between Afghanistan and Iraq and was in the process of obtaining a nuclear bomb. This order of priorities derived from the administration's considerations regarding the future of NATO, the threat of another terrorist attack of a 9/11 magnitude, the danger of a nuclear war in Southern Asia, and the president's low approval ratings (one must keep in mind that wars have a tendency to bedevil an American president's term).

In light of the above, the United States' other priorities, including Iran and Middle East peace, had to compete for the administration's attention and resources. Moreover, Obama's presidency focused more on domestic policy (health, unemployment, etc.) than on foreign policy.

As an aside, a jihadist revolution in Pakistan would fundamentally alter the rules of the game in the international system and pose a direct threat to Israel, since Pakistan was a Sunni terrorist state with much greater nuclear military deterrence and capability than Iran. It should be noted that, as part of President Obama's agreement with the Pakistani prime minister, the former renounced any say over the country's nuclear program. There was also an assessment that a military takeover of the country would precede a jihadi coup.

Obama's priorities being what they were, it was clearly not in the United States' interest to stir up any trouble in its relations with Iran. After the 2009 Iranian elections, some in the US administration voiced their belief that any American support of the opposition in Iran would be a "kiss of death" because pressuring Ahmadinejad while he was weak could be perceived as an attempt to exploit his vulnerability and increase hostility against the United States.

The prevailing assessment in government circles was that if Israel were to attack Iran and if it were to respond, the United States would not be able to stand by. But an attack on the United States or on its forces in Iraq or Afghanistan following Israeli action against Iran would cause serious damage to Israeli-US relations.

The United States-Pakistan-Afghanistan triangle had significant implications for Indian-Pakistani relations. The Indians were concerned over the weakness of the Pakistani regime. The Pakistanis feared that the Indians would exploit their weakness. In light of this, the Pakistanis gave up their nuclear safeguards, that is, the physical separation of their nuclear warheads and their means of delivery.[1] The Indians interpreted this as a sign of intent and raised their level of alertness. A possible outcome of this situation was the continuation of terrorist attacks in India originating in Pakistan, which would be followed by an Indian response, and then, potentially, escalation in the form of Pakistani nuclear readiness. An Israeli observer should be reminded that for a combination of economic, political, and demographic reasons, relations between India and Iran were close, and it was hard to imagine that the improvement of Israel's relations with India would affect India's relations with Iran. Even after Indian prime minister Narendra Modi's highly publicized visit to Israel in July 2017, and even though India today is the second-largest client of the Israeli defense industries, Indian spokespeople advise Israel that, rather than exhibiting hostility toward the Iranian regime, it is preferable to show sympathy for the Iranian people. These spokespeople either ignore or are not aware of the complete hold that the regime has over the people of Iran, thanks in part to the IRGC, which is now the central force in the country, controlling the army, nonconventional weapons, the economy, and, to a greater and greater extent, the ayatollahs. It is the IRGC that is exhibiting hostility toward Israel.

The informal assessment of the US State Department was that engagement with Iran would not yield a satisfactory agreement on Iran's nuclear program but that if an agreement were to be reached it would postpone the final product and allow Iran to continue accumulating low-enriched uranium until a decision was made regarding a breakout (that is, a declaration and/or an experiment). The thinking was that gaining more time was preferable to having an immediate confrontation. However, disagreements on the question of Iran arose between Secretary of State Hillary Clinton and the White House, with Clinton demanding a tougher approach and the setting of a timetable for negotiations, as well as open expressions of support for the

Iranian opposition. She argued that it was impossible to negotiate only with carrots and with no stick. It became more and more apparent that the administration could not adhere to red lines in relation to Iran's nuclear program, even though both the White House and the State Department knew that it was impossible to conduct negotiations with no limits. Period!

The claim that the United States was too biased when it came to Israel, to the point of any criticism against Israel being considered illegitimate, was increasingly heard both within the Democratic Party and within the administration, at least until President Trump took office in early 2017. Many American officials grew tired of hearing Israel's argument that a nuclear Iran was an existential threat and adopted the view that the Iranians were rational and therefore would not use nuclear weapons against Israel, if and when they had them. This assessment is very dangerous and far-reaching if one remembers that what is being discussed is the possibility of a nuclear event, with the decision maker being the spiritual leader who, according to Shiite belief, cannot make mistakes. In this context, it should be stated that the power of the Jewish lobby in the United States is not what it used to be.

In his Cairo speech, Obama said that no country was entitled to determine which country had the right to acquire nuclear weapons. But a nuclear Iran would trigger a nuclear arms race in the Middle East, which was contrary to the interests of the United States. This meant that the United States was afraid, not of a nuclear Iran, but of a nuclear Middle East. In other words, the United States seemed likely to accept Iranian hegemony in the Middle East, which was of great concern to moderate Sunni Arab states and, of course, to Israel.

The Obama administration was examining alternatives that would prevent the next stage of regional nuclearization and was looking for ways to curb proliferation, from Pakistan, with its unstable regime, to the rogue state of North Korea and to China and Russia. In the interest of reaching a consensus with Europe on this issue, the administration tried to define a red line that would be the lowest common denominator accepted: that is, that a Western response would come only after a nuclear or other nonconventional attack on Israel.

Another idea that was considered was the German-Japanese model of a two-month threshold for acquiring a bomb. According to this model, in order to reach an agreement or understanding with Iran, Iran would be allowed to advance to the point of being two months away from a bomb. Of course, such a deal would not solve the problem of the arms race throughout the entire region.

At the end of the day, toward the end of Obama's tenure, there was no chance of any intelligence picture motivating the administration to take action against Iran. The tendency was to believe that there was still time and that the hour had not yet come for action. This would be the approach until Iran carried out a nuclear test, after which the administration would adopt an approach that would try to persuade the Iranians not to repeat it.

Another American stance derived from the following logic:

- There was a connection between Iran's march toward nuclear weapons and the Israeli-Palestinian conflict.
- If the Israeli-Palestinian conflict was resolved, it would be difficult for Iran to attain nuclear weapons in the resulting atmosphere of reconciliation.
- Iran was aspiring to reach the breakout stage within a year or two, and there was therefore still time for negotiations and an agreement based on the 2004 model (see below).
- Iran should not be required to make concessions regarding Israel, such as ending its support for Hezbollah, because that would make it more difficult to reach an agreement on the nuclear issue.

From my perspective, what I identified in the Obama administration was confusion and a lack of determination. This was an administration for whom foreign policy was a nuisance, for whom Israel was a nuisance. It displayed a tendency to appease the "bad guys" rather than confront them. I will address President Trump's position later.

It should be noted that the 2004 model mentioned above was not an American-Iranian agreement that led to Iran halting its military nuclear development for a period of time. Iran made the decision unilaterally following the US invasion of Iraq. That is, the decision was made following a clear military move by the other side, and not as the result of a policy of engagement or of verbal deterrence.

Iran: A Case Study in Obstinacy and Wearing Down the Enemy

Iran emerged defeated from its nine-year war with Iraq, which ended in 1990 on the eve of the outbreak of the First Gulf War. After this war, when the Iraqis were busy invading Kuwait and fighting against the international coalition led by the United States, the Iranians were drawing lessons from their war against Iraq. They concluded that their defeat in the war was the result of the combination of two weapons that the Iraqis had introduced into their ranks during the crucial stages of the war—rockets and missiles launched at Iranian population centers, including the capital Tehran, and chemical weapons, which had been used by the Iraqis on the front lines. The Iranians had no response to these two types of weapons.

As a result of the lessons it learned, Iran decided to invest its efforts into developing nonconventional military capabilities in order to build up its strategic power. For the first time, it was decided to build chemical and biological capabilities in parallel, as well as missile and rocket launching systems. The internal debate over whether to expand the efforts to build nuclear capability as well continued for a long time. The initial position of the first spiritual leader, Khomeini, based, inter alia, on religious grounds, was to rule out nuclear development. Later on, however, he was brought around by the proponents of nuclear development, headed by members of IRGC, and he gave his blessing for the launching of a development program.

One can assume that over the course of the discussions the question arose as to whether Iran should build up its military capabilities only to deal with the Iraqi threat in the future or whether it should build strategic capabilities that would support a foreign policy that aspired to turn Iran into a regional hegemon.

In any case, the second position was the one that was adopted, and Iran embarked on an arms race with long-term plans and budgets and with deceptive plots for the concealment of its programs to obtain military nuclear capability, long-range missile capability, and chemical and biological military capabilities. Later, submarines were added to the list.

The first proof of the new Iranian strategic doctrine made its way to Israel when intelligence was received indicating that the Iranians were extending the range of the Shihab 3 missile, the first to be developed under the new doctrine, to 1,300 kilometers. This range covered the entire State of Israel with launchers stationed in western Iran. Today they have missiles with a range that allows them to place the launchers deep inside Iran and still cover the entire State of Israel. During the first half of the 1990s, ample evidence of Iran's activity to realize its strategic capabilities accumulated, with a central element of this evidence being its intensive acquisition of Western technologies.

The Israeli quest to convince the world that Iran's ambition was to become a military hegemon in the Middle East began in 1991. I remember how I would go from country to country, from the head of one intelligence agency to the next, from one military commander to another and from one decision maker to another, trying to convince them that a strategic threat was developing against Israel, one that would also constitute a regional threat. I must say that at first I was taken for a lunatic. Later, I would receive the response, "Leave us alone, you're talking about a threat that's way off in the distance— we're busy dealing with a long list of more urgent threats."

I relay this in order to point out that Iran's decision to develop nonconventional strategic capabilities was made in the early 1990s, almost twenty years ago (at the time of writing) and more than twenty-five years before this book was published. Today, no serious person carries any doubt about Iran's intentions to develop military nuclear capability. It is also now impossible to deny that for twenty years the Iranians managed to deceive the world and sell it the story (which was convenient for the world to buy) that their nuclear program was solely for peaceful purposes. Today, with the Iranians already having obtained long-range (3,500 km) missile capability and chemical and biological capabilities, and with nuclear military capability just around the corner, they have already begun to realize their goal of strategic hegemony in the Middle East. The first Gulf state to announce its recognition of this development was Qatar, which had already concluded several years earlier that the United States could not be relied upon and had aligned itself with Iran. Moreover, Iran now has a heavy military presence on the ground in Iraq, and the two countries can be defined as "sister states," with their common denominator being Shiite Islam. Iran has a massive presence, both directly and through groups of foreign fighters (Chechens, Turkmen, and others) in Syria and Lebanon, and Iran has also been taking an active part in the civil war in Yemen.

The Iranian move in Lebanon was astute, and today Hezbollah, with its high-trajectory strategic capabilities, is a first-rate threat that Israeli policy planners cannot ignore. The military experience that Hezbollah acquired in the war against ISIS in Syria should not be underestimated; today it should be treated as a regular army and not as a terrorist organization.

The evacuation of US military forces from Iraq will turn it into a vacuum to be occupied by Iranian strategic influence. The Iranians have been operating inside Iraq for years, expanding their base of influence, with their natural allies being the Shiites, who constitute a clear majority of Iraq's population. As of 2017, Iranian military forces and security advisers belonging to the IRGC are fighting side by side with the Iraqi Shiite army against ISIS in order to try to drive it out of Iraq. Following the departure of the American forces, the next aim of the Iranians and their Shiite allies will be to strike and terrorize the American civilian organizations that are likely to replace the US Army. Washington will not go to war again to protect these American citizens. They will leave Iraq, the issue will disappear from the media's agenda, and Iraq will become a de facto protectee of Iran. It should be remembered that among the Shiite leaders in Iran and Iraq there is not only religious solidarity but also family ties. Many Shiite clerics from Iraq studied in Iran and at various points also sought political asylum there.

In light of all the above, today's world, with the United States at its helm, is at a crossroads; its attention is turning more and more toward postnuclear issues. One of them concerns what Iran's postnuclear strategy will be. In this context, there is a view that the attitude toward nuclear weapons is culturally dependent and not necessarily determined by military considerations. For example, the Soviet regime banned their bombers from flying freely over the skies of the Soviet Union with nuclear bombs on board. Why? To prevent a Soviet pilot from being tempted to drop a bomb on the Kremlin. Will the Iranians also think this way? Will they ensure that a missile launcher with a nuclear warhead can under no circumstances direct a missile at an Iranian target?

Another issue is that Iran's nuclearization is likely to lead to increased demand for nuclear technology in the Middle East. Those who will undoubtedly star in this show will be members of the group known as the "A. Q. Khan boys" (Abdul Qadeer Khan was the undisputed leader of the Pakistani nuclear project and is the world's number one proliferator of nonconventional weapons). If this happens, very little will remain of the global nonproliferation regime to which President Obama devoted so much of his time, because the North Koreans, the Chinese, and even the Russians will want to take part in this lucrative market.

A third issue concerns nuclear deterrence. We are familiar with the concept of the unitary deterrence rational actor, whereby, in the dialectic of nuclear theories, logic prevails for everyone in all cases, leading the nuclear states to tone down the conflict between them. The answer to the question of whether these rules will apply in the case of Iran is not evident. Our judgment of what is rational refers to everything that is reasonable in our eyes and ignores fundamental differences in the adversary's database, the filters through which it sees things, the focus of its identity (Its country? Its religion? Its culture?).

In this context, it is worth mentioning the US Department of Defense's practice of "deterrence profiling." This profile includes the following elements: the enemy's history, its self-image, the degree to which it complies with authority, its past responses to reward and punishment, its sources of motivation (be they religious, economic, ideological, political, personal, or collective), the filters through which it receives information, and the degree to which it believes in explanations that seem to us "unreasonable." There is no doubt that this is a very interesting measurement tool, and one in which the Americans have invested a great deal of thought and experience. However, it does not claim to be scientific, nor is it based on any scientific methodology. And when one is dealing with issues of survival, it takes a lot of courage to make decisions only on the basis of this profiling tool. I believe that an intelligence officer, from the IDF or the Mossad, relying only on an intelligence assessment based on an analysis of the enemy and precluded from assessing Israel's own capabilities with regard to the Iranian nuclear issue (as this is done by the political leader and the body that works under him or her, such as the National Security Council), will be forced to present the decision maker with an intelligence assessment that is based on a very pessimistic scenario.

The instinct of survival triumphs over every other instinct. But does it stand up to the Iranian ideological and theological test that sanctifies death if it achieves the ultimate goal of restoring the global Islamic caliphate? To further complicate this dilemma, one can point to two cases in which the Iranians preferred reason over the ideological imperative. The first time was in 1988, when Supreme Leader Khomeini, who saw that Iran was being defeated by Iraq, made a unilateral decision to end the war. In explaining his decision, he wrote that for him it was like "drinking a cup of poison." The second instance was in 2004, following the US invasion of Iraq; the Iranians, fearing they were next, unilaterally decided to suspend their military nuclear program temporarily. Here, too, logic prevailed over religious considerations. This example is weak, however, in view of the fact that what the Iranians reacted to was a huge military move and the American invasion of Iraq, rather than a verbal threat.

Below are some other dilemmas related to the decision on courses of action against a nuclear Iran:

- Experience has taught that a defensive approach alone in reaction to provocation (for example, the launching of missiles on the southern city of Sderot) is not only ineffective but also liable to exact a prohibitive price.
- A carrot will be perceived by the other side as a weakness if it has not been preceded by a stick or a credible demonstration of power.
- Targeted assassinations of members of the leadership are, in my view, a very effective strategy in general, but not a sufficient one.
- True deterrence occurs only when the adversary understands that the steps it is taking are illogical, as not only will they not achieve its goal, but they will even lead to negative results in areas that really matter to it. Here again, the question arises of whether this definition applies to an adversary that is irrational.
- Will the mechanisms that have been in place in the nuclear arena since the Cold War—safeguards and permissible access links— be accepted by the Iranians if and when they obtain nuclear weapons?
- To what extent will the taboo on using a nuclear bomb, which has existed since World War II, be maintained by the Iranians, or at least be an additional consideration for them? The conflict that comes closest to testing this taboo today is the Indian-Pakistani conflict. The conventional theory is that both sides having nuclear capacity acts as a moderating force. In the case of Iran, the question is whether the divine command of self-sacrifice for the sake of the global Islamic caliphate will lead to the violation of the taboo or whether it will be preserved despite this edict.

- During the Cold War, the messages conveyed between the two powers took the form of actions, except for the Cuba crisis, during which President Kennedy conveyed his messages via declarations. In a nonstate situation, declarations are the only means of communicating with the adversary, and their influence, by definition, is weaker than actions that display strength. A situation in which the adversaries are nonstate actors refers to the possibility that terrorist organizations will gain control of, or be given by a state, nuclear weapons, be they advanced or not.

Khamenei is becoming weaker in relation to the IRGC. As discussed, the regime is increasingly assuming the character of a pretorian regime in which the IRGC is controlling the political leadership by taking over of the centers of power—the security services, the economy, and the channels through which information is passed to the leader. IRGC members are being appointed to key positions in both the president's administration and the office of the spiritual leader. In this reality, the question is how much influence the IRGC will have on the nuclear decision-making process, not to mention on potential nuclear activity.

Even if the Iranians agree to transfer part of their stockpile of LEU (low-enriched uranium) abroad to continue enrichment, as long as this option is consistent with the projected Iranian course of progress, it will be preceded by long and exhausting negotiations on the conditions and arrangements for verification, and afterwards it will not even be possible to ensure that they do not continue to secretly enrich the LEU by themselves. Regarding the timetable, the working assumption is that they will not reach breakout capacity until they have enough material for at least ten bombs. That is, even if the Iranians agree to such an arrangement, they will not give up their desire to acquire nuclear weapons.

The events surrounding the 2009 Iranian elections only boosted the regime's determination to march forward with the nuclear program. The regime's assessment was that American pressure or an

American "green light" for Israeli military action should not be feared. They judged that their determination to continue progress on the program would strengthen the regime. There is evidence that the North Korean case served as a model for Iran. If this is true, one could expect that Iran, in its negotiations with the United States and Europe, would reach understandings and then withdraw from them in order to extract further concessions. Indeed, in the negotiations between Iran and the United States and the other world powers, there were signs that the Iranians had learned from North Korea's patterns of behavior.

Another lesson from the North Korean case is that Iran would prefer to demonstrate its capability on the basis of the assumption that there will be no rollback, so if it crosses the line (that is, carries out an experiment or otherwise demonstrates its military nuclear capability) it will have achieved the desired status, and the subsequent discussions will be about a freeze and avoiding the repetition of a similar experiment.

Here it is worth examining the North Korean case and its implications for Iran's behavior during the Trump era. Perhaps we should start from the end (just before the summit of Trump and Kim in June 2018) and say that Trump's "strategy," expressed via tweetstorms and frenetic, spontaneous statements from every stage, including the 2017 UN General Assembly, is already steering the North Korean leader even further toward brinkmanship. But if we assume that Kim Jong-un will be guided by his survival instinct, he might read Trump as follows:

- Trump wants to kill terrorists and does not want to get involved in major wars.
- Trump enjoys the support of only a minority of Americans. The American majority finds him repugnant, as do the American media.
- Trump is a serial violator of international agreements. These include the Trans-Pacific Partnership, of which twelve countries are

members, and the Paris Agreement on climate change, signed by 195 countries. He maintains a hostile attitude toward NATO, whose members believe America can no longer be trusted, and finally, he pulled out of the nuclear deal with Iran.

Some of Kim Jong-un's other considerations may be as follows:

- He believes that in situations of brinkmanship, China will continue to support him and will not "throw North Korea to the dogs," because as its buffer state with South Korea, which enjoys the support of the United States, North Korea is a strategic asset that China will not easily give up.
- Russia also has allied itself with North Korea and probably promised it its veto in the UN Security Council, as part of its strategy of obstruction against any American move.
- If the United States withdraws from the nuclear agreement with Iran, all that is left for it to do is impose additional sanctions against Iran, to which the other parties to the agreement will not join. An American attack on Iran's nuclear facilities is inconceivable.

The conclusion that the North Korean leader is likely to reach is that he can continue his show of brinkmanship vis-à-vis Trump, with the exception of a physical attack on American territory (including Guam), without risking a direct American attack on his country. He will not initiate a direct attack on the United States but will respond to any attack by it.

As for the United States, it is quite possible that Kim will succeed in knocking Trump off balance, but if the latter wants to attack, the American system will stop him from doing so.

The issue of the status of the spiritual leader also poses a difficult dilemma for Western decision makers. Two approaches can be found among the Iranian spiritual leadership. Khamenei's view is that the spiritual leader is the sole decision maker. He is infallible and speaks the word of God. The view of Grand Ayatollah Hossein Ali Montazeri is that the spiritual leader's role is to make recommendations and act as a consultant, not to be the sole decision maker.

In trying to assess what the future holds, one cannot refrain from quoting Khamenei's remarks to a foreign critic: "My mission on earth is to bring about the destruction of the State of Israel, and a nuclear Iran is a tool designed to impose the will of God and Islamize the world."

Russia: Playing the Iran Card in Order to Regain Its Superpower Status

From the October Revolution in Tsarist Russia in 1917 and until the Khomeini revolution in Iran in 1979, there was hostility between the Soviet Union and Iran. In his time, Stalin encouraged the establishment of a communist party in Iran that would lead to increased Soviet influence and neutralize Western influences. The Soviet Union adopted a policy of "realpolitik" toward Iran, which had some successes here and there. But apart from the period of the Marxist republic of the Tudeh Party in northern Iran between 1942 and 1947, supported by the Soviet Union, and the period of Prime Minister Mossadegh (1951–53), who overthrew the shah and enjoyed Soviet support, Iran was a consistent ally of the United States.

The Khomeini revolution in 1979 was initially supported by the Soviets, but this changed in the wake of a series of developments:

- The Soviets were disappointed by Iran's choice to be independent of any superpower.
- Iran displayed a negative attitude toward communist atheism.
- The Soviets were miffed by Iran's support for the Mujahidin in Afghanistan in their war against the Soviet invasion of their country.
- Iran was affronted by the Soviet Union's coercive policy regarding oil prices.

After the collapse of the Soviet Union in 1991, a situation developed in which Russia needed Iranian support to prevent the infiltration of radical Islam into Russia and the Asian republics, and Iran needed Russian weapons and technology.

President Putin's policy since 2000 has aspired to restore Russia's former superpower status. Ideally this would be done with the consent of the United States, but if that is not possible, Russia will still continue to pursue this goal. Still, post-1991 Russia does not have the power to dictate to the United States, so the only strategy it can adopt to advance its goal is to use its "nuisance value." This is how Russia has turned into the "spoiler" trying to throw spokes in the wheels of any American international initiative.

Russian officials, both past and present, have spoken in closed circles about the humiliation the US administration has brought upon Russia since 1991. Since the demarcation of the Soviet Union's borders at the end of World War II, Russia had not shrunk in size to the extent it did after the Cold War and the collapse of the Soviet Union in 1991. Russia lost all of eastern Europe and the Baltic states and is still trying to maintain some influence in Ukraine; first it seized the Crimean peninsula and annexed it, and later it took control of territory in eastern Ukraine. The conflict, as of late 2018, is still in full swing. In terms of conventional strategy, the western gateway to Moscow is no longer protected. Russia lost the Asian republics, an event that had far-reaching implications with regard to energy. It lost Georgia, which had "imported an American president from the United States," thereby exposing Russia's southern underbelly.

All Russian political, international, or strategic decisions are made on the basis of the extent to which the decision will bring Russia closer to being recognized once again as a global superpower. In 1992, I met with Yevgeny Primakov, then head of the KGB, in Moscow, at his invitation. At the end of a long and exhausting day of discussions, which were conducted through an interpreter, we shook hands and were about to part ways. Suddenly, Primakov switched over to fluent English and told me: "I want you to convey to your political masters in Israel that Russia was a superpower, Russia has the potential of a superpower, and Russia will again be a superpower."

On January 20, 2009, as President Obama entered the White House, I sent him a letter via an envoy. I recommended that the Obama administration's foreign policy priorities begin to include the Iranian threat. The first step on this path needed to be a visit by Obama to Moscow and a proposal to Putin that in exchange for Russian support for sanctions against Iran, the United States would retract its intentions to deploy a missile defense system in eastern Europe. Dealing with the Israeli-Palestinian conflict would be much simpler *after* the Iranian threat had been dealt with.

I never received confirmation that the letter had reached its destination. But on July 9, 2009, the *New York Times* noted that during a visit to Russia "President Obama today offered to scrap plans for a missile defense shield in Eastern Europe if Russia helped to stop Iran developing a nuclear bomb" and that he told graduating students of the New Economic School in Moscow, "I want us to work together on a missile defense architecture that makes us all safer. But if the threat from Iran's nuclear and ballistic missiles programs is eliminated, the driving force for missile defense in Europe will be eliminated. That is in our mutual interest."

The Russian response to Obama's proposals was only lukewarm. From then until 2010, the United States abandoned President Bush's original missile defense plan in eastern Europe, though the Russians did not really join the American-European camp against Iran's nuclearization. It can only be assumed that the price that the United States was willing to pay the Russians for joining their efforts did not satisfy them. What the Russians want from the United States in exchange for their joining the anti-Iranian Western front is the recognition of their status as an equal power. (In the years that followed, the United States and Russia—together with other powers—cooperated in putting pressure on Iran, including sanctions, which led to the signing of the nuclear agreement in 2015. However, the agreement does not fully reflect the initial demands that the United States presented to

Iran, and various actors, particularly Israel, regard it as a capitulation to Iran.)

Russia is apparently not worried about a nuclear neighbor to its south because its own nuclear power—today and in the future—will deter Iran from threatening it, since Russia can easily wipe Iran off the map altogether. Russia does seem to be concerned about Iran's imperial ambitions, which will be bolstered by military nuclear capability, at least in the Middle East, but that is not enough to convince it to join the United States. Perhaps the Russians have some other hidden consideration? An Israeli attack on Iran's nuclear facilities would certainly serve Russian interests:

- Russia would benefit greatly from the repairing of Iranian infrastructure following its destruction in an Israeli attack.
- Russia would be the one to refill (for a price, of course) the Iranian weapons depots.
- Russia would benefit from the increase in energy prices after such an attack.
- Russia could—after an attack—serve as mediator between Iran and the rest of the world.

In general, Russian-US relations toward the end of 2018 seem to be closer to what they were during the Cold War era than to the short period of Trump's rise to power, during which it appeared that he and Putin would be partners in building a new global architecture.

Options, Priorities, and the Day After

The following is a list of options, in decreasing order, of possible action against Iran:

A. A diplomatic solution through negotiations could offer the Iranians incentives that would lead them to agree to cancel or freeze their nuclear project.

B. Iran might agree to a one- or two-year breakout time, when it would have enriched uranium with a high enough level of fissile material to make ten bombs. It is quite possible that the United States will concede to this. Some say that in an extreme case the United States may agree to a one-month breakout time, believing that after their first experiment the Iranians will commit to not advancing any further. The Europeans will be satisfied with either of these two options.

C. A solution through sanctions may work if a number of conditions are present: (1) the sanctions are really tough (e.g., the cessation of the sale of refined petroleum to Iran, a complete economic boycott, the termination of investments in energy development); (2) Europe is fully on board with the sanctions; (3) Russia fully joins the sanctions regime; and (4) China, while not being required to join in, does refrain from blatantly violating the sanctions. The most problematic of these conditions is Russia's full compliance with the sanctions program. It is not at all certain that the United States will agree to grant Russia full recognition as an equal power, and it is doubtful whether Russia will settle for less.

D. An American attack did not appear to be a realistic option during President Obama's term, for three reasons. First, it would be an admission of the failure of the president's engagement strategy. This strategy embodied the vision that Obama brought with him to the White House—that he would be the president who would bring about reconciliation between the United States and the Muslim world. Also, the United States was embroiled in two major wars—in Iraq and Afghanistan—whose end and extent of continued American involvement are still difficult to foresee. Finally, there was a domestic economic crisis.

E. An American attack in the Trump era would appear particularly problematic at this point in time (in late 2018, about a year and a half after Trump's entering the White House):

1. On the Iranian nuclear issue, as with all of the major issues Obama dealt with, Trump adopted the contrary position.

From his first day as president, he voiced his stance against the nuclear deal with Iran, which had been signed by the world's powers (and Germany) in addition to the United States.

2. On various occasions in the first half of 2017, Trump stated his thoughts, ideas, and even threats regarding pulling out of the agreement and imposing new sanctions on Iran. He also hinted that in October 2017 he would not sign a document confirming that Iran was complying with the requirements of the agreement, contrary to statements by the military and security echelons of the United States and the European body in charge of oversight. In response, Iran's foreign minister announced that if Trump carried out his threat, Iran would consider announcing its withdrawal from the agreement and would renew and possibly even accelerate its nuclear development program.

3. The withdrawal of the United States from the agreement was a slap in the face to Great Britain, France, Germany, Russia, and China, who had invested two years of negotiations with Iran before the agreement was signed.

4. The United States' withdrawal from the agreement set a precedent that may cause great difficulties in finding a solution to the crisis with North Korea.

5. It is impossible to know at this point in time (2018), even after the Trump-Kim summit, whether and how the crisis between the United States and North Korea will be resolved. As to Iran, the first round of the resumption of sanctions is already in place, to be followed by harsher sanctions toward the end of 2018. Discussions in Washington are whether US strategy should aim for a change of regime in Iran or just denuclearization.

F. An Israeli attack would only occur as the result of the crossing of a red line. Right now this red line is probably set at a very extreme condition. What is it?

In the early 2010s, many articles on the conditions that would justify an Israeli attack on Iran's nuclear facilities began to be published, both in the press and in academic publications.[2] On the basis of these articles, inter alia, I assess the threshold to be as follows:

1. Proven Iranian possession of the technology to produce highly enriched, weapons-grade uranium (HEU)
2. Iranian possession of enough HEU to produce at least one bomb
3. Iranian possession of enough HEU to produce an arsenal of at least ten bombs
4. The existence of proven military capability, that is, a combination of bombs with launching facilities, deployment, and a combat doctrine
5. An Iranian provocation that would lead to an Israeli attack in response

When it comes to an Israeli attack, the question is whether the "red line" is any one of these conditions separately, or all of them together. When it comes down to it, this will have to be decided upon by the Israeli decision maker at that time.

What kind of Israeli attack are we talking about?

1. A clear "blue and white" attack (with no possibility of denying Israel's responsibility and no attempt to deny it)?
2. An attack that would leave room for deniability?
3. An attack on nuclear targets alone, when the working assumption would be that it is possible to strike only some of the Iranian nuclear targets?
4. An attack on both nuclear and government targets, including economic infrastructure, with the aim of toppling the regime?
5. Would the United States be informed in advance? And if so, at what point?
6. Would the home front need to be prepared for a possible response by Iran and/or Hezbollah? If so, at what point? And how? (This constitutes a major operations security problem.)
7. What would the day after look like?

Iran would certainly respond with conventional means, but it might also respond with chemical or biological weapons or both. Hezbollah would most likely react with its entire arsenal of high-trajectory weapons against military and civilian targets throughout the State of Israel. Hamas, if it still existed at this time, in the Gaza Strip might sit on the fence for a day or two, in order to see where the wind was blowing before deciding to respond. Iran would also respond in some way against the United States in Iraq and Afghanistan.

What would the American response be? Professor Zbigniew Brzezinski, who headed the National Security Council under President Carter (from January 1977 to January 1981), expressed the White House's attitude toward a possible Israeli attack by saying: "The United States will have to bring down the Israeli planes on their way to bombing Iran"(!). If an Israeli attack had been carried out during the Obama era, Obama would probably have seen it as a stab in the back of his engagement policy. An Israeli attack in the Trump era would be possible, in my opinion, only on the basis of Israeli-American cooperation or at least a quiet American nod. If this scenario were to take place today (October 2018), I would not see Trump agreeing to an attack given all the constraints he is under, including the circle of generals around him, who in my opinion would do anything to prevent him from approving a decision to attack Iran, be it American or Israeli. If John Bolton or others who shares his views, at such time, are still serving in the NSC, the decision may be different!

Europe would condemn Israel out of fear of rising energy prices and the disruption of the regional, and perhaps even the global, order. Europe would never be able to forgive tiny Israel, whose standing in world public opinion is at an all-time low, for allowing itself to do what no other country in the world would dare.

Russia would also express condemnation but would harvest the fruits of the Israeli attack by rehabilitating and rearming Iran.

The rest of the world would also criticize Israel, and while the condemnation of any one particular country would not do any harm, all of them together could create a movement to impose sanctions on Israel.

An Israeli attack could mark the end of the era of global nuclear proliferation.

This entire description of the "day after" would apply only to an Israeli attack that achieved results that were less than the destruction of the entire Iranian nuclear infrastructure and/or the collapse of the regime. An attack that brought about the collapse of the regime would win Israel much praise. This is based on the precedent of the Israeli attack on the Iraqi nuclear reactor (Operation Tamuz), which was a successful "closed case" that did not provoke any extreme reactions against Israel.

■　■　■

In June 2015, on the eve of the signing of the nuclear agreement between Iran, the United States, and its allies, the first question I asked myself was "Will there be an agreement?" And the answer I gave myself was "Apparently so!" And the main reason was that President Obama saw the agreement as a seminal achievement for his legacy as president. The Iranians, who understood this, would use all of their negotiating talents to extract more and more concessions. On what basis did I determine this? On the basis of the fifty years I had been working on Iran, two and a half of which I spent living and working in that country. My greatest teacher of the Persian language was the Tehran bazaar. As noted earlier, the bazaar is not just a shopping center but the center of the Persian art of negotiation. And regarding that art, there is no contest between Western culture and Persian culture.

Following the Iran-Iraq War, which continued throughout the 1980s, and after the Cold War and the First Gulf War, revolutionary Iran consolidated its national security doctrine and defined its future strategy. The Iranians reached the conclusion that Iran needed comprehensive strategic capabilities (chemical, biological, nuclear, and means of delivery), first, to ensure Iran's immunity from external aggressions, including American threats, and second, to enable Iran to realize its imperial foreign policy goals and become a regional power. As far as Iran is concerned, military nuclear capability is a necessary condition for the realization of these two objectives.

As a culture that was already an empire in the sixth century BCE, and then again from the seventh century until the Khomeini revolution in 1979, Iran does not recognize or accept the Western concept of "time being of the essence." As noted earlier, when it comes to achieving a goal through negotiations, there is no match for the Persian. He has immeasurably more patience than the American, who has a history of only two hundred years—thus my prediction that the Iranians will exhaust the Americans and their allies and squeeze more and more concessions out of them. In the course of time, they will fulfill their part of the agreement, first of all until the sanctions are lifted and their relations with the West return to normal. Down the road, the world will have to deal with problems and crises as they arise. Presidents and heads of state will change, and the Iranians will begin to chip away at the agreement, gradually and with small steps, none of which will cross any of the lines set out by the West. At a point in time that suits them—perhaps at the time of the agreement's expiration, but it is certainly possible that it will happen earlier—they will declare themselves a nuclear state. At that moment, they will have realized their first goal of achieving immunity and will set out to achieve their second goal—making Iran a regional power—in a much more determined and brazen way.

At this point, when the world will have to treat Iran as a country with nuclear capability, it will have to grapple with the million-dollar question: Will a nuclear Iran act as a pragmatic state or as a messianic state? This question is not theoretical at all. One mustn't forget that the person with his finger on the nuclear trigger is the spiritual leader, who speaks the word of Allah and is therefore infallible. It should also be remembered that the Shia does not recognize coexistence with anyone other than Shiites and that the realization of the caliphate, the supreme and ultimate goal of Shiite faith, sanctifies a jihad against the infidels.

The question posed in the simplistic form of "messianic versus pragmatic" does not reflect the subtleties of the dilemma. When Iran becomes a member of the club of nuclear states, the situation will be fundamentally different from what it was during the Cold War, when the global order was dictated by two nuclear blocs that created a system of tools and capabilities that ensured stability and the prevention of errors. In a system of nuclear states between whom there is no symmetry, who have different interests, and for some of whom the well-being of the human race is not a priority, all it takes is one provocation that party A sees as tolerable but that party B defines as a *casus belli* (a justification for war), and you have a nuclear event whose end cannot be predicted.

The bottom line is that the thought of a fanatical Shiite ayatollah with his finger on the nuclear trigger is terrifying.

CHAPTER THREE

INTELLIGENCE AND NATIONAL SECURITY

Military Doctrine in the Absence of Strategic Depth

This chapter was conceived at the beginning of 2016, when a delegation of Chinese (apparently retired) generals came to visit IDC (Interdisciplinary Center) Herzliya and asked to hear a lecture on the subject of intelligence and national security. I thought that a good joke at the beginning of my lecture would help to break the ice, and so I asked our guests if China was suffering from a lack of strategic depth. I did not succeed in getting them to crack a smile.

Israel's *military* doctrine, in contrast to its national security doctrine, began to crystallize after the War of Independence. With the signing of the armistice agreements, the nascent State of Israel covered an area of twenty thousand square kilometers. Its Jewish population numbered about 750,000 (approximately 600,000 of whom were already there before the establishment of the state and another 150,000 of whom had arrived during the war) and a minority population of about 120,000. The tiny country was surrounded by Lebanon, Syria, Jordan, and Egypt, relations with which were based on a regime of armistice agreements. Iraq, which had taken part in the war, had refrained from signing an armistice agreement, so under international law Israel and Iraq are in a de facto state of war to this day.

During the first twenty-five years of independence we experienced five wars: the War of Independence from 1947 to 1949; the Sinai Campaign of 1956; the Six-Day War in 1967; the War of Attrition from 1970 to 1971; and the Yom Kippur War in 1973. During these twenty-five years, the first generation of Israeli independence, the building blocks of its military doctrine were formed.

The first building block is deterrence, the practical meaning of which is the creation of a balance of terror in which the enemy knows—or thinks—that a provocation will cost him a price that is too heavy to bear, namely prohibitive retaliation. The principle of deterrence as one of the building blocks of a national security doctrine applies to any country that has enemies, let alone a small country like Israel, which was surrounded by enemy states in those years.

The second building block is early warning, which has double layers: strategic warning, which requires intelligence infiltration at the decision-making level in order to uncover the enemy's intentions, and tactical and operative warning, which relates to the timing of the outbreak of war and the enemy's war plans.

The third block is "subjugate/vanquish," which means comprehensive military capability that guarantees absolute superiority over the enemy.

The rationale behind these three building blocks is that *even if deterrence fails, and even if there is no warning, we still have the ability to defeat the enemy.* This was the case in the Yom Kippur War, with one difference—we did have a warning, but it was interpreted incorrectly by those in charge of assessing national intelligence—and a warning that is not interpreted correctly is the same as no warning at all.

The fourth building block is the principle of moving the war into enemy territory as quickly as possible. The rationale underlying this principle is the absence of *strategic depth*, and the understanding that Israel as a general rule does not embark on preventive wars. Additional considerations are to try to turn the enemy from an attacker into a defender in minimal time and to minimize damage to the home territory and its citizens. The necessary conditions for the realization of these objectives are qualitative intelligence on the enemy's capabilities and operational intelligence on targets in the enemy territory.

From all of the above, we can see that Israel's lack of strategic depth required it to adopt and develop an offensive defense doctrine, with the exception of the option of preventive war. The absence of preventive war from Israel's strategic arsenal is anchored in the political explanation that if Israel attacks first it will be accused of aggression, not only by the Arab states, but by the entire world. Israeli governments have always attached supreme importance to the world's perception of it—in the West in general, and in the United States in particular—as a country whose wars are forced upon it and who goes to war only to defend itself against aggressors.

The prestate military doctrine was a hybrid; that is, it was varied and not entirely coherent. The pre-independence Jewish community, the Yishuv, lived in very difficult conditions: the two populations, the Jews and the Arabs, mingled on the same territory. The number of Palestinian Arabs far exceeded the number of Jews. The Palestinian Arabs had unlimited strategic backing in the form of the entire Middle East, full of Arab states, all of which had regular armies.

The Jewish military response took the form of secret militias operating under the British Mandate. These militias arose and operated in a political environment in which the political parties were preparing themselves for the struggle for power in the future independent state to be established upon the end of the British Mandate. The largest and most important of these militias was the Haganah, which was subordinate to the Jewish Agency for Palestine and controlled by the Labor parties (Mapai and Mapam). The Haganah established and operated a body that was similar to Military Intelligence in its organization and objectives—the Information Service ("Shai"). The Shai included a network of regional controllers who operated Arabic-speaking officers recruiting agents from among the Arab population for HUMINT (human intelligence)—the only intelligence discipline at the time. Here and there one could also see the very modest beginnings of intelligence gathered from listening in on communications. The intelligence product was the "village files," which contained all of the intelligence needed for military or diplomatic action. The other militias—Etzel and Lehi—made do with the collection of specific intelligence for planned operations, mainly against the Mandate authorities.

Five Arab states—Egypt, Jordan, Lebanon, Syria, and Iraq—sent armies to destroy the State of Israel immediately after its declaration of independence. The number of casualties of the War of Independence is estimated at about six thousand, that is, one percent of the Jewish population. The war ended with armistice agreements, not with peace agreements. The IDF was created over the course of the war and came out of it battered. The period immediately following the war was a formative one for the establishment of Israel's national security doctrine and the expansion of its military doctrine, with the lack of strategic depth being a decisive variable in strategic thinking.

David Ben-Gurion, founder of the state and its first prime minister and defense minister, defined the national security doctrine, which built upon the military doctrine that has just been discussed. Ben-Gurion's definition included the following elements:

1. Israel needs a strategic ally that is a superpower.
2. Israel needs regional alliances (the concept of the northern and southern "triangles").
3. Israel needs to have military supremacy over all its enemies.
4. Israel needs strategic military capabilities.
5. Israel needs to have economic supremacy.

6. Israel needs to have scientific and technological superiority.
7. Israel must nurture and maintain its national resilience, which is expressed by its citizens' belief in the justness of its cause and their willingness to sacrifice what is necessary in order to ensure its national survival.

The 1950s were a formative period for the IDF's rehabilitation and its transformation into a modern army and for the development of an offensive security doctrine. The IDF's command was made up of commanders of great stature. I will mention two of them here, whose contribution was unique. The first is Ariel Sharon, whose contribution to deterrence and decisive victory, through Unit 101 and the paratroopers, was extremely significant. The second is Avraham Arnan, who made a unique contribution to the building of the doctrine and capabilities of intelligence warfare, one that offered the possibility of early warning in the absence of strategic depth.

The Six-Day War in 1967 gave the State of Israel a quantum leap in terms of strategic depth. From a position of strategic inferiority on the eve of the outbreak of the war, in only one week of military action the IDF succeeded in defeating three Arab armies. The IDF's conquest of Sinai added sixty thousand square kilometers to Israel's strategic depth, an area three times larger than that of the entire country. The IDF occupied the West Bank to the Jordan River, a victory that added both territory and a border that acts as a natural military obstacle. The conquest of the Syrian Golan Heights brought Damascus closer within the range of Israeli artillery.

Israel's entry into space, both in terms of communications and in terms of imagery, added even more to Israel's strategic depth. The satellite era contributed significantly to Israel's intelligence doctrine. The insight that the IDF could reach targets far outside of its borders greatly enhanced Israel's deterrent capability. VISINT satellites significantly improved Israel's intelligence capabilities, even in theaters of action far from its borders, affecting both deterrence and early warning.

The threat of high-trajectory weapons forced Israel to add a defensive dimension to its traditional offensive doctrine. Israel, because of its size, its sensitivity to human life, and the density of its economic infrastructure, decided to invest in the development of a three-tiered impenetrable defense system against all types of high-trajectory weapons: the Iron Dome system against tactical high-trajectory weapons with ranges up to one hundred kilometers; the David's Sling system against medium-range missiles; and the Arrow system against long-range ballistic missiles. This three-layer antiaircraft defense system, together with the upgrading of offensive capabilities, such as the F-35 (Lightning stealth multirole fighter) jets and the expansion of its submarine fleets, made a significant contribution to Israel's deterrent capability and increased the IDF's prevention capabilities.

The cyber age has introduced variables of a whole new kind into the world of strategic thinking. The first is that cyber capabilities completely nullify the dimension of strategic depth. You can now attack any target from any point on earth. The second variable is that the potential damage of a cyberattack is equivalent to the damage of an attack by nonconventional weapons such as chemical, biological, or nuclear weapons. The third variable is that it is difficult, if not nearly impossible, to identify the attacker and/or his location. The significance of this is that in the cyber world it is impossible to apply the system of rules that existed in the strategic thinking of the Cold War era with regard to the balance of terror. The cyber affair that was revealed during the last presidential campaign in the United States clearly illustrates the potential damage of this tool, even when it is not being employed to destroy state infrastructures.

The cyberattack that took place during the US elections was professionally designed for the purposes of psychological warfare. There is no doubt that the damage caused by this attack has been tremendous. It completely disrupted the relationship between the incoming president and the American intelligence community, an unprecedented phenomenon in the history of relations between the White House and the number one intelligence community in the world. It sowed distrust and doubt with regard to the electoral system in a democratic country among many constituencies in the United States. It also proved that the United States, along with many other countries in the world, still lacks a fundamental, systematic, and comprehensive doctrine of cyber warfare. President Obama's response to the Russian cyberattack—the expulsion of thirty-five Russian diplomats from the United States—was taken out of a Cold War rule book. At that time, it was customary to expel diplomats in response to the exposure of espionage. The extent of the damage in this particular cyberattack was immeasurably greater than any damage that a spy could cause, even a "top spy." Assuming that the Americans had unequivocal evidence that the Russians had a hand in the attack, a more appropriate reaction would have been to respond in kind—a counter-cyberattack against Russian targets that would cause the Russians the same degree, or an even greater degree, of damage than that caused to the United States. It is reasonable to assume that the imbalanced American response stemmed from Obama's unwillingness to escalate relations with Russia on the eve of his departure, or from his lack of firm proof that the Russians were responsible, or perhaps a combination of both.

The world of cyber warfare is double-layered, comprising the development of defensive capabilities against an attack by one's adversaries and the development of one's abilities to attack the adversary's systems. The building up of cyber warfare capabilities is based primarily on high-quality intelligence and sophisticated intelligence operations, whose purpose is also twofold: to learn the enemy's attack capabilities in order to build your defense system, and to learn the enemy's defensive capabilities in order to build your own attack capabilities. A condition for victory in this type of warfare is to get ahead of the adversary by at least one and a half generations, in the area of defense as well as in the area of attack. The one-and-a-half-generations rationale is based on the assumption that if the adversary catches up to you, you will still have the advantage of being half a generation ahead.

Only one more thing remains to be said on the issue of strategic depth, globally, in the context of nonconventional weapons. Strategic depth is dialectically relevant to two aspects: resilience and "second-strike capability." Regarding resilience, a country with a small territory and high population density and concentration of infrastructures in a relatively small area requires the ultimate deterrence. If deterrence fails, there is a danger that one barrage could incapacitate the country. Second-strike capability strengthens deterrence, as it conveys to the enemy that it does not have the ability to defeat you. In addition, with your second-strike capability you may be able to defeat the enemy, or at least inflict enough damage to convince it that its decision to initiate the first strike was unwise.

The National Intelligence Assessor

The structure of the State of Israel's intelligence community—Military Intelligence (MI), the Institute for Intelligence and Special Operations (the Mossad), and the General Security Service (Shabak)—was established in the early 1950s by the first prime minister of the independent State of Israel, David Ben-Gurion. As an avowed democrat, he correctly believed that the unnecessary concentration of power in the hands of one body should be prevented as much as possible. He recognized that intelligence is power and that an intelligence community must therefore be built in such a way that there is no single center of power. An excess of power has the potential for corruption and abuse.

Ben-Gurion decided then that the head of MI would be subordinate to the defense minister, through the IDF chief of staff; the heads of the Mossad and the Shin Bet would be subordinate to the prime minister. The cynics asked what the value in this was, as Ben-Gurion filled both of these roles at the time, so that all the power would be concentrated in his hands anyway! The answer to this question lies in the historic story of the establishment of the state. Ben-Gurion understood that the only guarantee for the survival of this miracle called the State of Israel was to establish a strong IDF as quickly as possible. He took this task upon himself, in his capacity as minister of defense. Once the state was established and the IDF would indeed be able to guarantee its survival, the time would come to implement the principle of the decentralization of power in the intelligence community.

Ben-Gurion defined not only the hierarchy of the young intelligence community but also the areas of responsibility and the boundaries of the three intelligence services. The IDF Intelligence Corps is supposed to be the most central and largest service, since it is responsible for early warning and for preparing intelligence for the IDF for future wars. Territorially speaking, MI gathers intelligence from within the State of Israel and abroad. The Mossad is responsible for intelligence gathering for MI, as well as for its own operations and for special operations: that is, any operation for the State of Israel that no other body is capable of carrying out. Finally, the Shin Bet, which is responsible for internal security, fighting subversive activities of any kind and engaging in counterespionage, operates within the borders of the State of Israel.

It is important to note that at its inception the intelligence community consisted of three intelligence services, of which only the most senior—MI—developed research and evaluation capabilities from the very beginning. The other two services dealt mainly with intelligence gathering and did not have research and evaluation capabilities, with the exception of intelligence research on their operations.

In the community's early days, a mechanism was built to direct intelligence collection. Since MI was the only service that also conducted research and assessments, it was natural for it to be the one to identify and define Israel's threats and translate them into EEI (Essential Elements of Information) to then be distributed to the Mossad and the Shin Bet, who were "subcontractors" of MI in everything related to responding to the national EEI.

The intelligence collection system between MI and the Mossad and Shin Bet created a very interesting symbiosis over time. At first, the process was one-way: Military Intelligence would brief the other two services and give them assessments of the material they had provided as well as more briefings; the Mossad and the Shin Bet would then brief MI with specific information regarding the operations they were responsible for, and MI would provide them with relevant intelligence from its sources.

Over time, MI researchers understood the potential of the other two services' sources and asked to assess not only the information they provided but also the quality of the sources themselves. The assessment of the sources was an important tool for the two intelligence-gathering services—the Mossad and the Shin Bet. It evolved from a one-time event to a periodic, annual, and special assessment mechanism.

At a later stage, MI's intelligence collection system assigned a representative of its own, a midlevel officer, as an attaché to the Mossad's HUMINT unit. The permanent presence of an MI officer in the Mossad significantly improved the work process. First, this presence enabled the two bodies, MI and the Mossad, to work in real time, twenty-four hours a day, every day. Second, the Mossad revealed all of the secrets behind its work—both intelligence and operational—to the Military Intelligence representative so that, through him, the top echelons of MI could better understand and appreciate the intelligence product provided by the Mossad. Third, the exposure enabled MI, through its representative at the Mossad, to focus its briefings on the individual source and its identified potential.

The development of the direction of intelligence collection was further enhanced when Military Intelligence's research department requested that its analysts be included in the meetings in which sources were debriefed, and the Mossad agreed. In retrospect, to the best of my judgment, at this stage the system began to "fake it." Why do I say this? The answer requires a slightly lengthy explanation, which is related to the ethos of HUMINT in the Mossad, which I experienced during the first decade of my service. HUMINT is like the "aircraft carrier" of the intelligence professions, first of all because of its historical age, which had its beginnings in the era of Joseph and his brothers in Genesis, but no less because of HUMINT's advantage over the other intelligence disciplines. This advantage is expressed in the fact that an intelligence collection officer, who is also an intelligence officer by training, can engage in live dialogue with his or her sources. In all of the other disciplines of intelligence—COMINT (communications intelligence), SIGINT (signals intelligence), VISINT (visual intelligence), and OSINT (open-source intelligence)—the intelligence officer can receive a piece of intelligence on a particular subject at a particular place at a particular time but cannot pose questions. The live dialogue between the collection officer and his or her source is the best way to gather intelligence on the enemy's intentions.

The classic ethos of the Mossad intelligence-gathering officer is that of someone who knows how to recruit sources, how to control them, and how to debrief them. I will allow myself to trust the opinion of my commanders, who considered me to be such an officer. MI's request to the Mossad that its researchers be integrated with the Mossad's collection officers was accepted by the Mossad as innocent and professional, since the addition of an intelligence researcher to the debriefing of a source should ensure a higher-quality intelligence outcome. In fact, the Mossad became a kind of a travel agency for MI researchers, for whom traveling abroad for a few days (during the period of the 1960s and 1970s) was a temptation that was difficult to resist and was therefore exploited, whether or not it was justified.

Intelligence collection officers, who were taught that the intelligence product of their work was the reason for their existence, witnessed a regression and the creation of a new form of status based on their recruiting talent rather than the quality of the intelligence they produced. I see in this a distortion of priorities, in which more importance is attributed to a skill that is a tool than to the ultimate goal—the intelligence for which the organization you serve exists. In light of this, during my period as director of the Mossad, the method I employed was based on approving the inclusion of MI analysts for meetings with sources only in those cases where it was justified, and not as a matter of norm and routine.

Since the 1950s, reality has changed almost beyond recognition, and with it the threats facing the State of Israel. We, the members of the community, and the entire nation of Israel, should be proud that all of the branches of the intelligence community have adapted to these changes surprisingly quickly with respect to the training of human resources, technological tools, and doctrines of warfare.

Beginning in the mid-1970s, the Mossad was charged with the additional task of thwarting hostile activities, namely global terrorism, in Target Countries and in the Base Countries. In the late 1970s, the Mossad also began to take on the responsibility of thwarting the buildup of nonconventional weapons by Israel's enemies. As a result of these tasks, for which the Mossad was involved in both intelligence gathering and prevention, there grew a vital need to develop research and assessment capabilities in these two areas within the Mossad; this was how the regime in which Military Intelligence was the sole body for research and assessment in the community began to change.

The annual intelligence assessment was—and still is—the peak of the community's intelligence work throughout the year. From the establishment of the state until the recommendations of the Agranat Commission, formed following the Yom Kippur War in 1973, it was agreed by all that MI was the national intelligence assessor of the State of Israel. MI's research division was the national clearinghouse to which all raw intelligence produced by any party in the country flowed. The IDF Intelligence Corps was not only an investigator and an assessor but an independent intelligence producer in all fields of intelligence, which continued to grow until it reached the proportions of a powerful country. MI's research division was a giant enterprise that produced research, assessment and position papers, EEI, and briefings on a daily, weekly, monthly, semiannual, and annual basis.

The partners who were considered junior members of the Israeli intelligence community—the Mossad and the Shin Bet—had no direct input into the annual intelligence assessment, which as mentioned was the peak of the community's annual work cycle, apart from the raw intelligence material they provided for MI's research throughout the year.

For many years and throughout my career in the Mossad, I maintained close working relationships with the top ranks of the Intelligence Corps. I learned to admire them for their successes in achieving remarkable things in the face of the State of Israel's existential challenges. But even the best systems fail from time to time! And when the operational culture of the system advocates excellence that constantly expands its performance envelope, it is impossible not to take into account the existence of a virtual red line, the crossing of which means failure—sometimes a colossal failure.

The main qualities required of an intelligence officer in a decision-making position are:

- A continuous aspiration for excellence.
- In the right circumstances, knowing when to decide not to take action, in a work environment where taking action is the benchmark.
- Skepticism and, when in doubt before making a decision, remembering to apply the adage "Whenever there is any doubt, there is no doubt." (This is a statement that has practical significance— do not let yourself wrestle and debate without end. Make a decision!)
- Knowing how to constantly test your self-confidence, which is acquired over time and experience, and remembering that modesty is sometimes also an option.

As the Hebrew prayer goes, "I have been young, and now am old," and in the world of intelligence I have seen it all. I admit that I, too, have suffered, more than once, from one weakness or another relating to the essence of the qualities I mentioned above. And what is the message encapsulated in my words? I will say it in the most blunt and simple way possible: had I been the head of Military Intelligence after the Yom Kippur War, I would have demanded from the prime minister, in addition to the recommendations of the Agranat Commission, that an external, professional, and extrajudicial body examine MI's intelligence products, as well as those of the Mossad and Shin Bet, following the establishment of their research bodies, in accordance with the recommendations of the Agranat Commission. Every attempt since the commission to establish a National Security Council, a national security adviser, an intelligence adviser, and so forth, amounted to a failed attempt that did not rise to the tasks as I defined them.

I will touch upon only one of these attempts, which I took part in, and which to the best of my knowledge has not been made public so far. The Agranat Commission completed its work and the State of Israel descended into a political spiral, as well as into a national trauma. Head of Military Intelligence Major General Eli Zeira resigned, as was recommended by the Agranat Commission, and was replaced by Major General Shlomo Gazit, a protégé of Moshe Dayan. IDF chief of staff David Elazar ("Dado") also resigned as per the commission's recommendation and with pressure from Dayan was replaced by General Motta Gur, who had been the IDF attaché in Washington during the war.

Defense Minister Dayan resigned, for the most part in the wake of public pressure. Prime Minister Golda Meir also resigned because of public pressure, but I think that in her case the deterioration in her health and her overwhelming stress and feelings of regret also contributed to her departure.

The door was open for Pinchas Sapir to become prime minister. The "professional politicians" of Mapai, of whom Sapir was one, wanted him in, but Sapir himself did not want the post. He believed that Israeli prime ministers should have a security orientation, and he did not feel that he fit the bill, especially after a war that had left the Israeli public wounded and questioning Israel's ability to continue to face its security challenges.

Yigal Allon, commander of the Palmach and perhaps the most prominent combat commander of the War of Independence, considered himself a natural candidate for prime minister, but Allon's political power was already depleted. As a member of the Ahdut Ha'avoda Party, which Mapai veterans had always viewed with suspicion, he knew that there was no chance that the majority of the Labor Party, who belonged to Mapai, would accept him as Golda's heir.

This situation led to Sapir, along with most of the Mapai oldtimers, choosing Yitzhak Rabin as Golda's successor. Rabin wanted the job, but in his ow right, and not because he was someone's "man"—Golda's or his patron's from his Palmach days, Yigal Allon. Rabin needed a period of calm without any tremors, in the political arena as well as in the military. The man whom he saw as someone he could lean on was the director of the Mossad, Zvi Zamir, a friend from his time in the Palmach, who had stood by Golda throughout the war and who had come out of the war and the Agranat Commission relatively unscathed. Rabin wanted him by his side as a special intelligence adviser to the prime minister. Zamir was prepared to consider this proposal but suggested that the prime minister appoint a committee whose role would be to examine a range of issues related to the organization of the intelligence community in the post–Yom Kippur War era and to present recommendations for changes and improvements.

Such a committee was appointed on April 26, 1974. Its members were Zvi Zamir, who served as its chairman; Mordechai Gazit, director general of the Prime Minister's Office; Major General Shlomo Gazit, head of Military Intelligence; Yossef Harmelin, head of the Shin Bet; and Avraham Kidron, director general of the Foreign Ministry. The committee's mandate was to submit recommendations regarding the organization of the intelligence community, including:

1. The delineation of areas of activity and responsibilities between the research departments of the General Staff/Military Intelligence, the Mossad, the Ministry of Foreign Affairs, and the Shin Bet
2. Methods for the dissemination of information from the collection units to the research units, the distribution of assessment papers among the assessment bodies, and the distribution of assessments from the assessment bodies to the decision-making parties
3. The authority and modus operandi of the special adviser for intelligence to the prime minister, as recommended by the Agranat Commission

The rationale that guided Zamir in his response to Rabin's request was that a door was opening for him to be the one to establish the recommendations of the Agranat Commission and turn the intelligence community into a pluralistic organism. From the mandate that was given to the Zamir Committee, one can see that Zamir did not limit himself to shaping the role of the prime minister's intelligence adviser but rather sought to make fundamental changes to the way the community had functioned until the Yom Kippur War.

Zvi Zamir appointed me as secretary of the committee. Under his guidance, a platform was prepared for discussion, entitled "The State Intelligence Assessment." The document contained seventeen pages. The committee held two lengthy discussions, after which a report comprising recommendations and reservations was submitted to the prime minister on May 8, 1974. Following a discussion with the prime minister held on August 18, 1974, the report was returned to the committee in order to reprocess its proposals and recommendations. Discussions to bridge the gaps continued until August 25, when the final text was prepared for submission to the prime minister.

At this stage, the committee's work was completed and there was no continuation. The final version of its recommendations was never discussed with Prime Minister Rabin. Zamir refused to be appointed intelligence adviser to the prime minister and retired from the service.

What had happened behind the scenes? The head of MI, Major General Shlomo Gazit, fought throughout the committee's deliberations to preserve MI's status as the national assessor. The head of the Shin Bet, Yossef Harmelin, supported Gazit's position, and the director general of the Prime Minister's Office, Mordechai Gazit (who was, incidentally, Shlomo Gazit's older brother), was absent from the committee's meetings because he was busy accompanying US secretary of state Henry Kissinger, who was visiting Israel at the time. Avraham Kidron, director general of the Foreign Ministry, was the only one of the committee's members who supported Zamir's position.

Throughout the period of the committee's work, Zamir was in regular contact with Rabin, and in conversations between them Rabin led Zamir to understand that he did not want to impose Zamir's opinions and recommendations on the IDF in general and on MI in particular so soon after being appointed prime minister. Rabin did not rule out the possibility that such a confrontation had the potential for a crisis in government. It is also possible that Rabin, who had been caught up in struggles and even disputes with Defense Minister Shimon Peres since his first day as prime minister, feared that accepting Zamir's recommendations might provide Peres with another pretext for dispute. Rabin thus refrained from adopting Zamir's recommendations. Zamir, for his part, drew the necessary conclusions and retired.

One more small comment I want to make with regard to the relationship between Military Intelligence and the Mossad: those Mossad directors who came to the Mossad following dozens of years of military service—Meir Amit, Zvi Zamir, and Yitzhak Hofi ("Haka")—were decorated generals who had served in the IDF for many years (Amit had also served as head of MI), and were treated as the "elders of the tribe" of the IDF. As for myself, who became head of the Mossad not after a long and glorious military service but after twenty-three years of service in the Mossad itself, all of which were wrapped in a cloak of secrecy, I did not find a red carpet laid out for me at the entrance to the "heads of services" club. I did not see this as a shortcoming but simply as a fact of life.

The establishment of the research department at the Mossad was a dramatic change. To use a metaphor, it changed the Mossad from being a marionette operated by Military Intelligence to being a living organism with its own wisdom that over time began to take a stand when its assessments did not match those of MI.

The transition from a world of conventional wars, which broke out once in a while, to a dynamic environment of real-time threats and battlefields that were not limited in area, such as the Western Desert in North Africa, but rather spread out across the urban world, required a new and revolutionary combat doctrine. This new doctrine needed to be appropriate for an environment that was a completely transparent "global village," with real-time communication from one end of the world to the other and constant dynamic threats that took on different forms. In this reality, the intelligence picture needed to be created and translated into operations in real time, or the intelligence would become worthless. This threat environment was a tremendous catalyst for the development of intelligence capabilities that had not existed in the past, most of them in science and technology, but also for innovative intelligence warfare doctrines. It also required the integration of intelligence and operational capabilities among all the bodies in the intelligence community. Indeed, over the course of time, the overall intelligence and operational cooperation between the members of the community proved itself to be a force multiplier, without which it is doubtful whether the threats could have been successfully dealt with. The close and intimate cooperation that developed between the branches of the community, each of which brought its relative advantage to the joint effort, enriched the wisdom, experience, knowledge, and skills of the Mossad and, I assume, also of the Shin Bet.

In conclusion, when you are the master of your own research and assessment abilities, and when you become a central axis in the intelligence war, you reach a maturity that gives you the ability and the right (which I believe is mandatory) to make your voice heard on everything from assessments, to EEI priorities, to the overall work plan of the community, including the allocation of resources. The Agranat Commission was indeed a catalyst for changing the research and assessment system from one that was monolithic to one that was pluralistic, but the interpretation of the issue of pluralism, as given by Shlomo Gazit, who was appointed head of Military Intelligence after the Yom Kippur War, was that it should be implemented *within* the Intelligence Corps and not in the entire intelligence community. The system he implemented was, in effect, pluralism between the research branch of the General Staff and the intelligence departments of the three IDF commands. This method had no professional logic, and it eroded the central role of the intelligence of the regional command—to be the intelligence officer of the arena for which it is responsible—but it enabled MI to continue to claim sole ownership of the title of national intelligence assessor. Reality proved that it was a rearguard action, which over time proved to be a failure.

During my tenure as director of the Mossad (1989–96), I worked with four MI heads. The first was Amnon Lipkin-Shahak, who was an officer and a gentleman. In late July 1990, we both accompanied Defense Minister Moshe Arens on an official visit to Washington. The visit's main purpose was to present Secretary of Defense Richard Cheney with the Israeli perception of the threat of Iraq's unconventional weapons. For the visit, the Mossad put together a "white paper" containing all of Iraq's transgressions with regard to WMD to pass on to the Americans. The briefing to the secretary of defense, on either side of whom sat about a dozen US generals as well as a few others in civilian dress, following Moshe Arens's opening remarks, was given by the head of the Mossad's WMD division and myself (I will expand on this in the chapter on the First Gulf War of January 1991).

The next head of Military Intelligence with whom I worked was Uri Sagi. Sagi's perception of his role was unambiguous—he believed that he, as head of MI, bore the national responsibility for intelligence assessment and therefore that he should be the one to approve the Mossad's annual work plan, the priorities in the Mossad's operational activities, and even the Mossad's budget! This view, which he never raised in a formal discussion with Prime Minister and Minister of Defense Yitzhak Rabin, at least not in my presence, greatly strained the course of our ongoing work, so much so that I decided to raise the subject with Rabin, with Sagi present. As an aside, I would like to point out that in my seven years of service as director of the Mossad I brought only two cases in which I had disagreements with another head of service before the prime minister for discussion and for his decision. My view was always that my job was to help the prime minister solve problems, not burden him with more problems.

During the discussion with Rabin, I presented my position and explained it, and Uri Sagi explained his. Rabin concluded the discussion by saying that the definition of the head of Military Intelligence as the national assessor was too far-reaching. MI should assume ultimate responsibility *only in matters of early warning*. In all other matters of the EEI, there had to be pluralism in research and assessment. This decision was in writing. I do not recall that any work was done to translate it into doctrine and work procedures. Personally, I breathed a sigh of relief following this decision regarding our ongoing work, as the "intellectual" dispute over the issue of who was superior to whom had finally subsided.

On National Security and the Media, and on the Internet as the Ultimate Medium

Ya'akov Karoz was Isser Harel's right-hand man for many years and later served briefly as Meir Amit's deputy.[1] I met Ya'akov personally only in the latter part of his life, when I was already director of the Mossad. One day he called and asked to see me. At that point he was no longer driving on his own, so I sent a car to bring him into the office. He was slightly hunched, and his voice was quiet and soft but full of determination. As we were speaking, I saw the image of the man I had first seen thirty years ago. I remembered him from the year 1964. It was his last year of service and my first. I had seen him once or twice on the sidewalk of the old Mossad headquarters. The gossip during that time centered on the changing of the guard in the top echelons of the Mossad and the fact that Ya'akov was completing his service. I remembered that in the late 1970s he would sometimes appear at the entrance of the Hadar Dafna building, accept an envelope from the doorman, thank him, and leave. This was the way in which Ya'akov, who had already then cultivated a journalistic career as a security affairs commentator in the newspaper *Yedioth Ahronoth*, began receiving open-source intelligence on the Middle East from Hatzav— an OSINT unit. It was a sort of internal arrangement with an old colleague, one that was harmless but useful to a journalist.

Back to our meeting—Ya'akov wanted to talk to me about his book. As someone who for many years had been entrusted with the carrying out of clandestine activity and the keeping of secrets, he had been struggling with the question of whether he had the right to write his memoirs and publish them as a book. He described these dilemmas in detail, tackling the problem from both professional and moral perspectives. Professionally, does the statute of limitations justify the publication of information that belongs to the state? And morally, are people at the top of the hierarchy entitled to rights not granted to regular employees?

These deliberations, Ya'akov told me, caused him much agony, which increased with his illness. In the end, he decided to write the book. He felt, he said, that he owed it to his family, who had stuck by him and supported him throughout his years in the service. I could discern a tone of urgency in his words, as if he sensed that his time was running out. I could not then, as I cannot now, keep myself from thinking about the words he did not say, the things that could only be read between the lines. Ya'akov had served a giant, Isser Harel, and had become his deputy; he had then served another great man in the same position, Meir Amit, albeit for a short period of time. These two idols' lives were commemorated by the state, the people, and themselves. Ya'akov's place as a "number two" in the heroic narrative of the establishment of the state and its security institutions remains unknown. If I am wrong in my interpretation of that meeting with him, I plead his forgiveness.

Since my personal acquaintance with Ya'akov, may his memory be blessed, did not go beyond that one meeting, I cannot elaborate any more than what I have said so far; I thought it might be appropriate to say a few things about the relationship that exists between the two professions Ya'akov chose over the course of his life—that of intelligence and security and that of journalism and media.

The weighty influence of the Israeli media, as is the case in all developed countries, is pronounced. The media to a large degree shape our national agenda. They are controlled by a small number of stakeholders, who are heavily involved in other sectors in the country as well. The media created a situation in which politicians are greatly dependent on them. They directly and indirectly (through advertising) affect our culture of speech and discussion; what we eat and how we dress; and the level and nature of our cultural taste in literature, cinema, theater, and music. In short, the media affect, at least indirectly, our national strength. Therefore, it is necessary and even vital to discuss the series of connections between the media and national strength.

The classic questions regarding the place and role of the media are:

• Is journalism a profession/occupation that is essentially different from other professions? An uneducated person could never be a surgeon but could certainly become a top journalist. An uneducated person could never be a teacher but could certainly become a successful politician. Therefore, a common denominator between a politician and someone who works in the media is that neither field requires formal education or testing. But this is where the common denominators end. There is no question that to be a politician requires national responsibility. As for the journalist, this issue is controversial.

- Is freedom of expression an absolute value? Thomas Jefferson, one of the founding fathers of the United States and its third president, said: "Were it left to me to decide whether we should have a government without newspapers, or newspapers without a government, I should not hesitate a moment to prefer the latter." The First Amendment to the American Constitution in 1791 (which was accepted in large part because of Jefferson's influence) states, "Congress shall make no law . . . abridging the freedom of speech, or of the press." But in practice, from the days of George Washington and through all of America's wars up to the war in Afghanistan, the opposite has been proven. In all its wars, the US government has employed various ways of keeping information from the media, ways that in most (if not all) cases have won public support.

- Does the principle that it is just to restrict the media during times of war also apply to us? Remember that in our case we are talking about a war that has been going on for almost seventy years! The question is whether restricting freedom of the press as a norm, indefinitely, because of a seemingly endless state of emergency, is appropriate.

- Is using the media for purposes related to national strength and security, or for other issues of public interest, a no-no? Is it acceptable to treat information as a national resource like manpower, minerals, oil, technological know-how, and so on? If so, when a state is conducting a war it is essential for the state to control information, as it does other resources under its control. On September 11, 2001, the American media voluntarily enlisted to serve the state. In one conference call of only a few minutes, the managers of the major networks decided not to take and broadcast any close-ups of the collapsing towers, and they all stood by the decision. There was not a single exception. Is the voluntary mobilization of the media merely a function of the magnitude of the blow and the resulting shock?

With my wife Yael in Italy, 1990.

With Yael in Bali, 1991.

Yael at a hotel overlooking the cataracts
of the Nile, opposite the Aswan Dam.

At the Tigris-Euphrates delta, 1967.

Myself with Yael and with David Karon in Iran.

(*above*) Yael at the Evrons'
pool in Tehran, 1966.

In Kurdistan, 1973.

At the Nimrodi family's pool in Tehran. From right: Ambassador Meir Ezri, me, Rehavia Vardi, and Yaakov Nimrodi.

In Kurdistan (in sunglasses) with my group of bodyguards, 1973.

Washing bulls in the river in Kurdistan, 1973.

David Karon and a friend in Kurdistan, 1973.

Sailing with colleagues during a visit with the CIA, November 1993.

At the first McDonald's in Moscow, November 1992.

With the director of the South Korean national intelligence service.

Working meeting with the director of the South Korean national intelligence service in Seoul.

With Prime Minister Yitzhak Shamir, his wife Shulamit Shamir, and Defense Minister Moshe Arens at our daughter Michal's wedding, 1990.

With IDF chief of staff Raful Eitan at Michal's wedding.

With Prime Minister Yitzhak Rabin at our daughter Ruthie's wedding, 1995.

A "historical" meeting between Prime Minister Yitzhak Shamir and former Mossad director Isser Harel at our daughter Ruthie's wedding.

With Bernd Schmidbauer, coordinator of the German intelligence agencies, aboard a German coast guard boat on the Neckar River near Heidelberg, May 1993.

With Bernd Schmidbauer, Bernd's wife Elke, and their daughter Sara during their visit to Israel.

With Prime Minister Yitzhak Rabin in China, at a meeting with the commander in chief of the Chinese army, May 1993.

With the third-ranking official of the Chinese Politburo, responsible for all of the country's intelligence and security services, May 1993.

With the director of the Chinese national intelligence service, May 1993.

Landing in Jakarta ahead of our meeting with President Suharto, 1995.

Prime Minister Yitzhak Rabin's meeting with President Suharto in Indonesia.

With the head of the Omani internal security service in Oman.

With Sultan Qaboos, 1994.

On a flight to the Gulf, 1994. *From right*: former Mossad director Efraim Halevy, Prime Minister Yitzhak Rabin, me.

With Colin McColl, former head of MI6, his wife, and myself at the International Institute for Counter-Terrorism's first international conference.

On a boat on the Red Sea as part of the International Institute for Counter-Terrorism's first international conference, with Jim Woolsey, former director of the CIA; Bernd Schmidbauer, former coordinator of the German intelligence agencies; and Sir Colin McColl, former head of MI6.

(*above*)
At the Great Wall
of China, April 1991.

In Petra, Jordan, 1993.

In India with Yael,
March 1993.

(below)
New Year's greeting from
the Jordanian royal family.

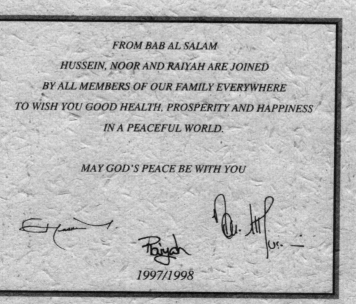

FROM BAB AL SALAM

HUSSEIN, NOOR AND RAIYAH ARE JOINED

BY ALL MEMBERS OF OUR FAMILY EVERYWHERE

TO WISH YOU GOOD HEALTH, PROSPERITY AND HAPPINESS

IN A PEACEFUL WORLD.

MAY GOD'S PEACE BE WITH YOU

Raiyah

1997/1998

(*From left to right*) King Hussein, former director general of the Mossad Nahum Admoni, former Mossad director Yitzhak Hofi, me, and Jordanian prime minister Zaid al-Rifai.

With Prince Hassan of Jordan on the anniversary of the signing of the peace agreement.

King Hussein presents the gift he received from the Mossad directors.

Shooting poison arrows in Malaysia.

In Kuala Lumpur, Malaysia.

Leah Rabin visits the Mossad.

Unveiling the Yitzhak Rabin memorial at the Mossad.

Yael in the Churchill Suite at Hotel La Ma'amounia in Marrakesh, 1993.

On a state visit to Korea, at a sculpture garden on Se-Ju Island.

Meeting with my professional counterpart on a visit to South Korea.

- In the age of the Internet and social networks, where there is no monopoly on information and no one can block its dissemination, is it justified to break all rules and norms and act according to the norm of "catch as catch can" (in the sense that "if I do not publish this, someone else will and I'll be the 'sucker'")?
- What should be the norm with regard to reporting on a conflict from the enemy's point of view? Journalist Oded Granot's interview with Yasser Arafat brought this issue under heated debate. Until the First Gulf War, the American journalistic norm refused reports from the enemy's point of view.

During the First Gulf War (1991), Saudi Arabia severely restricted journalists' access in general and to the border areas with Kuwait and Iraq in particular, and the US military imposed its own restrictions on journalists. As a result, newspaper editors agreed to accept materials originating in Iraq, even if they smelled of psychological warfare by Saddam Hussein's regime.

In the Israeli debate over freedom of the press versus the preservation of the security of the state, those who prioritize the former use the United States as their standard. They advocate the adoption of the American model of freedom of the press and the public's right to know. The military censor has become an archaic institution, and the Israel of the twenty-first century is expected to resemble other enlightened nations. I would like to state for the record that the public norm in the United States on this issue is interpreted in Israel in a distorted, or at least inaccurate, manner.

Totalitarian states favor state security over freedom of speech, although they sometimes use the excuse of security as a cover-up to conceal failures. Should the equation in democratic countries be automatically reversed? Every nation strives for security as an existential instinct, regardless of any ideology. It may, of course, be argued that the principle of freedom of speech contributes to national security in some respects. But it is impossible to refute the claim that absolute freedom of speech, without limits, is liable to harm state security. Sir William Stephenson, who was the liaison between the intelligence services of Britain and the United States during World War II, wrote in his book *A Man Called Intrepid*:

> The weapons of secrecy have no place in an ideal world. But we live in a world of undeclared hostilities in which such weapons are constantly used against us and could, unless countered, leave us unprepared again, this time for an onslaught of magnitude that staggers the imagination. And while it may seem unnecessary to stress so obvious a point, the weapons of secrecy are rendered ineffective if we remove the secrecy. One of the conditions of democracy is freedom of information. It would be infinitely preferable to know exactly how our intelligence agencies function, and why, and where. But this information, once made public, disarms us. So there is the conundrum: How can we wield the weapons of secrecy without damage to ourselves? How can we preserve secrecy without endangering constitutional law and individual guarantees of freedom?

In my humble opinion, security as a value should take precedence over freedom of speech. Even so, a healthy society must recognize the constant tension between the needs of national security and freedom of speech. A healthy society must accept the existence of these two principles and give each of them the appropriate weight. The United States, in this respect, is a healthy society.

In Israel, the military censor continues to function, though as a shadow of its former self. This institution has not been dismantled because in Israel no alternatives have yet been established whose role is to balance this tension, such as those that exist in the United States. For example, in the United States there are voluntary, nonpartisan, nonprofit bodies that study the media (in the style of *Consumer Reports*). These bodies have set for themselves the goal of placing the media on the agenda of public debate, instead of allowing the media themselves to determine the agenda of public debate.

The media in the United States, as well as here in Israel, have become the eyes and ears of the modern state. They have largely replaced traditional institutions such as schools, religion, and family with regard to social values, and they determine the patterns of public consciousness. What the media teach and convey can make or break people, ideas, and institutions. The media also see themselves as the main watchdogs of the democratic regime. The question is then, of course, who is watching the watchdogs? In the United States, which enshrines the principle of national security, the institutions responsible for watching the watchdogs are the Constitution, the House of Representatives, the Supreme Court, and voluntary institutions such as the Center for Media and Public Affairs, one of whose studies I used for this chapter. This institution conducts its research using scientific and statistical methods. Each statement made by a critic or journalist is characterized, catalogued, and fed into a computerized database. The statistical results of these databases provide media coverage profiles that serve as diagnostic tools for the accuracy and reliability of the source, journalist, or media outlet.

> The behavior of the media is intimately related to the unity and clarity of the government itself, as well as to the degree of consensus in the society at large. This is not to say that the role of the press is purely reactive. Surely it made a difference, for instance, that many journalists were shocked both by the brutality of the war and by the gap between what they were told by top officials and what they saw and heard in the field, and were free to report all this. But it is also clear that the administration's problems with the "fourth branch of government" resulted in large part from political divisions at home, including those within the administration itself. . . . It is hard to see how, short of a real turn to authoritarian government, political doubt and controversy could have been contained much longer.

Sound Israeli? It sure does! But these were the words of Dean Rusk, US secretary of state, during the public debate over the role of the American media in the Vietnam War. Rusk added that there was no point in having censorship in Vietnam until censorship was introduced in Washington, because most of the leaks originated in Washington. That too sounds like something an Israeli would say! As the Talmud teaches, the foundations of the world are one and the same.

The Center for Media and Public Affairs conducted a comparative study of the Vietnam War and the First Gulf War through the lens of the media, defining the former as "the Living Room War" and the latter as "the Instant Replay War." During the Gulf War, for the first time in history, the world could watch the crisis and the war unfolding live before their eyes. This war had a second front: the struggle for control over television content, the struggle between the Pentagon and the media. This was the story of the American effort to prevent a second Vietnam and to try to influence America's future in the global village that was increasingly being shaped by the media. It was the story of an independent opposition media that found itself in conflict with the American citizen, who expected the media to support "the good guys." The media lost this battle. The Pentagon succeeded in blocking and controlling the media's endless thirst for more information.

During and after the war, opinion polls were conducted by the Times Mirror Company, which owned major publications including the *Los Angeles Times* and *Newsday*. According to these polls, eight out of every ten Americans rated the media's performance during the war as good. An even higher number viewed the censorship imposed on the media as being justified and approved of the "pool" method (in which free access to combat zones and security information was given, not to any journalist who requested it, but only to those representatives of the media selected by the Pentagon, who then distributed their stories and broadcasts to all media outlets) that was employed during this war. A high percentage of respondents said that they would have approved even more severe censorship than that which was actually imposed. Similar polls conducted after the war produced even higher numbers of those who approved censorship. The traditional distribution of responses to public opinion polls in the United States on the question of whether to allow the media to publish stories that they believe should be brought to the attention of the public or whether to censor when it comes to preserving national security has always been 50-50. But in the post–Gulf War polls the distribution was two to one in favor of censorship. On the margins of these polls were, of course, also the extremists, from the camp of General Schwarzkopf, the commander of all the coalition forces in Iraq, who accused the media of helping and encouraging the enemy, to the left-wing circles who hurled the opposite accusation—that the media acted as the "cheerleaders" of the war.

The television coverage of the Gulf War was the most extensive in the history of this medium. An analysis of the coverage reveals interesting data. Three out of every five statements (59 percent) regarding government policy about the war were negative. On the other hand, statements about the American soldiers and American weapons were generally positive. The results of the Times Mirror polls showed that more Americans participated in demonstrations in support of the war than in those that opposed it, but the media coverage of that period revealed that more coverage was given to antiwar demonstrations.

The most evident conclusion of the data arising from an analysis of the media is this: When there is a conflict between the media and the government, the public usually supports the media and their duty to fulfill the public's right to know. But when it comes to matters of life and death, the equation changes. In such a situation, the public prefers to censor some information in order to protect the lives of those who are protecting it. This conclusion raises the question: What about Israel? It would be correct to say, with some degree of generalization, that Israelis have been in living in a life-or-death situation since the establishment of the state, and we do not know any other reality. Therefore, the answer to the question of the need for censorship—not the institution but the concept—should be obvious.

Public opinion polls in the United States have for years pointed to two other negative aspects of the media: the arrogance of journalists and the mediocre level of professionalism. The public as a whole exhibits a negative attitude to the journalistic tendency to get a story at any price and to emphasize negative stories over positive stories. These days one can easily identify attitudes according to which the press is "them" versus the public that is "us." Within a generation, the image of the journalist in the United States has transformed from one of the poor and wretched soul fighting for his reputation through integrity and good values to one of the stereotypical rich and famous "celeb." There has been a distinct change from a culture in which the average person sees the journalist as someone who truly represents him or her to a culture in which the ordinary citizen feels alienated from the press.

In Israel, within a generation, we have witnessed a revolution from a press owned, operated, and mobilized by political parties to a commercial press whose outlets fight among themselves over small market shares in order to survive; for this purpose the ends justify the means, including competition among the journalists over who can irritate the military censor the most. I have been told that at least some in the Hebrew press have tried to incorporate positive information in their reports to the public but that the readers consistently ignored it. Assuming that this is true, the question arises as to whether this is not another surrender by the media to ratings. After all, even the simplest rules require some sort of balance, if only for appearance's sake.

"Irangate," the Pentagon Papers, and Watergate are cited over and over again by advocates of freedom of the press as milestones of the American media. What the public may not be aware of is a very long list of laws and rulings that constitute the other side of the equation.

The Freedom of Information Act, which advocates of freedom of speech are so proud of, and rightly so, also incorporates the principle of the state's right to censor information. To establish this governmental right, a separate executive order was signed in 1983, which states that it is permitted to censor information whose unauthorized publication may cause damage to national security.

The US Espionage Act of 1917 prohibits the passing of information to an enemy that may cause harm to the United States. It does not cover in its definition the leaking of information by government officials or by journalists. But in the case of an American citizen who worked as a researcher in the US Department of Defense, and on the side was also an editor for a British newspaper, and who gave the paper classified satellite photographs of Soviet vessels, a federal court ruled against him under the Espionage Act, arguing that the danger to the United States was the same whether the information was delivered to an agent of an enemy state or leaked to the press.

The Atomic Energy Act of 1954 prohibits the publication of information that will harm the United States or grant an advantage to its adversary or competitor. In the well-known precedent of *United States v. Progressive, Inc.*, 467 F. Supp. 990 (W.D. Wis. 1979), in which the publication of an article about the hydrogen bomb and how the United States attained it was examined, the article's author proved that the piece was written on the basis of openly available material, and yet the court ruled in favor of the state, on the basis of the test of damage caused.

Richard Welch, the CIA station chief in Athens, was murdered in December 1975, less than a month after his name was published in the media by Philip Agee, also a former CIA officer. As a direct result of this case, a legislative process began that resulted in the 1982 passing of the Intelligence Identities Protection Act, which defines as a federal crime the exposure of the identity of a secret agent, including by a person who has legal access to classified information. Philip Agee was denounced both by the American media and by the judiciary. In Israel, however, following the publication of Victor Ostrovsky's book, which included the names of Mossad employees, no similar law was passed, and the Israeli media was more interested in interviewing him than in denouncing him.

The Invention Secrecy Act deals with patents, even those of private individuals, whose uncontrolled use may be detrimental to national security.

The Export Control Laws of 1976 limit exports that could harm state security if they were to reach an enemy or adversary.

The legal precedent of Grenada is particularly interesting. In a lawsuit filed against Secretary of Defense Weinberger, the court decided that a ruling on the issue was unnecessary since the media blackout had been lifted prior to the case being heard. However, if the court did have to rule, it would not be against the defendant, since such a ruling would limit the number of options available to commanders in the field, thereby jeopardizing the success of military operations, endangering human life, and severely harming national security.

Does the American norm with regard to the media and national security denote a healthy society? There is no doubt that the answer is yes—this is a healthy society in which there is a wall-to-wall consensus that certain information concerning national security must remain secret. Revealing everything means exposing the nation to risks and threats from potential enemies. On the other hand, in assessing the norms of the Israeli media, unfortunately I do recognize some symptoms of recklessness.

The exposure of military plans, strategy, military power, and deployment provides a huge advantage to a potential adversary. R&D of weapons systems, details of nuclear technologies, and the like can spell disaster if handed over to an adversary. The leaking of secrets about advanced technologies, such as lasers, kinetics, and computers, can mean the victory of one side over the other. The ban on scientific publications in the United States that deal with issues of strategic significance has become a bone of contention between the administration and academia, with the latter losing the struggle, even when academic freedom is at risk.

There is no doubt that security measures are necessary to ensure the proper functioning of the security services. Exposing the identity of agents or sources undermines their ability to continue collecting information and endangers their lives and the lives of others. The publication of methods and means and information about cryptology encourages adversaries to develop countermeasures and impair our abilities. Further, the inability of a government to keep its secrets leads friendly countries to lose their confidence in us and decreases their willingness to share their secrets with us.

Secrecy also plays a major role in diplomacy. Kissinger's first visit to China proved that diplomatic initiatives can open channels of communication with hostile actors only if they are kept secret. The Oslo Accords with the Palestinians were made possible only by the secrecy with which they were achieved. The lack of progress in negotiations with Syria was in large part due to President Assad's refusal to open a secret channel of dialogue. Covert talks allow representatives of both sides to say things to each other that, if spoken publicly, could cause internal rifts, coalition trouble, and so on. Confidentiality encourages negotiations that are focused on content and helps prevent stagnation resulting from the desire not to be seen as giving up, losing face, or "blinking." To paraphrase a Jewish American judge, "Secrecy eliminates the need for the dangerous cosmetics of international political theater."

A robust economy is an indicator of national security. Military and other exports are often conditional, from the buyer's perspective, on confidentiality. A violation of the confidentiality of such transactions may have a negative impact on employment. In such cases, which principle is stronger? The right of the public to know or the preservation of jobs? In the renowned ruling of *New York Times v. United States*, 403 U.S. 713 (1971), commonly known as the Pentagon Papers Case, Justice Potter Stewart, who was one of the six majority judges, wrote: "In the absence of the governmental checks and balances present in other areas of our national life, the only effective restraint upon executive policy and power in the areas of national defense and international affairs may lie in an enlightened citizenry— in an informed and critical public opinion which alone can here protect the values of democratic government. . . . Yet it is elementary that the successful conduct of international diplomacy and the maintenance of effective national defense require both confidentiality and secrecy."[2]

Reading this thoughtful opinion of a great judge, who started his career as a journalist, from a double point of view—both as citizen in a democratic state and as the head of an national intelligence organization—I conclude that the gist of Justice Stewart's ruling is that in a democratic society, which accords much weight to the freedom of debate and freedom of the press, preserving national security is not about a police state imposing restrictions but rather about the existence of a consensus, both within the government and outside it, regarding the need to protect certain types of information from exposure. The US Constitution recognizes the dual responsibility of maintaining freedom of speech while also protecting national security by restricting freedom of speech. And it expects the compliance of the judicial, executive, and legislative branches, as well as that of the "fourth estate," which is the media.

Is there such a consensus in Israel? Does Israel's "fourth estate" comply to any degree?

Friends of mine from the world of media accuse me of being naive, asking, "Are you not aware that the sources of the leaks are politicians and army officers? Do MI's periodic assessments just make their own way to journalists (usually specific ones) prior to their official publication, or are there those who want to leak them? Was Daniel Ellsberg, who released the Pentagon Papers, an irresponsible traitor or a patriot who did a great service for American national security? And why don't you mention the comments made to the media by Mossad chief Dagan, Shin Bet chief Diskin, and IDF chief of staff Ashkenazi on the subject of attacking Iran's nuclear sites, when they thought that such an attack would bring unprecedented disaster on Israel? When they feared that the prime minister and defense minister were leading Israel toward suicide, was it not their duty to take action by all means necessary, including via the media? And what about Snowden—traitor or patriot?" Here are some of my responses to these issues.

First, it is a mistake to make an equal comparison of these issues between the United States and Israel, because the test is not one that is universal, but rather one based on the outcome of the expected damage. The United States, because of its size and power, can absorb a kind of damage that Israel cannot. Second, Ellsberg, Snowden, and their ilk in the United States, because of their roles and status, were not able to take into account all of the variables needed to justify the kind of decisions they made. It is clear to me that activity within the framework of the tools that Western democracy provides to us involves many frustrations and obstacles along the way, but it still does not justify the choice to leak information to the media that will harm national security and undermine the foundations of the democratic system.

As for the Israeli officials mentioned, for whom it is impossible to claim that they were not exposed to all of the elements of the Iranian nuclear issue, their actions can be compared to those of the biblical prophets who stood, wrapped in cloaks, at the gates of the city and chastised the decision makers in the name of God. Jewish tradition asserts that there have not been any prophecies since the destruction of the Temple; the three men mentioned above did not claim that they were doing what they did in the name of God, but in my opinion they should have exhausted all means possible using the legitimate tools available to them. Left with no choice, they should have unanimously submitted their resignation to the prime minister and defense minister. The impact of that move would have caused a much greater earthquake than going to the media.

There is no doubt that a government should be prohibited from using the pretext of state security to cover up bureaucratic errors, political scandal, or illegal activity. However, it should be taken into account that it is difficult for courts to establish clear and unequivocal standards of the degree of potential or real harm resulting from the disclosure of information. Diplomatic developments and foreign relations are the result of innumerable components, forces, and events, making simple categorizations by the court impossible. The disclosure of critical information can generate a chain of events and developments that may only later turn out to have an effect on national security. One of the limitations of the method is that whether it is a demand to prevent publication, or a discussion, in retrospect, of information that has already been published, the political or security damage has already been done.

As a major force in our society, the press should be a loyal ally of the public. It must act responsibly in all matters relating to the publication of information that is liable to harm state security. Self-discipline and cooperation with the government can guarantee against revelations that can harm national security.

The resolution of the tension between national security and freedom of the press does not have to be a zero-sum game. In other words, it is not true that increased freedom of the press negatively affects national security, nor is it true that increased national security erodes freedom of the press. These two things can and must co-exist peacefully, with each supporting the other. The subtext of this statement is that a journalist must not shirk his or her personal national responsibility when a person in an official position has made a transgression!

It is possible—but not necessary—to discuss the internet revolution as part of the debate on national security and the media. I have chosen to do this for two reasons. The first is the Snowden affair, which touches the heart of the dilemma over what is permitted and what is forbidden in the disclosure of state secrets. The second is the initiation of revolutions through the medium of the internet (as was the case in some of the countries that experienced the so-called "Arab Spring"), which also touches upon the issue of national resilience.

The internet is the technology that has produced the greatest change in human society in recent decades. More than any other technology, it has transformed the world into a completely transparent global village where an unlimited amount of information flows from any point on earth to another in real time. The internet enables anyone to become a media superstar if he or she is able to release even a scrap of information that someone else wants to conceal or prevent from being publicized.

This ability has produced what is commonly referred to as "breaking the fear barrier." When you can communicate with anyone and send them a text or a photograph in real time, ahead of all the professional media networks, turning any type of censorship into a joke, you have nothing to be afraid of. And as the internet fills up with more and more users, even the slightest bit of fear that remains inside you disappears.

Today, the internet is both a battleground and a weapon that is at the disposal of every individual, organization, or country, with each being free to define the enemy and fight it with the means and methods it deems necessary. There are still no "laws of war" for this battlefield or for the doctrines of warfare practiced on it.

It is said that about 90 percent of the intelligence needed by any intelligence body comes from open sources. These days, the internet is the largest source of open intelligence, and from it one can derive strategic intelligence, tactical intelligence, and even intelligence for specific operations, down to a terrorist's or other wanted person's flight details, photograph, passport number, and rental car at his destination.

Through the internet, hostile groups can be infiltrated. Through the internet, psychological warfare campaigns can be conducted, the result of which can be a drastic change in the views of the members of the group that has been targeted. Moreover, the internet enables the creation of groups that share common values and opinions, through which national and other interests can be advanced.

Through the internet, disruption and sabotage campaigns worthy of the best suspense movies can be carried out, and *revolutions can be launched*. The trouble is that though we may regard revolutions as constructive acts carried out by the masses in order to topple a tyrannical regime in favor of an enlightened one, at this point in time we are in between these two poles. No one can say with certainty that the revolutions that have already taken place and those that are currently emerging will result in enlightened regimes at the end of the process.

The intellectual—or ideological, if you like—tension that Israelis and Jews find themselves in with regard to the tsunami sweeping the Middle East has been articulated by two well-known commentators. According to Gadi Taub, of the three possibilities—*democracy, dictatorship*, and *Islamic fundamentalism*—it's sometimes best to choose the second, not just to preclude the third, but also to prevent the first from engendering the third.[3] The subtext here is that certain peoples have not yet proved sufficient maturity to enjoy the fruits of democracy. Therefore, it is preferable that they remain under the rule of a tyrannical ruler (an enlightened one, if possible) with political maturity, who understands the need for security and stability, and to wait for the long historical process (which can take decades or even longer) during which the need for a democratic regime will naturally develop as a result of the adoption of democratic values. In contrast, Assaf Sagiv writes that "the Jewish people cannot lend a hand to the degradation and repression of other nations. We cannot ignore the cry of the persecuted merely because the persecutors proffer their friendship, and we cannot afford to nurture an anti-democratic mood," because, as says the divine command, "Remember that you were slaves in Egypt."[4]

Popular wisdom states that "the truth lies in the details." If this is the case, let us step down for a moment and take a closer look into the countries undergoing the revolutionary processes we are talking about. And let us begin with Iran, where the model upon which today's events are based developed. The revolution that ousted the shah took place in 1979. The first governments that arose following the revolution were civilian and liberal and survived for only a short time, until Khomeini's radical Islam seized power and turned the country into a Shiite sharia state. The second half of the first decade of the twenty-first century in Iran was characterized by intensive activity by opposition forces, which was generated by social networks and the internet. To date, the power of the internet has not succeeded in toppling the government, which has no qualms about using any means necessary in order to survive. It is hard to predict the future, but at least for the moment it seems that the "internet squads" will need assistance in order to defeat the regime, most likely from the outside or perhaps through some kind of internal eruption.

The recent wave dubbed "the Arab Spring" began in Tunisia, a North African Arab country whose western European image stood out in comparison to the other North African countries (take, for example, its female traffic officers in trousers). The match that sparked the revolution on December 17, 2010, came in the form of a young university graduate who could not find a suitable job and therefore sold fruit at a market stall in order to make a living. Following an episode of harassment by the police, he set himself on fire. In January 2011, President Ben Ali fled to Saudi Arabia. The political body then seen as the most powerful was al-Nahda, a Muslim party modeled after the ideology, organization, and structure of the Muslim Brotherhood in Egypt. Its leader, who had spent more than twenty years in exile in England, returned to Tunis and organized his supporters to run for power. In the elections to the Constituent Assembly held in October 2011, the country's first free elections, the al-Nahda Party won a majority. In late January 2014, in parallel with the approval of the new constitution, the government under the leadership of al-Nahda resigned and a government of independent bodies was set up to prepare the country for the first presidential elections, which were held in December 2014. This time, a secular party won the elections and the presidency, with al-Nahda becoming the second largest party. During a year of unrelenting activity by terrorist organizations, a "national dialogue" was held between the four largest parties in the country in an attempt to reach a national consensus. For this, the "Quartet" received the Nobel Peace Prize, as well as the praise of President Obama and Secretary of State Kerry.

From the self-immolation incident in December 2010 up to the present day, Tunisia has not seen quiet. What began as demonstrations and mass disobedience against the previous ruler, unemployment, and the low standard of living turned into terrorist activity that has claimed thousands of victims. Tunisia has witnessed the killing of foreigners and the destruction of its cultural assets, the political murder of opposition leaders, and the spread of riots across the country. The terrorist activities were attributed to jihadist elements, and in July 2013, for the first time, to al-Qaeda.

The 2011 elections, as well as those of 2014, were held in the shadow of ongoing terrorism and political instability. The secular ruling party led by President Essebsi and the second-largest party, the Islamic al-Nahda led by Rached Ghannouchi, adopted a pragmatic approach in an attempt to establish a coalition to address the issues currently facing the Tunisian public—namely, economic growth, development, unemployment, and working conditions. Will they succeed? This is a major question. President Essebsi is ninety-two years old. His party was established only a few years ago and is identified with President Bourguiba's authoritarian rule, and his potential partner Ghannouchi, founder and ideological leader of al-Nahda, as noted spent a generation in exile in England. These starting points do not seem to guarantee long-term success. It is a bit like mixing fire and water.

Let us remind ourselves that Tunisia's neighbor to the west, Algeria, had a similar experience in the early 1990s when the radical Muslim GIA Party took part in democratic elections. The party's leaders declared in the election campaign that they would participate in the democratic political game but that if and when they won they would declare a sharia state. GIA did indeed win the election, but at the last minute the military leaders decided to prevent it from taking power. From then until now, for more than twenty years, what is for all intents and purposes a civil war has been raging in Algeria between the military government and the Muslim underground.

And what happened in Egypt? In 2011, the internet brought millions of people to Tahrir Square. These masses, who persevered with their presence in the square for many days, were indeed a necessary condition for the overthrow of the regime, but they were not a sufficient one! President Obama provided the other necessary condition when he chose the will of the masses over what had been the United States' most important ally in the Middle East since the early 1970s. And what next?

The power of social networks lies in their ability to mobilize the masses and bring them out into the streets. The weakness of social networks is that at least to date they have not been able to produce leaders who know how to harvest the fruits of the revolution. Since Tahrir Square did not produce a real leader (Mohamed ElBaradei and Amr Moussa's appearances in the square were pathetic), the Egyptian army took over power, established a civilian government under its rule, and prepared the country for the first multiparty democratic elections since the Nasser revolution in 1952.

At the head of the council overseeing this transitional period was General Tantawi, an old fox but a sick and weak leader. The main dilemma facing the council's generals was their fate the day after free elections, with a new president and parliament who were elected by the people and whose source of authority would be the people and not the military, as had been the case until that point. The generals understood very well that they were the link between the old, hated regime and the future that was supposed to be democratic. Who could guarantee that the elected government, under the pressure of the masses, would not take the same approach as Friedrich von Schiller's character in the play Fiesco, that is, "The Moor has done his duty, the Moor can go," or even worse?

Meanwhile, the crowd in Tahrir Square dictated to the council and the government what to decide on its behalf. At the same time, the foundations of the previous regime were destroyed, the ruling party was disbanded, the Ministry of Internal Security almost ceased to function, prisons were demolished and tens of thousands of prisoners escaped, crime skyrocketed, public security deteriorated, and the economy crashed.

The most prominent political actor in Egypt is the Muslim Brotherhood. Their involvement in political life in Egypt has experienced many ups and downs, but no regime—not those of the kings or those of Nasser, Sadat, or Mubarak—has succeeded in expunging them. This is due to their dual identity—both that of a religious movement and that of a political organization. When their political activity is banned, it is still easy for them to survive and continue to exist as a religious movement. Their physical and organizational infrastructure easily serves both identities. Each mosque is also a party branch, and each imam is also the secretary of the branch. Every contribution to the mosque is also a contribution to political or social activity, and for any political activity a religious cover story can be crafted. It seemed that the Muslim Brotherhood was acting with great political wisdom when they informed the public—in order to reassure them—that they had no intention of putting forward a presidential candidate and that they intended to participate as a political party only in the parliamentary elections. Their goal in these elections, they claimed, was to create a political bloc in the parliament that would have the power to block initiatives of the soon-to-be-formed government—in other words, to be a force of balance. If they succeeded in realizing this goal, it would serve as a basis and a springboard for the realization of additional goals in the future, whose ultimate goal would be to take control of the state and impose sharia.

In fact, the Muslim Brotherhood did put forward a candidate of their own—Mohamed Morsi—for the presidential elections, and won; for the first time in its history, Egypt had a president who was also a leader of the Muslim Brotherhood. Morsi removed incumbent defense minister Tantawi and appointed General Abdel Fattah el-Sisi in his stead. Before long, el-Sisi initiated a "quiet revolution" in which President Morsi (who was tried on various charges, convicted, and sentenced to death, though the sentence was not carried out and it is doubtful that it ever will be) was deposed. El-Sisi took power and was elected president in the general elections, and the rest is history.

Tunisia and Egypt are cases in which the phenomenon of social networks succeeded in generating revolutions that have still not reached their conclusions, which are difficult to predict. There is no guarantee that a democratic regime awaits these countries at the end of the road.

The other Arab states in North Africa (Libya, Algeria, Sudan, and Morocco) and the Middle East (Syria, Saudi Arabia, the Gulf States, Jordan, Yemen, and Lebanon) are at different points in the revolutionary process. It is still too early to point to any successes of the social networks in these cases. Therefore, Tunisia and Egypt should be seen as the exception rather than the rule.

To paraphrase Thomas Friedman in his *New York Times* column: the revolution was inevitable, but the revolutionaries may not succeed in rising to democracy, only to the height of the minaret of the mosque!

CHAPTER FOUR

A DIPLOMATIC
PERSPECTIVE

Rabin and the Peace with Jordan

On November 5, 1995, the day after Yitzhak's murder, I issued the following order to the Mossad's employees:

Re: In memory of our Prime Minister Yitzhak Rabin

The Prime Minister of Israel, Minister of Defense and our commander, Yitzhak Rabin, is gone.

The bullets of a Jewish murderer cut his life short.

His life was an ongoing contribution to the rebirth of the State of Israel, and to its security and strength.

Peace, towards which he focused his efforts since the Madrid Conference, is, in his view, another dimension to the securing of the existence and strength of the State of Israel and her people. With his passing, it is as if a limb has been severed from the nation and State of Israel.

He had a special place in his heart for the Mossad and its staff; we last heard his warm wishes when he came to greet us on the eve of Rosh Hashanah.

We send our condolences to the family and we all mourn together with them.

May his memory be a blessing.

November 3, 1995, the day before the murder, was like any other Friday. On Fridays, Prime Minister Yitzhak Rabin, who also served as defense minister, used to work in his office in the IDF's headquarters in Tel Aviv. These Fridays were crammed with discussions about security, ranging from presentations for approval for operations and sorties to consultations on weighty security issues with the heads of the defense establishment, either separately or together in various groups, depending on the case.

Friday, November 3, was just like that. A consultation took place that morning between the defense minister; IDF chief of staff Amnon Lipkin-Shahak; head of Military Intelligence Moshe ("Bogey") Ya'alon; a representative of the Shin Bet; and the director of the Mossad (myself). We discussed two issues—the ongoing challenge of terrorism and the strategic issue of the buildup of nonconventional weapons in the Middle East in general and in Iran in particular. During the first part of the discussion, reference was made to the extreme Right's protest activity. Rabin, the defense minister, dismissed it casually. None of the people around the table could have imagined that thirty hours later the prime minister would be murdered.

On Saturday night, November 4, I was sitting at home with my wife, Yael, watching the rally on TV that was being held in the square outside of Tel Aviv's city hall. At about 10 p.m. the phone rang. It was Danny Yatom, Yitzhak's military secretary. "Yitzhak has been shot by an assassin," Danny said. "He's on his way to Ichilov Hospital."

"I'll be right there!" I said, and hung up the phone. I do not remember the trip from my home in Ramat Hasharon to Ichilov Hospital in Tel Aviv, but in my memory time seemed to have stopped. I went down to the hospital's operating room and found a corner where I stood leaning against the wall, contemplating. The area around the operating rooms was filling up with cabinet ministers, foreign ambassadors, senior officers, and friends. Leah Rabin sat inside one of the rooms that had been cleared for her, together with other family members. The whole crowd awaited news of Yitzhak's condition.

It seemed that an eternity had passed by the time the director of the hospital, Prof. Gabi Barabash, came out of the operating room. His statement was laconic: "Prime Minister Yitzhak Rabin has died."

I made my way into the room where Leah was, my vision blurred. I squeezed her hand and said to her, "Leah, he went by a whirlwind into heaven." And that was the moment I decided that my time as director of the Mossad must come to an end.

That same night another impromptu government meeting took place at IDF headquarters in Tel Aviv, in which Shimon Peres was appointed as acting prime minister and decisions were made regarding the arrangements for the funeral and mourning period.

I remember nothing of my journey home. All that night I lay awake in my bed, staring at the ceiling.

I informed Shimon Peres about my decision to step down from my job during our first work meeting. When he asked about my reasons for leaving, I explained to him that over the past six months I had already been speaking to the late prime minister Rabin about completing my tenure. I added that six-and-a-half intensive years on the job, working with two prime ministers as different from each other as Shamir and Rabin, had left me fulfilled and I felt it would be very difficult for me to continue in the role working with a third prime minister. Peres, in his thick voice, began by saying that it was not every day that a prime minister was assassinated in Israel, that Shin Bet head Gillon had already taken it upon himself to resign, and that an additional announcement that the director of the Mossad was also resigning would have a devastating effect on public morale. His reasoning resonated with me. I was convinced that it stemmed from genuine concern for the country. We agreed that I would remain in my position for another six months and that the official announcement would be made ahead of the next elections, when I would have served as Mossad director for seven years.

The director of the Mossad is directly subordinate to, and appointed by, the prime minister. Generally speaking, the prime minister tends to consult with other people, including of course the defense minister, on the matter of whom to appoint, but it is the prime minister who makes the ultimate decision. I was chosen to be the head of the Mossad by Yitzhak Shamir. Rabin, who was the defense minister at the time of my appointment, had suggested Amnon Lipkin-Shahak, then head of Military Intelligence, for the job. This did not interfere with the development of a close relationship between Rabin and me—both a working and a personal one. We had also had the opportunity to get to know each other previously, when I was the head of a department in the Mossad and he was defense minister.

As the Mossad director is directly subordinate to the prime minister, the nature of my relationship with Rabin when he was defense minister was not hierarchical. I would present him with joint IDF and Mossad operations and hold debriefs with him from time to time. When Rabin was appointed prime minister, I had been serving as director of the Mossad for three and a half years, so the work relations, trust, and mutual esteem, as well as the personal relations that made me and my wife Yael regular guests in Yitzhak and Leah's home, developed very quickly. The fact that he had supported another candidate to be Mossad chief never even came up between us.

"Silence is praise to you," it says in Psalm 65 about God. Rashi, the great Jewish commentator, explains that since there is no limit to the glory of God, there are no words that can describe it. Therefore, the best way to describe his glory is silence. Similarly, it seems that when you try to describe the personality and virtues of Prime Minister Yitzhak Rabin, you cannot find the right words, and silence is what best describes what you are trying to say.

When I found myself among those standing helplessly outside of the operating room in the basement of Ichilov Hospital, waiting for

Prof. Gabi Barabash's report while the doctors tried desperately to resuscitate the prime minister, time seemed to stand still. The situation was like a time tunnel, with your stream of consciousness working overtime and questions arising in your mind about eternity—the eternity of man, the eternity of the nation, the eternity of the divine spirit.

In the Judaism of "free will," "permission to kill" exists only among fundamentalists, who dare to pose as God Almighty himself. The only thing from which there is no way back is death, and therefore on issues relating to the Land of Israel it is inconceivable that the authority to permit the killing of a Jew would lie in the hands of man. The sentence of the degenerate who cut short the life of the prime minister is infinitely more in the realm of the true divine spirit.

Yitzhak's roots, which connected him to the Jewish people and the Land of Israel, were as deep and entrenched as the history of this people. The perpetuity of the people and the land was the number one concept that guided him, above and beyond any political or public debate. He did not mention these issues very often, but there was a rare event at which I heard him discussing them. It was during his state visit to China, while he was touring Beijing University. Almost spontaneously, several hundred (perhaps even thousands) of students gathered in a spacious hall to welcome him. He took the stage and delivered a long lecture in eloquent English, without any notes or prior preparation, about the history of the Jewish people and its state. The main message of his lecture to the Chinese students was that while the great Chinese nation had been around for six thousand years, the tiny Jewish nation had also survived for more than five thousand years, and would continue to do so for all eternity.

The man radiated wisdom—not the kind acquired at school or university but the kind attained in the school of life. It was a wisdom that reflected personal experience, the result of carrying the burden and working for decades toward one great purpose—the existence and security of the Jewish people in its land.

The prime minister's superb analytical abilities were well known. His unique talent lay in the fact that he could grasp complex situations and issues, break them down into simple elements, and in straightforward Hebrew, in four- or five-word sentences, draw out the essence and make it clear and understandable for everyone around him. Often, after hearing him analyze an issue, I would ask myself how it was that I had not seen it that way before and would marvel at how simple and understandable it seemed after the prime minister's analysis.

He always put the country first. When I look back on all of my years of work with him, I cannot point to a single case in which a decision of his was tainted by personal or party considerations. I do not remember him ever taking advantage of the tremendous power that was concentrated in his hands as prime minister and defense minister for a cause that was not in the best interest of the state. He forbade us, the members of the intelligence community, to place considerations of discretion and security above national considerations, even in extreme cases in which the result would be sacrificing intelligence or security activities.

Yitzhak Rabin was a leader. In the security-intelligence establishment there is a hierarchy in which each level examines itself in comparison to the echelon above it and also seeks from it reinforcement and inspiration. This interrelationship is both logical and wise when dealing with activities in which the risk calculation between the benefits of success and the damage of failure is taken from a world of concepts with which the public is unfamiliar. This is an industry that pushes the envelope of human ability, that dares to bend the laws of physics, and whose threshold for risk is beyond imagination. The person at the top of such a pyramid must exhibit a similar kind of leadership. Rabin would approve the most daring of operations, but not before he was convinced of the need for them and was certain that the chosen course of action involved only the risks that were absolutely necessary. And from the moment he approved the operation, he radiated a quiet confidence that was felt by the entire hierarchy. Whenever he was presented with an idea, an operation, or a plan, you got the feeling that for him it was "déjà vu," that he had already been here before. Thus, as the executor of the plan, you yourself could be calm and self-confident.

He was not a man with whom you would sit and have a long chat. The chummy, slap-on-the-back culture was not his style. He would sit across from you, leaning back on his chair, or leaning forward on his knees, the perpetual cigarette between his fingers, staring at you with his piercing blue gaze, examining you and listening to you and examining you again, and only after countless tests deciding you were worthy of his trust and support. But once he did, you knew that he would always have your back.

Yitzhak Rabin lived seventy-three years that were rich in deeds and made a unique contribution to the revival of the Jewish people in its country. Like Moses, he was stopped when he was just on the verge of completing his mission. Even had it been in his hands, he could not have planned a better time to leave us. He did so at the height of his life—he went by a whirlwind into heaven. This is, of course, my subjective view, and this is not the place to enter into a rational-empirical discussion in order to prove it.

The world's response and the immense respect that global leaders paid him at his funeral were a profound testimony to his greatness.

There is no doubt that Rabin was murdered against the background of the Oslo Accords. There is no doubt that the rally in Jerusalem's Zion Square on October 5, 1995, was a formative event in this matter, as was the October 10 event at the Wingate Institute, which was a direct continuation of the previous one. The unbridled demonstrations in front of Rabin's home, against him and his wife Leah, broke all the rules.

Without going into a political polemic, I feel that some would find it interesting to hear the insights of the director of the Mossad at the time (myself) regarding Rabin's position on the Oslo process.

The Oslo talks were conducted as a secret intelligence operation of the highest order, without discussion or approval by the government or cabinet. They were run by a group of people who, in my humble opinion, were acting on behalf of themselves. I remember my reports to Yitzhak on the talks and his reactions. At first he would listen to my reports and not respond. Later he would respond to my reports by saying that he did not believe anything would come of it. At a later stage, whenever I reported to him, he would respond by saying, "I know about it." I would like to emphasize that my perception of my relationship with the prime minister was based on my understanding that I reported to him and that he had the right and the authority to respond—or not to respond—to these reports. Only rarely and in extreme cases did I ask for explanations, and in those cases, too, the decision whether to explain was his. It is also important to note that according to the intelligence community's "Magna Carta," the Mossad does not engage in intelligence gathering on and surveillance of Israelis. The Mossad personnel deployed in Europe, being skilled intelligence agents, came upon the Oslo talks incidentally and indirectly, and not by virtue of a mission assigned to them by anyone.

On the Palestinian issue in general, and with regard to the Oslo talks in particular, Rabin was passive and lacking faith, and he detested Arafat. We asked ourselves why, then, he gave his consent to Oslo, and one of the possible explanations was that Rabin assessed that if he were to refuse Peres's demand to allow him to advance Oslo, Peres would work within the Labor Party to oust him from his position.[1] We also found, from the same source, that on June 7, 1993, two and a half months before the signing of the Oslo Accords, Rabin sent Peres an official letter demanding that he stop the talks. He then retracted it. That same month, in June 1993, Rabin sent a high-level personal envoy to London for a meeting with Nabil Sha'ath, a member of the PLO's Executive Committee, to assess the credibility of the Oslo process.

Rabin's position on the Oslo process was also derived from the peace negotiations with Jordan, which were taking place at the same time and in which Rabin strongly believed. He thought that they had a very real chance of succeeding, greatly admired King Hussein, and took a very active role in leading the talks. The intensive diplomatic activity that took place in the second half of 1993 included not only the Jordanian and the Palestinian tracks but also the Syrian track. In early August 1993, Rabin gave US secretary of state Warren Christopher the famous "deposit" in which he defined—conditionally and hypothetically—Israel's conditions for a future settlement with Syria and the Israeli willingness to withdraw from the Golan Heights.[2] Assad refrained from responding substantively to the "deposit," sticking to his precondition that Israel commit to withdrawing from the entire Golan Heights. Rabin, who did not want to give up on the Syrian track so easily, sent me to ask King Hassan II of Morocco to check directly with President Assad if he was serious about the peace process and what he would be willing to give in exchange for an Israeli withdrawal from the Golan Heights. The answers that the Moroccan king returned with did not satisfy Rabin's minimum conditions, and the process failed.

Rabin also assessed that the Oslo process, which was taking place simultaneously, secretly and completely independently from King Hussein, could make progress on the negotiations with Jordan difficult. When the Oslo signing ceremony was decided upon in Washington, Rabin did not even intend to participate, and he did so only under pressure from President Clinton. I remember a meeting between Rabin and King Hussein on the eve of the signing of the agreement, held at the king's palace in Amman. At the end of the meeting, after they had finished discussing all the issues, the king turned to Rabin with a sarcastic smile and said, "I understand that you are going to Washington for the signing ceremony of the Oslo agreement." When Rabin nodded, the king added, "Until now I'm the one who has had to suffer Arafat's wet kisses—now it's your turn!"

Yitzhak and I did not have the chance to analyze the Oslo affair together, but in my opinion, over time, during Yitzhak's second term as prime minister, he became convinced that the State of Israel could not continue to live by the sword and that no opportunity to break through the wall of hostility should be neglected. This is the logical explanation for his conduct in the three tracks: the Palestinian, in a completely passive manner until it ripened; the Jordanian, in a very active way throughout, until the signing of the peace treaty; and the Syrian, which he managed directly until it failed.

In my opinion, the Israeli-Jordanian peace agreement was the peak of Yitzhak's achievements and his greatest contribution to the resolution of the historical Arab-Israeli conflict. What a pity that he did not receive the Nobel Peace Prize for this accomplishment. After his murder, we set up a commemorative corner in Yitzhak's honor in the lobby of the Mossad building, and each year, on the anniversary of his death, the Mossad employees hold a memorial ceremony, which is attended by representatives of the Rabin family. At the memorial ceremony that took place on October 24, 2007, Eitan Haber, who had been Yitzhak's bureau chief, delivered a speech to the Mossad staff. I think it is appropriate to include it here:

History does not recognize the term "if." Because there is no "if" in history, for the past twelve years, I have consistently refused to answer "if" questions: "What if" Rabin would have said this or done that, what would Rabin have done and said about what is happening today "if" he were here . . . "if" and "if" and "if."

However, there is one "if" that I feel like I can respond to today with confidence: if Rabin was standing here today in this foyer, as he often stood on these steps, if he were here with you, I know for sure that he would say thank you from the bottom of his heart for what you do and for who you are. Many of you knew him, and how he would discuss and analyze the dangers that threaten us and our existence, and he would tell you that each and every one of you holds the key to the security of the State of Israel. If he were here, he would ask you, demand of you, to continue your work with all of your energy, "not to fall asleep on the watch," and "not to worry—I will give you all the backup you need." I knew him and I know many of you; when he would tell you that you are doing the most important job for the state, you would believe his every word, because it was Yitzhak Rabin, and he really meant every word. And those of you who have been here a long time will nod and say, "That's true," when I tell you that there have been prime ministers who praised the Mossad more than Yitzhak Rabin. There have been prime ministers who criticized the "office"—as you call it—more than Yitzhak Rabin, but there has not—there has not!—been a prime minister who admired the Mossad as much as Rabin did, respected its people as much as he did, and used its abilities in a better and more intelligent way. Many of the Mossad's incredible achievements took place during his tenure as prime minister. In those days, this "office" brought him what no other intelligence organization has ever brought to its country—and that was a peace agreement.

The truth is that I miss those days here, in the office, in Jerusalem and in Amman. I even miss the white van with the curtains hiding the people inside it, the refined man named Hussein, the king of Jordan, who was always a gentleman and did not say out loud what he thought of the late-night meals that were offered to him here on the hill, and I miss the sleepless nights that produced, thanks to this office, a peace agreement.

I would like to take this opportunity to thank my friends Shabtai and Efraim, and of course, Yitzhak Rabin, for giving me the opportunity to take some small part in such a great deed.

To the people of "the office," I do not presume to offer you any advice. As someone who was asked to speak here this morning on behalf of the murdered prime minister, I will say this: That redhead, who was never great at expressing emotion, would have stood here this morning moved by your actions, your contributions. That man who came into your lives examining and demanding the tiniest operational details, who had to be present for the exercises ahead of the operation, the man who knew how to take responsibility and always supported you, would be moved without you noticing it. He would even be embarrassed of his emotions. But in the car after leaving here, he would always get angry and criticize me, saying, "Again with you and your crazy schedule! Could not you have given me another hour or two in the Mossad?"

And one last "if":

My friend Haim Hefer once wrote: "This nation would like to say thank you to the people of the secrets and the riddles. This nation would like to give a warm word of thanks—*if* only it knew who to say it to."

As someone who knows who to say it to, I want to tell you, in his name, thank you.

Ironically, the small and poor kingdom of Jordan saw itself and the State of Israel as having identical strategic interests. Jordan never made such a declaration, but the ties between the two countries, which until the peace treaty were kept secret, have made this Jordanian thinking entirely clear.

The first contacts with Jordan were made in the 1960s and were led by Yaakov Herzog, the director general of Prime Minister Levi Eshkol's office. After the Six-Day War, senior Israeli politicians and officials regularly met King Hussein. On the eve of the Yom Kippur War in October 1973, the king sent us a warning about the impending outbreak of war. Between 1974 and 1977, meetings were held between Prime Minister Rabin and King Hussein, in which Yigal Allon and Shimon Peres also took part. During these meetings, the Israeli side expressed its willingness to discuss a partial Israeli withdrawal along the Jordan River as part of peace negotiations, but the king demanded a full withdrawal, including Jerusalem. In late 1977, a meeting was held in London between Moshe Dayan and the king, the outcome of which was silence until 1982 (it would be interesting to know what was said during this meeting). From 1982 onwards, a tradition began in which periodic meetings were held between the head of the Mossad and his Jordanian counterpart in various European cities. One might say that the significance of these meetings was the very fact that they took place.

From 1984 to 1987, a channel was established between Shimon Peres and the king under the auspices of the British Lord Mishcon.

The Mossad was not a player in these talks, which began as a secret. It was not until 1987 that the British became aware of their existence. In April 1987, Peres and the king arrived at a draft peace agreement, but it was not accepted by Prime Minister Shamir. This draft later became known as the London Agreement.

Only three months after the London Agreement in July 1987, the first meeting between Prime Minister Shamir and the king took place in a castle outside London. The meeting lasted for two days—Friday and Saturday—and included many hours of talks in various constellations, including private meetings between Prime Minister Shamir and King Hussein. This meeting shaped the future relationship between the two men, which was characterized by genuine chemistry and mutual trust, despite differences of opinion on core issues.

In 1988 there was a meeting in Paris between the king and then-defense minister Yitzhak Rabin. This meeting did not yield results, and until early 1990 only lower-level meetings were held. It should be remembered that at the end of 1987 the First Intifada broke out, and in the summer of 1988 the king announced that he was washing his hands of the West Bank and the Palestinian cause. In March 1990, Mossad deputy director Efraim Halevy met with King Hussein in London. This meeting opened a new chapter in the relations between the two countries—the chapter of the First Gulf War.

As mentioned, King Hussein sided with Iraqi ruler Saddam Hussein. In meetings held on the eve of Saddam's invasion of Kuwait, we warned King Hussein not to allow Saddam to use Jordanian territory. This issue led to the next meeting between the king and Prime Minister Shamir, which took place in the first week of January 1991, about a week before the outbreak of the First Gulf War. At this meeting, the king pledged not to allow the Iraqi air force to use Jordanian airspace.

The Gulf War left King Hussein on his throne, and the Kingdom of Jordan suffered no physical damage. Hussein saw this as a great achievement and attributed it to the agreement with Prime Minister Shamir.

Throughout 1991, frequent meetings were held, the main subject of which was the upcoming Madrid Conference, which was intended to open another chapter of initiatives to end the conflict.

In meetings held in 1993, the king expressed his concern over the Oslo talks. We maintained that no significant importance should be attributed to them. When the signing ceremony was held on the White House lawn, the king saw himself as having been betrayed and deceived and as having his back against a wall, with Egypt and Saudi Arabia against him and the United States imposing a naval blockade on Aqaba. Prime Minister Rabin saw it as his duty to try and appease the king, so we worked on preparations for a meeting between the two, which took place in October 1993 in Aqaba with an Israeli commitment to maintain total secrecy. The king's explanation for the need for secrecy was that after the Gulf War he had only one ally— Syrian president Hafez al-Assad—and the disclosure of a top-level meeting with Israel could seriously damage Jordan-Syria relations.

The main bone of contention at the Aqaba meeting was the strategy of peace negotiations between the two countries. The king believed that minor agreements should be reached over a period of time and that once these agreements reached a critical mass they could all be wrapped into one peace agreement. Rabin's position was that there was no time for this and that it was preferable to conduct one negotiation in which the parties would bridge all gaps and reach a full peace agreement. The meeting ended with no consensus. The following morning the Israeli media released a report on the meeting. The result was another crisis followed by stagnation.

In 1993 and 1994, marathon negotiations were held between the two countries, led by Rabin and the Mossad. These included achievements but also a number of crises and obstacles, both objective and otherwise:

- Jordan had joined the Iraqi camp in the First Gulf War, versus the American coalition, which included nearly all of the Arab countries.

- There were countless players with opposing agendas, including the Americans, the Egyptians, the Shin Bet, Shimon Peres, supporters of Syria in Jordan, and some in Israel as well.
- The national assessor—Military Intelligence—persisted in its assessment that Jordan would not sign a peace treaty with Israel by itself.
- The Oslo process took place in parallel to the negotiations with Jordan.
- Those who rejected the peace negotiations with Jordan and those who believed that there was no chance for a separate peace with Jordan found support for their positions in Jordan's consent to Hamas's presence on its territory and the terrorist activity emanating from Jordan.
- The king's strategy of incremental progress differed from Rabin's view that a peace agreement should be reached in one short process.

Much has been said about the peace treaty between Israel and Jordan, and still there is more that we don't know about the process than what we do know. The negotiation process lasted for two years, with hundreds of meetings taking place in various arrangements across different continents and countries. These negotiations had to find the common denominator among an array of global, regional, local, and personal interests (issues of "honor" threatened the success of the agreement every week).

On November 2, 1993, only one month after the failed meeting between Rabin and the king in Aqaba, Foreign Minister Peres asked for Rabin's approval to try his hand at setting the wheels back in motion. Peres's meeting with the king was arranged by the Mossad, and its deputy director, Efraim Halevy, accompanied Peres to Amman and participated in some of the meetings. Peres succeeded in putting pressure on the king during a marathon meeting and in extracting a draft peace agreement. The king told Peres that in his upcoming annual speech to the Jordanian parliament (a kind of Jordanian State of the Union), he was planning to begin preparing the parliament and the people for peace. He asked Peres to keep their agreement a secret between them until after the speech, and Peres committed to doing so. Upon his return to Israel, Peres briefed Prime Minister Rabin on the meeting and its results, and that evening, as he left the meeting, he told journalists, "Remember November Second." In our next meeting with the king, he delivered a statement of his own, one that struck us like lightning: "You have put out a contract on my life." The draft agreement that Peres had obtained was filed away in the archives.

From November 1993 until March 1994 nothing happened on the Jerusalem-Amman track. On the other hand, negotiations on the Washington-Jerusalem-Damascus track began to gain momentum. Then, in March 1994, Efraim received an invitation from the king to come and visit with his wife for a few days. During the visit, the blueprint of an agreement was drafted, which Efraim brought back with him to Israel. He returned on April 12, Memorial Day, the same day that Hamas carried out a major terrorist attack on a bus in Hadera. The entire State of Israel—Rabin, Peres, Military Intelligence—came down hard on the king, viewing him as at least partially responsible for the attack. The Mossad, through Efraim, succeeded in navigating the crisis and in salvaging the situation. At a meeting in London on May 11, 1994, the blueprint that Efraim had obtained was adopted as a detailed memorandum of understanding, initialed by Elyakim Rubinstein and the Jordanian crown prince, Prince Hassan. The memorandum of understanding was translated into a detailed agreement, with appendices, by the negotiating teams of the two sides, with the two leaders acting as troubleshooters whenever the negotiators got stuck on a particular issue.

It was after midnight. King Hussein and Yitzhak Rabin shook hands at the king's palace in Amman, after agreeing on the last details that required their final decision. At that moment, someone in the room said that the Americans, who until now had been out of the loop, ought to be informed. The king and Rabin decided to update President Clinton directly and asked to contact the White House. When the president got on the line, they told him that they had just shaken hands, signaling that the peace agreement had been finalized.

From there things moved quickly. It was agreed that a meeting would be held in Washington, which would continue with the signing ceremony in Ein Evrona near Eilat and Aqaba and an official public visit by Foreign Minister Peres to Jordan. The rest is history. On a personal note, I would like to mention that around midnight, the day after the ceremony in Washington, I received a call at home from the king's plane. He was on his flight back to Amman and was dropping Efraim off on the way. The king wished to thank me personally for my role in achieving peace. It was a gracious gesture on the part of the king that I will always remember.

The operation of achieving a peace treaty with Jordan succeeded. The secret of its success lay in the presence of two essential conditions. One was the long history of the Mossad's secret ties with the Jordanian royal family, including the personal chemistry between Efraim Halevy and the king and Prince Hassan. The other was the close personal involvement of the leaders, Yitzhak Rabin and King Hussein, in the negotiation process, including the chemistry that formed between them and their willingness to solve in real time any problem that the negotiating teams could not resolve on their own.

King Hussein viewed the continued survival of the Hashemite Kingdom as his primary goal. He saw several factors as necessary in ensuring this survival, including:

- Good relations with Israel: Hussein regarded Israel as a strategic pillar, with an interest in the continued survival of his kingdom; this was a necessary, though in his eyes not a sufficient, condition for its survival.
- Strategic ties with at least one other Arab country. Hussein understood that Jordan must have at least one major Arab country

from the Middle East as its ally—Syria, Saudi Arabia, Iraq, or Egypt.

• A guarantee of support from the United States.

An understanding of these considerations seems necessary in order to understand developments in the Middle East and the steps taken by Jordan both leading up to and after the peace agreement with Israel. The only explanation, I believe, for the thirty-year-plus relationship between Israel and Jordan is the late king's view that relations with Israel were valuable and essential for the survival of the kingdom. If anyone needed proof of this thesis, I would refer them to the events of "Black September" in Jordan in 1970, when, in response to the Jordanian massacre of Fatah, the Syrians sent a military force southward toward Jordan, and only the deployment of Israeli forces in the southern Golan Heights convinced the Syrians to abandon their military advancement and withdraw their forces.

These considerations also influenced King Hussein's strategy in everything related to the march toward peace, throughout that entire period and during the years of negotiations. There was a radical difference between the king's strategy and that of Israel. As mentioned earlier, the king adopted a step-by-step approach. He tried to persuade his Israeli interlocutors to "focus on small agreements; we'll accumulate one agreement after another, and when we reach a decisive amount of small but important agreements, we will wrap it all up in the package of a peace agreement." This approach of the king was based, in my estimation, on his belief that the Arab world would tolerate small, measured moves toward peace but would not accept a single major comprehensive move that resulted in a full peace agreement.

Israel's approach was always the opposite: to do everything quickly and in one shot, and to know that the deed was done. Negotiations for peace, therefore, carried on for many years, moving constantly between these poles—the willingness to go in the direction of small agreements and the desire to achieve one big agreement.

Another reason on the Israeli side for difficulties and for the prolongation of the negotiations was the different agendas and preferences of the various parties involved in the process, with each pulling in a different direction. These bodies included the intelligence community, the foreign ministry, the Shin Bet, and others. The different preferences stemmed not only from different interests but from varying assessments; there were those who maintained that the Syrian track should be the first focus, those who preferred to begin with the Jordanian track, and those who argued that the Palestinian track should take priority. Over the years, the entire process was conducted according to an agenda that was dictated by the United States, which did not always coincide with the agenda of Israel or Jordan. There was never a complete overlap among all of the parties. And, of course, Egypt's agenda also had to be taken into account.

One of the greatest worries for Israel was the assessment, maintained for a long period of time, that Jordan would not sign a peace treaty with Israel alone. This assessment was well founded and well reasoned, and was held by players who could not be easily dismissed with a wave of the hand. Another major difficulty stemmed from the presence and role of the radical Islamic organizations in Jordan, first and foremost Hamas. They had been present in Jordan for many years; every time an attack was carried out in Israel and its source was traced back to Jordan, it was seen as additional proof of the belief held by some in the Israeli camp that Jordan would never sign an agreement on its own and that it was impossible to reach an agreement as long as Jordan provided shelter to radical Islamic organizations. Each time Israel complained about the extremist Islamic organizations in Jordan, the answer was: "We will expel them if you want, but if we do then we lose control. They will go to Libya or Algeria, and from there they'll be able to do whatever they want. At least here in Jordan we have full control over them, and we can monitor them, restrict them, and thwart their terrorist plans."

Decision makers in Israel faced a dilemma, in which all the intelligence officers felt that they had a direct relationship with the subject about which they were collecting information. The Israeli intelligence-gathering and assessment bodies had to collect intelligence about Jordan, while at the same time maintaining personal contact with those on whom they had to gather information. The dilemma was whether this personal contact led to better understandings and assessments or whether the personal acquaintance colored the evaluation, leading to biased and inaccurate assessments and analyses of the situation.

The Mossad people believed, in large part on the basis of personal familiarity, that they were on the right track and were talking to people who really wanted peace; they believed that Jordan would agree to sign a peace agreement on its own, subject of course to a few necessary conditions. Other members of the intelligence community, who did not have personal relationships with the Jordanians, were much more suspicious and reserved. The end result showed that the optimists were right, and that is a good thing.

In my capacity as director of the Mossad, I was quite involved in the subject and in the peace process with Jordan. The person who bore the main burden of negotiating with the Jordanians on behalf of the Mossad was Mossad's deputy director Efraim Halevy, whose role and contribution to the peace process were crucial.

The communications between King Hussein and the prime minister of Israel, whether it was Yitzhak Shamir or Yitzhak Rabin, spoke of Halevy as "our trusted emissary," who faithfully delivered messages back and forth between the two sides. And this trusted emissary at a certain point became "our trusted negotiator." This is a lesson that shows that the messenger does not necessarily "get shot" by the end of the process. Sometimes one can go from being a mere go-between to being a negotiator with one's own input into the process. Many times, at crisis points, of which there were many, the emissary was the one who was able to suggest ideas that bridged the gap and made it possible to continue negotiations.

The genuine smiles on Hussein and Rabin's faces in the famous photographs that epitomize the Jordanian-Israeli peace process in the eyes of the public did not necessarily characterize the period of the negotiations. This stage came only at the end of the process. There were times when suspicion and disappointment overcame trust and hope, and things even became hostile now and then.

As an illustration, let us return to the year 1993 and examine it in more detail. Throughout the year contact was maintained, messages were conveyed and negotiations were held. Everything was done in complete secrecy. The king's situation was very difficult: the United States, which did not forget his support for Saddam Hussein during the Gulf crisis, turned its back on him and made his life miserable. It imposed a closure on the port of Aqaba as part of the blockade of Iraq and inspected every ship on its way to Jordan. Egypt and Saudi Arabia also took a stance against the king because of his position in the Gulf War. Despite all this, and perhaps in part because of it, he continued to negotiate with Israel but implored for the contacts to remain secret. Throughout the negotiations in 1993, Hussein would occasionally say to his Israeli interlocutors, "Something is happening with the Palestinians." The Israelis would reply that this was not the case. The king continued to insist that something was developing on the Palestinian issue, and the Israelis continued to insist that they knew nothing. Then Hussein said, "I am telling you that things are happening in Oslo." The Israelis responded, with the consent of Prime Minister Rabin, that the peace negotiations with Jordan were the prime minister's top priority.

A short time later, the Oslo Accords became public.

Of course, Jordan as a state and Hussein personally favored the agreement and supported understandings with the Palestinians. However, one of the pillars of Jordan's strategy had always been to be involved in what was happening between Israel and the Palestinians, whether actively or passively, and this position had been acceptable to the Israelis. As mentioned, over the course of 1993, Hussein repeatedly told the Israelis that there was something going on between Israel and the Palestinians, and the Israeli negotiators, knowing nothing about it, denied it. This indicates that while there are advantages to clandestine contacts and secret negotiations, if the top ranks of the intelligence community are not all in on the secret, such situations may occur. The fact that the Israelis denied that something was indeed happening on the Palestinian track undermined Hussein's confidence in them. Another event that increased this mistrust occurred in October 1993, when Prime Minister Rabin met with the king in Aqaba. The meeting took place under a cloak of secrecy, at the king's request, but even so, the following morning the meeting was reported in the Israeli media. And I have already mentioned the statement that Shimon Peres, then deputy prime minister and minister of foreign affairs, leaked to journalists following his meeting with the king in Amman, during which far-reaching understandings were reached ahead of an agreement: "Remember November Second." As stated, this series of events led within a few months to the king lashing out at his Israeli interlocutors at one of the meetings, saying, "You have put out a contract on my life," a declaration that accurately reflected the anger and despair that he felt as a result of the leaks.

In conclusion, it is worth pointing out the relationship between the two leaders and their ability to look beyond the peace agreement and examine the potential for solving the problems of the entire Middle East. Once it was clear that there was to be an agreement, but before it had been drafted and signed, the two men discussed the potential role Iraq could play in solving all the problems of the Middle East. Iraq was a country that had it all: large areas of arable land, a relatively small population in comparison to its land area, and unlimited water and energy resources. Only such a country—in the post–Saddam Hussein era, obviously—could contribute to solving the issues of water, energy, refugees, and population surpluses in the Middle East. This is what the two leaders discussed while the agreement between the two countries was still brewing.

Since its establishment, the Mossad has been responsible for establishing secret contacts with countries that have not had diplomatic relations with Israel. It has also used its capabilities to organize clandestine meetings with leaders of countries with which Israel does maintain diplomatic relations but where, because of certain circumstances, both sides preferred the relations to remain secret.

Yitzhak Rabin was in favor of secret diplomacy. It gave him the opportunity to get a better and more direct sense of "friend" and "foe" (to use air force jargon). He enjoyed the secret trips that broke up, if only briefly, his busy routine. He liked to be with the people of the Mossad, who planned the meetings, prepared for them, and carried them out far away from the prying eyes of the media. Particularly top-secret trips were planned in such a way that his absence from the country was not even felt, though in any case there was always a suitable cover story.

The most dramatic visit during my tenure was Rabin's visit to Indonesia and his meeting with President Suharto in October 1993. The Indonesia visit followed his trip to China, which was the first official visit of an Israeli prime minister to that country. The Mossad was involved both in initiating and in planning for the visit to China, through the Mossad's channel with the Chinese intelligence service. Because the visit was official and public, the delegation was large and the prime minister's plane was full of representatives of the Israeli media.

The delegation was housed in the official guest village, a luxurious villa complex in downtown Beijing. Chinese leader Jiang Zemin held a reception and state dinner in honor of the prime minister and his wife, attended by the political and military leaders of China.

In the working meetings with the Chinese prime minister and his team, Rabin instructed me to sit close to him, as part of the Israeli delegation at the table, which led to my being photographed by the local media for the first time since I had begun my term.

I attended a meeting with the head of China's intelligence and security services and was present at Prime Minister Rabin's spontaneous lecture on the history of Zionism and the State of Israel, delivered in English and with no prior preparation, to hundreds of Chinese students during a visit to Beijing University. Following the official portion of our visit in Beijing, we continued, accompanied by members of the media, to Shanghai. The highlight of our visit there was an excursion to the former Jewish synagogue, which was now a museum that documented the warm welcome and assistance extended by the Chinese to Jewish refugees who had fled the Holocaust in Europe and ended up in China.

The prime minister's most important insight from the visit to China, which I shared with him, was undeniable—the emergence of the China as a major world power, second only to the United States in terms of its global potential, both economic and military. It was clear that Israel would have to formulate its own strategy vis-à-vis China, whose main focus would be the building of a relationship that would encompass as many issues as possible on which there was a convergence of interests. I recommended to the prime minister that the Israeli ambassador to China have a status similar to that of Israel's ambassador to the United States. He or she should be the personal appointment of the prime minister, like the ambassador to Washington, and should report directly to the prime minister.

The Mossad has guided Israel's relations with Indonesia, the largest Muslim country in the world (with 250 million Muslims dispersed throughout some seventeen thousand islands) since 1963. During the "agricultural" era of Israeli foreign policy, Israeli agricultural experts, under the auspices of the Mossad, set up an impressive farm for President Sukarno. There was a dairy farm there as well, and Mossad personnel who visited Indonesia sometimes took with them small stainless-steel containers containing the semen of the best Israeli cattle in order to enhance the breeding of the cows on the farm. During that period, Israeli agriculture bolstered its relations with many countries around the world with which it did not have diplomatic relations.

Prior to the visit to Indonesia in 1993, the Mossad made great efforts to arrange a meeting between Prime Minister Rabin and President Suharto of Indonesia and succeeded when the conditions were ripe. It was agreed that the visit to Indonesia would coincide with the visit to China, which greatly complicated the logistics of the trip. The meeting with Suharto was scheduled for a Friday, at his private home in Jakarta. The prime minister's plane was scheduled to land following Friday prayers in the mosques, after the worshippers had dispersed. It was clear that we could not stay in Jakarta overnight, so we planned to fly from there to Singapore, about an hour's flight. We would have to arrive at the hotel in Singapore before the start of the Sabbath. Rabin remembered the government crisis that had broken out in 1976 following the landing ceremony for the first F-16s that arrived in Israel, which had taken place after the start of the Sabbath, and he was not willing to risk another crisis of this sort. Another problem was that the Indonesians had stipulated that the meeting be kept secret by both sides until its conclusion. They announced categorically that if news of the meeting were leaked prior to its taking place, the prime minister's plane would not receive a landing permit from the control tower of the Jakarta airport.

The biggest challenge was hiding from the dozen or so Israeli journalists who had been invited by the prime minister to participate in his important trip to China the fact that after the visit they would suddenly find themselves in Indonesia. Before the trip, they were briefed that following the visit to China the prime minister's plane would be flying west and refueling in Azerbaijan and that from there it would continue to Nairobi for a meeting between the prime minister and the president of Kenya before the return to Israel.

After midnight between Thursday and Friday, I received a phone call at my hotel room in Shanghai. It was Danny Yatom, the prime minister's military secretary, inviting me to come up to the prime minister's suite. There, in addition to Yitzhak Rabin, his wife Leah, and Danny Yatom, were the prime minister's bureau chief Eitan Haber, director general of the Prime Minister's Office Shimon Sheves, and the captain of the plane. The problem: the captain was required to fill out a flight plan and distribute it to the control towers in Shanghai and Jakarta as well as to his headquarters in Israel. If he were to write that his next destination was Jakarta, the result would almost definitely be a leak of the meeting, which would surely be canceled as a result. The second issue was when and what to explain to the journalists traveling with the prime minister.

After some discussion, it was agreed that the captain would fill out the flight plan details according to the route of the cover story, namely Shanghai to Azerbaijan to Nairobi to Tel Aviv. The journalists would be informed about Jakarta near the time of landing. The following day, Friday, we took off from Shanghai as planned. During the flight, the prime minister went to the back of the plane to talk to the members of the press. One of the journalists accompanied him back to the front, and Yitzhak introduced him to me and asked that I brief him so that he could fill in the rest of the journalists in turn. I briefed him and answered all of his questions completely frankly, doing my best to convince him that we had left the media in the dark only for lack of any other choice. I will not attempt to describe all of the journalists' reactions from that moment until the end of the journey, but I will mention that one of them threatened that upon the return to Israel he would file a lawsuit for kidnapping and imprisonment against his will.

The blue-and-white plane with the Star of David on it, which for the first time in history arrived in the largest Muslim country in the world, was a little ahead of schedule. The control tower instructed us to wait for a landing permit, which left us circling over the city of Jakarta. We eventually landed near the VIP guest hall. I will never forget the looks of astonishment on the journalists' faces when the plane door opened and the first people to enter were Hebrew speakers. These were, of course, members of the Mossad's advance team. Waiting in the parking lot was a limousine convoy sent by our hosts, along with security guards and escorts. They were joined by the prime minister's own security guards. The Indonesians had also determined that the two leaders be joined at the meeting by only one other person each, and the prime minister decided that I would be his "plus one." I got into the waiting limousine along with him, and the motorcade set out for President Suharto's private home. Eitan Haber and Danny Yatom displayed exceptional loyalty to their boss and managed to sneak into the limousine convoy by pretending to be security guards. Being typical Israelis, they anticipated that if they could get to Suharto's house they would probably be able to somehow get into the meeting, but their hopes were dashed; as "security guards," they stood on watch throughout the meeting on the porch of the house facing the street.

President Suharto greeted us at the entrance to his house, which looked to us like a modest home in a middle-class neighborhood. The two leaders shook hands and bowed to each other. We were led into the meeting room and seated on armchairs in a small sitting area. From the start, the atmosphere of the meeting was relaxed, intimate, and informal. We were served cups of tea and left alone. Suharto's military aide sat behind him and took minutes. I sat next to Rabin with a small notebook and a pen.

Rabin was the one who spoke the most during the conversation. He began by thanking the president for agreeing to meet with him and for his consent to have the meeting announced publicly by both sides immediately upon its conclusion. He then introduced me to the president and commended the long-standing relationship between the two countries, which was guided by the Mossad on the Israeli side.

The prime minister spoke at length about the situation in the Middle East and his efforts to promote peace between Israel and its neighbors. He delved into details regarding Israel's relations with each state—Egypt, Jordan, Syria, and the Palestinians. He praised Morocco for its instrumental role in advancing peace in the region and expressed his hope that Indonesia would also contribute to the advancement of peace. Suharto responded by saying, "Here we are, meeting, and it will soon be known to the world!"

The two discussed China. Rabin told Suharto about his visit, his meetings and impressions, and the two agreed that China would be a major player on the global level and certainly in East and Southeast Asia.

Suharto and Rabin were both people who spoke in understatement, but as a listener on the sidelines one could sense that as the diplomatic process in the Middle East progressed, progress could also be expected in the relations between Indonesia and Israel.

The meeting lasted about an hour and a half. At its conclusion, gifts were exchanged. Photographers came into the room to take pictures, and my photograph, God help us, also appeared in all the Jakarta newspapers the next day. The president escorted us to the exit, and the convoy set out for the airport, where our next mission awaited us—arriving in Singapore before the start of the Sabbath.

Until the Khomeini revolution in 1979, Israel had "contact" with the Persian Gulf from southern Iran. This contact enabled us to get a closer feel of Iraq as well as at least some of the Gulf States. It was only natural for us to aspire to develop contacts in the southern part of the Gulf also, across the Straits of Hormuz. The Sultanate of Oman, strategically located opposite and south of the Hormuz bays (i.e., at the entrance to the Gulf from the Indian Ocean), had a long tradition of British influence, in the form of a protectorate. In 1932, Said bin Taimur came to power as sultan, with the support of the British. He was deposed in 1970 by his son, Sultan Qaboos bin Said, who remains the country's leader to this day. Oman has an area of 212,000 square kilometers, with a population of less than a million people. The sultan comes from the Ibadi tribe, the largest of the various groups in the sultanate. The tribe originates from the Khawarij (who were the first to secede from the original Islam). Beginning in the eighth century they have appointed their own imams as their spiritual leaders. Oman's economy is based mainly on oil revenues, but it does not have oil reserves the size of Saudi Arabia's or Iran's. Its oil resources are depleting, which requires them to manage their economy wisely and cautiously.

The Mossad also had a presence in Oman, with the intensity of our activity there adapting according to changing needs and conditions. Prime Minister Rabin, as well as his predecessor, Shamir, attached great importance to our presence in the territory. Rabin, perhaps because of being a former military man, wanted to see and hear things firsthand; he was interested in meeting Sultan Qaboos and hearing his positions on issues related to the Israeli-Arab conflict and the problems and threats in the Persian Gulf. After considerable efforts over a long period in 1994, the sultan agreed to a secret visit by the prime minister and a meeting with him. The visit was planned to last less than twenty-four hours, with most of the members of the prime minister's bureau not being privy to it. We left in the afternoon and returned the next morning. We landed at Muscat Airport near the sultan's private terminal, and from there we were taken to the palace.

The meeting and the dinner that followed were held in a circular space about thirty meters in diameter, with 360-degree glass walls and decorations, including rare arabesques, that made us feel as if we were staying in one of Harun al-Rashid's palaces.

After both sides exchanged thanks and niceties, Rabin offered the sultan his views on the state of the world, the Middle East, and the conflict, as well as his perceptions of threats and prospects. When Rabin spoke about the Israeli-Palestinian conflict, the sultan muttered that he did not support Palestinians coming to live in his country. He had apparently drawn conclusions from the Kuwaiti experience with the Palestinians in the first Gulf crisis of 1991, when the overwhelming majority of Palestinians who were allowed to remain in Kuwait and worked there in very lucrative jobs supported the Iraqi invasion. The Iranian issue was also discussed, and both sides agreed that an increasingly powerful Iran—certainly with nonconventional weapons—was indeed a threat. The sultan gave the impression that the Gulf States looked upon Israel as a force capable of stopping the Iranians. The two leaders agreed to stay in contact and to share their assessments through their representatives. Following the conversation, an unimaginably vast meal bursting with Middle Eastern aromas and flavors was served, a feast that could have fed an entire company of soldiers for a few days—or, indeed, one thousand and one nights.

Following an exchange of presents and farewells, we returned to our waiting plane. In the air, the prime minister summed up the visit by saying that an Israeli foot on the ground in the Persian Gulf was important and necessary.

One last story: Rabin believed in the paradigm that power creates deterrence and deterrence enables increased flexibility and room to maneuver in diplomatic negotiations. Israel's relations with Germany, since the early years of the state, have been unique. During Shamir and Rabin's terms, Bernd Schmidbauer, the minister in charge of co-ordinating the intelligence and security services in Chancellor Kohl's government, served as the link for all matters that needed to be dealt with discreetly.

We were flying to Germany on a small business jet. We took off, in secret, from Ben Gurion airport in the afternoon and landed at the airport in Cologne. We set off in a convoy to the chancellor's private residence in Bad Godesberg, one of the towns surrounding Bonn, which still served as the capital, although the process of transferring official institutions to Berlin was already in full swing. The chancellor was a mountain of a man, and his presence overshadowed everyone else. We were seated around an intimate dining table and were served a modest dinner. The main topic discussed at the meeting was German aid to Israel in the form of submarines, but the two leaders also took advantage of the meeting to exchange views on the state of the world and Rabin's efforts to advance the peace process. Approximately two hours later we were already on our way back to the plane. I summed up the trip by saying that while a business jet does not come cheap, the deal Rabin had "closed" with the chancellor justified the cost of the flight.

And a few words in closing: this man, who felt at home in the courtyards of kings, presidents, and heads of state, took as a given his participation in exercises for special operations in target countries; even after a long and exhausting day of work, he could spend an entire night in the middle of the Negev or the Golan Heights with combat soldiers, talking to them and asking them questions, checking everything to the very last detail, and giving his comments before disappearing. He was also known to insist on observing the exercises of operational squads at various hours of the day on the noisy city streets and to marvel that the people in the area had not understood and could not explain what had happened right before their eyes.

I loved the man. His personality and his knowledge filled me with confidence. Wherever I was, I had the feeling that if I looked behind me I would see him, giving me a wink.

There was no precedent to the unique and personal attention Yitzhak gave to the combatants and employees of the Mossad, and unfortunately, since his passing no one has lived up to the standard he set. I miss him every day.

On the Israeli-Palestinian Conflict

This section was written in a time tunnel. It was penned in mid-2016, but its content and the opinions expressed in it date back to the decade between September 2001 and September 2010, though I do occasionally slip in the views I hold today. This lends validity to the statement attributed to the late Moshe Dayan, that "only donkeys do not change their minds!" The opinions I hold today are expressed in detail in the following section "A Parallel Arrangement—An Alternative to Bilateral Negotiations."

In September 2001, I was in the midst of making the shift from my second career to my third. My first career was, of course, the thirty-two years I spent in the Mossad, the pinnacle of which was my service as its director from 1989 to 1996. In my second career, I served as the CEO of Maccabi Healthcare Services, the second-largest HMO in Israel, between the years 1996 and 2001. Then, in August 2001, I began my third chapter in the business world in the field of energy, advancing the natural gas agreement between Egypt and Israel.

On the afternoon of September 11, 2001, I was sitting in my office, engrossed in some energy-related reading material, when the phone on my desk rang. I picked up and immediately recognized the voice of an old friend, the former head of the CIA's Near East Division.

Skipping the usual opening niceties characteristic of phone calls, he said "Shabtai, turn on CNN and call me back." I hurried into the next room and turned on the TV just in time to see the second plane crash into the second Twin Tower. I sat down on the couch, stared at the television screen, and murmured to myself and to the people who had begun to gather in the room, "As of today we live in a different world." I returned to my office, closed the door, sat down, and began to imagine what the post–September 11 world would look like.

In Judaism, Jews are commanded to engage in soul-searching once a year, on Rosh Hashanah; they are supposed to examine their actions over the year that has passed, both between themselves and their fellow man and between themselves and God. The Jewish New Year and the anniversary of the World Trade Center attacks usually occur in the same month—September. At the International Institute for Counter-Terrorism (ICT) at the Interdisciplinary Center (IDC) Herzliya, which I helped establish and of which I serve as chairman of the board, we decided to hold our annual international conference on the anniversary of the September 11 attacks.

In 2010, the ICT held its ninth international conference. We'd had almost an entire decade since that fateful day to remember, think, analyze, and compare the world that existed before September 11, 2001, and the one that followed it. I myself could testify that the world in 2010 looked worse, much worse, than I had imagined it then, just minutes after watching the disaster unfold on TV. In essence, the most dramatic element of the change was that the post–September 11 world had returned to an era of religious and cultural wars—a world in which Islam was trying to regain the hegemony it had lost, with radical Islam leading the way.

In the aftermath of the attack on the World Trade Center, the world looked to Israel, the Western country with the most experience to date in dealing with terrorism. In retrospect, I must admit that the scope of global radical terrorism was enormous even by our standards.

In the wake of September 11, the US administration underwent a major organizational reform, the largest since the end of World War II. The Department of Homeland Security, which was established following the attacks, is now the largest department in the cabinet. The need to respond to a threat of that scale, while at the same time engaging in fighting, resulted, of course, in a number of mistakes. But, to the Americans' credit, it must be said that they generally detect their mistakes and correct them.

There has been total intelligence and operational cooperation between the United States and Israel in the field of counterterrorism from the get-go. Both sides understood that they had something to learn from each other, as well as the fact that only international cooperation would make it possible to deal with the threat in the most effective way.

The phenomenon of Islamic fundamentalism interested me, especially in light of my extensive experience in the war against Arab terrorism, which at the time was characterized by nationalistic, secular, and class motivations. Here are a few things I learned, things that I think all people in Western society who consider themselves educated should understand.

When fundamentalist Islam burst onto the world stage, with its notorious and distinctive representative Osama bin Laden, who presented an apocalyptic religious vision of the eradication of all infidels and the establishment of a global Muslim caliphate, thinkers, opinion makers, statesmen, and politicians around the world were caught off guard and therefore did not want to deal with the insight that the world of the late twentieth century was returning to the era of medieval religious wars.

According to Samuel P. Huntington's classic book *The Clash of Civilizations* (1996), "A resident of Rome may define himself with varying degrees of intensity as a Roman, an Italian, a Catholic, a Christian, a European, a Westerner. The civilization to which he belongs is the broadest level of identification with which he strongly identifies." Huntington lists the major civilizations of the world as Western, Confucian, Japanese, Islamic, Hindu, Slavic-Orthodox, South American (Latin), and African. He describes civilizations as differentiated from each other by history, language, culture, tradition, and, most important, religion.[3]

For over a decade after the terrorist attacks of September 11, 2001, Western leaders, intellectuals, and educated citizens had refrained from defining the conflict between the Western and Islamic civilizations, which the attacks had brought to the forefront of the global agenda, as religious. The reason for this was the primal fear of a return to the medieval religious wars. It seemed to me that Bush's much-publicized visit to the Islamic Center in Washington immediately after the terrorist attack was an indication of this fear.

Upon further thinking, it occurred to me that the phenomenon of fundamentalist Islam was not purely one of religious war. Perhaps it was more accurate to define it as engaging in a religious war against those who held different religious beliefs that adopted the values of freedom and modernity. Fundamentalist Muslims represented only a small minority of Islam's 1.3 billion (in 2010) believers. Moreover, both Shia and Sunni Salafi fundamentalist Muslims viewed the Muslim majority that did not share their beliefs as heretics against the true Islam who must be fought, perhaps even before the war against the other religions of the world. For over a decade and a half, the Muslim fundamentalist minority had been able to set the global agenda, while the world's moderate Muslim leaders were not doing enough, likely out of concern for their lives, to promote the alternative vision of peaceful coexistence among civilizations.

Another important insight: civilizations are the sum not only of the relations between God and man, but also of relations between the citizen and the state, the individual and the collective, rights and duties, liberty and authority, and equality and hierarchy. The significance of this insight is that in a clash of civilizations, historical variables are mixed with cultural, national, and moral elements. Even so, there is no doubt that the religious element is the dominant one, and whoever tries to sweep it under the rug is ignoring the main point.

The frequent use of the term *crusaders* by Osama bin Laden and other fundamentalist spokespeople when referring to the West emphasizes the religious aspect of the conflict. The term *crusaders* is saturated with religious connotations and contains an element of colonialism. Many Muslim speakers and writers, including Palestinians, refer to us Jews and Israelis as "crusaders," implying that we belong to a different race and have seized Palestine from the Muslims. This use of language suggests that just as the Muslim Saladin liberated Palestine from the Christian crusaders in the twelfth century, Muslims of the twenty-first century will liberate Palestine from the Jews. Fundamentalist Islam's burning hatred of the West is so great that it distorts history. It claims that the "American Crusaders" intend to conquer the "land of the two holy mosques" (meaning Saudi Arabia, home of the Muslim holy cities of Mecca and Medina) and ignores the historical fact that in five cases between the 1990s and 2015—in Kuwait, Somalia, the Balkans, Iraq, and Syria—the United States embarked on military campaigns in order to protect Muslims. On the other hand, the common denominator for the assassination of President Sadat, the "fatwa" against author Salman Rushdie, the destruction of the monumental statues of Buddha in Afghanistan and Tadmor in Syria, the executions of women and homosexuals, and the attacks on the Twin Towers was the subcivilization of fundamentalist Islam.

The American invasion of Afghanistan, the Second Gulf War, and the Israeli-Palestinian conflict marked a dramatic change from the classical doctrine of war. Western civilization now found itself in a completely asymmetrical conflict with the subcivilization of fundamentalist Islam. Powerful, traditional armies found themselves at war against an enemy that was more virtual than real. This enemy operated according to a divine religious decree that commanded it to destroy the civilization of the infidels. The enemy sanctified death by virtue of the divine decree, found refuge among the civilian population, operated in small groups all over the world, and constantly sought the soft underbelly of Western civilization. The most important strategic significance of all of this was that the mighty Western armies could not effectively use even a fraction of their military power in this conflict.

In our case, the representatives of this enemy were Hamas, Islamic Jihad, Hezbollah, and ISIS. A very problematic feature of the hierarchy of the subcivilization of fundamentalist Islam was its leadership structure. In contrast to the two-tier system of command of Western armies, whereby the civilian, political echelon made decisions and the military echelon executed them, in the military/terrorist organizations of the fundamentalist Muslim subcivilization the command system was three-tiered, with the top tier being the religious-spiritual leader, followed by the political and military levels. Why was this three-tiered system a problem? Because it required you to deal with ethical dilemmas that were nonexistent in classical wars. You were dealing with an enemy whose religious-spiritual leader was involved in all decisions down to the tactical level, and you were forced to make decisions that you would rather avoid, such as causing harm to clerics or religious institutions.

I concluded that the history of the Israeli-Palestinian conflict and the history of terrorism and the struggle against it were one and the same. The parallel between the two had been burned in our consciousness, even without our having noticed it, many years ago. There were various opinions regarding the historical point at which terrorism had begun to rear its head in our country. There were those who spoke of 70 years of terror, the age of the State of Israel, implying that terrorism had emerged as part of the conflict. Some speak of 120 years of terror, beginning with the arrival of the first Jewish pioneers in the late nineteenth century. This point marked the beginning of the realization of political Zionism, as well as the beginnings of Arab terrorism.

In a world in which human society is made up of the weak and the strong, terrorism is the weapon of the weak. The weak can be the poor, the disadvantaged, or the conquered. As a generalization, it can be said that terrorism is a means whose use derives from economic, social, national, or religious factors, either individually or in groups of more than one factor. The term *terrorism* has a negative and illegal connotation in the eyes of the general public and therefore, when countries (such as Iran, Syria, and North Korea) use terrorist methods or support terrorist organizations, they are defined as "state sponsors of terrorism" who are criticized by the free world, and against whom various measures can be taken.

The conclusion to be drawn from what has been said thus far is that the total elimination of the phenomenon of terror will apparently be possible only in a world in which the dichotomy between the strong and the weak does not exist. As an aside, it should be mentioned that global jihad emerged on the world stage only after the end of the Cold War and the era of the bipolar, bloc system. The global system in the Cold War era was much more stable than the situation of today, in which destabilization has created the conditions that have allowed terrorism to burst onto the scene.

The war against terror involves weighty moral questions, including whether what is permitted to the weak is also permitted to the strong. In a conventional war, there are international laws of war by which the actions of the two sides are gauged. In the struggle against terrorism (asymmetric or low-intensity warfare), no international laws have yet been made, and even the very definition of terrorism is still controversial. The enlightened world views the nuclear bombing of Hiroshima as a legal act of war. The enlightened world also sees the carpet-bombing of Dresden as a legal act of war. Would a similar bombing of Ramallah or Gaza by the Israeli air force be considered justified? Does the gap between the strong and the weak automatically invalidate the use of this means? Is the moral burden that lies upon the strong greater than the moral burden of the weak? Where is the moral line drawn with regard to measures that I—the strong— take to defend myself against the weak?

The international laws of war and agreed-upon international conventions were intended to establish moral and ethical norms determining what is permissible and what is forbidden to the two sides fighting a conventional war. Since to date there are no such laws regulating the war against terror, guerrilla warfare, and low-intensity wars, one cannot automatically expect and demand that the strong side adhere to and apply the regular laws of war while simultaneously forgiving the weaker side for blatantly violating them. And let us not forget that the murky environment in which we are trying to find the "golden path" is one in which lives are at stake. Every human life is of supreme value, and therefore in the kinds of conflicts we are dealing with I am willing to be moral and to limit myself only to the point at which it is beginning to cost me in human lives. This is what the poet meant in the Book of Psalms when he wrote, "The dead do not praise the Lord." In an extreme situation in which if I choose to be more moral I will pay with my life, I would rather be less moral and survive. I think this is the basic and natural instinct of all people.

We Israelis live in a divided and polarized society—there is economic polarization, ethnic polarization, religious polarization, and a polarization of values. Public debate is legitimate and healthy only to the point at which our national resilience and our belief in the justice of our path are being harmed. I want to believe that despite our polarization, we are anchored by one common denominator—that we all aspire to live in a Jewish-democratic state. If this common denominator does indeed exist, then anything that weakens it risks our very existence.

In a society as polarized as ours, should the right marker be the liberal intellectual elite, whose language is understood only by its own members? A resident of Sderot, who may not be familiar with all the nuances involved in democracy and Judaism, knows that he is a Jew, that the Land of Israel is the Promised Land, and that his children risk their lives every day as they make their way to Be'er Sheva. And the people who endanger them are Palestinian terrorists. Period. He expects his prime minister and the IDF to do everything possible in order for his children not to be in danger, without laboriously pondering the specific moral dimensions of the measure that should be taken to remove the risk. The things I am writing may come across as politically incorrect, and could even be painted by some as being fascist, God forbid. It is commonly agreed that the majority of Israelis support a two-state solution, but as long as no diplomatic negotiations are taking place, behavior is determined by what is happening on the ground. And what is happening is a violent conflict, in which, in my humble opinion, the calculation is between being more moral and dying, or being less moral and surviving. The second option is the one that will prevail because it is the product of a human existential instinct. Because I come from the world of practice and not from the world of thought, I try to challenge my views with those opinions that are, as I see it, the exact opposite to mine. In this context, I remind myself that my opponents would say that the real questions that need to be dealt with are whether, after fifty years of occupation, the Palestinian struggle is legitimate or not. Is every terrorist struggle illegitimate because it is defined as such? Can there be a national liberation movement that does not use terrorism? Well, my answer to the third question is—yes! And the examples that immediately come to mind are Gandhi in India and Martin Luther King Jr. in the United States (there may of course be objections to the second example, though I still think it has logical validity). As for the other two questions, I do believe that the Palestinian struggle is just. However, according to my yardstick, any struggle aimed at advancing political goals (for our purposes, the right to self-determination and independence) that chooses to target civilians as a strategy should and must be defined as terrorism. Leaving that aside, if I am asked whether the Palestinian struggle is just, as I said, I believe it is. The only way available to me as a citizen to help civilians realize their goals is through the democratic tools available to me. The problem is that I am writing from the point of view of a practitioner whose task is to deal with problems at the operative-tactical level. This being the case, my role is to ensure the safety of the child of the resident of Sderot, as well as that of the children traveling from Jerusalem to Kiryat Arba and from Ramat Hasharon to Yitzhar; I cannot tell these children's parents that because the Palestinian struggle is just I am prevented from protecting the lives of their young.

I am not suggesting, God forbid, to do to Ramallah and Gaza what the Allies did to Dresden during World War II, but I am also in no way prepared to agree to the definition of the separation fence as a war crime. This is one of the measures that Israel has taken in order to reduce terrorism, and any empirical test will show that this measure justifies itself every single day.

Former prime ministers Ehud Barak and Ehud Olmert will be remembered as having touched upon the core of the conflict. A large portion of the Israeli public has since come to terms with the parameters they and Clinton offered. Unfortunately, the reality in which we find ourselves today (2019) is a harsh one. Therefore, while we must continue to aspire to advance the diplomatic process, we must act simultaneously with a strong hand against terrorism, in all its manifestations.

My view in 2010 was that Israel had only two red lines vis-à-vis the Palestinians: Israel could not renounce, certainly not de jure, its sovereignty over Jerusalem; and Israel could not accept the Palestinian demand for the "right of return."

Regarding my first assertion, relinquishing Israeli sovereignty over the Temple Mount would undermine Israel's Jewish identity and sense of historical belonging, and the justness of the claim that the Land of Israel historically belongs to the Jewish people. This statement may reflect a kind of gut instinct that I carry with me from childhood, which perhaps does not deal with the democratic notions of majority and minority, but it comes from the heart. However, being a pragmatist, I believe today (2019) that even in Jerusalem a solution can be reached on the ground that leaves us with Jewish sovereignty.

Regarding the second statement, I know of only one Arab position on the refugee issue and the "right of return," and that is the "all or nothing" approach. It must be remembered that the Arab demand is for Israeli consent to the "right of return" as a precondition for any negotiations to resolve the conflict. Under the conditions of the Middle East, an Israeli compromise on the "right of return" would destroy it as a democratic state with a solid Jewish majority. I discuss the issue of the "right of return" in the chapter about UNRWA (the United Nations Relief and Works Agency for Palestine Refugees in the Near East).

By the term *red lines*, I mean that even if the parties reach agreements on all of the other issues of the conflict, if the Palestinians do not recognize our (de jure) sovereignty over the Temple Mount, I will oppose the deal. I emphasize "de jure" recognition because within such a framework all kinds of arrangements can be made that will satisfy the other side. Whoever adheres to the belief that the Temple Mount is the Holy of Holies of the people of Israel must be prepared to fight for it and, if necessary, die for it. This, indeed, is what happened in the Six-Day War! Apart from Jerusalem, in my opinion, it is possible to conduct negotiations on any territory in Judea, Samaria, and Gaza. Although Israel has historical rights to Bethel, Hebron, Anatot, and Shiloh, in order to ensure its future it must demonstrate a willingness to relinquish the realization of these rights. Even the Israeli demand to keep control of the Jordan Valley now seems to be up for negotiation. This demand stems from the need to protect Israel from an eastern front that, while not a threat today, may be in the future.

The dragging on of the conflict and the evasiveness of the Palestinian enemy causes harm to our national strength, our economy, and our basic democratic values. It is almost certain, for example, that if the conflict were to be resolved, the Israeli GNP would double, every citizen's sense of well-being would completely change, and Israel would become a country no less wealthy than Switzerland or the Netherlands. It is therefore clear that if relinquishing territories can bring an end to the conflict this concession must be made. Despite all the pain involved, giving up land in exchange for an end to the conflict is a worthwhile goal. And from a different, moral, angle, there is no doubt that human life is worth more than a piece of land. This is all the more true since over time, from the Biltmore conference and onwards, the territory of the State of Israel has continued to expend.

However, because I think Israel will not accept legal Palestinian sovereignty in Jerusalem, because Israel cannot absorb Palestinian refugees, and because Israel must demand that the Palestinians withdraw their demand for the "right of return," the conflict will not end in the immediate future (I said this in 2010). In the near future, the gap between Israel's existential needs and the basic demands of the Palestinians will not be bridged. Therefore, as the failures of Ehud Barak and Ehud Olmert proved, as of 2010 it seemed impossible to reach a permanent agreement. Instead, I argued, a strategy should be developed that would allow both sides to gradually reduce the areas of disagreement between them. Long-term Israeli-Palestinian coexistence that would not be based on a peace treaty needed to be fostered. Only after a decade or longer of such coexistence would there be a chance that Israelis and Palestinians would be able to deal with the fundamental issues of the conflict. At the time of this book's writing, it can be said with certainty that any new diplomatic initiative will require a window of between half a decade and a decade in order to mature into a permanent settlement. I believe that today the chaos that prevails in the Middle East can serve as a window of opportunity for the realization of a permanent agreement within the framework of a regional arrangement that will follow the era of ISIS and al-Qaeda.

Long-term Israeli-Palestinian coexistence must be based on a new balancing point between the parties. Only if such a point can be found will it be possible to shape a new diplomatic reality, not just an agreement, that will last for many years. In order to give long-term coexistence a real chance, another condition must be fulfilled—an economic "Marshall Plan" for the Palestinian Authority, to boost the Palestinian economy and standard of living. Such a program should be carried out by the Organisation for Economic Co-operation and Development (OECD) countries led by the United States and the rich Arab countries, with Israel, too, contributing its share. Its results would need to be seen immediately in order to strengthen the moderates in Palestinian society against the extremists.

Much has been said about the advantages of an agreement as opposed to the unilateral option. An agreement is preferable, of course, but is possible only when you have a partner in dialogue and when there is a willingness to compromise. Since the Biltmore Conference (and perhaps even earlier), the Palestinian side has rejected any proposal for a settlement involving a compromise, and each time it has taken a stronger blow as a result; after each blow the Palestinians become even more stubborn, while the territory of the State of Israel continues to expand.

The Israeli-Palestinian conflict is unique due to several variables:

- The Palestinian side does not recognize Israel's right to exist as a Jewish and democratic state.
- There is no reconciliation between the parties.
- Both sides have claims on the same piece of land.
- Israel cannot use the full force at its disposal when the conflict degenerates into violence.
- The Palestinians, who are our adversaries, are located geographically within us.

Our peace agreements with Egypt and Jordan only reinforce the distinctiveness of the Israeli-Palestinian conflict. The obstacle of the "three no's" in Khartoum was shattered and the era in which peace was an unattainable dream is far behind us. In other words, it is possible, through compromise, to attain peace with the Israelis. The fact that this has not happened with the Palestinians is rooted in the unique characteristics of the conflict, as described above.

Another area in which both sides are lacking is in leaders of the same stature as Begin, Rabin, Sadat, and Hussein. Therefore in 2010

I predicted that the maximum that could be attained was coexistence of one kind or another, from which would emerge one of two types of leaders—either those that would strive toward finding an agreement, or those that would aim to improve their positions for another round of violence.

The unilateral option is not the preferred mode of action but rather the fallback option, a path to be taken when there is no one to talk to, and yet you want to make progress on solving the conflict. The examples of the one-sided options that I myself supported did not yield heartwarming results. I am referring, of course, to the unilateral withdrawal from Lebanon and the evacuation from the Gaza Strip. These Israeli concessions, which did not demand anything in return, expanded the scope of conflict rather than reduced it. Moreover, in both cases Israel did not stand behind its declarations that it would respond harshly to any provocation after the unilateral moves, and for that it paid a price in its deterrent capability. The only case that has proven to be a success over the test of time has been the security fence, which was intended to block the infiltration of suicide bombers from the territories into Israel. The reason that as of 2016 the fence has not yet been completed was the resistance from the extreme Right.

We are all lovers of life and most of us are also peace-loving, and we often ask the question "Shall the sword devour forever?" I am among those who ask this question. But in 2010 I assessed that the conditions for ending the conflict were not ripe. I hoped I was wrong. But, I concluded, if I was not, all we could do was adopt a strategy of continuing to manage the conflict in an attempt to keep it on as low a burner as possible, identify issues, even small ones, on which we could agree, and proceed to take controlled unilateral steps to prevent stagnation. And until we could finally achieve peace, we had to maintain our deterrent capability, our ability to achieve decisive victories, our economic and technological superiority, our alliance with the United States, and our national strength.

To sum up, in 2010 it seemed to me that despite our will and desire to achieve peace, to my great regret, a cold analysis of the current global, regional, and local conditions led to the conclusion that the best that could be achieved is a delicate coexistence, accompanied by efforts to create an environment of mutual interests between the parties, which at some point down the road would hopefully develop into a peace agreement.

Over half a decade passed, and the optimistic hopes I held in 2010 had not been realized. In mid-2016 I found myself involved in another attempt at a unilateral move, initiated by the movement "Commanders for Israel's Security." The movement's plan was based on a realistic approach that recognized that current conditions were not yet ripe for a discussion on the core issues of a final status agreement. The plan adopted an approach that was somewhere between a final status agreement and a capitulation to the reality of terror, international pressure, and boycotts. It was designed to change the situation in the short and medium term and to prepare Israel for possible extreme scenarios—the ripening of conditions for a diplomatic process to resolve the conflict, or the collapse of the Palestinian Authority and the chaos that would ensue. The plan's principal ideas included the following:

- It was an Israeli initiative that was not conditional upon the existence of a partner for peace.
- Comprehensive responsibility for security in the entire area needed to be in the hands of the IDF until a final status agreement was reached.
- There had to be a separation from the Palestinians—we needed to be living side by side and not among each other.
- We were committed to the two-state solution.
- Practical steps had to be taken in the fields of security, civilian and economic life, and diplomacy, to be applied in Judea and Samaria, Jerusalem, and Gaza.

A Parallel Arrangement: An Alternative to
Bilateral Negotiations

By my count, the history of the Israeli-Palestinian conflict began in the 1860s with the arrival of the first Jewish pioneers, full of Zionist motivation, from eastern Europe. The founding of the Hashomer defense organization in 1909 marked the beginning of the armed struggle between the Jewish and Palestinian populations. Since then, the political conflict between the two peoples has not ceased for a moment.

A key insight that applies to the various junctions and milestones throughout this protracted political struggle is that whenever the parties have been faced with a concrete proposal advanced by the superpowers and international bodies, the Israeli side has generally agreed to it and the Palestinian side has refused. A second insight is that whenever the conflict has flared up in violent confrontation, the Israeli side has usually prevailed, but Palestinian obstinacy has become more extreme after every defeat. It is quite possible that this insight is what led to the Israeli saying, "There are no second chances in the Middle East." A third insight states that at every new round of the peace process the Palestinians have demanded that the starting point of the negotiations be the Israelis' last concession in the previous round.

Global politics of recent years have been characterized by a great deal of change, which has created a general geostrategic picture of instability and unrest in many areas, particularly the Middle East. The Soviet Union, which in the 1950s and 1960s had established a status in the Middle East similar to that of the United States, was expelled from Egypt in 1972 but partially retained its status in Syria. Today, Russia is trying to regain a much more active role in the Middle East through military intervention in Syria and the establishment of Russian-controlled land, naval, and air infrastructures for an unlimited period of time. This is a strategy that President Obama chose not to oppose.

There were indications that President Obama was interested in reducing American involvement in the Middle East. If these indications were true, I think his approach was wrong. Either way, the United States cannot afford to abandon the Middle East. Even those who argue that the areas of instability in the China Seas (the Japan-China and Philippines-China conflicts), the Korean Peninsula (between North Korea and South Korea), and the India-Pakistan border are important and sensitive cannot ignore the destructive potential of the Middle East as an almost eternal boiling point and as the region in which the "clash of civilizations" between the West and radical Islam has been most prominent in recent decades. The United States, if it wants to influence and contribute to stability in the Middle East, will not be able to do so without a physical presence—and not necessarily a military one—in the area.

The perception that the main source of instability in the Middle East is the Arab-Israeli conflict, which in the past few decades has been largely confined to the Israeli-Palestinian conflict, is completely misguided. However, solving this conflict could create the potential for increased stability in the region and a significant bolstering of US influence in it, diplomatically and without the involvement of military forces.

For many years, in fact since 1949, the year in which the armistice agreements with the Arab states were signed following the War of Independence, Israel has sought to reach peace agreements with its neighbors and with the Palestinians through bilateral negotiations with each party separately, usually (but not always) with the mediation or involvement of the United States; it has generally expressed reservations or even vehement opposition to negotiations with a pan-Arab coalition. Israel has taken this position for many reasons, though this is not the place to discuss them or to assess whether they were justified.

The bilateral approach has yielded two peace agreements thus far—one with Egypt, which was achieved with the intensive involvement of the United States in most stages of the negotiations, and the other with Jordan, which was attained without American involvement.

On the other hand, attempts to reach a peace agreement or long-term arrangement with the Palestinians, both those that were discussed bilaterally without the involvement of an outside party and those involving the United States, have thus far failed. The Oslo Accords did not live up to the hopes that were pinned on them, as even those who supported them will agree.

Some Arab thinkers have expressed the view that one of the main reasons for the protraction of the Israeli-Palestinian conflict has been the Arab states' desire to keep it "on a low flame" as a conceptual "glue" to unite the entire Arab nation. The notion of Pan-Arabism, which once served as a unifying "glue" for the Arab countries, dissolved over the years until it finally died in the 1991 Gulf War, when Arab states fought against their fellow Arab country of Iraq.

I argue that the Arab states, certainly the more moderate among them, are tired of the Israeli-Palestinian conflict, are interested in ending it, and see the Palestinians as the ones who have mounted obstacles and have adopted destructive approaches throughout the history of negotiations. To clarify this point, I will offer a few examples from my personal experience on this issue in meetings with Arab leaders during my tenure as director of the Mossad (1989 to 1996):

- In a three-person meeting with a certain Arab leader, whenever the subject of Arafat or the Palestinians came up, he would use words in Arabic that are not suitable for print.
- In a meeting with another leader, when I asked him how many Palestinians were in his country, he glared at me and said, "There are no Palestinians in my country, nor will there ever be."
- During many meetings with King Hussein, whenever the name of a Palestinian leader came up, he would let out a despairing sigh. And as I noted earlier, on the eve of the signing of the Oslo Accords, King Hussein told Prime Minister Rabin, "Until now I'm the one who has had to suffer Arafat's wet kisses—now it's your turn!"

- In a meeting with another leader, King Hussein described the Palestinians as "the headache of the Arab world."

The meetings described above, as well as many others, were secret and attended by only a few individuals, without any recordings or written records. Therefore, I believe that the attitudes that were expressed toward the Palestinians and their leaders were authentic, unlike those expressed in documented official meetings where speakers are naturally cautious in their statements.

At the conclusion of the First Gulf War in 1991, during which Arafat supported Saddam Hussein, the ruler of Kuwait expelled, within forty-eight hours, about three hundred thousand Palestinians who were living there. Since then, they have not been allowed to return to Kuwait.

In light of the failure of bilateral negotiations, the time has come to consider a different direction—a parallel arrangement that will include a permanent solution to the conflict between Israel and the Palestinians and that will be achieved through negotiations involving a coalition of those Arab states that have agreed in principle to peace with Israel. The vehicle through which to advance such negotiations already exists, in the form of the Saudi Initiative of 2002, which was officially adopted by the Arab League in 2003 and has since been periodically ratified by the League.

To understand the potential for success of such negotiations, we must go back to a ceremony that was held more than twenty years ago in Cairo. On May 4, 1994, Israeli prime minister Yitzhak Rabin and PLO chairman Yasser Arafat were invited to Cairo to sign the Gaza-Jericho Agreement. This agreement, which was the continuation and implementation of the Declaration of Principles signed on the White House lawn on September 13, 1993, established the self-governing Palestinian Authority (PA), with legislative powers, and the transfer of the Gaza Strip and the Jericho area to the Palestinians. Egyptian president Hosni Mubarak and the foreign ministers of the United States and Russia were invited to attend the ceremony as witnesses.

An incident took place during the ceremony: Rabin realized that Arafat had avoided signing the maps that were attached to the agreement and that formed an integral part of it. There was a sharp exchange, and the ceremony was suspended for half an hour. Arafat stood his ground, and there was fear that the agreement would not be signed. Mubarak, who from the beginning of the incident had not hid his anger toward Arafat, approached him and on live television (!) cursed him in Arabic and told him, "Sign, you dog!" with the whole world watching. Arafat gave in and signed.

Neither John Kerry of the United States, nor Laurent Fabius of France, nor Ban Ki-moon of the United Nations, can stand up to Abu Mazen or any other Palestinian leader and demand, "Sign, you dog!" But the Saudi king, the Egyptian president, the princes of the Gulf States, and others can. They not only have the ability to do so because they are among the financial backers of the Palestinian Authority, but more importantly, they have the moral authority as leaders of the Arab world. The event described here convinces me that were there to be negotiations involving Saudi Arabia, Egypt, Jordan, and the Gulf States, there is a reasonable chance that pressure from these participants would affect the Palestinians' signing. Even if it didn't, it would still be worth a try.

So what is the Arab Peace Initiative that was initiated by Saudi Arabia?[4]

The Council of the League of Arab States at the Summit Level, at its 14th Ordinary Session:

Reaffirms the resolution taken in June 1996 at the Cairo extraordinary Arab summit that *a just and comprehensive peace in the Middle East is the strategic option of the Arab countries*, to be achieved in accordance with international legality, and which would require a comparable commitment on the part of the Israeli government.

Having listened to the statement made by his royal highness Prince Abdullah Bin Abdullaziz, the crown prince of the Kingdom of Saudi Arabia in which his highness presented his initiative, calling for full Israeli withdrawal from all the Arab territories occupied since June 1967, in implementation of Security Council Resolutions 242 and 338, reaffirmed by the Madrid Conference of 1991 and the land for peace principle, and Israel's acceptance of an independent Palestinian state, with East Jerusalem as its capital, in return for the establishment of normal relations in the context of a comprehensive peace with Israel.

Emanating from the conviction of the Arab countries that a military solution to the conflict will not achieve peace or provide security for the parties, the council:

1. Requests Israel to reconsider its policies and declare that a just peace is its strategic option as well.
2. Further calls upon Israel to affirm:
   a. Full Israeli withdrawal from all the territories occupied since 1967, including the Syrian Golan Heights to the lines of June 4, 1967, as well as the remaining occupied Lebanese territories in the south of Lebanon.
   b. Achievement of a just solution to the Palestinian refugee problem to be agreed upon in accordance with U.N. General Assembly Resolution 194.
   c. The acceptance of the establishment of a Sovereign Independent Palestinian State on the Palestinian territories occupied since the 4th of June 1967 in the West Bank and Gaza strip, with East Jerusalem as its capital.
3. Consequently, the Arab countries affirm the following:
   a. Consider the Arab-Israeli conflict ended, and enter into a peace agreement with Israel, and provide security for all the states of the region.
   b. Establish normal relations with Israel in the context of this comprehensive peace.
4. Assures the rejection of all forms of Palestinian patriation which conflict with the special circumstances of the Arab host countries.

5. Calls upon the government of Israel and all Israelis to accept this initiative in order to safeguard the prospects for peace and stop the further shedding of blood, enabling the Arab Countries and Israel to live in peace and good neighborliness and provide future generations with security, stability, and prosperity.

6. Invites the international community and all countries and organizations to support this initiative.

7. Requests the chairman of the summit to form a special committee composed of some of its concerned member states and the secretary general of the League of Arab States to pursue the necessary contacts to gain support for this initiative at all levels, particularly from the United Nations, the security council, the United States of America, the Russian Federation, the Muslim States and the European Union.

Reactions

President Obama was quoted as saying that he might not agree with every aspect of the proposal but that it took great courage to put forward something so significant.

Brent Scowcroft and Zbigniew Brzezinski, who at various times had served as US national security advisers, wrote that the major elements of such an agreement were well known and that the US president ought to declare publicly that the basic parameters of a fair peace should contain the following four principal elements: 1967 borders, with minor, reciprocal and agreed-upon modifications; compensation in lieu of the "right of return" for Palestinian refugees; Jerusalem as the capital of the two peoples; and a demilitarized Palestinian state. In addition, something more might be needed to deal with Israeli security concerns, which a Palestinian government would be incapable of providing. This could be dealt with by deploying an international peacekeeping force, such as one from NATO.

The well-known journalist Thomas Friedman complained that the Arab League did not know how to properly "sell" the proposal.

According to him, King Abdullah of Saudi Arabia should have flown to Israel (as Sadat had) and make four stops: the Al Aksa Mosque in East Jerusalem; Ramallah, where he could address the Palestinian parliament; Yad Vashem, and finally the Knesset—the Israeli parliament—where he could formally deliver his peace initiative.

Ban Ki-moon was quoted as saying that the Arab League initiative sent a clear signal that the Arab world, too, craved peace.

The almost automatic negative Israeli response can be explained by the Israeli interpretation of the proposal as "take it or leave it" and by the fact that it mentioned UN Resolution 194 in the context of the refugee issue. The last point that bothered the Israelis was that according to the proposal Israel would receive the promised changes only after it fulfilled its part. However, it should be noted that in the various rounds of negotiations that have taken place between the parties since 2002, quite a few elements of the Arab League's proposal have been softened. On the territorial issue, the component of land swaps was added, as well as the Palestinian consent to the settlement blocs remaining in the territories under Israeli sovereignty, in exchange for appropriate territorial compensation. The Palestinians have relaxed their position on the refugee issue relative to the wording in the League's proposal, and they have also shown signs of willingness to be more flexible on the subject of Jerusalem. It is also agreed that the Palestinian state will be demilitarized.

In January 2007, the Arab world signaled to Israel that the initiative was not set in stone but rather was a basis for negotiations. On July 8, 2014, the Saudi prince Turki al-Faisal published an article in *Ha'aretz* in which he explicitly stated that the proposal was not a prescription but a template for negotiations.

Discussion

The use of the Saudi Initiative as a tool for advancing a regional settlement will require the diplomatic and intellectual efforts of all parties involved. It will necessitate thinking creatively, "outside the box" of many of the paradigms that both sides have established throughout the history of the conflict. As mentioned, the Israeli-Palestinian conflict is unique in several ways:

- There is no real and reciprocal recognition of the other's right to exist.
- There is no mutual reconciliation.
- There is a mutual claim on the same piece of land.
- The nature of the armed conflict (asymmetric) and the arena of the conflict (the civilian battlefield) do not allow Israel to exercise its full military capability.
- Our enemy—the Palestinians—lives geographically within our borders.

Our peace with Egypt and Jordan only reinforces the uniqueness of the Israeli-Palestinian conflict, and the objective difficulty in finding a solution to it. Of the core issues of the conflict, two are anchored in the Palestinian national, cultural, and religious ethos. These are, of course, the "right of return" and the holy places in Jerusalem ("the Holy Basin").

I propose a symmetrical formula by which the Palestinians understand that the "right of return" is an unrealistic dream rooted in the values of their national-historical culture. In the same vein, I suggest that the Israeli equivalent of this dream is the vision of a "Greater Israel," and that the same logic applies to Jerusalem. The belief or aspiration of "it's all mine" will have to be abandoned by each side. Both parties will have to learn to live with each other's fantasies and refrain from interpreting them as a *casus belli*. Living side by side over time will dull the intensity of the fantasy on both sides. To truly adopt the process I describe here, it is essential that we have leaders of the stature of Begin and Sadat or Rabin and Hussein.

The "Arab Spring" in the Middle East has created instability in this region of a kind that we have not seen since the end of the First World War. The factor that distinguishes this instability more than anything else is the religious component, which has brought the world back to the era of the "clash of civilizations." The reader may well ask, "How can a Middle East in such a state of chaos move forward with an initiative for a peace agreement?" Well, within this chaos one can identify a series of variables, some necessary and others desirable, around which one can sketch a geopolitical and strategic architecture that is worthy of examination.

At the implementation level, there is no doubt that the initiative will require American involvement, and perhaps even a deep commitment. Such involvement is likely to be achieved only after the next US presidents are convinced that both the Israeli and the Arab sides are genuinely willing to accept the principles outlined in the initiative. This persuasion would be achieved not by public pronouncements, but, at least in the early stages, through secret contacts.

A necessary condition for the advancement of the initiative is the conviction of the parties, and especially of their leaders, that its implementation and success will create a win-win situation. Obviously, if any party remains unconvinced that it stands to profit from the initiative, its chances of success will be greatly reduced. I believe that all of the parties involved could benefit from the Saudi Initiative, as I explain in detail below.

The United States

The United States' involvement in resolving the Arab-Israeli conflict would make it a key partner in the creation of a Middle East characterized by peace development, in the weakening of radical Islamic groups, and in the bringing about of calm in the entire Islamic world.

In terms of US relations with Saudi Arabia, which has traditionally been considered the United States' most important ally, American involvement in such an initiative, which originated in Saudi Arabia and in which Saudi Arabia is a key partner, would greatly improve relations between the two countries (which have suffered recently because of Saudi Arabia's fundamental distrust of Iran and its reservations about the nuclear agreement signed with it) and will contribute quite a bit to strengthening Saudi Arabia and the Gulf States as a buffer against Iranian expansionism. An American return to the Middle East on the platform of a new regional order and an Israeli-Palestinian agreement would be a huge coup that would restore the status of the United States as the leading superpower, contain radical Islam, curb Russia's re-emergence in the region, and stop the spread of Iranian influence.

Saudi Arabia

As explained above, American involvement in advancing the Saudi peace initiative will undoubtedly improve and strengthen relations between the two countries. It can be assumed that it will also reduce the pressure sometimes felt by the United States to take steps toward democratizing the kingdom, which the Saudi regime is wary of. In this context, American decision makers should consider the following lesson from the Arab Spring revolutions: opposition to authoritarian rule and the attempt to impose democracy soon lead to radical religious dictatorships. In the eyes of Saudi leadership, what the Americans call "democratization" is likely to increase tribal tendencies, to the point of a return to the situation that prevailed during the Ottoman Empire, before the Ibn Saud family succeeded in uniting all of the tribes together under one regime. Tribalism is a threat that hangs over the Saudi regime like the sword of Damocles, so much so that despite the drop in oil prices in recent years from around $140 per barrel to $50 or less a barrel, the regime has not reduced its social welfare allocations even slightly, preferring to deal with a budget deficit than to risk domestic social unrest.

It can also be assumed that such an initiative, in which Saudi Arabia plays a leading role, would be seen by its rulers as a worthy long-term investment that would strengthen their strategic alliance with the United States and alienate and isolate Iran, Saudi Arabia's main rival both in the religious struggle for the leadership of the Islamic world and in the geostrategic rivalry in the Middle East and the Gulf.

Egypt

Egypt has the largest population among the Arab states. Despite all its efforts, Egypt has not been able to effectively reduce its birthrates, and every ten months the country has a million new mouths to feed. Egypt's sources of income are meager: the Suez Canal, tourism, energy (but in quantities that are not comparable to those of Saudi Arabia and the Gulf States), and foreign workers (Egyptians who work abroad and send money to their families). The majority of the population still live in villages along the banks of the Nile, and the land is worked using methods that are outdated and inefficient. Most of Egypt's territory is desert that cannot be used for agricultural purposes.

Though in 1948 Egypt led the Arab states that invaded Israel with the aim of destroying the nascent Jewish state, it was also the first to embark on a diplomatic process with Israel. In 1979, it signed a comprehensive peace agreement, despite opposition from the PLO, which was recognized by the Arab world as the legitimate representative of the Palestinians.

Like many Arabs—perhaps the majority of them—in the Middle East, the Egyptians, and especially those in the ruling and military circles, view the Palestinians as ungrateful "troublemakers" who do not appreciate the many sacrifices that the Arab nations, chief among them Egypt, have made for them. It can be safely assumed that Egypt would support a solution to the Israeli-Palestinian conflict that it deems as being fair, certainly if it enjoys the support of the two countries on whose assistance Egypt is entirely dependent—the United States and Saudi Arabia.

Moreover, such a solution would help the Egyptian authorities defeat ISIS and their associates in Sinai, as well as to solve the Gaza problem, which, while not their main concern, is a nuisance that they see as needing to be dealt with before it becomes a real threat. A solution to the problem of the Gaza Strip will be possible only within the framework of an Arab and international initiative. This will require the abolition of UNRWA, which perpetuates the Palestinian refugee issue (I will delve into this issue in a separate section below).

Jordan

Since the establishment of the Kingdom of Transjordan by the British in 1927, there has been a conflict between the Bedouin tribes, most of whom are loyal supporters of the Hashemite family that controls the monarchy, and the Palestinian population, which constitutes a majority in the kingdom and parts of which are suspected of being disloyal to the monarchy.

The survival of the current regime in Jordan, which until 1949, and to a certain extent for a few years after, was entirely dependent on Great Britain, today relies on the support of three actors: the United States, as a strategic partner; Israel, which since its inception theoretically represents Jordan's strategic depth and which has a vested interest in protecting it against attempts, especially by Syria, to undermine its existence, as happened in September 1970; and Saudi Arabia, on which Jordan is reliant for economic support. Despite the historical hostility between the Ibn-Saud family that rules Saudi Arabia and the Hashemite family, Saudi Arabia has been financially supporting Jordan since the days of King Abdullah I of Jordan, the grandfather of the current king, who reached an understanding with Ibn Saud that the Saudis would help finance the Jordanian monarchy; this agreement has held strong, even during the First Gulf War in 1991, in which Jordan sided with Iraq while Saudi Arabia was a key member of the US-led coalition against Iraq, as well as the launching ground for the forces that liberated Kuwait.

If achieved, an agreement between Israel and the Palestinians on the basis of the Saudi Initiative would strengthen the foundations of the Jordanian monarchy and would pacify the large Palestinian population living in that country. It can be assumed with a great deal of certainty that Jordan would support it.

In the framework of a new regional order, the first since Sykes-Picot, the Kingdom of Jordan could benefit in the eyes of world public opinion, which would be a major achievement for the country.

The Gulf States

The Gulf States are generally pro-American, pro-Saudi, and anti-Iranian. An Israeli-Palestinian agreement in the context of a regional arrangement based on the Saudi Initiative satisfies all of these interests. Qatar is an exception that aligned itself with Iran when it realized that it could not necessarily rely on the United States.

The Palestinians

Since the Palestinian National Council's 1988 decision to move forward to resolve the conflict peacefully, the Palestinians have found themselves trapped, making progress difficult and even impossible. They feel a commitment to the Arab refugees and their descendants and are unwilling to give up the "right of return," and on top of this the Arab world expects them to be the guardians of the holy places in Jerusalem. Israel, for its part, does not make it easy for them and raises suspicions (some of them justified) among them that it wants to take over additional areas in the West Bank and change the status quo on the Temple Mount.

An agreement that has the seal of approval of the moderate Arab world, leaving the extremist groups aside, under the patronage of the American superpower, and that will ensure generous and long-term financial aid from Saudi Arabia, is the best and perhaps the only escape from this trap. And if the endorsement of the proposed agreement is in the hands of the participating Arab states, the Palestinians will not be able to refuse it.

Israel

Realistic Israelis—who represent the overwhelming majority both of the Israeli leadership across the political spectrum and of the Israeli population—understand that if and when a solution to the conflict with the Palestinians is achieved, it will be based on a combination of the parameters proposed by Ehud Barak to the Palestinians at Camp David II, the Clinton Parameters, President George W. Bush's "Road-map," and the (unsigned) agreement between Ehud Olmert and Abu Mazen, all of which are basically variants of the same solution. The Saudi Initiative is close to these parameters. If Israel really wants to resolve the conflict—and I believe it does—it will be willing to adopt the Saudi Initiative as an effective tool for moving forward toward a solution based on these lines. It should be reiterated that since the basic proposal of 2002, changes have been made in order to appease Israel.

If this move is taken, Israel will regain the support of the world and recognition of its positive contribution to regional peace and stability. Such peace and stability will free Israel from the burden of the occupation, and it will be able to deal more efficiently and successfully with its internal issues, such as social problems, education, health, and infrastructure. Such an agreement will also yield huge economic dividends for Israel.

Roadmap

As someone who served in the Mossad for thirty-two years, I am a devotee of the secret approach to negotiations. My unequivocal recommendation is that the endeavor to pursue a parallel arrangement must, from its inception and up to a certain point, which I will discuss later, be conducted in secrecy.

The initiative for a regional settlement must begin with a meeting between the Israeli prime minister and the president of the United States, the goal of which would be to agree upon the following:

1. Joint participation in the initiative, which will take place with complete confidentiality up until the point that the partners decide to make it public.

2. The initial participants will be the United States, Israel, the Palestinian Authority, Saudi Arabia, Egypt, Jordan, and the Gulf States. Further down the road, and depending on needs and conditions, other actors can be added (for example, Morocco and Tunisia).

3. Each party—Israel and the United States—will carry out staff work separately and in absolute secrecy, based on the Arab League's 2002 proposal. Israel will summarize its response to the proposal and the changes that have been added to it—its agreements, objections, alternatives, red lines, and open questions. In addition to the permanent status agreement between Israel and the Palestinians, the United States will also address issues related to the desired regional settlement at the interpower and interregional level (this stage can be completed over three intensive months).

4. Upon completion of this stage, a series of secret meetings will be held under the leadership of the president of the United States, the prime minister of Israel, and a small team representing each of the parties for a joint presentation of the results of the parties' respective staff work, with the aim of reaching the maximum number of understandings and planning the follow-up processes.

5. Assuming an understanding is reached between the US and Israeli positions, the United States will take it upon itself to persuade or recruit Saudi Arabia, Egypt, Jordan, and the Gulf States (in this order) and, if and when Israel announces that it accepts the 2002 Arab Peace Initiative, to respond positively to the changes that have been added to it in the rounds of the negotiations since then as a basis for final status negotiations between Israel and the Palestinians.

6. If and when the United States succeeds in the aforementioned task (point 5), Israel can then make a public declaration. From

that point on, negotiations can proceed in various constellations depending on the matter at hand, in public or in secret, as necessary.

Of course, this roadmap is only a suggested outline, which would be likely to change as progress is made, but it should be emphasized that the stage of secret talks is a vital condition for success.

A New Regional Order in the Middle East: The Only Way Out of the Deadlock

This section was first written after the release of a November 24, 2015, photo of Secretary of State Kerry and Prime Minister Netanyahu, in which the facial expressions of the PM and the secretary testified both to the deep freeze in relations between Israel and the Palestinians and to Israel's relations with the United States. I thought at the time that our geographic location in the Middle East, which had turned into a boiling cauldron, would suck us into it as well if we did not take preventative steps to prevent it and did not think, in an out-of-the-box manner, about what kind of Middle East Israel wanted—and needed—to strive toward after the chaos died down.

Since then and up to the time of completing this book (in late 2017), the world and the Middle East have undergone many changes and upheavals. But all these changes do not negate the central idea of this section, which proposes that the "good guys" outline what the day after should look like in order to help shape the plans that are being put together. It must be understood that the Middle East is witnessing changes that are similar in scope to the Sykes-Picot Agreement, which lasted for a hundred years!

Back in 2015, the Israeli and international media were full of editorials and opinion pieces by various pundits that grappled with the dilemma between security and morality in the context of the Western democracies' approach to fighting ISIS. My personal, somewhat

Machiavellian view was that if we chose morality over security with regard to the enemy in question, then what we would achieve would be dying with the proud knowledge that we had died as more moral beings.

Russia is fighting ISIS, but it is clear to all that what is more important to it than defeating that terrorist group is its aspiration to firmly establish its military presence in Syria and preserve the regime of Bashar al-Assad. To a great extent, this is also true of Iran, which, in addition to its desire to uphold Assad's regime, aspires to create a continuum of territorial influence from Iran to the Mediterranean (the "Shia Crescent"). In my estimation, the Western democracies would have been capable of dealing with ISIS and bringing about its elimination, even without Russian and Iranian assistance, if they had demonstrated determination and perseverance in this mission.

Achieving the goal of destroying ISIS requires integrated air and ground force activity. The aerial activity is already in place at the time of the writing of this chapter, but it is not sufficiently intensive or effective. The only effective ground activity is that of the Iraqi Kurds, but it is also not sufficient.

I believe that the following elements, if realized, can lead to ISIS's defeat:

- A joint command and control center must be established by the United States, France, and other NATO members (Britain? Turkey?) whose main task is to come up with targets based on all of the partners' intelligence and to send in air forces in coordination to strike these targets.
- Iraqi Kurds, to be made capable of achieving victory over ISIS, must be equipped with armored vehicles and a mobile artillery unit to give them room to maneuver and firepower, as well as coordinated air support.
- There is room to increase the number of American military advisers to support the Kurdish forces.

- To appease the Turks, who oppose any assistance to the Kurds, an agreement can be reached by which most of the heavy weapons supplied to the Kurds will be borrowed and returned to the United States with the end of the campaign against ISIS.
- The intelligence effort in producing targets, with the contribution of the Kurds, who are on the ground, will reduce collateral damage.

However, as important as eliminating ISIS is, it is not the number one challenge of today, nor was it then, at the end of 2015. Today, as then, we must focus our efforts on outlining the geostrategic architecture of the future—if you will, a new "Sykes-Picot model"—that will best serve the Middle East and the world. Once this architecture is defined, it will be possible to derive the optimal operational plan to achieve it. In other words, if a coalition goes to war against ISIS without having a clear plan for the day after the war, the results will be similar to those of the wars in Afghanistan, Iraq, and Libya.

It is true that in the Middle East arena there are too many cooks in the kitchen, from global and regional powers, to individual states both large and small, to terrorist gangs. It is not realistic to hope to find a common denominator that will satisfy all the interests of each player. Therefore, at the end of 2015 it seemed to me necessary and possible to reach a consensus that the most urgent priority was to eliminate the threat posed by ISIS, and that before embarking on this campaign, we had to form the contours of the Middle East as we wished it to emerge the day after the campaign. I will try to do this in the following paragraphs. As of 2017, this outline seemed even more likely to me than it did at the end of 2015.

The building blocks of the new Middle East, after a hundred years of the Middle East of Sykes-Picot, should in my opinion be as follows:

If *the United States* wants to maintain its influence in the world, not only must it not abandon the Middle East, but it must deepen its involvement, not necessarily militarily, but diplomatically, economically, and internationally.

Iraq, which until the Second Gulf War was ruled by the Sunni minority, has become a Shiite state, which, as a result of all of its upheavals, is now under Iran's strategic influence. In the new Middle East, I see a shrunken Iraq, without the territories occupied by the Sunnis and without Iraqi Kurdistan. The United States and NATO countries will condition their recognition of Iran's influence on Iraq on the former severing its ties with Hezbollah and agreeing to an independent Kurdish state in the Iraqi-Syrian area.

The independent *Kurdistan* within the borders of northern Iraq and northern Syria will gain the support of the United States and NATO and will serve as a buffer state between Turkey and the Middle East to the south. Already today, Iraqi Kurdistan is independent for all intents and purposes, lacking only a formal declaration of independence. In addition, the Kurds have constituted the most effective ground force in the war against ISIS and have rightly earned the realization of their aspiration for independence.

Syria, which is a multiethnic state ruled by an Alawite minority and reliant on Russian weapons, will shrink in territory and fall under Russian influence. In exchange for recognition of this influence, the United States and NATO countries will present Russia with a series of demands (relating to Ukraine, the Baltic states, etc.), including that Syria abandon its support for Hezbollah.

"Sunnistan" will be a new country whose borders will be Kurdistan in the north, Iraq in the east, Jordan in the south, and Syria in the west. This new state will be under Western patronage. Its role will be to provide a solution for the large Sunni population in the Middle East, which to this day has no territorial expression. It will also serve as a buffer between the Iranian-Iraqi bloc to the east and Syria and Hezbollah to the west.[5]

The demilitarized *state of Palestine* will be established on the basis of a peace agreement between Israel and the Palestinians, with American and Arab League assistance, as part of the new regional order. This peace agreement will be achieved through negotiations without preconditions but will be based—as nonbinding elements—on the 2002 Arab League proposal and the proposals of Prime Minister Barak, President Clinton, President H. W. Bush, and Prime Minister Olmert. Israel will strengthen its diplomatic coordination with the United States, and Palestine will enjoy the support of the United States and generous assistance from the moderate Arab states.

The most significant event that took place on the world stage from the end of 2015 until the beginning of 2017 was Donald Trump's election as president of the United States. The Obama doctrine is done, Trump's is still in the making, and there is no certainty that a coherent doctrine will emerge. Judging from the nine months that have passed since Trump entered the White House, the United States is being run with no direction, no staff work, no orderly decision-making process, many scandals, and a president who uses Twitter as his primary tool.

In the new regional political structure, there will be a balance between the United States and Russia, albeit not an entirely symmetrical one but one that is acceptable, provided that Trump, unlike his predecessor Obama, is prepared to invest in shaping the new Middle East. The United States will have a lot of room to maneuver vis-à-vis Russia should it choose to reestablish its presence and influence in the region.

Putin's ultimate goal is to gain American recognition of Russia as a superpower, as it was during the Cold War era. It is hard to predict whether Trump will be willing to grant this to Putin. At least some of Trump's advisers would oppose this and would do everything in their power to dissuade him from doing so. However, even given this situation, there is still a lot of room for negotiation between the United States and Russia on the Middle East following ISIS's obliteration. In order to get Putin to agree to the outline mentioned above, Trump can legitimize Russia's status and influence in a minimized Syria. Putin would consider this a significant reward—Syria as a strategic Russian military base in the Middle East with the possibility of direct access to the Mediterranean Sea. Access to the "warm waters" has been a dream of Russia's since the period of the tsars.

In return for American recognition of Russia's status in Syria, the United States and its allies will demand recognition of their status and influence in independent Kurdistan, independent "Sunnistan," and other pro-Western countries in the Middle East. It would be only natural to give the Sunni community in Iraq its own independent territory, especially given the fact that the Sunnis make up the majority of the land already. "Sunnistan" will enjoy the natural resources on its territory, especially oil and natural gas, and will serve as a transit state for energy from Iraq to the Mediterranean Sea.

As for the Israeli-Palestinian conflict, following decades in which the Israeli government insisted on bilateral negotiations (with each of the Arab parties separately), the time has come to try a strategy of multilateral talks (this was discussed extensively in the previous section). The United States has a key role to play in leading the process, and the moderate Arab states—Saudi Arabia, Egypt, Jordan, and the Gulf States—will contribute by persuading the parties to narrow the gaps between them on the road to the final agreement. The Palestinians will have to find a satisfactory solution to Gaza, regarding which the Arab countries involved in the process will also have a significant influence. The resolution of the Gaza issue will be based on an economic solution in the form of a "Marshall Plan" of one kind or another, funded by the rich Arab world, the United States, and international bodies. The containment of Hamas as a terrorist organization will be possible against the backdrop of the new Middle East, which will banish the phenomenon of radical Islamic terrorism.

The foundation of a bold new architecture in the Middle East, following a century of Sykes-Picot, should have the backing of an agreed-upon international body either within or outside of the United Nations, whose sole role will be to turn this vision into a reality.

To anyone reading this chapter whose immediate reaction is a lack of faith, I suggest taking a pause before coming back and reading it again.

UNRWA: "J'Accuse!"

The title of this section is borrowed, of course, from Emile Zola's open letter about the Dreyfus case. I chose this title because I think it inspires curiosity in the reader, who may ask him- or herself, "Who is he accusing and of what?"

Well, the deeper I delve into the Israeli-Palestinian conflict, the more I become convinced that all of us, and especially the Israeli governments throughout the years, bear the main burden for the Palestinian refugee problem and its swelling from about 700,000 refugees in 1949 to about 5 million in 2015. We are to blame for the birth of the "right of return" ethos, which is based on the idea of refugeehood, and for turning it into a major obstacle, perhaps even the main obstacle, to the resolution of the conflict.

Today it is widely agreed that the conflict's core issues are (1) Jerusalem, (2) territory, (3) borders, (4) security arrangements, and (5) refugees. But I believe that the refugee problem, combined with the "right of return," is far more influential than the others. I also believe that as time passes, the weight of the refugee problem continues to grow and become an obstacle to peace that may even overshadow the challenge represented by all of the other core issues put together.

The first time that the problem of refugees was dealt with in an international framework was after the First World War. The destruction caused by the war, and even more the massive border changes, created a serious refugee problem. The League of Nations, which was established at the end of the war, appointed a special commissioner for refugee affairs. This was Fridtjof Nansen, the Norwegian ambassador to the League of Nations, the first researcher to reach the North Pole, a renowned zoologist and oceanographer, and a world record-breaking ice skater with a reputation for being impeccably honest and decent. In his capacity as the League of Nations' high commissioner for refugees, he devised the "Nansen passport," a document of identity for people in foreign countries, and helped them emigrate to countries that were willing to absorb them. More than fifty countries—the vast majority of the world's countries at that time—recognized the Nansen passport, and it helped tens of thousands of people in their efforts to resettle in other countries. Among the famous personalities who emigrated using the Nansen passport were the painter Marc Chagall, the composer Igor Stravinsky, and the ballet dancer Anna Pavlova. Nansen also managed to raise substantial funds to help the victims of the famine that hit Russia in 1919 to 1922, following the civil war. Perhaps his greatest achievement was the role he played negotiating the population exchange agreement between Turkey and Greece, in which more than a million Greeks left areas under Turkish control, and half a million Turks left Greek-controlled territories, all in an organized and orderly manner that also included some financial compensation. For this and his other accomplishments, Nansen was awarded the Nobel Peace Prize in 1922.

The refugee problem at the end of the World War I was dwarfed by the problem that was created in 1945, at the conclusion of World War II. Tens of millions of refugees throughout Europe needed to be resettled, and this was on top of the rehabilitation of the continent from the terrible destruction caused during the war. The years immediately following the war were used by the powers to reshape and rehabilitate the world. It took five years for the United Nations to establish the Office of the United Nations High Commissioner for Refugees (UNHCR) in 1950, which defined the term *refugees* under the UN Refugee Convention, ratified in 1951. According to this definition, *a refugee is a person who is outside his/her country of nationality; has a well-founded fear of persecution because of his/her race, religion, nationality, membership in a particular social group or political opinion; and is unable or unwilling to avail himself/herself of the protection of that country, or to return there, for fear of persecution.*

The UNHCR's mission, from its inception onward, was to resolve the problem of refugees *by resettling them*, and it has indeed succeeded in this mission. To this day, the agency continues to address and solve the problems of people around the world who have become refugees as a result of various wars.

The struggle to establish the State of Israel, the War of Independence that broke out immediately upon the declaration of the establishment of the state, and the responsibility that Israel took upon
itself with regard to the survivors of the Holocaust and Jewish refugees are, I believe, comparable in magnitude to the horrors of World
War II itself. This is the only explanation I can offer to the question
of why the founding fathers of Israel and each successive Israeli government failed to understand the obvious: that the unfortunate 1949
vote at the United Nations (a year before the establishment of the
UNHCR) to establish the United Nations Relief and Works Agency
(UNRWA) was a seed that was planted by the Arab and Muslim countries, using their automatic majority in the UN, with the inention of
perpetuating the Palestinian refugee problem. The seed sprouted and
became a plant, a tree, and then a jungle that may now be impossible
to contend with.

In my estimation, Ben-Gurion's priorities in those days were,
first, the establishment of the state, its institutions and an orderly
government, in the midst of armed struggle and war; and second,
mass immigration to Israel, both as the state's duty toward Holocaust
survivors in Europe and as a way of changing the country's demographic balance. Ben-Gurion saw the resolution of the conflict and the
achievement of peace as a vision for the future but not as a goal that
could be realized in the foreseeable future. This was because the Arabs
did not contemplate any kind of coexistence with the Jewish state but
sought only to destroy it. This was the logic that guided the Arabs as
they applied pressure to come up with a definition for the Palestinian
refugee that was fundamentally different from the definition of any
other refugee; they sought to preserve the status of the Palestinian
refugees and not to solve their problem. They therefore stubbornly
insisted that Israel accept the principle of the "right of return"
totally—by which all those who were defined as refugees, without exception, could return to their places of residence. This is a principle
that is not applied to any other refugee, in any place or in any war.
This demand was also formulated in "all or nothing" terms—that is,
there was a refusal to enter negotiations on the number of refugees

who would be allowed to return, the criteria of those who would be allowed to return, timetables, and so on.

This rigid stance, as detailed below, was convenient for Israel, which demanded recognition of the link between peace negotiations and the solution of the refugee problem. As long as the Arabs stood their ground on the "all or nothing" principle, Israel could avoid dealing with the refugee problem relatively easily. There was a body that would finance the refugees' basic needs without any of the financial burden falling on Israel (which was then poor and struggling to pay for the absorption of penniless immigrants whose number far surpassed that of the local population, a challenge that no country has ever met). Moreover, following the collapse of the Lausanne Conference (discussed below), there was no international pressure on Israel to participate in solving the problem. The refugees became an eternal quandary.

The UNRWA decided, for obvious reasons, to give Palestinian refugees a unique definition. UNRWA voluntarily took upon itself the eternal responsibility to sustain this one group of refugees in the world who did not meet the territorial conditions of refugee status, since they were not citizens of a state but subjects of the British Mandate. UN officials debated and likely argued over the definition of Palestinian refugeehood and came up with a wily definition that I, for one, am not at all certain stands any legal or moral test.

The agency determined that Palestinian refugees would be defined as *"persons whose normal place of residence* [interesting definition! Why not use the term *permanent residence?*] *was Palestine during the period 1 June 1946 to 15 May 1948* [the date of the termination of the British Mandate!] *and who lost both home and means of livelihood as a result of the 1948 conflict. The descendants of Palestine refugee males, including legally adopted children, are also eligible for registration (as refugees)."*

The UN officials who formulated the definition of a Palestinian refugee took the liberty of inventing a new kind of human being—an eternal refugee, both him and his descendants, until the end of time.

These officials saw it as being under their authority to make the State of Israel, too, a "debtor" for this insurance policy. The reasoning behind the definition was that the refugee problem would be only a temporary one because it was only a short matter of time before the Arabs would defeat the Jews and the refugees would all return to Palestine. This was also an attempt to define Israel as a debtor in all future negotiations, which would be conditional upon the Jews' prior consent to allow the return of the refugees. This is how the term *right of return* was born.

UNRWA also granted itself the liberty of defining the lowest possible threshold imaginable for acceptance onto the Palestinian refugees' "insurance policy"; anyone who lived at a certain point on the planet for less than two years, as well as their descendants and those adopted by them, would benefit from that policy until the end of time.

According to authoritative estimates, the number of Arabs living in the territory of the British Mandate before the outbreak of the War of Independence was between 1.3 and 1.4 million. Approximately 400,000 of them remained in the territory captured by the Jordanian Legion (the "West Bank"). About 150,000 were in the Gaza Strip, which was captured by the Egyptian army. (These figures include both the original inhabitants of these areas and those who moved or were transferred there during or as a result of the war.) Approximately 105,000 Arabs remained in the State of Israel, and this number increased to approximately 156,000 after Israel agreed to accept some 50,000 Arabs within the framework of family unification. These figures show that the number of Palestinians displaced from their homes in 1948 was between 600,000 and 750,000. In 2015, however, the "Palestinian refugee club" numbers about five million members, with the forecast for 2020 reaching six million!

In his book *The Birth of the Palestinian Refugee Problem, 1947–1949*, the historian Benny Morris emphasizes that the idea of a transfer never developed in the minds of Zionist leaders as a party platform or master plan.[6] He also stresses that there was never a decision to expel the Arabs. In a November 2003 conference on refugees and the "right of return," Morris stated that the displacement of a large part of the population, perhaps even a majority of the 700,000, was not *outside of Palestine* (i.e., the territory of the British Mandate), but *within* it, and that consequently these persons were not refugees according to international norms or law.

Moreover, he argued, their descendants should not be recognized as refugees. From the end of 1947 to May 1948, the bloody clashes were actually a "civil war" initiated by the Arabs against the Jewish community in British Mandate Palestine (the Yishuv). The Jews had the upper hand because they were more willing and determined. Furthermore, the goals set out by most of the Arab leaders when they instigated hostilities in November–December 1947 and when they invaded in May 1948 were to destroy the Jewish state and perhaps even the Yishuv. The Yishuv feared that that the Palestinians, and later the Arab states, would try their hand at producing a Middle Eastern version of the Holocaust, less than three years after the end of World War II. In this context, it should be remembered that one of the most prominent leaders of Palestinian nationalism at that time was Haj Amin al-Husseini, an avowed admirer of Adolf Hitler, who never masked his support for the idea of annihilating the Jewish people. The commander of the "Arab Liberation Army" which fought in the north, Fawzi al-Qawukji, was also sympathetic to the Nazis and lived in Germany for a period during World War II.

Benny Morris explains that the Palestinian refugee problem unfolded over four-and-a-half stages between 1947 and 1950.

The first phase, from the end of November 1947 until the end of March 1948, took place when some one hundred thousand refugees left their homes *voluntarily*. This exile of choice was a continuation of a similar phenomenon that occurred during the Arab Revolt of 1936 to 1939. It should be noted in this context that almost all the members of the Arab Higher Committee were outside of Palestine until March 1948, as was the political leadership of the cities and some of the villages. And when the leadership is absent, the flock scatters. In the closing remarks of his book, in which Morris details the reasons for the Arab flight during the first stage, from November 1947 to March 1948, in which, as mentioned, some one hundred thousand Arab residents left towns and villages that were intended to be part of the State of Israel in accordance with the UN Partition Plan, he does not attribute to the Israeli side any act intended to force or encourage the Arabs to flee, although almost every day during this period there were clashes between the two populations in the mixed cities, as well as along roads and in agricultural areas.

The second phase took place from April to June 1948. During this period, another three hundred thousand Arabs left, fled, or were expelled. The component of expulsion, though not a policy determined by the Israelis, was the result of the conviction that an invasion by the Arab states' regular armies would take place immediately upon the termination of the Mandate on May 15, 1948, and that until that time everything must be done to prevent the formation of a "fifth column" who would fight alongside them. Neither "Plan D" (see below) nor any other document included an explicit deportation order, either from the territories of the State of Israel according to the Partition Plan or from other territories. However, there was a general understanding that the smaller the number of Arabs in the Jewish state, the better, and "Plan D" left the discretion regarding this matter in the hands of the brigade commanders.

The Arab Higher Committee, in anticipation of the invasion of the Arab armies, urged Arab residents to evacuate women, children, and the elderly from their places of residence. Their encouragement had results on the ground, with many Arabs responding to their call. Thus the Mufti al-Husseini contributed significantly to the mass flight of the Arabs.

The third phase occurred from June to September 1948. During this period, the Israeli government made a strategic decision not to allow the refugees to return to their places of residence. This was a correct and appropriate decision that ensured the survival of the State of Israel (a view also shared by Benny Morris). During the "Battles of the Ten Days" in mid-July 1948, Israeli forces raided Lod,

Ramle, and Nazareth. About fifty thousand Arabs were expelled from Lod and Ramle (the largest expulsion of the war). The reason for this was that these two cities blocked the passage from Tel Aviv to the east and were at the rear of Latrun, where Arab control was the main obstacle to the liberation of the road to Jerusalem. In contrast to Lod and Ramle, where orders were issued to expel the residents, no such command was issued in Nazareth. There the residents who did not flee remained in their homes and continued to live in the city even after its occupation by the Israelis.

The fourth phase took place from October to November 1948. During these months, Operations "Hiram" in the north and "Yoav" in the south were launched. In the north, there were forced expulsions from some places and voluntary flights from others. In the south, there was mainly expulsion. During this phase, another two hundred thousand Arabs became refugees when they fled or were ejected from their homes.

The final phase lasted throughout 1949 and even into 1950. The State of Israel expelled some of the residents of Zakaria (outside of Jerusalem), Iqrit and Bir'am (along the Lebanese border), and Majdal (Ashkelon), some within the borders of the state and some outside of them. These expulsions were defended as being due to security considerations in the context of preventing the aiding of infiltrators and future attacks from beyond the border.

I am a Jew and an Israeli patriot, and I do not profess to be objective, but when I read about the decision-making processes of the Yishuv leaders during this period, led by David Ben-Gurion, I must say that I am proud to be a Jew and an Israeli. In reading these, it is very easy to recognize that the leaders of the Yishuv, some more than others, agonized over each decision concerning the future of the Arab inhabitants of the country, not only at the general strategic level, but also when it came down to examining the case of each individual Arab village—this, though there is no dispute that the Arabs were the ones who instigated the hostilities and violence against the Jewish community immediately after the UN vote on the Partition Plan and that the Arab armies invaded Israel upon the termination of the Mandate without provocation or real cause.

The principal document of the Jewish Yishuv regarding the fate of the Arabs in the Mandate area, in between whose lines one can identify the moral dilemmas involved, is "Plan D," which was prepared in March 1948 by a group of commanders led by Yigael Yadin. Yadin was the Haganah's head of operations and throughout most of the War of Independence served as the de facto chief of staff. The plan was intended to defend the Jewish state that was to be established and the Jewish blocs outside its proposed territory from the expected invasion of the Arab armies after May 15, 1948. It was clear to the leaders of the Haganah that defeating the irregular Arab forces (the so-called "gangs") was a necessary precondition for their future capability to confront the regular Arab armies. In order to control the roads and strategic areas, the Arab towns and villages that dominated them needed to be "quieted"—that is, they had to either surrender to the Haganah or be evacuated and destroyed.

It must be emphasized that "Plan D" was prepared on the basis of military considerations and by military commanders, not by politicians. The formulators of the plan did not work on the basis of any political directive to expel the Arabs of the Land of Israel. The plan determined, for the first time in the history of the Haganah, that villages and towns should be either conquered and held or destroyed. The occupied areas were to be searched for weapons and irregular forces. *If resistance was encountered, the armed forces were to be annihilated, the residents were to be expelled, and a garrison was to be stationed in the village.* In some of the brigades' operational orders, commanders were granted the discretion to "seize or destroy" as they saw fit. At that stage of the war, even before the declaration of the state, the reality on the ground was such that few of the commanders actually had to deal with this dilemma, as most of the Arabs did not wait for an expulsion order—they fled on their own initiative.

Until April 1948, there was no sign of a general policy of expelling Arabs in any of the institutions of the Yishuv. The mass flights of the

Arabs surprised even the hawks among the Yishuv's leadership. Reading the documents from that period, one is struck by the sense of uneasiness felt throughout the ranks of the Jewish leadership, from Ben-Gurion downwards, which reflected a dilemma that contained a clear tragic element—the recognition that for the sake of ensuring the sovereign existence of the Jewish people in its land there was no option but to change the demographic balance but, at the same time, the feeling that all those involved in this matter were doing so reluctantly and with displeasure. Here and there, one can find expressions of relief voiced by the leaders of the Yishuv regarding the Arab flight, for example Ben-Gurion and Israel Galili, who said that the Arabs "made it easier for us" or "did the work for us." The ideological Left, represented most prominently by Mapam, advocated a binational state but reluctantly accepted the flight of the Arabs and the prevention of their return. Ideology and land are apparently two separate matters—Mapam's Hashomer Hatzair kibbutz movement saw no ideological barrier to taking control of the Arabs' lands after they fled, in many cases also taking over the lands of villages whose residents were expelled. Particularly conspicuous is the case of Kibbutz Bar'am, which was built on land belonging to the village of Bir'am, whose residents were promised that they would be allowed to return, which never happened. Most of the commanders who were ideologically affiliated with Mapam's Left did not hesitate to expel and destroy the Arab residents when military necessities overcame ideological considerations.

The question of the return of the refugees to their homes arose for the first time when the first truce came into effect in June 1948, as a result of the "trickle" of refugees returning to their homes and the Arab pressure to enable this return. The government, headed by Ben-Gurion, was forced to deal with this issue in two contexts; the first was internationally, in the framework of Israel's foreign relations with the United States, the United Nations, and the Arab states, and the second involved the relations between Mapai, the ruling party, and its coalition partner Mapam, which called for a binational state.

A compromise resolution was adopted at a June 16 cabinet meeting: there would be no return of refugees as long as the war was in progress. At the conclusion of the war the issue would be revisited. This decision gave Israel some breathing room vis-à-vis its foreign relations and also ensured the survival of the Mapai-Mapam coalition government.

International treatment of the refugee problem began in 1948, in parallel with the War of Independence. Three international actors were involved:

1. Count Folke Bernadotte, the UN mediator, who demonstrated a hostile attitude toward Israel during his six weeks on the job. Before being assassinated by members of the Lehi—a prestate paramilitary organization—he left an interim report in September 1948 that became his "will and testament" and that was indeed honored by the UN and the superpowers. The basis of Bernadotte's report was that the refugees' right to return to their homes and lands was *absolute* and could not be disputed by any party.

2. The United States, via the State Department and President Truman's personal representative to the United Nations Palestine Conciliation Commission, Mark Ethridge, a Baptist from the South who maintained direct personal correspondence with the American president and who supported Count Bernadotte's views and recommendations.

3. The British government, whose representatives on the ground had to contend with the reality of the Balfour Declaration and its concrete implications, on the one hand, and, on the other, a solution to the refugee problem that the Arab states that invaded Palestine at the end of the Mandate period placed as a precondition to any negotiations for resolving the conflict. At the foundation of the British approach was the colonial consideration that obliged good relations and cooperation with the greater Arab world in the entire Middle East over support for the tiny State of Israel.

Bernadotte's statement on the refugees' "right of return" was discussed by the General Assembly on December 11, 1948, and it was indeed treated as his last will and testament, to be honored. Article 11 of the General Assembly's Resolution 194, which was adopted at the end of this discussion, stated, *"The refugees wishing to return to their homes and live at peace with their neighbors should be permitted to do so at the earliest practicable date."*

Despite the clear support for the general idea of the return of the refugees, the decision qualified it by determining that the return was conditional on the "practicable" circumstances that would allow it. This resolution also established the Conciliation Commission, whose task was to assist in the implementation of the decision.

The United States was chief among the Western powers that supported General Assembly Resolution 194. This decision, from the moment it was passed, has been a headless nail of the Arab-Israeli conflict. As Benny Morris points out, almost everyone believed that its realization would be hindered by two factors—first, Israel's likely refusal to permit a mass return, and second, the expected refusal of at least some of the refugees to live under Israeli rule. In early 1949, for example, the mufti Haj Amin al-Husseini was one of the most outspoken opponents of the return of the refugees to areas under Israeli rule.

All those involved in dealing with the refugee issue, including Bernadotte and Ethridge, understood by the end of 1948 that the real solution to the refugee problem was their resettlement in areas held by the Arabs and in the Arab states, in particular Syria and Iraq. However, they believed that it was only just that Israel contribute to resolving the problem by absorbing 250,000 to 300,000 refugees in the State of Israel.

The reality was, though, that the demographic balance of the State of Israel at the time was such that the absorption of this number of refugees was tantamount to national suicide. At the time of the signing of the armistice agreements in the summer of 1949, the population of the State of Israel was estimated at approximately 1 million, of which about 156,000 (15 percent) were Arabs. The absorption of a quarter of a million Arab refugees would have increased the percentage of Arabs in the country to 36 to 37 percent; beyond the security issues this would involve, it would have placed a huge economic burden on the young state, which was expected to absorb over a million Jewish refugees from Europe and the Arab countries in the coming years. (According to Ben-Gurion—see below—such a large minority, part of which was hostile, in a democratic state threatened its very existence.)

The Arab states, for their part, categorically refused to absorb the refugees, out of a complex set of considerations. They identified the Western powers' concern that the prolonged existence of the refugee problem would play into the hands of the Soviet Union in its efforts to expand its influence by recruiting weak and suffering groups to the ranks of the Communist Party. The Arab countries also believed, correctly to a large degree, that Israel's stubbornness would lead to the superpowers increasing their pressure on it, on humanitarian grounds. And a final consideration was that if Israel agreed, under pressure, to absorb the refugees, or at least some of them, the result would be the economic and political, and perhaps military, undermining of the State of Israel from within.

The Conciliation Commission saw it as its duty to try to bring the positions of the two sides closer together. The committee members— the United States, France, and Turkey—tried to persuade the parties to agree to a solution according to which both Israel and the Arab states would agree to take upon themselves the absorption of some of the refugees.

As a result of the pressure placed on Israel by Ethridge, the American representative to the Conciliation Commission, Secretary of State Dean Acheson, and even President Truman, Israeli foreign minister Moshe Sharett wrote to his American counterpart, Acheson, on March 14, 1949, that "Israel would be prepared, under certain circumstances, to allow the return of a certain proportion of [Arab refugees], although this willingness will depend on the nature of the peace to be discussed."

The Americans were not satisfied with this and demanded that Israel agree to absorb a quarter of all of the refugees. This demand was attributed to President Truman himself.

The Conciliation Commission pushed for an international conference to address the refugee problem, as well as the other core issues of the conflict, in order to forge a comprehensive peace settlement. Such a conference was indeed held in Lausanne, Switzerland, and convened discussions in two rounds, from April to September 1949.

Ben-Gurion, in a meeting with Ethridge on April 18, 1949, presented a relatively conciliatory stance. He expressed his willingness to compensate the refugees who were farmers for their lands, to offer advice on how to absorb refugees in Arab countries, and to allow a small number of refugees to return to Israel on the basis of family reunification.

The Lausanne Conference convened at the end of April 1949, and by the end of May there was nothing remarkable to report. The Americans' frustration grew, and at the end of May President Truman sent Ben-Gurion an extremely strong-worded letter. Among other things, Truman wrote that the US government did not see the current approach of the Israeli government as being consistent with the principles upon which US support of Israel was based. "The US Government is gravely concerned lest Israel now endanger the possibility of arriving at a solution of the Palestine problem in such a way as to contribute to the establishment of sound and friendly relations between Israel and its neighbors. . . . The Government of Israel must be aware that the attitude which it has thus far assumed at Lausanne must inevitably lead to a rupture in those conversations," the president wrote.

At the end of June 1949, the deliberations of the Lausanne Conference were suspended for three weeks. Representative Ethridge resigned and made no secret of the fact that his reason for doing so was the inflexibility of the Israelis. This did not improve—to put it mildly—Israel's status in the eyes of the Americans, especially not in the eyes of President Truman, who was Ethridge's patron and personal friend. Teddy Kollek, whose opinion Ben-Gurion greatly respected, wrote to Ben-Gurion from London that the refugee problem, as it was perceived abroad, was becoming the main difficulty in Israel's foreign relations and that in order to avoid a crisis it was necessary to change direction.

While Ben-Gurion did say in internal discussions that Israel must not give in to pressure that threatened its vital interests, there is no doubt that Truman's letter made a strong impression on him. The US administration also threatened to suspend a $100 million loan to Israel that had already been approved—this was an enormous sum in those days, and one that Israel needed like air to breathe. These factors, together with Kollek's warning, led to Israel's proposal during the second round of the Lausanne Conference to absorb 100,000 refugees. The proposal was rejected outright by all of the Arab states, which continued to insist that Israel absorb all of the refugees.

Two other initiatives that arose during the suspension of the Lausanne Conference—and both ended in failure—should be mentioned parenthetically. One initiative was talks between Israel and King Abdullah of Jordan regarding a separate bilateral peace agreement, with Jordan gaining control of the West Bank. The second was the idea of handing over the Gaza Strip—with its 150,000 residents and 250,000 refugees—to Israel, and for this to be considered Israel's contribution to the solution of the refugee problem as well as a way to help open the door for negotiations for final peace agreements with the Arab states. This plan grew more and more complicated as Britain, with quite a bit of American support, introduced all kinds of imperial considerations, such as territorial exchanges. Israel was not enthusiastic about the idea but for diplomatic reasons decided not to reject it. This time, too, the Arabs did the Israelis' work for them—the Egyptian government opposed the idea, and it was dropped.

The government of Israel was subject to heavy pressure throughout the deliberations of the Lausanne Conference, first of all by the bloc of Arab states, which took an all-or-nothing stance, insisting that Israel absorb all the refugees into its territory and that otherwise there would be no progress toward peace agreements. The position of the United Nations was presented as neutral, but in practice it adopted an anti-Israel stance from the outset of the process. The person who shaped this position was Count Bernadotte, who was guided by a set of considerations that he regarded as moral but that lacked even an iota of pragmatism. He placed demands on Israel of the sort that one did not need to be a great genius to understand that no Israeli government could ever accept.

The US administration, from its official representative Ethridge to Secretary of State Acheson to President Truman, believed in the principle of a compromise by which the two sides should be partners in solving the refugee problem. But the American demands of Israel—that it absorb about a quarter of a million refugees—far exceeded the absorption capacity of the Israeli government.

Britain's contribution was negative because of grudges from the past and imperial considerations, which saw the establishment of the State of Israel as contrary to Britain's interests in the Middle East.

In light of all this, the young Israeli government, which was waging a war with one hand and dealing with the absorption of Holocaust survivors with the other, found itself facing enormous pressure from the rest of the world. Because of its refusal to agree to completely impossible conditions, it was losing the sympathy of the international community, to the point that comparisons were being made between the Zionist actions vis-à-vis the Arabs in the Land of Israel with the actions of the Nazis against the Jews during the Third Reich! At home, too, the government did not enjoy a consensus.

While in the process of formulating the agreement to accept 100,000 refugees, the government attempted another move intended to demonstrate that it was willing to compromise and perhaps gain some sympathy from the international community, and especially from the United States. On June 15, 1949, Foreign Minister Sharett announced a family reunification plan in the Knesset that would enable families who were split up during the fighting to reunite in Israel. There was much hubbub surrounding the announcement of this plan within Israel and among its supporters, but the results were underwhelming. By September 20, 1951, about 2,000 refugees had entered Israel under this program; it was a drop in the ocean, and it did not ease the pressure on the government in the slightest.

On July 5, 1949, Sharett suggested during a cabinet meeting that Israel declare its readiness to absorb 100,000 refugees in exchange for peace. Most of the ministers supported the proposal, but Ben-Gurion objected. It was therefore agreed to put out feelers to see if the suggested number would indeed even satisfy the Americans. To make a long story short, Secretary of State Acheson's response was a demand for 250,000 refugees. President Truman, on the other hand, thought (according to the testimony of one of his aides) that the 100,000 offer might break the deadlock. On July 28, Israel officially announced its willingness to absorb 100,000 refugees. The announcement sparked a domestic political storm, with the voices against it surpassing those who were in favor. Once again, the Arabs made Israel's job easy by rejecting the Israeli proposal out of hand and refusing even to discuss it.

Benny Morris concludes that the Arab rejection of the 100,000 offer did not cause Israel much disappointment. In reality, its leaders were quite comfortable with the situation of no-war-and-no-peace. In mid-June, Ben-Gurion described Abba Eban's thinking as follows: "He doesn't see the need to run after peace. An armistice is sufficient for us. If we run after peace, the Arabs will demand of us a price—borders or refugees or both. We will wait a few years." In quoting Abba Eban, Ben-Gurion must have been conveying his own opinion as well. Secretary of State Acheson described Israel's way of thinking as follows: "Israel prefers the status quo. The objectives of the Israeli government appear to be: (1) absorption of almost all Arab refugees by Arab states, and (2) de facto recognition of the armistice lines as boundaries."

On August 3, Israel formally submitted the 100,000 proposal to the Conciliation Commission, where it was rejected out of hand. At the end of August the delegates wrapped up their discussions, and on September 12 the Lausanne Conference broke up and was not reconvened. The Conciliation Commission continued to distribute reports on the refugee problem into the 1950s.

Benny Morris summed up the end of 1949 as follows: "Palestine's exiled Arabs would remain refugees to be utilized during the following years by the Arab states as a powerful political and propaganda pawn against Israel. The memory or vicarious memory of 1948 and the subsequent decades of humiliation and deprivation in the refugee camps would ultimately turn generations of Palestinians into potential or active guerrillas and terrorists and the 'Palestinian problem' into one of the world's most intractable."

The next chapter of the saga of the refugees took place on the sidelines of the 1956 Sinai Campaign. The war began after the establishment of a French-British-Israeli coalition. The goal of the two powers was to regain control of the Suez Canal, the nationalization of which Egyptian president Gamal Abdel Nasser had announced at the end of July 1956. France had another important interest—the weakening of the Egyptian president, who was providing military, political, and financial aid to the organization FLN, which was fighting for Algerian liberation from French rule. Israel joined the coalition because its goals were in line with its own interests. The war began on October 29, 1956, and ended on November 7, but not before the Soviet Union threatened to intervene and implied that it would consider using nuclear weapons, and the United States, which was not a partner in the coalition, expressed its displeasure with the operation. US president Dwight D. Eisenhower demanded that Israel immediately withdraw from the Sinai.

In the days that followed, the Israeli government held marathon discussions on all issues related to the withdrawal from Sinai and what would happen after its completion. Israel was engaging in extensive diplomatic activity with the United States, the Europeans, and various blocs in the UN. This short war created another 200,000 refugees—residents of cities and towns in northern Sinai and the Gaza Strip who fled their places of residence to Gaza and joined the 150,000 residents of the city. (There are those who claim that the number of those who fled was significantly lower and did not exceed 120,000.)

On November 25, 1956, the Israeli government announced the beginning of the IDF withdrawal from Sinai—a withdrawal of about twenty kilometers and the evacuation of two brigades (in fact, more than two brigades were evacuated, but Ben-Gurion preferred not to reveal the full extent of the retreat). At that time, a cabinet meeting was held that opened with a report by the director general of the Prime Minister's Office, Teddy Kollek, on his impressions from his visit to the United States. Kollek said that Israel, which at the time did not have any television broadcasts, could not grasp the enormous influence of American television on Israel's standing in the eyes of the American public. He spoke of the impact of "This Is Israel," a thirty-minute CBS documentary filmed in Israel in February 1956 by the legendary journalist and commentator Ed Murrow; Murrow had interviewed Ben-Gurion, Chief of Staff Dayan, Air Force Commander Ezer Weizman, and Arab refugees from the Gaza Strip, who said, "We do not like Israel, and we did not like Egypt, but we hope that Israel will make a real attempt to solve the refugee problem. Egypt has done everything it can to keep us refugees."

The diplomatic challenges facing the government were (1) the withdrawal from Sinai; (2) the future of the Gaza Strip; (3) the Suez Canal; (4) Sharm el-Sheikh and the Straits of Tiran; (5) Taba; and (6) the international force stationed at the entrance to the Gulf of Eilat.

According to Kollek, in the United States there had already been talk in favor of Israel's remaining in Gaza, not only in circles close to the administration, but within the administration itself. Kollek expressed confidence that if Israel succeeded in prolonging the withdrawal and holding on to Gaza and Sharm for two or three more weeks, then the public diplomacy efforts in the United States, both within the administration and among the American public, would inevitably bear fruit.

During a cabinet meeting, a discussion was opened in which unanimity was expressed regarding the military necessity to control

Gaza. On the other hand, there were grave doubts regarding Israel's ability to assume responsibility for the refugees in the city. When Interior Minister Haim Moshe Shapira, the leader of the National Religious Party, said, "I am very anxious about the prospect of 250,000 Arabs being added to the State of Israel. What would that mean?" Ben-Gurion interjected, "In the present circumstances of the political regime in Israel, this would mean Arab rule of the country!"

When the ministers asked Ben-Gurion to elaborate, he said the following:

> I am strongly opposed to the demilitarization of Sinai [a proposal raised by Minister Shapira]—this will only strengthen Nasser's position against demilitarization. I reject here and now the declaration that we will be prepared to take responsibility for some of the refugees, the reason being that we do not know where we will settle them. In Gaza today we are already feeding them, providing medical assistance, and establishing municipalities, and the residents themselves, not only the refugees, are destitute and in need of our help. Therefore, it is not advisable to rush to commit to doing more than that. In Israel's existing regime of twenty parties, the Arabs will control us. There are all kinds of ideas. For example, Ezra Danin thinks we can offer the Christian Arabs financial compensation and send them, with their consent, to Argentina, but I am not sure if this is possible. Some say that we can settle a small portion of the refugees in El-Arish, which is a possibility, but not before experts examine this idea and come back to us with a well-founded opinion. Some say that it is possible to bring a thousand Arabs into Jaffa, and it is worth examining this idea. In any event, we cannot just commit ourselves to absorbing 300,000 Arabs from Gaza—it's still early.

Toward the end of the meeting, Prime Minister and Defense Minister Ben-Gurion proposed announcing a series of actions already being carried out in Gaza to benefit its residents and the refugees. His proposal was accepted, and at a later meeting held that day it was decided to announce the following:

We decide:
1. To renew the activities of the local authorities in Gaza and elsewhere in the Gaza Strip.
2. To cooperate with UNRWA in providing food and services to refugees in the Gaza Strip.
3. To allow the resumption of fishing in the Gaza Strip.
4. To allow free passage between towns and villages in the Gaza Strip.
5. To provide Gaza residents with essential foodstuffs at reduced prices from government warehouses.
6. To establish arrangements that will enable the agricultural areas of the Gaza Strip to market their produce and export their surplus of oranges and dates.
7. To renew the operation of banks and other financial institutions in the Gaza Strip.
8. To improve the supply of water, electricity and services in the Gaza Strip.

In response to Minister Zalman Aran's question, "What is the point of announcing all this after the UN has decided that we have to withdraw from the Gaza Strip?" Ben-Gurion replied, "In my opinion, there is tremendous value in us announcing this to the world. It does not necessarily mean that the Asian countries will say that the Gaza Strip should remain in our hands. *But it has value, if over the course of time we have thoughts about settling the refugee problem, either partially or entirely!*"

On December 23, 1956, a marathon government meeting was held while IDF forces retreated to El-Arish. According to the original plan, the IDF was supposed to complete the retreat by January 1, 1957. For various reasons, the deadline was postponed. It can be gleaned that the Israeli government had an interest in postponing in order to gain time for further discussion and the formulation of a policy for the postwar period. Another reason for the delay was the renewal of Fedayeen operations from Jordan, inspired by the Egyptian attacks. Dayan, as IDF chief of staff, coordinated the postponement of the withdrawal with General Burns, the emissary of UN secretary general Dag Hammarskjöld, who was not considered to be pro-Israeli in Israel and who persisted in exerting pressure on the Israelis.

Ben-Gurion steered the government wisely and with a vision that sometimes bordered on prophecy, certainly with a rare political astuteness, while allowing space for all his coalition partners to express themselves. But when, at the end of each meeting, the time came to decide on the language of the "decision" items, it was his own views that were reflected. It was rare for him to have to present his proposals for a vote in the government. In most cases, he gave the ministers the opportunity to express themselves and in the end he convinced them to adopt his view. In other cases, the discussion did not even reach that point, and the ministers simply accepted his opinion, even if they had some reservations.

At a meeting on December 23, 1956, Ben-Gurion focused the discussion on what he dubbed "the Gaza problem," "especially what will happen after the first week of January (1957) when we reach El-Arish. We have more time for consultations. There are two more weeks. That's why I wanted Abba Eban, to the extent possible, to clarify the position of the American government, as it largely determines matters at the UN."

In analyzing the Gaza issue, it is worth quoting Ben-Gurion's exact words:

I want to say that on the matter of Gaza I had no opinion for a long time, because I saw both the negative and the positive aspects of all of the proposals. Some say that the State of Israel should annex Gaza. There are those—not here—who say that Gaza should be internationalized. It is now clear that the news of a few days ago that Egypt does not intend to return to Gaza is incorrect. Fawzi announced that Egypt does intend to return to Gaza. One thing that everyone can agree on is that Egypt should not return to Gaza, and we must try to stop it from doing so. After examining the matter closely, I think that the *annexation* of Gaza, that is, making Gaza a legal part of the State of Israel—would be *a disaster for Israel*. We cannot absorb another 300,000 Arabs in the country. . . . Complete UN control of Gaza poses a danger to security. . . . The matter of demilitarization is in great doubt, though it is being discussed in many places. But England and France will not have much influence at the UN General Assembly this year, and the fact that Selwyn Lloyd [the British foreign minister] supports demilitarization does not mean anything. We do not know what the others are saying, because there is firstly the problem of sovereignty. If they demand demilitarization here, too—we have a small country and every bit of land is important.

The Egyptians did not intend to settle the Sinai. It cannot be settled, it is only a military base. We have no land that is only a military base. It is therefore doubtful whether there will be demilitarization. If the UN has full control of Gaza, it will become a Fedayeen base, which will be difficult to fight. Even if it is not the Yugoslav army there, let's say it will be a Danish army, even the most friendly one, it will not be able to prevent Fedayeen attacks, and we will not attack a UN army there.

Therefore, it seems to me that the best way out—and this is not to say that this is already a given politically, but that this is what we should strive towards, which will require taking certain actions—the best option, in my opinion, is *de facto rule by the State of Israel, de facto rather than de jure*. This means that the State of Israel will provide all services, transportation, for example—by the way, at the moment the only way to reach even El-Arish is via Haifa. The food that UNRWA sends to Gaza must be sent through Haifa, and we then transfer it by train to Gaza.

We will have to provide all services to Gaza, and assistance to the refugees, which is UNRWA's business. We will open legal services, schools, transportation services, and police services there. If we put the Israeli Police there—even if they are Arab policemen, and there will have to be Arab policemen there—we can be sure that there will be no Fedayeen operations.

My proposal is that we be there on the ground, but without an-nexation. I am sure that there is no possibility, even if we were not facing increased (Jewish) immigration, for us to absorb 300,000 more Arabs. There is no way for this small and miserable country to take in another 300,000 Arabs.

From there, Ben-Gurion moved on to the events taking place in the Soviet bloc, such as the revolt in Hungary and the immigration of Jews from Poland to Israel. He then predicted: "It is not impossible that there will also be an immigration from Russia. I'm not saying that it will be today or tomorrow. It depends on political develop-ments in the Soviet bloc, perhaps also in China. . . . But we must not rule out the possibility that in the coming years we will face an influx of immigrants from Russia, and if there is a wave of immigration from there, it will be the final redemption of the State of Israel. We must reach four million Jews in the State of Israel. This can be provided by Russian Jewry."

He then returned to the refugee issue:

In the current reality, we do not have the ability to absorb 300,000 Arabs. The annexation of Gaza would make us respon-sible for 200,000 refugees and another 100,000 residents. Among the latter there are many who have no income. I think what we should strive towards, and it does not depend on us, but I think that it is possible, is not to let the Egyptians back there. There is a legal basis for this; it cannot be claimed that this is a sover-eign territory—they [the Egyptians] invaded it. The world has ac-cepted that the armistice agreement is no longer relevant—even

Hammarskjöld says this when he has to make claims against us. This has been accepted. *Egypt has no hold in Gaza.*

In response to a question from one of the ministers, Ben-Gurion stressed that this was not about occupation and annexation but about governing de facto, without committing to a specific period of time. He added:

> What will be with the refugees at the end of the day? I believe we must take a stance. In any case, when I am asked what will happen to the refugees in Gaza, I say that they are part of the refugee problem in general, and that we must find a solution for all the refugees. This solution cannot be found in Israel. The solution can be found only in Iraq and Syria, but it is clear to me that this solution will not happen without peace. As long as there is no peace, Iraq and Syria will not agree to settle the refugees because they are holding the refugees as a political weapon against us. A temporary governing regime can last thirty years or even fifty years. I do not believe that there will not be peace for another thirty years or fifty years, though it is impossible to know.

In response to another question, Ben-Gurion said:

> There are various proposals. For example, [Walter] Eytan, [director general] of the Foreign Ministry, raised the idea that we be given a mandate over Gaza. I don't think this is acceptable, and I am sure others will not be prepared to give us a mandate over Gaza. They will not hand over a mandate on Arab territory to the State of Israel. But there is *de facto rule.*
>
> We may have to agree, and I am very willing to agree, to some kind of UN supervision. A UN representative will be based there, or we will have to send a report on Gaza each year. In any case, I regard *annexation* as a great risk. If I had to choose between annexation and the United Nations, I would choose the United

Nations. So while there are quite real security dangers, they are hypothetical nonetheless, and can be prevented. But with annexation we would receive 300,000 Arabs who would need to be dealt with right away, and this would immediately change the affairs of the state.

Ben-Gurion continued to lay out his doctrine as follows:

For Israeli rule in Gaza to be well-grounded, the economic connection between Israel and Gaza must be strengthened. One link is already in place—transport via train. At present it is impossible to get from Egypt to Gaza by train, but it is possible to get from Haifa to Gaza by train. In everything that we can we should integrate the economic life of Gaza with the economic life of Israel. After all, there is a desert between Gaza and Egypt—this cannot be changed. You can make a road, you can make a train, but a desert cannot be changed. Gaza is inside Israel—Israel surrounds it on two sides—the east and the north. All efforts should be made to ensure that the integration is as robust as possible, because we have time; first of all, we are only going to reach El-Arish on January 7th. I think that we will need to "take the pulse" to figure out how to delay the withdrawal from there, because in the meantime, from November 2nd until today [December 23] seven weeks have elapsed and we are still far from El-Arish. It will also be some time before we get from El-Arish to Rafah. We have a number of weeks. Over the course of these weeks, we will have to take several economic steps that will integrate Gaza more into our economic life. I heard a suggestion that I think is an important one from Eshkol—laying pipes so that there will be a source of water in Israel for the people of Gaza so that they will be able to cultivate a larger portion of their land, plant orchards, and be dependent on water from Israel. This is another economic project that will link Gaza with Israel, and is by no means an annexation of Gaza by Israel, which would turn Gaza and its refugees into Israeli citizens. . . . If we adopt this position on Gaza, we will need to establish a few projects that will integrate economic life and connect a large number of the permanent residents to Israel's economic life. This is something which Egypt cannot do and which the United Nations cannot do.

Several cabinet ministers at the meeting expressed opinions that were different from those of Ben-Gurion. The meeting ended without a decision, but there appeared to be a clear majority in favor of Ben-Gurion's approach.

On February 11, 1957, the government convened to formulate its position ahead of the UN General Assembly's annual discussion on UNRWA's yearly report. This discussion was set to take place shortly after the Sinai Campaign, in the wake of which Israel became responsible, de facto if not de jure, for the fate of more than 200,000 refugees in the Gaza Strip, as well as about 60,000 local residents (other versions claim much larger numbers of up to 150,000), most of whom had no livelihood.

It was clear that the Israeli representatives at the annual meeting would have to adopt a stance, as the Gaza Strip was in our hands and we were being pressured to return the Strip to Egypt as part of the evacuation from Sinai.

Israel's traditional position was that it was the UN's job to process the plans for the permanent settlement of the refugees, including the Gaza refugees. Israel would make a *full contribution* to these plans, though it refrained from going into detail about what this contribution would be. Now that Israel was under pressure with regard to the Gaza issue, the question arose as to whether it should go into specific details and figures regarding its willingness to absorb refugees and resettle them.

Ben-Gurion wanted his government's opinion and so convened the meeting (though he was absent due to illness). The question presented to the ministers was: Can we authorize our representatives to the General Assembly to interpret the term *full contribution* that we use not only relating to *compensation* but also to *resettlement*?

After a discussion of several hours, and after all the participants had asked their questions and voiced their reservations and views, the government concluded as follows:

We decide:

1. The Israeli government grants power to the UN General Assembly to propose solutions to the refugee problem in Gaza by the United Nations in various ways, including in Israel.
2. (With a majority of six in favor and three against) we decide to inform the delegation alone that Israel would be prepared under Article I to resettle a small number of Gaza refugees (not to exceed 15–20,000) within the borders of Israel. The delegation is not authorized to use this number externally.

Regarding the 15,000 to 20,000 people to be resettled "within the borders of Israel," the intention was actually to settle them in Gaza, an area included in the British Mandate for Palestine, which was conquered by the Egyptian army during the War of Independence and came back under Israeli control during the Sinai Campaign.

During the cabinet meeting, the question arose as to whether, in the wake of Israel's reoccupation of the Gaza Strip, UNRWA would cease its activities. The given answer was that the United States would not allow this to happen. This question remains hypothetical, as we know, because Israel's desire to retain at least the Gaza Strip in its hands was not realized. American pressure forced Israel to withdraw to its armistice line with Egypt, exactly as it had been before the operation.

In the period between the Sinai Campaign (1956) and the Six-Day War (1967), the issue of the refugees occasionally came up on the Israeli government's agenda. At the October 29, 1961, cabinet meeting, Foreign Minister Golda Meir reported on her meetings with UN envoy to the Middle East Joseph E. Johnson, who had told her that following his meetings with the parties he had gotten the impression that neither side saw the refugee problem as a fundamental issue. He claimed that for Israel the fundamental issue was Israel's existence. And for the Arabs, the fundamental issue was the destruction of Israel as an independent political entity. Neither of the parties believed that comprehensive negotiations should be initiated on the refugee issue, because the solution to the refugee problem would still not solve the conflict.

Golda explained to Johnson that as long as the Arabs did not change their position on Israel's existence, there was no point in working to solve the refugee problem. Only after the Arabs recognized Israel's right to exist would the latter agree to participate in the resolution of the refugee problem, their resettlement, and so forth. In her explanation to Johnson, the foreign minister emphasized that if the principle of free choice were to be included in a solution to the refugee problem (UN General Assembly Resolution 194, Article 11), which effectively granted every refugee the right to return to his or her place of residence before the war, if he or she so wished, Israel would not be willing to cooperate in the process.

At the same cabinet meeting, Golda also discussed the report submitted by UNRWA director John Davis, whom everyone involved, including the Americans, considered to be so radically pro-Arab that he needed to be replaced. Davis, the foreign minister grumbled, was supposed to carry out a census but didn't, and therefore could not say how many refugees there were, though he was able to say with certainty that every one of the refugees wanted to return to Palestine. He could also say for sure that they could not be absorbed in their countries of residence, because they were farmers and their host countries did not have enough agricultural resources to enable them to be properly assimilated. According to Golda, Davis's reports became worse with every passing year.

Golda also reported an Israeli attempt to enlist a coalition of twelve countries, headed by the United States, to submit a draft resolution together with Israel that would include the following points:

1. All Arab countries had to take steps to resolve the refugee problem.
2. The refugee problem would not be resolved prior to peace negotiations between Israel and the Arab countries.
3. The mandate of the Conciliation Commission was to bring both sides to the negotiating table.

At the August 18, 1962, cabinet meeting, the foreign minister reported that that year, the question of extending UNRWA's mandate was also on the agenda:

> It is increasingly clear that the American Mr. Davis, the head of UNRWA, is completely aligned with the Arab position. Parts of Davis's annual report have already been published in the press, and they read as if they were written by an Arab! Israel is trying— it is not certain whether we will succeed—to recruit other countries to join the proposal that the UNRWA mandate be extended for one year only, and that the General Assembly instruct the UN Secretariat to examine all of UNRWA's work methods. There are objective people around the world who have researched this and have come to the conclusion that it is unheard of for it to take 14–15 years to take care of this issue, and it seems as if the main goal of this organization is to preserve its existence, and to this end it must continue to maintain the refugee problem.

Golda noted that Israel was not demanding that UNRWA be dismantled or that it stop being funded but was claiming that

> what the organization is doing has no precedent in the world. After the First World War there were many millions of refugees, but today there is no trace of this refugee problem. Somehow the issue was resolved. There were all kinds of constructive steps taken, both small and large. Here it is an eternal refugee problem, and a great deal of capital has been poured into it every year for

14 years. No one knows how many refugees there are. Someone can own a large business and still hold a refugee card that entitles him to support. Someone could have died years ago, but still be entitled to a food allowance. If nothing is done to correct this, we will be informed that this year the number of refugees is 1.2 million refugees, and next year they will announce that it has reached 1.3 million, and so on. The head of the organization and its people are mostly Arabs. They have no interest at all in moving things forward.

Finance Minister Levi Eshkol, after listening to Golda's remarks, responded that in his opinion Israeli policy should be to cope directly with the matter, working toward a permanent solution, contrary to the opinion of many Israelis who supported the maintaining of the status quo. According to Eshkol, if there was going to be an "explosion," this was the time. The longer the situation carried on, the harder it would become for Israel, he claimed. "We let the cobra get warm beneath our lap," he said, and expressed his hope that at least someone would investigate and study the matter.

At the cabinet meeting on November 29, 1964, Abba Eban, in his capacity as deputy prime minister, reported that the refugee clause would "catch fire," as he put it, in the General Assembly in January 1965. A worrying new development was that the Arabs were demanding recognition of the delegation to the annual discussion not as a refugee delegation but as a Palestinian delegation; there was a bloc of twenty Arab and Muslim countries that supported this demand. But there was also a ray of hope in Abba Eban's report. In a conversation he had with the person responsible for the UN in the US Department of State, two points were raised. The first was the impatience of those in the State Department involved in the refugee issue with UNRWA's rampant malpractices and manipulations. They were urging the new UNRWA director, Dr. Michelmore, to tighten procedures. The removal of the deceased from the list of refugees was only the first demand of him; he was also under pressure to greatly reduce the number of refugees, removing not only those who had died but also those who had been absorbed into the economies of their countries of residence. The second point was that more and more people within the State Department were in agreement that the Arabs were using the refugees as a pawn and that UNRWA was providing them with international support. The State Department's conclusion was that the humanitarian dimension of the refugee problem had been exaggerated.

On June 17 and 19, 1967, a few days after the end of the Six-Day War, two—in my opinion pivotal—government meetings were held that dealt with the refugee issue. In hindsight, these meetings can be seen as a watershed between the nineteen years after the War of Independence and the era that began with the Six-Day War and that continues to this day.

The protocols of these meetings show the balance of power and influence around the table as follows. On one side was a group of ministers—Pinchas Sapir, Zalman Aran, Eliyahu Sasson, Mordechai Bentov, and Yisrael Yeshayahu—who viewed this as the ideal time for Israel to come up with an initiative to solve the refugee problem once and for all, from a position of power. Opposing them was a single minister—Defense Minister Moshe Dayan—who categorically rejected their approach and claimed that, since Israel was in a position of power, the problem it was facing was a *territorial problem and not a refugee problem*—namely, how we could preserve the new borders we had attained in this war.

Between the two camps stood Prime Minister Eshkol, who hardly uttered a word and certainly did not lead the discussion or direct it toward a decision. History has proven that Dayan's position was the one that prevailed in this debate. I leave it to the reader to decide, with the wisdom of hindsight, whether that position was the right one.

The basis for the discussion in the government was a draft document that was prepared in advance in order to assist the government in making a decision regarding the stance Israel would take in the discussion in the General Assembly, which was supposed to submit its recommendations to the Security Council. During the discussion, various numbers were waved around by some of the ministers in order to illustrate the scope of the problem. There was no consensus about the numbers, but it was generally assumed that the number of Jews in the State of Israel in 1967 was 2.3 million, and the number of Arabs in the territories under Israeli control was 1.5 million. If these figures were correct, then the demographic balance between the two populations should have worried, to say the least, the participants in the discussion.

Here are some excerpts from Dayan's remarks at these meetings:

The refugees are not a problem that belongs to this war. They were not created in this war and they will not be resolved by the question now facing the General Assembly and the Security Council. Any attempt to tie the refugee problem to the question we want to answer now [the question of territory] will only complicate things and is not practical. We have conquered up to a certain point and they are now demanding that we withdraw to the armistice lines. This is the subject of discussion. If we say that there is a refugee issue, it will only raise the problem, and it will not relieve us of the pressure on us to withdraw. When the Egyptians were in the Gaza Strip, UNRWA controlled the refugee camps. We got the territory from Egypt; we did not get the refugee camps from UNRWA. At the General Assembly, we don't need to jump the gun and discuss the refugee problem. Our position should be that at this stage we are not publicly proposing any plans to settle the refugees. We must investigate and check, but we are not announcing plans for the settlement of refugees. If we do then we are making ourselves responsible for the problem.

Dayan proposed the following formula:

Peace—or we remain on the borders we attained in the war. We mustn't intertwine, certainly not at this point in time, ahead of the first discussion in the UN, other issues, including the refugees. . . . As for the refugee problem, responsibility for the Arab refugees, both in the Gaza Strip and the West Bank, will remain in the hands of UNRWA, in accordance with the agreement reached between the Government of Israel and UNRWA representatives. This was a tremendous achievement for us, for UNRWA to agree to continue to take this issue on as its responsibility. Here we are, twenty years after the War of Independence, and we have ceased to be responsible for this matter called the refugees. . . . UNRWA is formally responsible for them. God forbid should we try to change one thing about this arrangement and accept responsibility while there is no solution, when UNRWA is agreeing to continue to bear this responsibility.

■ ■ ■

Whoever came up with the idea of a special refugee agency for the Palestinian refugees, whoever conceived of the notion of subordinating this agency to the UN General Assembly, whoever formulated the definition of Palestinian refugeehood, whether it was one person or the collective brainchild of a group of people—was a genius.

In 1949, it would have had to be a genius, with the ability to see into the future, to construct a diplomatic architecture that would perpetuate a conflict between two peoples. The reader may glean that according to my analysis, in the eyes of the Arabs at the time, the conflict was and would always be a zero-sum game. First, they defined their defeat in the War of Independence as "Nakba," which was the associative counterpart of the Holocaust, and by doing so attempted to create a conceptual symmetry between the two peoples—the Jews and the Palestinians. The connotation of such an association was that if the world saw the Holocaust as a reason and justification for a Jewish state, then it must recognize the need to establish a Palestinian state after the "Nakba." And since the two peoples had claims over the same territory, and in the first round of the war over this territory the

Palestinians lost, it was necessary to build a m
which the Palestinians' "War of Independence"
until they could claim victory. And the victory, acc
estinians, was the elimination of Jewish existence
rael and the establishment of a Palestinian state u.
mechanism that the Arabs built was UNRWA, together with a definition of Palestinian refugeehood that was different from that of all
other refugees of all the wars that had taken place on the planet since
World War II. Later, beginning in the early 1960s, when an independent Palestinian national consciousness began to emerge, the Palestinian organizations, headed by the PLO, adopted these claims.

The perception of perpetual war until final victory is achieved is
rooted in the Islamic faith. When there is a vision or a dream (for example, the Islamic caliphates), its realization sometimes involves innumerable rounds of struggles and wars. The achievement required
in each round of war is not necessarily a complete victory. Survival is
enough of an achievement, and a victory in itself. Why is this? Because survival leaves hope for the next round and the one after that,
until the ultimate victory is achieved.

By definition, Palestinian refugeehood opposes the principle of
resettlement. Moreover, it recognizes the descendants of refugees
(including those who have been legally adopted) as refugees in every
respect. This is how the number of refugees swelled from 700,000 in
1949 to more than 5 million in 2018, even though about 4.5 million
of this figure were not born in the territory under dispute.

The concept of Palestinian refugeehood has, from its inception,
included the principle of the "right of return." This principle has become a stumbling block to any attempt to negotiate a diplomatic solution to the conflict. How so? Since the War of Independence in 1948
and to this day, the true positions of the parties do not even allow
them to begin talks. The Palestinians insist on the precondition of Israel's recognition of the "right of return," which according to the Palestinian understanding means the right of *all* refugees to return to
the Land of Israel. Israel's position is that the negotiations must take

ce without any preconditions. Israel undertakes to "contribute its share" to resolving the refugee problem within the framework of a peace agreement. Prime Minister Netanyahu went one step further in increasing the gap between the two sides' opening positions in negotiations with his demand that the Palestinians recognize Israel's right to exist as the state of the Jewish people. Such Palestinian recognition would imply the renunciation of the "right of return," as the Palestinians interpret it.

The UNHCR was established in 1950. UNRWA was established on December 8, 1949, and began operating on May 1, 1950. Both are under the umbrella of the UN. Why did UNRWA continue to operate after the establishment of the second agency? The answer to this is that the Arab League countries in the UN, with the help of the bloc of Muslim states and the nonaligned bloc, insisted on the continued existence of UNRWA as a separate entity that would perpetuate the idea of the "right of return." The only country in the United Nations that could have intervened was the United States. The question is, Why didn't it?

The United States' vote on the establishment of the State of Israel was a last-minute miracle; a Jewish friend of President Truman's succeeded in influencing him, against the advice of the State Department, Secretary of State Marshall, and others who argued that a Jewish state in the Middle East would not survive. When the proposal to establish UNRWA was discussed in the United Nations, the Americans saw no reason to object to it, especially given the continued American dependency on Saudi oil, as well as the United States' alliance with Britain, whose imperial considerations dictated support for the Arabs rather than the State of Israel.

In addition, the truth is that nowhere is there even a hint that there was any Israeli initiative (or that one was even considered) to persuade the United States to stop the establishment of UNRWA and/or influence the definition of Palestinian refugeehood. This was because it was convenient for Israel for foreign money to free it from the heavy burden involved in providing for Palestinian refugees.

We have already seen that international treatment of the refugee problem began in 1948, while the War of Independence was being waged in full force on all fronts. On the American side, the parties dealing with this issue were the State Department and President Truman's representative to the Conciliation Commission established by the UN, Mark Ethridge—a personal friend of Truman's who corresponded with him directly and who supported the views of Count Bernadotte, who displayed a hostile attitude toward Israel. The US was one of the first to come out in support of UN General Assembly Resolution 194, which was adopted on December 11, 1948, and whose Article 11 recognized and established the "right of return." This resolution has since become a major stumbling block to resolving the Arab-Israeli conflict.

The first Israeli concession on the return of refugees to the State of Israel was made in March 1949, the result of pressure by Ethridge, Secretary of State Acheson, and President Truman. Israel's willingness in principle to make concessions was never translated into action because of the US demand that the Israeli government absorb a quarter of all of the refugees (this figure was attributed to President Truman himself). As mentioned earlier, in late May 1949, President Truman wrote a very strongly worded letter to Ben-Gurion, in which he stated, "The US Government does not regard the present attitude of the Israeli Government as being consistent with the principles upon which US support has been based. The US Government is gravely concerned lest Israel now endanger the possibility of arriving at a solution of the Palestine problem in such a way as to contribute to the establishment of sound and friendly relations between Israel and its neighbors. . . . The Government of Israel must be aware that the attitude which it has thus far assumed at Lausanne must inevitably lead to a rupture in those conversations."

In the 1956 Sinai Campaign, the Americans feared that the coalition of Britain, France, and Israel could lead the Soviets to intervene on behalf of Egypt, and that this in turn was liable to lead to a nuclear confrontation between the United States and the Soviet Union. This concern explains Eisenhower's uncompromising position, which demanded that Ben-Gurion withdraw immediately from all of the territories it had conquered, down to the last centimeter (or inch).

Developments during the Sinai Campaign made it clear to Ben-Gurion that Britain and France were at best second-rate powers and that the final decision on any matter was in the hands of the United States. Therefore, throughout the government's discussions on the withdrawal from Sinai, Ben-Gurion assigned Abba Eban, the Israeli ambassador to Washington and the UN, the responsibility for clarifying directly what America's exact position was on all matters related to the subject.

At the end of the Six-Day War, Israel had the opportunity to take unilateral measures to find one solution or another to the refugee problem. It didn't use this opportunity. As discussed above, Defense Minister Moshe Dayan, who steered Israeli policy on the territories occupied in the war, declared that Israel should focus on preserving the territories it had captured and that the other issues were trivial. This "sit and do nothing" policy, which left the issue of refugees in UNRWA's hands, has remained unchanged to this day.

Toward the end of 2005, Israel gave in to heavy American pressure and agreed to hold general elections in the territories, although many claimed that these would lead to an unprecedented strengthening of Hamas. The elections were held in January 2006, and the warnings proved to be well founded. A year and a half later, in June 2007, Hamas took control of Gaza, systematically eliminating Fatah members in the Gaza Strip. Hamas immediately began its campaign to take control of UNRWA, and that same year, in the elections for the UNRWA workers' union, out of the twenty-seven members of the union, twenty-five Hamas members were elected.

UNRWA employs thirty thousand people in the territories, about ten thousand of whom are in Gaza. UNRWA's annual budget is about $1.25 billion, and the United States contributes a fifth ($250 million) of that amount. I do not risk slander if I say that the US government, which initiated legislation against funders of terrorist organizations, has itself contributed to this day about $16.5 billion to an organization that has become a terrorist tool. If the US government should request it, Israel would be able to present it with an irrefutable case full of legal evidence that UNRWA is today an organization operated by Hamas.

Even putting aside the issue of terrorism, it is hard for me to believe that US president Donald Trump would be indifferent to a waste of $250 million a year that is clearly intended, not to solve a problem, but rather to perpetuate the same problem and inflate it more and more each year. Many believe that the Palestinians have moderated their position on the "right of return" of refugees and will eventually agree to the return of a symbolic number of refugees to the State of Israel, with the rest receiving financial compensation. I doubt this, because of the cumulative weight of all of the following considerations:

- There is no group of refugees in the world that has received as sweeping a definition as the Palestinian refugees. This definition has increased the number of refugees from seven hundred thousand in 1948 to five million in 2016.
- There is no other group of refugees in the world whose full right to return to their homeland has been recognized by the UN (see General Assembly Resolution 194 III). This resolution created the ethos of the "right of return."
- The Palestinian leadership has done everything, from 1947 to this day, to maintain the refugees as such. In other words, the leadership has condemned millions of Palestinians to give up their lives, their futures, their pride as human beings, and their standard of living in order to preserve and nurture their status as refugees.
- Since 1947, the Palestinian leadership has adopted the approach of *all*, that is, Israel must agree to accept all the refugees into its territory as a precondition for the opening of diplomatic negotiations, or *nothing*, that is, the Palestinians will not agree to a diplomatic solution.

- The Palestinian leadership has built an education system that sanctifies the values of refugeehood and hatred for Israel.
- The Palestinian leadership created and maintained all of the above knowing that objectively there is no chance that Israel will agree or be able to absorb five million refugees.

After sixty years of presenting and nurturing this twisted version of reality to millions of refugees, can the Palestinian leadership abandon it and agree to the return of only a few thousand refugees to the State of Israel? I doubt it.

However, there is no need to wait for the Palestinian leadership to take this step, which will almost certainly never happen. My view is that the Israeli government should urge the United States, UNRWA's main sponsor, to reconsider its position vis-à-vis this organization, which carries the main responsibility for perpetuating the refugee problem and which is ruled by Hamas, a terrorist organization by any definition, including that of the United States.

The change of power in the United States opened the door to a drastic change with regard to the refugee issue. President Trump has shown much sensitivity on the subject of terrorism. If the Israeli government presents him with the data laid out in this chapter and suggests that he fundamentally change the policy of the United States on the refugees, there is a good chance that he will be open to the recommendation that the responsibility for Palestinian refugees be transferred from UNRWA to the UNHCR. Events in Syria have created millions of refugees who are treated by the UNHCR. Today, the only party that has an interest in the continued existence of UNRWA is Hamas. There is no reason for the United States, Israel, the Western countries, and the world in general to serve this Hamas interest.

CHAPTER FIVE

WARS

The Yom Kippur War—October 6, 1973

In the summer of 1972, my family and I returned to Israel after seven years of service abroad in two different countries. Upon my return, I realized that I had become unfamiliar with the office, and I felt like a fish out of water. I was appointed to a job that did not meet my expectations. It consisted mainly of "paper-pushing"—I was providing intelligence and administrative services from the "desk" at headquarters to the branches it was responsible for abroad. In late 1972, I informed the unit's commander that I was not ready to continue in this position and requested that I be offered another job, even in another unit. I was only thirty-three years old at the time, and I told myself that unless I was offered something interesting and challenging I would consider retiring from the Mossad. The agreement that was reached was that my name would be put forward for the summer 1973 discussions on job assignments, as a possible candidate for the role of head of the Mossad's Operations Directorate; until then, I would spend a few months in Kurdistan as the head of our mission there.

In mid-1973, I returned to Israel and was indeed appointed head of the Operations Directorate. Taking on this position meant that I was going from being in charge of certain issues in a single unit to being responsible for matters that were pertinent to the entire institution, inter alia, as the Mossad's liaison to the other agencies in the intelligence community. The new role also brought me closer, both physically and professionally, to the bureau of then-Mossad director Major General (res.) Zvi Zamir.

In my new position, I participated as an observer in the weekly briefing by the head of Military Intelligence. This forum was led by the head of MI at the time, Major General Zeira; by his side were his assistant for research and the heads of the various divisions of MI's research department (at that time it was still a department). There was a weekly brief by which each sector head of regional department reported on the main developments in his sphere of responsibility and suggested points and issues that needed monitoring. The assistant to the head of MI for research gave his comments on these remarks, and the head of MI then summed up the discussion and dictated the EEI (Essential Elements of Information) for intelligence gathering in the coming weeks. I would write down the main points brought up during the briefing and send a concise report to the director of the Mossad to keep him updated.

Another task I was responsible for was to write, every week, a summary of the "political review" that was given every week at the Mossad Unit Heads' Forum (Rasha, Hebrew acronym for heads of units), headed by the Mossad director. The political review was given by the forum's "senior intellectuals"; in my time, these were David (Dave) Kimche and Yitzhak Oron. They based their reviews on the intelligence collected by Mossad sources, on MI's intelligence bulletins, only a small portion of which were distributed to the Mossad, and on information received from friendly services. The Mossad was then an intelligence-gathering agency without a research body. Intelligence wisdom was relatively poor.

At that time, the head of Military Intelligence had the supreme responsibility of being the single national assessor of intelligence; under his direct command were four intelligence-gathering agencies. The head of MI had at his disposal what was then the largest research body of its kind in Israel. The Mossad, at that time, dealt exclusively with intelligence gathering and special operations (any activity on behalf of the state that no other official body apart from the Mossad had the capacity to carry out).

Moreover, the Mossad's intelligence gathering was carried out under the express direction of MI. Within Mossad's HUMINT division was a section of MI called Modi'in 11, staffed by an officer with the rank of lieutenant colonel, whose job was to receive from MI all of the EEI (briefings about the information requested from one source or another) and to pass them on to specific point people in the HUMINT division, down to the level of which EEI to direct to which source! This shows how familiar the MI representative to the Mossad was with each and every source. This officer was also the first to see the raw intelligence material that came in and was privy to all of the secrets of the Mossad's sources. Later, another section, Modi'in 12, whose function was identical to Modi'in 11's, was established within the unit dealing with friendly intelligence services.

A periodic assessment of the Mossad's sources was carried out by MI research officers—the consumers of the material. These officers were regularly involved in the investigation of Mossad sources abroad and in talks with analysts from the friendly intelligence services. The Mossad disseminated all the information it collected to MI, without exception. On the other hand, Military Intelligence distributed the products of its research and evaluation to the Mossad selectively—very selectively. The choice of what to disseminate appeared to be almost arbitrary and was always explained as being due to reasons of "information security." As a result of the situation I have described, in practice the Mossad was prevented from dealing with research and evaluation, even with regard to the information collected by itself, and certainly with regard to information gathered by the intelligence community.

The analysis I propose in this chapter regarding the progression of the early warning of the Yom Kippur War challenges the prevailing thesis of the public and media discourse on this war. In my analysis, the early warning of the Yom Kippur War was a rolling, continuous event that had an ample basis in intelligence collected over the years, which reached its peak on the eve of the outbreak of the war.

In my capacity as a head of the Operations Directorate, my attention was directed mainly toward the activity of the Mossad's operational units and less, if at all, toward the intelligence products of this activity. However, I remember that beginning in mid-1973, especially in the forum of the Mossad's unit heads, more and more surprise was expressed about the fact that Military Intelligence did not agree with, or take seriously, the growing mass of intelligence from the Mossad's sources that indicated a deterioration toward war. At least some of the heads of the units around the table believed that Military Intelligence must have had other serious sources that contradicted Mossad intelligence. The feeling of those in the forum was that we needed to focus on how to bring higher-quality intelligence without engaging in the research and evaluation of this intelligence, which was not included in the Mossad's mandate and which it therefore did not have the professional tools to carry out.

The director of the Mossad at that time was Zvi Zamir. He was more in tune than others to the research and evaluation significance of Mossad intelligence because of his military background, in particular the years in which he served as GOC Southern Command. In addition, since he had also served as the head of the IDF's training division, he was able to read the intelligence materials from Egypt and Syria, which dealt with strategic issues, combat doctrine, training, and exercises, with an authoritative eye, and he interpreted them as preparations for war. Moreover, Zamir used to meet selectively, depending on the matter, with the Mossad's top sources in various arenas in order to hear from them directly. He would question them, brief them, and hear the intelligence straight from their mouths, without any "filters"; this enabled him to formulate his opinion according to the net intelligence, without any background noise. We were always taught the adage "It is not forbidden for an intelligence officer to use his intelligence." Zvi Zamir did exactly this by examining and integrating the intelligence that was coming in from a variety of Mossad sources—all of which pointed to war.

I remember that on Friday, October 5, 1973, I returned home just before the beginning of the Sabbath on the eve of Yom Kippur. When I got home, I asked my wife to pack my army backpack for me, because the next morning I would be going off to join the war. I made this statement on the basis of an extraordinary mass of intelligence alerts that had come in from various Mossad sources over the last week. *None of these alerts came from Ashraf Marwan*, though Marwan, son-in-law of former president of Egypt Gamal Abd-El Nasser, and one of the closest aides to Nasser's successor, President Sadat, was one of the best sources of the Mossad. Marwan's last warning came on September 8, 1973, and the next time he reported in was at 21:30 on October 4, in a telephone conversation in which he mentioned the code for war for the first time. On October 6, at 02:55, the office of the head of the Mossad informed the head of Military Intelligence that about half an hour earlier the Mossad had received the code word for war from the source. I will elaborate on the further unfolding of the early warning later in this chapter.

In the late morning of Saturday, October 6, 1973, I was in contact once an hour with the assistant to the head of MI's intelligence-gathering department to hear "firsthand" about what was happening on the front. At 12:00, my interlocutor reported to me that our sentries along the Suez Canal had reported that the earthen ramparts along the Canal had been breached with water cannons. "And what is your assessment?" I asked him. His response was, "Our assessment remains that this activity is part of the Egyptian military exercise!" I said goodbye to him and added, "See you after the war." I kissed my wife and children, got into my car, and drove to my unit and the Syrian front of the war.

I returned from the war after the cease-fire came into effect and found myself in an internal discussion at the Mossad about whether it was wise for Mossad employees exposed to sensitive state secrets to participate in wars in combat units and on the front lines. This discussion was particularly germane because it took place following the Syrian capture of an intelligence officer from unit 848 (which later became 8200) at the Hermon outpost. The information that the officer, Amos Levinberg, gave up in his interrogations by the Syrians caused great damage to the IDF's intelligence apparatus.

The state commission of inquiry headed by Chief Justice Shimon Agranat was a direct result of the failings revealed by the Yom Kippur War. Mossad chief Zvi Zamir was among those who received advance notice from the commission that he would be summoned to testify. He prepared for his testimony by establishing an interunit team to assist him and appointed me as its head. The objective of the team's work, as defined by Zamir, was to present the Mossad's intelligence contribution to the war. The period of time examined by the team was between the end of the War of Attrition on August 8, 1970, and the outbreak of the Yom Kippur War on October 6, 1973.

The Mossad director formulated his theses or insights related to the war during the three years that preceded it, based on his personal and intensive handling of Ashraf Marwan, meetings with other top sources, the reading and approving of all of the intelligence that came through as raw material throughout this period to the highest-ranking officials, and working meetings and consultations with the top security and political echelons, with the exception of those with Defense Minister Dayan, to which the head of the Mossad was not invited. There is no doubt that the Mossad chief's military past helped him in reading the vast intelligence material and in understanding the strategic and doctrinal issues, as well as the tactical ones. Zamir presented his theses on the war to the team and instructed us to review all of the intelligence material from the Mossad's sources throughout the period under investigation, in order to either confirm or refute his thesis. It was decided that the material would be examined through its division into four sections: (a) Egypt/Syria—strategic intentions; (b) Egypt/Syria—military buildup; (c) Egypt/Syria—sources' descriptions of the nature of the next war; (d) Egypt/Syria—possible dates for war (early warnings).

I accompanied the Mossad director to all of his appearances before the Agranat Commission. My main role was to support his testimony by presenting the intelligence material that backed up his theses. The materials submitted to the commission filled several binders and reflected the contribution of the Mossad's sources to Military Intelligence on the topics I mentioned above, as well as others. The following are only a few samples from the sea of material, which have already been published in the past and which I therefore do not see an issue with presenting here, forty-three years later.

Breaking the Deadlock by Way of a Limited War

Anwar Sadat came to power in Egypt at the end of September 1970, less than two months after the cease-fire that ended the War of Attrition. At the end of that year, he had begun to make it clear that while he saw no chance of defeating Israel militarily and of liberating the territories by means of war, he did see it as crucial to wage a war with a limited operational objective, the essence of which would be to "unfreeze" the conflict from its current state of stagnation. The longer the stalemate dragged on, the more he insisted on this. It is remarkable that this strategic political outlook was held not only by Sadat but by the entire Egyptian leadership.

Below are some examples of intelligence sources:

1. In April 1971, a reliable source reported that Egypt was going to engage in limited warfare in order to test the reactions of the United States and Israel, after it despaired of arriving at a diplomatic solution.

2. In November 1971, at a meeting with the Soviet leadership, Sadat said, "The current situation is the best one for America and Israel. . . . Israel is asking the United States why they should be rushing to find a solution. . . . Egypt cannot do anything. . . . My fear is that the world will stop taking an interest in the problem. . . . In light of this, there is no choice but to make a move and make the world interested in the problem again—for the sake of a peaceful solution—by limited military action."

3. In February 1972, during a visit to Moscow, Sadat told his hosts: "We need to carry out a limited military operation in the second half of 1972, for example at the passes [i.e., the Mitla and Gidi passes, which lead from the Sinai Peninsula to the eastern bank of the Suez Canal]. After achieving this goal we can emphasize our desire to find a peaceful solution and to open the Canal."

4. In January 1973, Sadat wrote the following to Soviet leader Leonid Brezhnev: "Our belief is becoming stronger that as long as Israel is not convinced that we can resist its forces, defeat them and change the military situation, it will not agree to withdraw from our occupied lands."

5. In April 1973, a reliable source reported there was no diplomatic solution on the horizon. Sadat had serious intentions to resume fighting in the near future in order to break the deadlock, even in the knowledge that the chances of success were small and that he might lose his position in the event of failure. This was a move of desperation.

The Determination to Go to War

In February 1973, Sadat said, "A basic principle of history is that as long as our armed forces do not enter into battle, our people will lose their manhood for the next millennium. It is a thousand times more honorable to die fighting than to continue to stand as we are until it ends in our surrender."

Military Action as Part of a Plan to Gain
International Support

In August 1972, Sadat was presented with a memorandum on Egyptian policy planning for 1972–73. The author of the memorandum was Hafez Ismail, the president's national security adviser. Ismail recommended:

1. Repairing relations with the Soviet Union with a view to ensuring the supply of weapons. This was after the expulsion of the Soviets from Egypt in July 1972.
2. Conducting a comprehensive campaign to gain diplomatic support, with the main focus being western Europe, along with efforts among the nonaligned and Latin American countries.
3. Raising the issue at the UN General Assembly, and after it (in 1973) at a special UN Security Council meeting to approve the Egyptian interpretation of Resolution 242.
4. Maintaining contacts with the United States.
5. Maintaining contact with the Arab states in order to bring about the exertion of pressure with regard to Western interests.
6. Recruitment of the "domestic front" in Egypt.
7. Taking into account that a military clash between Egypt and Israel and the United States was almost inevitable. (My interpretation of the inclusion of the United States in this phrase is that it was only figurative/emotional and was not intended to suggest a clash between Egyptian and American military forces.)
8. Considering the possibility of limited Egyptian military action in the winter of 1972–73.

The crux of Ismail's view was that Egypt should rely mainly on "diplomatic action," in which the military forces would play only a supplementary role. And indeed, Egypt did carry out most of Ismail's plan, though the military campaign was postponed until October

1973. The results of the Egyptian diplomatic efforts were evident on the eve of the war, during it, and in its wake.

The "Détente" and Its Implications for the Conflict

The "détente"—the process of the thawing of relations between the two blocs, which began in the late 1960s—convinced the Egyptian leadership that there was no longer any chance for diplomatic efforts and that it could not rely on the two powers for salvation, especially not after the second summit of the leaders of the United States and the Soviet Union in Washington in July 1973. The Security Council debate on the Middle East, which was held around the same time and which ended with an American veto (as Israel had hoped), was the final stroke.

- In May 1973, the American assessment was that despite the low likelihood of an Egyptian military initiative, there was a greater risk of it now than there had been in the past. There was logic in taking military action to break the conflict out of its deadlock. Most of the other options were blocked. Sadat could not expect anything from Brezhnev at the upcoming summit, and Brezhnev would not endanger the détente because of Egypt. Only military action could get the superpowers to take the conflict seriously.
- In June 1973, a European intelligence service assessed that because none of Egypt's diplomatic initiatives had achieved results, and because Egypt was disappointed with the outcomes at the UN, the possibility that Sadat would go to war had to be taken into account.
- In June 1973, a reliable source reported that if the Nixon-Brezhnev summit did not lead to a change in the Middle East, the Egyptians would try to take over Mitla Pass.
- In July 1973, an analysis of the significance of the détente for Egypt was prepared by Ismail Fahmi, then minister of tourism, who immediately after the war (in November 1973) was ap-

pointed foreign minister. His conclusions were that Egypt could not expect salvation from either superpower; the Soviet Union "could not and did not want" to bring about a solution, and the United States "could but did not want to." Egypt must strive to reach a state of "autarky" (independence), enlist the support of the Arab countries and the nonaligned countries, and rely on its own political and military capabilities.

- In August 1973, an intelligence report on the public mood stated, inter alia, that concern and tension among Egyptian citizens had recently been increasing as a result of feelings of despair and pessimism about resolving the conflict and the fear for the country's future, especially after recent global developments and their negative implications (this was in reference to the summit and the discussions in the Security Council).
- In September 1973, a source reported that a decision had been taken to cross the Suez Canal and occupy the crossings in an attempt to reach a diplomatic settlement.

Early Warnings—Potential Dates for the Launch of the War

From the vast intelligence material dealing with the potential dates of the expected war, the Mossad compiled seventy items containing clear warnings, all from important and highly valued sources. They were all based on HUMINT sources or on reports from the intelligence services of friendly foreign countries, indicating that contrary to what was understood from the discourse in the Israeli media, the warnings about the war were not based on a single source, namely Ashraf Marwan. The fulfillment of the intention to go to war was conditional on Egypt's readiness, which was not achieved before the middle of 1973. The desire and intention to go to war were present before then, of course, but the Mossad's sources clearly indicated that the realization of these intentions was far off or even nonviable, as the Egyptians were still in the preparation stage and did not consider themselves ready to go to war.

For example, while Sadat determined that 1971 was the "year of decision," according to a November 1971 report, he had informed the Soviets one month earlier that he still lacked critical munitions without which he could not start a war. These only began to make their way to Egypt in 1972. Another example: in November 1972, the Egyptian defense minister told the Syrians that Egypt wanted to go to war in January 1973. The Syrians said in response that they would not be ready before April 1973.

According to our sources, from the summer of 1972 three main times were discussed as possible times for the launching of the war: (a) late 1972 to early 1973; (b) between late April and early June 1973; and (c) September–October 1973. The fundamental differences between these three early warnings were as follows:

1. Regarding the first potential time, planning and preparations had not yet been completed and there were no reports of preparations on the ground.

2. Regarding the second warning, April–June, the main planning and preparations had already been completed, but there were very few reports of preparations on the ground. Egypt and Syria had not yet closed all of the existing gaps (for example, depth, electronic warfare, and antiaircraft missiles). In addition, the Soviet Union sought to postpone the deadline, promising Sadat that if the forthcoming summit (in Washington in July 1973) ended with no results, the Russians would supply Egypt with the offensive weapons needed for attacks deep inside enemy territory.

3. The third date, September–October, appeared to be a direct continuation of the second, postponed, date. The stage of planning on both fronts was essentially the same as what had been reported to us regarding April–June, and armament had now been completed. An unprecedented number of reports of preparations on the ground were coming in as this date neared.

Some Mossad sources also held the opinion that Sadat would not go to war. These views were based on the assumption that just as Sadat had not fulfilled his promises to go to war in the past, the same would be true this time around. Such views were expressed as late as mid-September 1973. *But from Rosh Hashanah onwards, during the last ten days before the outbreak of the war, sources reported only the intention to go to war, with no reservations whatsoever.*

Time A: Late 1972 to early 1973

Among the explanations for this possible time were:

1. The academic year at the universities was set to begin on October 31, and this was a particularly sensitive time in terms of domestic pressures.
2. It would put pressure on the United States ahead of elections.
3. It would also put pressure on the upcoming UN General Assembly discussions.

It should be noted that the reports coming in about this possible date were received from many sources.

From a military perspective, going to war on this date would have been a strain. There were still not enough offensive weapons. Syria was going to begin receiving them only at the end of 1972, and some would arrive only in the first quarter of 1973. Syria requested to postpone the date to April 1973. (The following items had still not been supplied in full: MiG-21s; Sukhoi-20s; SA-6, ZSU-23, SA-3, and improved SA-7 missiles and antiaircraft systems; a Luna artillery rocket system; antiaircraft missiles; and Mirage and Lightning aircraft.) There were no reports of detailed operational planning or preparation on the ground for this date, as there were for the dates that followed.

Time B: Late April to early June 1973

Among the reasons for these possible dates were:

1. Hafez Ismail's visit to the United States had failed, and therefore one could not expect any "miracles" from the July summit meeting unless military action was launched.
2. Sadat would not be able to hold on to power if he did not carry out military action. Defeat would be preferable to the current stalemate.
3. It would put pressure on the superpowers ahead of the summit and might influence the Security Council's discussions.
4. The military preparations were completed.

In contrast to the earlier warning, this time our sources reported concrete plans for the attack and—to some degree of detail—indications of evidence on the ground. For example, reports came in that some units were being brought closer to the front lines and that transport battalions were being mobilized, that a brigade was being advanced, and that a Mirage squadron had arrived in Egypt from Libya. There was also a report about a plan to launch the war with artillery shelling along the length of the Canal, deep attacks on Israel's heartland (on Israeli ports), and the construction of ten bridges on the Canal. It was also reported that a detailed Syrian operational plan had been completed.

Two reasons were given for postponement of the date. First, there was Soviet pressure to postpone the date for the launch of the war, with the promise that if the summit did not bring about any change, the Soviet Union would provide offensive weapons. There was strong pressure on Assad to postpone during his visit to the Soviet Union at the end of April 1973. Second, reliable sources also reported that the Egyptian army was still lacking in its offensive capabilities and that the army was not ready.

The first (undetailed) report on Egypt's decision to postpone the launch of the war came in May 1973. Among the reasons given were the need to complete preparations and to receive new weapons from the Soviet Union, and the Syrian request to postpone for the same reasons. At the same time, a report was received from another source claiming that the signs of imminent war had disappeared.

Isolated Early Warnings about July–August 1973

A single source reported on a plan to open fire simultaneously on both the Egyptian and Syrian fronts on July 15, 1973, *which would begin with a comprehensive army exercise* on July 3. Another source reported on the possibility of the war being launched between August 10 and August 15, adding that July 23, Egyptian Revolution Day, had also been mentioned.

Time C: September–October 1973

"Time C," September–October 1973, was the direct continuation of "Time B"—late April to early June 1973, but at Time C, the armament that had been the condition for Egypt's readiness for war had been completed. Leading up to this date, an unprecedented number of reports came in describing preparations on the ground. From mid-July 1973 to October 6, the date that the war broke out, the Mossad provided twenty-three unambiguous warnings from its most reliable sources, including Egypt's and Syria's detailed war plans. It should be noted once again that all of the early warnings that came in between September 8 and October 5, fifteen in total, were from a variety of sources. Not one of them came from Ashraf Marwan.

The early warning that Marwan provided to Israel on the eve of the war has preoccupied many researchers and journalists who have written tens of thousands of words on the subject. Some of them genuinely tried to expose the truth about the "failure." Others were looking for support for imaginary, even delusional, assertions.

Here is a brief summary of how things unfolded. At 22:30 on October 5, a meeting began between the source, the head of the Mossad, and the source's regular handler. After the meeting, the Mossad director phoned his bureau chief and gave him a report in code, which the bureau chief deciphered. The bureau chief then passed on the message by telephone to the prime minister's military secretary, Brigadier General Israel Lior, at 02:45, to the head of Military Intelligence, Major General Eli Zeira, at 02:55, and to the Minister of Defense's military secretary, Brigadier General Yehoshua Raviv, at 03:10. The warning read as follows:

- According to the plan, the Egyptians are going to attack toward evening. [They] know that today is a special holiday [Yom Kippur] and think they can descend before dark.
- The attack will be carried out according to the plan we are already aware of.
- In [the source's] opinion, Sadat cannot postpone the attack because of commitments he has made to other Arab heads of state, which he wants to keep down to every last detail.
- The source estimates that despite Sadat's hesitancy, the chances of an attack are 99.9 percent.
- In their [the Egyptians'] opinion, they will win, so they are very concerned about any early disclosure that could lead to outside intervention, which may deter some of their partners who may reconsider whether or not the attack is worthwhile.
- The Russians will not take part in the attack.

At 9:50 a.m. on Saturday, October 6, additional reports came in from Marwan, following his warning of the previous night. The most interesting of these was that on September 25, Sadat decided to launch the war on October 6 but did not share this decision with anyone. On September 29, Sadat convened the National Security Council and informed its members of his decision to violate the cease-fire in the near future, explaining that this was now the most opportune time to do so from a political point of view. On September 30, Sadat convened the Supreme War Council and conveyed a similar message to its members, again without specifying the precise date. On October 2, just four days before the date set for the start of the war, Sadat relayed the date of October 6 to his minister of war, Ahmed Ismail, and ordered him to update the representatives of the Syrian general staff in Cairo and to fly to Damascus the following day for further coordination.

Sadat's Goals and General Outline for the War

Sadat's strategic goal beginning with his rise to power in 1970 was and remained the extrication of the conflict from its stagnation by means of a military operation that would lead to a diplomatic process. The detailed war plans progressed and matured toward the end of 1973, and symmetry evolved between the general methods outlined in the Egyptian and the Syrian war plans. They both intended to open with air strikes and artillery fire. This would be followed by the infiltration of infantry divisions (five Egyptian and three Syrian) to secure a bridgehead (ten to fifteen kilometers in Sinai and six to eight kilometers in the Golan Heights). Assuming that the securing of the bridgeheads was successfully completed, the armored divisions would advance through them, in the Egyptian case, to the Mitla and Gidi crossings. The war plans mentioned two stages, without specifying a precise timetable between the first and second stages. On the eve of the war, in the complete report from the meeting that was received on the morning of October 6, it was stated that the first stage was intended to capture a strip ten kilometers east of the Canal and that the effort to move eastward into Sinai would be decided on the basis of the results of the first stage; that is, for the first time there was an element of interlude added between the two stages.

Military Buildup and Closing Gaps in Preparation for War

In 1972 and 1973, the Mossad provided hundreds of intelligence reports from its best sources on Egypt's and Syria's armament and on the closing of the gaps that were defined as a condition for going to war. These reports came from HUMINT sources (agents) and friendly intelligence services. Most of them came as authentic original documents. The following are some of the insights that emerged from the plethora of intelligence material:

- The Egyptian planners spoke of two levels of existing gaps. The first was in the Egyptian army's capabilities in the field of defense. In this area, the Russians were more willing to come to Egypt's aid. The second level involved closing the gaps necessary to attain the capability to achieve the objectives of the war. Here the Soviet approach was more rigid. Sadat had defined 1971 as the "year of decision." The commanders of the Egyptian army did not believe that the army was ready for war that year, as it lacked some vital types of weapons—armaments to deter Israel from attacking deep inside Egypt; electronic warfare equipment (the Egyptians recognized that Israel was light-years ahead of them in this area); self-propelled air defense systems that would provide cover for the attacking Egyptian forces; bridges; and advanced tanks.

- In December 1971, an arms supply agreement was signed between Egypt and the Soviet Union. There were delays in its implementation during 1972. Moreover, the Egyptian planners argued that the types of weapons included in the agreement provided a response only to the "first level" of gaps—those in Egypt's defensive capabilities. Sadat, with the support of his army commanders, continued to demand additional items from the Soviets, as well as increased quantities. When he realized that the Soviet Union was not responding to his demands at the pace he expected, Sadat expelled the Soviet military presence from Egypt.

The Soviets continued to supply arms only in accordance with the signed treaties. At this point, however, they decided to balance the removal of their military presence in Egypt by intensifying their military presence in Syria, and the way to do so was to adopt a more liberal weapons policy vis-à-vis the Syrians. Following the amendment of Egyptian-Soviet relations in early 1973, a new arms deal was signed in February during the Egyptian minister of war's visit to Moscow. This deal included a lot of amphibious equipment, APCs outfitted with Sagger antitank missiles, additional bridges, Volga antiaircraft missiles, another battalion of SA-6 missiles, and eighteen electronic warfare aircraft that were given on loan. The reason for the addition of the bridges, crossing equipment, and mobile antiaircraft vehicles was probably related to the changes that the Egyptians put into the war plan, namely, the increase of crossing forces in the first phase of the war from three divisions to five. The equipment and armaments included in the agreement were supplied with unprecedented speed, with most of them reaching Egypt in April–May 1973. In May or June of 1973, the Soviets also supplied Egypt with Scud ground-to-ground missiles.

- Two additional insights to help understand the entire picture. The first is that while Sadat was prodding the Soviets to expand the supply of offensive weapons, the Russians were preparing for the second summit meeting in July 1973 in Washington. It would be fair to assume that the Russians restricted the types of equipment they provided to Egypt before the summit, and there was indeed evidence of this in the Mossad's intelligence material. According to one source, in a meeting between Sadat and Brezhnev the latter told Sadat explicitly that only if the summit did not produce satisfactory diplomatic results with regard to the Egyptian-Israeli conflict would he supply Egypt with the offensive weapons it needed. The summit did indeed end in failure when it came to this issue. Even so, at the end of the day it appears that the Soviets did not satisfy all the Egyptians' desires.

Evidence of this is Sadat's agreements with Libya that it would provide Egypt with two Mirage squadrons, with Saudi Arabia and Kuwait that they would provide squadrons and "Lightning" aircraft, and with Iraq that they would provide a "Hunter" squadron. In the area of electronic warfare as well, the Egyptians did not settle for what the Soviets supplied them, and in March 1973 they purchased electronic warfare equipment from French and British companies. And as early as mid-1972, the Egyptians purchased water pumps from British and German companies for the purpose of breaking through the ramparts on either side of the Canal.

• The second insight relates to the dates of the war. Reading the enormous amount of intelligence material about the Egyptian-Russian negotiations on the supply of weapons, the signing of contracts, the supply times, and so on, it is clear why the first date set for the launch of the war—late 1972 to early 1973—was postponed until the late April–early June 1973, and why this date was in turn postponed to the third and final date. The months between June and October 1973 were essential for Egypt to receive the equipment it had been lacking and to begin putting it to use before the war began.

Strategic Aspects of the Preparations for War

In early May 1973, a Mossad source reported that Sadat was about to conclude negotiations with the oil-producing Arab states regarding the cessation of the supply of oil to Western countries immediately following the outbreak of the war.

• Toward mid-1973, the Mossad reported an Egyptian decision to impose a closure on the Straits of Bab al-Mandeb (between the Red Sea and the Indian Ocean) and to deploy commando fighters at the entrance to the Gulf of Eilat immediately upon the outbreak of hostilities.

- At the end of 1972, the Mossad reported a Syrian demand for co-operation with Jordan, asking for the latter to commit to securing the southern flank of the Syrian front in order to prevent the IDF from crossing into Jordan and reaching the southern front. As the war neared, intelligence came in confirming that King Hussein had indeed agreed to the Syrian request.

Conclusion

In the forty-three years that have passed since the Yom Kippur War, from time to time pundits of various kinds pop up—particularly in the media—who see it as their duty to relieve Military Intelligence of the burden of complete responsibility for the colossal failure and to assign some of this burden to the Mossad. Every year when the anniversary of the outbreak of the war, October 6, approaches, the level of noise emanating from the media begins to rise. Documents and reports related to the war and the Agranat Commission are published from time to time, based on arbitrary rules derived from the laws regarding the publication of classified information. Each one of these episodes reopens all the wounds of the trauma of the Yom Kippur War. It must be remembered that the Agranat Commission investigated only the first three days of the war. The question must be asked: For how many decades can we continue the ritual of this self-torture? Answers such as "The public has the right to know," "The obligation to investigate is growing," and "We must get to the root of the problem" often conceal the interests and motives of various parties.

In spite of my intensive involvement in the Agranat Commission, which I described at the beginning of this chapter, I was indifferent to the subject whenever it came up on the media's agenda during the forty years between 1973 and 2013. In mid-2013, following the authorization to publish an additional segment of the Agranat Commission report (which had been confidential until then), a well-known journalist launched into a diatribe in three long newspaper columns, casuistically concluding that then-Mossad chief Zvi Zamir was guilty of the failures of the Yom Kippur War. This cracked my indifference and compelled me to come out publicly in defense of the Mossad and its director during the war.

I did not invent the maxim that if the intelligence is good there is no need for assessment, but I do maintain, from my personal familiarity with every detail of intelligence that the Mossad provided to MI, that if there is a historical case that proves the truth of this statement, the Yom Kippur War is it. Moreover, I believe that any intelligent reader looking over the samples of intelligence I present in this chapter cannot help but reach the same conclusion—that with such intelligence, assessment is superfluous.

The wealth of intelligence material clearly pointing to Egypt and Syria's intentions and capabilities (examples of which have been presented here) casts the total reliance on the warning provided on the eve of the war in a completely different light. This intelligence was already being systematically transferred to MI by the Mossad by the end of the War of Attrition, and therefore all explanations regarding the "concept" must be directed toward MI and not others. The "concept" is the name given by the State Committee of Inquiry headed by Chief Justice Agranat to a theory that was developed and formed by the MI in the early 1970s. According to the "concept," Egypt would not go to war against Israel unless it had certain advanced weapons— low-flying bombers and/or long-range surface-to-surface ballistic missiles—which would grant it strategic balance vis-à-vis Israel, and Syria would not go to war without Egypt. The "concept" led MI to the assessment that the Arab military deployment in the days just before the breakout of the 1973 War did not necessarily indicate an intention to go to war, in spite of numerous signs to the contrary.

In early 2016, I was surprised to find support for my views from an unexpected source. Dr. Hagai Tsoref is the director of the State Documents and Commemoration Department of the Israel State Archives and has edited a memorial volume for Golda Meir, Israel's prime minister during the war.[1] Tsoref's clear advantage lies in his access to the State Archives' documentation of the conduct of the Prime Minister's Office during the war, in particular the diaries of the bureau and the cabinet meetings. Tsoref also had access to the complete protocols of the Agranat Commission (prior to their publication). The majority of those who have dealt with the Yom Kippur War—historians, journalists, and other researchers—did not have access to even a portion of the wealth of primary sources to which Tsoref was exposed. I will mention once again that the Agranat Commission investigated only the first three days of the war. Therefore, even if someone had access to all of the commission's protocols, he or she would still not come close to the abundance and authenticity of the materials to which Tsoref had access, which covered the period from October 3 to October 31, 1973, the date that the cease-fire came into de facto effect and the beginning of the diplomatic struggle.

Dr. Tsoref divided his research into three periods of time:

1. October 3–6, 1973: The days preceding the outbreak of the war and the war's first few hours
2. October 10–14, 1973: The end of the holding action stage and the launching of the attack phase
3. October 18–31, 1973: The end of the war and the transition to diplomatic activity

The core of Tsoref's research deals with the interfaces between the head of the Mossad, Zvi Zamir, and the Israeli political and military leadership. He describes the dynamic that developed between the main players over time, from which it emerges that the Mossad director, whose status was relatively low on the eve of the outbreak of the war, became the intelligence adviser to the prime minister as of October 10.

Tsoref's first insight is, "Much is said about the role of the Mossad and its director in the period leading up to the war, and about Zamir's warning of the outbreak of war which he received from Ashraf Marwan on October 5, 1973. But the Mossad chief's important role during the war remains almost completely unknown."

The status of the Mossad and its director was undermined when the warning of war in April–May 1973, which I have referred to in this chapter as "Time B," was not realized. According to Tsoref, "During the war, and as the days passed, the standing of the Mossad and its chief grew stronger and stronger. This process was likely influenced by the failure of Military Intelligence, headed by Eli Zeira, to predict the outbreak of the war. This is how the head of the Mossad became Prime Minister Golda Meir's chief adviser on intelligence affairs, especially during the final stages of the war. Without him, no decisive strategic decision was made. Zamir was in the Prime Minister's Office almost daily and participated in many of the consultations held there."

According to Tsoref, the Mossad, headed by Zamir, played an important role throughout the war in a number of areas:

1. Zamir met with Marwan twice more during the period under discussion, and the information he brought from these meetings played an important role in directing the government's diplomatic moves vis-à-vis the Americans and the Egyptians.

2. From the beginning of the war, Zamir warned that the IDF had not fully understood the change that the Egyptians had made to the war plan near its outset, which led to the IDF planners beginning to respond to these changes accordingly. This change had to do with the war's objective, which at first was ambitious and involved crossing the Canal and rapidly progressing to Mitla Pass; on the eve of the war the objective was modified to breaching the Suez Canal and capturing a narrow strip of ten kilometers to its east.

3. The intelligence information Zamir provided to the leadership saved Israel from major military threats.

This last statement refers to Zamir's advice regarding counter-attacks and the crossing of the Canal. Already on the night of October 7, at a meeting in Golda's office, Zamir warned against embarking on a counterattack on the southern front on the following day, October 8. Zamir is quoted as saying, "The Egyptians are waiting for exactly such an attack by us."[2] The IDF indeed played into the hands of the Egyptians, and in the counterattack on October 8 it suffered many losses, lost many tanks in an assault on infantry forces (which were equipped with Sagger missiles), and did not improve the IDF's position on the front.

On October 12, the seventh day of the war, with the IDF already weary, a discussion was held with the extended cabinet, headed by Golda Meir. Lieutenant General (res.) Haim Bar-Lev, who had been appointed as commander of the southern front a few days earlier, reported to the cabinet on the situation on the front and strongly recommended not to wait for the Egyptian counterattack but to launch an attack beyond the Canal the next day, on the thirteenth of the month, despite the many risks involved. The commander of the air force, Major General Benny Peled, supported Bar-Lev; IDF deputy chief of staff Yisrael Tal objected to his suggested course of action; Chief of Staff Dado was hesitant; and Defense Minister Dayan was also not convinced. The dilemma was serious. Then Zamir was called out of the meeting to receive some urgent information that had just come in. When he returned to the meeting he relayed that a reliable source had been told that the Egyptians were about to begin the second phase of their attack on the passes in the next day or two. Golda's reaction was, "Well, I understand that Zvika Zamir has ended our discussion."[3] It was decided to postpone the IDF counterattack and wait for the Egyptian army east of the Canal, where it would be "crushed" in its attempt to break through the crossings; from there the IDF would move from a position of superiority to a counterattack to the west of the Canal. The Egyptian army did indeed launch the second stage of its attack on October 14 and suffered a severe blow on the east of the Canal—between 150 and 250 Egyptian tanks were destroyed. On October 15 the IDF began crossing the Canal, and by the eighteenth it had established a clear position of superiority as it reached the Canal's west bank.

The head of the Mossad also made a major contribution to formulating Israel's strategy vis-à-vis the Egyptians and the United States. As mentioned, Zamir met with Marwan twice more, on October 19 and 29, and the intelligence he brought, especially the insight that the Egyptians and Syrians were not interested in a cease-fire and wanted to drag Israel into a war of attrition west of the Suez Canal, influenced Golda's decision to travel to the United States for meetings with Kissinger and Nixon. The Kissinger-Alexei Kosygin agreement on a cease-fire, which was achieved in Moscow on October 20 upon Kosygin's return from a secret visit to Cairo, during which he pressed the Egyptians to agree to the cease-fire, posed an obstacle but did not change Golda's decision to go to the United States.

Tsoref sums up his research as follows:

> Only twenty-seven days passed between October 3 and October 30, but in terms of the status of the Mossad and Zamir as its leader, it felt like light-years. On October 3, a critical discussion was held on the possibility of the breakout of war, and the Mossad director was not even invited to participate. On October 30, Zamir was the senior figure in everything related to intelligence assessments in the Prime Minister's Office. There is no clearer evidence than this meeting to indicate the strengthening of the Mossad's standing in the eyes of Israeli leaders and Zamir's important role in the conduct of the Yom Kippur War and the diplomatic struggle that accompanied it. This was due both to the information he presented to the leaders and to his assessments, which were based on his extensive military experience.[4]

Wise words indeed! One more thought to finish. Wars are conducted by people. In order to properly analyze them, it is not enough to know "who's who" and "who is for and who is against." To really get to the root of things—decisions, actions, and omissions—one has to understand the historical, political, personal, and even egotistical background of each of the players that make up the "command center." None of the security experts who surrounded Ben-Gurion accepted his decision to subordinate the head of the Mossad to the prime minister! This subordination was anathema to defense ministers, directors general of the Defense Ministry, and the heads of Military Intelligence over the years. Another point is that a person's rank was measured with the help of a strange political tool—did he identify with "Ahdut Ha'avoda" (such as Tabenkin and Yigal Allon) or with Mapai (like Ben-Gurion and his political circle)? Or was he a veteran of the Palmach or of another body (the Haganah, the British army, etc.)? Whoever wants to truly understand the background of the Yom Kippur War must be aware of the fact that Dayan and Zamir had a lukewarm relationship. Why? Because historically, Zamir was considered a close friend of Yigal Allon, Dayan's greatest rival. In addition, Dayan objected to Zamir's appointment as head of the Mossad, preferring another candidate. When he took office, Zamir made it clear to Dayan that he would work directly under Golda, which Dayan did not like. The relationship was so tepid that Zamir was not even invited to discussions with Defense Minister Dayan! The head of Military Intelligence, Major General Eli Zeira, was a favorite of Moshe Dayan's, and Dayan had tapped him to be chief of staff one day. Golda, who did not possess military knowledge and experience, and had no more than a formal relationship with Dayan, the hero of the Six-Day War, had difficulty dealing with the "Dayan-Zeira coalition" and accepted their assessments and recommendations almost automatically.

The Dayan-Zeira coalition disregarded the Mossad and its leaders, especially after the fruitless warning of "Time B," late April to early June 1973. In retrospect, there is no doubt that the failure was theirs, for they *failed to understand that the early warning of the Yom Kippur War was a rolling event, which had a complete basis in the intelligence that flowed in parallel to the unfolding of the warning.* I dare say, from the vantage point of a fly on the wall, that Dayan's cumulative contribution to the Yom Kippur War, certainly with regard to intelligence, was negative.

The First Gulf War, January 16, 1991

"I have personally experienced a great many historical events, too many, in my seventy-five years. I remember very clearly the outbreak of World War II in September 1939, when I was only twelve years old. I experienced the terrible days of the war, the Holocaust, our War of Independence, the loss of my loved ones, and all of the wars of Israel since then. Throughout all of these events I was on the passive side of the barricade, unable to influence the course of events. . . . I want to be remembered in my own consciousness, and perhaps also in the consciousness of some of my friends, as someone who contributed even the smallest share to the first Gulf War, and perhaps even to the second one."

This was written—though never published—by the person who, beginning in 1987, headed the Mossad department responsible for gathering intelligence and foiling efforts to develop nonconventional weapons in Arab countries. It seems to me that things like this can be written only by a member of the Jewish people, who experienced the Holocaust personally, and whose life as a survivor led him to a position where he could have an influence over the development of a similar threat, this time to the State of Israel, from a deranged and bloodthirsty dictator like Saddam Hussein.

Iraq, though it does not share a common border with Israel, was considered its fanatic enemy. Iraq is the only Arab country to have fought against Israel in the War of Independence, and it did not sign an armistice agreement with Israel upon the war's end; therefore, from the standpoint of international law, Iraq and Israel have been in a state of war from 1948 until today.

The 1958 revolution in Iraq overthrew the monarchy and turned the country into a military dictatorship that relied on the Sunni minority in a country with a predominantly Shiite population. General Abd al-Karim Qasim established the military dictatorship and changed the country's orientation from an Iraq that was pro-Western to an Iraq that tied its fate to the Soviet Union and the Eastern bloc.

After five years in power, Qasim was deposed in a coup initiated by his ally-turned-rival, Colonel Abdul Salam Arif. Arif was killed three years later in a helicopter accident and was briefly replaced by his weaker brother. His brother was then replaced by a general named Ahmed Hassan al-Bakr, who had participated in the pro-Nazi revolt in Iraq in 1941. Under al-Bakr's rule, a young citizen named Saddam Hussein quickly rose through the ranks to become appointed deputy chairman of the Revolutionary Command Council, the body that ruled Iraq in practice.

From its establishment as a monarchy in the Sykes-Picot Agreement of 1916, during the First World War, Iraq was a rich and powerful country. It had a large area of about half a million square kilometers, with a relatively small population of about fifteen million (in the 1970s). It had an abundance of water, with the Euphrates and Tigris crossing it from the north, from Syria in the northwest and from Turkey in the north, respectively, to the south and east into the Persian Gulf. Iraq was also rich in the energy resources of oil and gas, as well as in agricultural land, and it had a sea outlet in the Persian Gulf. The military dictatorship that ruled the country beginning in 1958 built up a large military force, with the help of the Soviets, in order to create a deterrent against Iran and Turkey; suppress the Kurds in the mountainous north of the country, who had always aspired toward autonomy and independence; develop a position of strategic superiority within the Arab world; and lead the Arab coalitions on the eastern front against Israel.

Despite being in Israel's "outer circle," with no shared border with it, Iraq was a major threat to Israel and a core element of its security doctrine. From its establishment until the outbreak of the "Arab Spring," Israel treated Iraq as a constant threat that had to be taken into account and regarding which a response had to be prepared in the event of any military flare-up in the Middle East.

Since its inception, Israel had adopted a strategy of containment toward Iraq, consisting of the following elements:

- Strategic cooperation with Iran, which had both an intelligence aspect and an operational aspect vis-à-vis Iraq, and which, of course, was halted following the Khomeini revolution of 1979
- Strategic cooperation with Turkey, which had experienced ups and downs over the years, but which in general had allowed Israel to get a "look and feel" for Iraq from the Turkish side of the border
- Strategic intelligence cooperation with the Kurds in northern Iraq, including the continuous presence of forces in the territory, with Iran serving as a territorial rear for this cooperation

Iraq had always been a concern of the Israeli intelligence community, but its place on the list of priorities of the EEI began to change in the early 1970s and onwards.

In 1970, Egyptian president Gamal Abdel Nasser died, and Anwar Sadat was appointed in his place. From the day he came to power in Egypt, Sadat concocted the idea of the Yom Kippur War, which he carried out in October 1973. In the wake of the war, the seeds of peace with Egypt were sown, and they grew into a peace treaty in 1979. After the war, Syria occupied the number one place on the Israeli EEI, though throughout the forty years that have passed since the Yom Kippur War, not a single bullet has been fired from Syrian territory into Israel. Jordan, during this period, was not considered a threat to Israel (unless the regime were to change). In Saddam Hussein's Iraq, on the other hand, there was the growing threat of strategic weapons that included military chemical, biological, and nuclear capabilities as well as surface-to-surface missiles. The Israeli air force attacked the nuclear reactor near Baghdad on June 7, 1981, rendering it useless. Exactly one year later, on June 6, 1982, the First Lebanon War began, which plunged the IDF into becoming a presence in Lebanon for many years; at the same time, Iraq went to war against Iran for eight years, all while continuing its efforts to develop its strategic capabilities.

From the end of the 1973 Yom Kippur War until the outbreak of the "Arab Spring" at the beginning of 2011, Syria was the number one priority on Israel's EEI. This fact had far-reaching implications for the directing of the efforts of the Israeli intelligence community, the allocation of financial resources, the allocation of human resources, and the development of capabilities in the areas of weapons and technology. This prioritization, which was decided upon by MI in its role as the "national assessor," was met with skepticism in the Mossad, especially in view of the growing Iraqi threat, which had not been degraded despite the Iran-Iraq War. The Mossad's doubts were connected to the fact that it was the Mossad that had led the intelligence gathering on and thwarting of Iraq's buildup of strategic capabilities. A dispute therefore arose between MI and the Mossad regarding the order of priorities vis-à-vis the threats facing Israel. In 1987, for example, Military Intelligence placed Syria in first place on the EEI and Iraq only third, whereas the Mossad placed the Iraqi threat, with regard to everything related to intelligence collection and prevention efforts, in first place.

In analyzing the historical background to the incongruence of the threat assessments of MI and the Mossad at that time, we must return to the Yom Kippur War. This was the first war since the establishment of the State of Israel that concluded with the establishment of a state commission of inquiry that investigated the issue of intelligence alerts and other aspects of the war related to intelligence. In other words—you have to pay for your mistakes, and the head of Military Intelligence, Major General Eli Zeira, indeed paid for his failure and was removed from his post. His dismissal, as well as that of IDF chief of staff Lieutenant General David Elazar, was a traumatic event for the IDF and the state. My subjective opinion, based on my long working relationship with Military Intelligence, is that this trauma had a psychological effect on the MI heads who served in the post after 1973 and that the decisions of the Agranat Commission became a kind of sword hanging over their heads. More than once I got the feeling that one MI head or another was operating as if he was there against his will and was counting down the days until the end of his term. This mental state may have influenced the fact that the subject of the early warnings of war with Syria occupied the highest place on the EEI year after year, with excessive resources being allocated to it. In retrospect, the Iraqi threat, which intensified in the second half of the 1970s and the 1980s, deserved a higher priority than it actually received, even though Iraq is in Israel's "outer circle," and despite the Iran-Iraq War. The thirty-nine Scud missiles launched from Iraq against Israel with the outbreak of the First Gulf War may attest to the fact that in the years leading up to it Iraq's strategic military buildup did not receive the appropriate prioritization.

The primacy given by the Mossad to Iraq's development of nonconventional capabilities yielded extraordinary achievements, both in the area of intelligence gathering and in the foiling of threats; these achievements saved Israel untold damage and casualties.

I will now say a few words about the dilemmas that concern decision makers regarding the proliferation of nonconventional technologies and weapons.

The matter of the proliferation of nonconventional weapons systems (chemical, biological, nuclear, and missile, surface-to-surface missiles in particular) is anchored in international law, under the auspices of the United Nations and the superpowers, in a long series of agreements and treaties. This has created common and fertile ground for cooperation between intelligence services, mainly Western ones, whenever a rogue state decides to develop these capabilities, in whole or in part. Counteraction against proliferation involves two elements—intelligence and prevention. The interservice cooperation on the subject was problematic where the Mossad was concerned, as there was a lack of symmetry between it and the other Western intelligence and security services on many questions, such as the priority each country attached to curbing proliferation, what resources each country was willing to allocate to the subject, whether the issue should be dealt with through overt legal means alone or also covertly, and how to tackle the issue of dual-use materials that could serve both civilian and military purposes. Another important question in counterproliferation doctrine concerned the optimal point in time for transitioning from the intelligence-gathering stage to the prevention stage. Our approach was, as a general rule, to be willing to take great risks at the intelligence-gathering stage—these risks yielded intelligence that proved useful beyond the isolated case at hand. We always aspired to obtain more intelligence than the minimum that was necessary for purposes of prevention. The operational significance of this was, of course, that we made an effort to postpone acts of prevention as much as possible in favor of gathering more intelligence, because any counteroperation put an end to the intelligence collection.

Another dilemma that arose again and again was whether preventative acts should be "blue and white" operations, that is, purely Israeli, or in cooperation with foreign intelligence services. The preference was for "blue and white" operations whenever possible. A joint strike with a foreign service was chosen only when there was no other way to do it or when the risks involved in acting alone were too high.

A few more insights on the subject of prevention: great powers can afford not to engage in thwarting their adversaries' capabilities. They can make do with building up deterrence against the enemy. Deterrence in this context means convincing the adversary that if he utilizes his abilities, the price he is liable to pay will be beyond what he can withstand. Small countries like Israel cannot adopt a strategy that relies solely on deterrence. In the case of Israel, even a combination of deterrence and the ability to achieve a decisive victory is not sufficient, especially in dealings with coalitions of enemy states, since Israel's territory is extremely small and its military and economic power is concentrated in a relatively small area, which does not allow it to develop and maintain the capacity to absorb blows. Israel must refrain from entering wars whose end cannot be seen on the horizon. A notable example of this was the Yom Kippur War in 1973. The war began on October 6. Sixteen days later, on October 22, a considerable number of IDF forces were already stationed west of the Suez Canal, having reached a distance of 101 kilometers from the Egyptian capital of Cairo. On the northern front, IDF artillery seized positions that would have allowed them to shell the center of the Syrian capital of

Damascus. But the two Arab rulers, Sadat and Assad, made no sign of desiring a cease-fire. On the contrary, Sadat expressed in internal conversations that Israel would not be able to withstand a war of attrition, something that greatly disturbed Israel's political and military leadership. The historical fact is that US secretary of state Henry Kissinger and the premier of the Soviet Union, Alexei Kosygin, agreed on a cease-fire during a secret meeting in Moscow. Kosygin forced the cease-fire on Sadat, assuring him that he had received a commitment from Kissinger that the United States would be able to pull the IDF out of its positions. As for Syria, which had emerged from the war battered and its capital Damascus threatened, it had no choice but to agree to a cease-fire rather than to stand alone against Israel. Moreover, the Russians had promised the Syrians that they would rebuild their army. The Israeli leadership breathed a sigh of relief when the threat of a war of attrition was lifted.

In light of all of the above, Israel adopted as part of its security doctrine the strategy of prevention, the reasoning behind which is to block the adversary from building up his power over time and to prevent him from bringing his capabilities to fruition. Sometimes aggressive retaliation is fully successful, as in the case of the direct hit on the Iraqi nuclear reactor Osirak, which resulted in the destruction of the reactor's core beyond reparation. The Iraqis, who had sought to achieve military nuclearization via plutonium enrichment, changed tracks to enriching uranium in centrifuges in the wake of the destruction of the reactor. Prevention can be achieved via sabotage that is either "loud" or "quiet," and without the adversary even being aware that he has been thwarted. Even if there is such a suspicion, the enemy may not be able to assert with full confidence that his efforts have been foiled. In the cyber age, preventive capabilities have become all the more sophisticated, and on this subject silence is golden.

It should be emphasized that the doctrine of prevention focuses, as a general rule, on nonconventional strategic weapons and not on conventional weapons. When it comes to conventional weapons, prevention is not worthwhile, even when it is possible. For example, the sabotage of one aircraft of an entire squadron that an enemy state has bought or received from a superpower does not pass the cost-benefit test, because the risks involved (the exposure of capabilities and intelligence sources, for example) are very large.

Back to the years 1987 to 1989. The Mossad, which had placed the Iraqi threat at the top of its list of priorities on the EEI, used all the tools and capabilities at its disposal, either directly or indirectly. Its direct capabilities included HUMINT, SIGINT, and all types of special operations. There was a body established within the intelligence community called Idan Hadash ("A New Era"). It was chaired by the head of the Mossad or his deputy, and its members were senior representatives from the Mossad, Military Intelligence, and the scientific community, all intelligence and prevention experts. The forum convened frequently, at the initiative of the Mossad director's bureau, though any member of the forum was entitled to call for a discussion if any developments took place that he or she thought justified the convening of the forum. The forum discussed the intelligence products that had been added since the previous meeting, reassessed the updated intelligence picture and the significance of the threat, steered the continuation of intelligence gathering, and took decisions regarding issues of prevention.

As discussed, the Iraqi reactor Osirak was bombed and destroyed on June 7, 1981, though the working assumption of those involved was that Saddam Hussein would not simply give up but would continue to pursue military nuclear capability. In the mid-1980s, we received information about the possibility of the renewal of French-Iraqi nuclear cooperation. Around the same time, news came in from Iraq regarding the establishment of centrifuges for enriching uranium, with the help of Pakistan and trained Iraqi scientists. One of the stunning successes of our prevention efforts was the transfer of information to two European countries regarding special material intended for the manufacture of centrifuges, produced in a European country, which was secretly transferred to a neighboring country and loaded onto an Iraqi commercial plane. The plane, along with its cargo and personnel, was stopped by the local authorities. It wasn't easy to convince the European parties to lend their hand to this complex operation. They gave their consent only after we presented them with unequivocal evidence that the material in question had no industrial or scientific use other than centrifuges for uranium enrichment.

Beyond the megalomania inherent in Saddam Hussein's personality, the Iraqi efforts to acquire surface-to-surface missile capabilities at the beginning of the 1980s stemmed from Iraq's relative inferiority in this area as compared to Iran. The Scud B missile that the Soviets had provided to Iraq had a limited range of only three hundred kilometers, which did not satisfy Saddam, and in 1982 he made intensive efforts to acquire an arsenal of surface-to-surface missiles with a variety of ranges, including missiles armed with medium- and long-range nuclear warheads. The "Al-Hussein" missile developed by the Iraqis was based on the original Scud, but its range was twice as long; this doubling of range to six hundred kilometers was made possible by reducing the weight of the explosive from 1,000 kilos to only 250 kilos. The result was a primitive missile with a primitive guidance system and a high chance of burning upon its return into the atmosphere, that is, before hitting its target. Still, despite these technological limitations, thirty-nine Al-Hussein missiles were launched from Iraq and landed in Israel during the First Gulf War (January–February 1990).

The question of whether the Iraqis had chemical warheads for the Al-Hussein missile was a difficult one for us to answer unequivocally. From all of the intelligence obtained during the years prior to the First Gulf War, a consensus was formed that assessed that the Iraqis did have chemical warheads but that Saddam would use them, if at all, only as a last resort. Foreign intelligence services did not reject this assessment.

The Badr-2000 missile was a global project, with the involvement of industrial and commercial companies from countries in Europe, South America, and the Middle East. Only a few government representatives from these countries were involved. The final product was designed to be a rocket with a solid-fuel engine, a range of 650 km, a length of twelve meters, and a diameter of eighty centimeters, with a high level of accuracy of 0.1 percent and the ability to carry a nuclear warhead. The original idea for developing the missile came from Argentina, and the code name of the project was "Condor," the giant bird found in the Andes. In 1984, the Argentinians presented the idea for the project to an Egyptian delegation led by the Egyptian defense minister, General Abu Ghazala, who recommended to President Mubarak that he enter into a partnership with Argentina to develop the missile. After Mubarak gave the green light, a request was put in to Saddam Hussein to participate in the project and to finance the lion's share of it. The intelligence gathering on this project brought the Mossad to all corners of the globe. In the end, the project, in which millions of dollars were invested, was permanently shelved, the Egyptian minister of defense was fired, and the infrastructures that had been established in some of the countries were closed.

The Al-Abbas missile, which was based on the Badr 2000 technology, but for a larger range of nine hundred kilometers, did not advance beyond initial experiments. The Tammuz 1 missile, with a planned range of two thousand kilometers, and the Tammuz II missile, designed to put a satellite into orbit, never passed the planning stage.

Saddam Hussein wanted to achieve strategic capability at all costs. Destiny brought him together with a Canadian-Belgian scientist named Gerald Bull, who for years had been trying to sell anyone who would listen to him the idea of a supergun with a 150-meter-long barrel, which would be positioned on the side of a mountain and would fire shells every few minutes, with a great degree of accuracy, toward targets in ranges of hundreds of kilometers. Bull saw the realization of his technological brainchild as his life's work and was so obsessed that he was willing to sell the idea to anyone who would pay for it and bring it to fruition. Political or moral considerations were of no interest to him at all. When the paths of these two eccentrics—Saddam and the Canadian scientist—crossed, the project began to take shape, despite attempts by many to dissuade the scientist from getting involved. This project, too, never bore fruit.

The Iran-Iraq War ended toward the end of the 1980s. Iran emerged from the war in an inferior position, licking its wounds and trying to draw lessons. Saddam Hussein emerged from the eight-year-long war thumping his chest, continued to develop his nonconventional capabilities and make threats against Israel, and prepared for his next military adventure—the invasion of Kuwait. On the global stage, the winds of change were blowing and bringing about the end of the Cold War era and the collapse of the Soviet Union. The Berlin Wall was destroyed on November 9, 1989.

A visit by Defense Minister Moshe ("Misha") Arens to Washington was set for the end of July 1990. It was agreed between the two sides that during this visit top US political and intelligence officials would be presented with the Israeli intelligence community's view of the Iraqi nonconventional threat. It should be noted here that in the systems regulating the exchange of intelligence between the American and Israeli communities, there were clear rules that were dictated by the Americans. They refrained from sharing intelligence with us about countries that were friends of the United States and hostile to Israel, and they were very stingy with regard to the intelligence they would share with us regarding nonconventional weapons, and especially on the nuclear issue. The Israeli defense minister's visit to Washington and the winds of war that were blowing in the lead-up to the First Gulf War created the conditions whereby the Americans were open to hearing from us how we saw the Iraqi threat. For this purpose, a special joint effort was made by MI and the Mossad, and a "white paper" was prepared, compiling a detailed intelligence picture for presentation to the Americans.

Since the Mossad was the leader on the issue of nonconventional weapons within the intelligence community, we were invited to join the defense minister's delegation, which also included Amnon Lipkin-Shahak, the head of Military Intelligence at the time; David Ivri, then-director general of the defense ministry; and others whom I cannot recall, and for this I ask their forgiveness. The Mossad was represented by Shlomo, head of the nonconventional weapons division, and myself. The official welcome ceremony of the Israeli defense minister by Secretary of Defense Dick Cheney on the Pentagon parade ground, with the honor guard, the flags, the orchestra, the salute battery firing cannons from the American Civil War—to me it was all like a scene out of a movie. The fate of "spies" is to live in the shadows, entering and exiting from back doors, adopting fictional identities, and so on—and here I found myself suddenly "in the limelight" for the first time. Almost automatically I began looking for a corner where I could see but not be seen.

My next memory of that trip is of a huge conference room adjacent to the office of the secretary of defense at the Pentagon. Sitting on one side of the large table was Secretary of Defense Cheney, surrounded by a dozen three- and four-star generals whose insignia almost blinded us, as well as a few civilians. On the other side of the table, Defense Minister Arens sat opposite Cheney, with the rest of our delegation next to him. The secretary greeted the minister and our delegation, and the minister thanked the secretary for his hospitality and willingness to hear from us, then gave the floor to me. I presented the key points of our information on and assessment of each of Iraq's nonconventional capabilities, as well as our assessment of Saddam Hussein's intentions. Afterwards, Shlomo gave his presentation with phenomenal proficiency—the papers were in front of him, but he did not need them at all. In English with a touch of a Hungarian accent, he performed the "libretto" of his life. All those sitting on the other side of the table were taking notes, and the secretary of defense was listening intently to everything that was being said. I will never forget the moment that Shlomo completed his presentation. Secretary Cheney buried his head in his hands and said, "Good Lord, this is exactly what we need now." He then turned to his men and asked them whether the things we had presented corresponded with what they, the Americans, knew. They responded that they had to check and that they would get back to him with an answer by the end of the day.

During the visit to Washington, briefings were held with Under Secretary of State Larry Eagleburger (Secretary James Baker was abroad), CIA director William Webster, our ambassador, and our military attaché. A professional highlight was our briefing to a joint forum of directors of analysis from the CIA, the DIA (the Defense Intelligence Agency), and the State Department, which was convened specially and was unprecedented in the Washington landscape. The briefing was attended by about sixty experts in intelligence analysis, to whom we presented our doctrine, led by Shlomo.

The following is an excerpt from an unpublished paper written by Shlomo:

> I stood there and lectured passionately on the danger posed to the world by the Iraqi nuclear weapons that would appear in Saddam Hussein's arsenal in a matter of only one or two years. . . . I shot off all of the data with a sense of security that did not beg any questions about their truth. . . . I could not shake off the thoughts about "where I had come from." From the beginning of my journey as a twelve-year-old boy, I set myself the goal of teaching myself every day, from a dictionary, fifty new words in English. This child's achievements came to a peak in this place, during this presentation.

The results of the Washington visit were real and immediate. The Americans agreed to continue, even more intensively, the exchange of information and assessments regarding Iraq's nonconventional capabilities, including the nuclear issue. The next step was the visit by an American delegation to Israel for further discussions and the establishment of joint action.

The defense minister continued his visit in the United States. Shlomo and I flew from Washington to London for a meeting with the head of MI6 and the personal assistant of British prime minister Margaret Thatcher. The meeting, in which we repeated the entire libretto, took place on August 2, 1990. While we were sitting with the two gentlemen, the assistant to the head of MI6 entered the room, whispered something in his ear, and left. The MI6 head turned to us and said, "Saddam Hussein invaded Kuwait!"

Shlomo continued from London to Munich in order to brief the head of the BND (the German intelligence service, equivalent to the Mossad) and its experts. I returned to Israel.

On the last weekend before the outbreak of the war, a secret meeting took place between Prime Minister Shamir and King Hussein on the latter's estate outside London. In addition to the prime minister, the Israeli delegation included IDF deputy chief of staff Ehud Barak, deputy head of the Mossad Efraim Halevy, Cabinet Secretary Elyakim Rubinstein, and director general of the Prime Minister's Office Yossi Ben-Aharon. In order to keep the meeting secret not only from the British but also from the Israelis, it took place on the weekend so that the absence of the prime minister was not felt. The delegation stayed at the king's estate for two nights. Because the delegation had a majority of those who observed the Sabbath and the rules of *kashrut*, the king's men made sure to provide new dishes and food from a kosher restaurant in London. The Sabbath dinner, in the presence of the king and his cousin, Jordanian prime minister Zaid Ibn Shaker, was conducted according to the rules of *halacha*, and Sabbath songs were sung. On Saturday night, the *havdalah* ceremony was held, marking the end of the Sabbath and the beginning of the new week. Over the course of the two days, several meetings were held in various constellations, in addition to three-way talks between the prime minister, the king, and Efraim, who documented the meeting (he relied on the principle of *pikuach nefesh*, whereby the preservation of human life overrides religious considerations, to justify his writing on the Sabbath). It was only the second meeting between the prime minister and the king, and from the very first moment there was a "click" between them. Those close to them used to joke that this chemistry was due to the two of them being able to talk to each other at eye level.

Moving on from the backdrop of the meeting to its content: at the heart of the talks between the king and the prime minister was the tangible tension on the eve of the outbreak of war between President Bush's coalition and Iraq. Even then, the prime minister was under heavy pressure from President Bush not to intervene in the anticipated war, for fear that Israeli involvement would endanger the coalition the US had built with most of the Arab states in the Middle East. The king's circumstances were no less difficult, for he had chosen to support Saddam Hussein in the impending war. According to what was later published in the press, the king took the time to explain to the prime minister the background and reasons for his decision. The prime minister, it was reported, asked the king to agree that in the unlikely case that it was necessary, the Israeli air force could cross Jordanian airspace on its way to attack targets in Iraq. The king refused, explaining to Shamir that for him it would be suicide—the Arab world would see him as a traitor and condemn him to death. After a lengthy discussion, the king pledged that he would not allow the Iraqi air force to fly over Jordan and would prevent Iraqi ground forces from entering the kingdom. The king requested and received the prime minister's word that Israel would not mobilize reserve forces for deployment on the Jordanian front and would not infringe on Jordanian sovereignty in its airspace.

About a week after Prime Minister Shamir's return to Israel, the First Gulf War broke out. It was January 16, 1991. During this period, the cabinet held its meetings at the base of the IDF general staff, in the conference room on the second floor of the Templar building—the same meeting room that had served the Israeli government in the early years of the state. The reason for this arrangement was to enable the IDF's high command to be near its headquarters and command posts, as opposed to dragging them to Jerusalem. The cabinet met every day to receive reports and updates, discuss domestic, foreign, and security issues, and make decisions to be carried out in real time. I participated personally in all of these meetings, from the very first day of the war.

Prime Minister Shamir was under increasing pressure from Defense Minister Arens and the top echelons of the IDF to authorize the

IDF to intervene in the war, first and foremost by activating the air force against the surface-to-surface missile launchers in western Iraq that were set to launch missiles at Israel. Later on, as a ground plan developed, according to which one of the elite units would enter western Iraq in a ground operation to locate and destroy the missile launchers, the pressure on the prime minister increased even further. As long as the rockets were not landing in Israel, the discussion in the cabinet remained theoretical and focused on the question of whether, if and when the Iraqis did launch missiles against Israel, we would respond and intervene in the war. From the moment the missiles did begin to land in Israel, the question became concrete and burdensome, either directly or implicitly bringing up all of the core components of the Israeli security doctrine. These included the arguments that we had never wanted or asked a foreign power to fight our war; that the absence of an IDF response to a direct attack on Israel seriously damaged its doctrines of deterrence and decisive victory; that the principle of transferring the battle into enemy territory as soon as possible would be dissolved; and that national strength and pride would suffer a blow.

Notwithstanding all of these concerns, there were other, no less serious, considerations to take into account. The superpower of the United States, whose support plays an immense, perhaps even decisive, role in Israel's security, had asked us not to intervene in the war so that the Arab coalition built by President Bush would not fall apart; the president of the United States had committed to making a special effort to eliminate Saddam Hussein's missile-launching capability toward Israeli targets, and to immediately reinforce Israel's air defense capabilities.

Beyond all these considerations, as the press later revealed, the prime minister had the guarantee he had received from King Hussein, namely his commitment that the Iraqi air force would not be allowed to fly over Jordanian airspace and that Iraqi army units would not be allowed to enter Jordan and threaten Israel.

The arguments for and against intervention were discussed daily at the cabinet meetings. The top echelons of the defense establishment, including the defense minister, urged intervention in the war. Most of the ministers around the table adopted a more passive stance and to the best of my recollection showed no real conviction in support of or against either position. Each day, at the end of the deliberations, no one demanded a vote, and the discussion ended with the clear understanding that we were not intervening and would revisit the issue at the following day's meeting. The prime minister found himself in the most difficult position—the defense minister and the top ranks of the IDF were against him, the rest of the ministers had not aligned in support of him, and he himself, as a former member and commander of the Lehi, was loath to exercise ongoing restraint in the face of attacks day after day; this position stood in sharp contrast to the worldview he had held since his youth. His decision against intervening was apparently a result of the axiom that was already being used in Israeli politics at that time, taken from the lyrics of a popular song: "What you see from here, you cannot see from there."

With hindsight, I have no doubt that the prime minister's decision not to intervene in the war was the correct one. The First Gulf War brought about at least two positive strategic results for Israel: the first was that the threat against Israel from the eastern front, which centered on Iraq, had disappeared. The second was that the First Gulf War, which was the first time that Arabs were pitted against Arabs, symbolized the end of the pan-Arab era in the Middle East.

And one more point in closing. In preparation for the publication of this book, I showed this chapter to Shlomo and asked his permission to include in it quotes from the unpublished paper he had written years earlier. Shlomo, in his great modesty, pointed out that the entire team that had worked with him also deserved mention and thanks. And so, I thank them here for their perseverance, their determination, and their extraordinary success in directing the gathering of intelligence and numerous prevention operations.

The Second Lebanon War, 2006

The Second Lebanon War has become ingrained in the consciousness of the Israeli public as a failure. The public's and the media's preoccupation with it became, I believe, second only to the Yom Kippur War. As a citizen of this country and as someone who still knew a thing or two about what was going on in Israel's security apparatus during the time of the war, I expressed my objections to the war's critics in closed circles. Today (in 2018), with the passage of time, it is worth trying to remove the mark of disgrace that Israel affixed upon itself after this war, with the generous help of the Israeli media and irresponsible politicians.

I will begin with the facts, about which there is no dispute. On July 12, 2006, a Hezbollah force commanded by Imad Mughniyeh and with the approval and blessing of Hezbollah leader Sheikh Hassan Nasrallah laid an ambush on IDF patrols along the Israeli-Lebanese border and attacked without any provocation, kidnapping two soldiers and killing eight others. The purpose of the operation was to capture Israeli soldiers in order to negotiate a prisoner exchange. It soon became apparent that the two soldiers had been seriously injured during the operation and had died immediately afterwards. The Second Lebanon War was a direct result of this event.

What were the main characteristics of this war? First, it was a war that was forced upon us and, from our point of view, a just war that, to the best of my judgment, met the conditions of the definition of a "war of no choice." My definition of the war as one of no choice will almost certainly provoke opposition and even hostility. Well, according to my interpretation, the definition of "no choice" is more complex and multifaceted than simply that a war is justified only when the alternative is the country's annihilation. When we withdrew from Lebanon in 2001, we warned Hezbollah that for every provocation on its part we would respond with a massive blow. Hezbollah systematically tested, with violent actions against us, the limits of what we were willing to withstand. We did not stand behind the threat we issued in 2001 and did not respond, so they continued to raise the bar with each new provocation. The provocation of July 12, 2006, immediately took eight soldiers from us, as well as two other soldiers who, from the outset, were estimated not to be alive (though for various reasons this was not officially confirmed) and who were kidnapped as bargaining chips for prisoner exchanges. Paying such a high price without a proper response would have completely shattered our deterrent capability.

Add to this the fact that on the Israeli side both Prime Minister Ehud Olmert and Defense Minister Amir Peretz were new in their positions and had no previous military or security background. Had they not responded, Hezbollah would have perceived it as weakness and would most certainly have raised the level of its provocations even higher. The international support for the justness of our cause, which is quite rare, also indicated that our response was warranted.

It was a long war (thirty-eight days), longer than any other Israeli war since the War of Independence, with the exception of the War of Attrition, which lasted throughout 1969–70. However, it was an asymmetric war in which a conventional army was fighting against a guerrilla force. As mentioned, the political and military leadership during the Second Lebanon War was inexperienced. The war was completely transparent because of the media's coverage of it in real time. There was a considerable element of psychological warfare in this coverage that inadvertently (and perhaps also intentionally) resulted in damage to national morale. This was the first war in which the moderate Arab world openly supported Israel (including the Lebanese government, albeit secretly). The Second Lebanon War was the first battle in our real campaign against Iran. It was the first major war in which the home front was the main front. (During the First Gulf War, thirty-nine Iraqi missiles fell on the home front, but Israel was totally passive and did not actively engage in the war.) It was a war without a clear victory for the IDF—I will refer to the significance of this in Shiite culture later.

Who were the players in this war?

Iran is a Shiite Muslim state that transformed overnight from a Western secular country into a radical Islamic sharia state in a bloodless coup in 1979. It is a country with huge energy resources, both oil and gas. The export of these energy resources in 2006 brought Iran $60 billion. Until the era of the sanctions imposed on it, Iran experienced growth of 6 percent per year and foreign exchange reserves of $65 billion, which constituted two and a half times the national debt. These data show that in 2006 economic considerations did not constitute a constraint on Iranian decision makers in all their decisions regarding Hezbollah.

Hezbollah is a group of the Shiite ethnicity, which was a minority in Lebanon at the time of the establishment of that country and which today is probably the largest of all the ethnic groups in the country. Members of the ethnic group live mainly in southern Lebanon, bordering Israel. This is a minority that was historically weak, poor, and suppressed and whose main livelihood was agriculture. The affinity of members of this group to Iran is based on their religious identity—the Shia faith. According to radical Shiite Islam, a violent conflict that does not end with a crushing defeat or surrender is considered a victory because, according to their belief, war is eternal, and in order to reach the final victory it is enough just to survive the battles on the way to this ultimate triumph. That is how the Shiites in Lebanon interpreted the IDF's evacuation in 2001. For them, it was proof that Israel was not invincible. Iran and Syria's military and other types of assistance to Hezbollah turned the organization into a force that could not be ignored. Over time, Hezbollah became a state within a state. As they increased their military power, they established a political arm that became a party represented in the Lebanese parliament and government coalition.

The Shiite leadership, unlike many others in Lebanon, is not tainted by corruption and expands its influence in the community through social activities, health services, education, and the like. There is no lack of funds for these activities. During the period under discussion, $100 million was transferred to finance them from Iran alone. Despite his simple origins, Hassan Nasrallah proved himself as a charismatic figure and has grown to be the unshakable leader of the Shiites in Lebanon, though his religious title is not particularly illustrious. Nasrallah's ties with Iran go back to the time he studied there and became acquainted with some of its current leadership.

Syria, a country controlled by the Alawite minority, also a Shiite sect, completes the Shiite Crescent, which includes Iran, Iraq, Syria, and Lebanon. Syria was established in the framework of the Sykes-Picot Agreement of 1916, which served as the basis for the political reality dictated by the victors of the First World War. Syria never recognized Lebanon's political sovereignty de jure, seeing it rather as an integral part of Syria, or at the very least as an entity under Syrian strategic influence and control. On Syrian maps, you will not find an international border between Syria and Lebanon. At the current border between the two countries, on the Damascus-Beirut road, there is only a Lebanese border crossing point, manned by Lebanese border policemen and customs. Since the Six-Day War in 1967, when Israel captured the Golan Heights from Syria, not a shot has been fired from the Syrian side of the border toward Israel. Syria has compensated for this by using Hezbollah in South Lebanon as its long arm to advance its strategic objectives. Thus a meeting of interests between Iran, Syria, and Hezbollah was formed. Syria's main role in this coalition has been to serve as a transit state for all Iranian weapons transferred to southern Lebanon, as a storage depot for some of these weapons, and as a refuge and activity base for the top echelons of Hezbollah. Syria's use of Hezbollah has allowed the Syrians deniability with regard to their direct involvement in terrorism, though Syria is considered a terrorist state (which was involved, among other things, in the assassination of Lebanese prime minister Rafik Hariri and has housed the headquarters of Islamic Jihad and Hamas).

In the wake of the First Lebanon War and the IDF's withdrawal from Lebanon in 2001, a balance of terror between Israel and Hezbollah quickly developed. How was this disconcerting situation created?

In 1999, Syria was forced to withdraw its military forces from Lebanon, but it maintained its close ties with Hezbollah and adopted the organization as its long arm against Israel. Iran also adopted Hezbollah as part of its strategy to become a regional power and as part of its deterrence doctrine. Iran sought to build up a threat on the Israeli border that could be used against Israel in the event of an American attack against Iran, as well as in the case of a possible Israeli attack. Israel evacuated its forces from Lebanon in 2001, declaring, as mentioned, that any provocation by Hezbollah would elicit a severe Israeli response. Unfortunately, Israel did not implement this policy. Hezbollah, for its part, occasionally tested Israel's declared policy and realized that Israel was not standing behind it.

What were the reasons for Israel's failure to follow through on its threats?

There is no simple answer to this question; rather, a series of factors must be taken into account. First, Prime Minister Ehud Barak, who pulled the IDF out of Lebanon and was the person who issued the ultimatum to Hezbollah, wanted to be free to pursue diplomatic activity. He initially gave priority to the negotiations with the Syrians over talks with the Palestinians and wanted a quiet border in the north. This quickly became irrelevant. When the Assad-Clinton meeting in Geneva failed, Barak gave up on the negotiations with Syria and turned his focus toward the withdrawal from Lebanon. Not long afterwards, the Second Intifada broke out, a challenge that quickly became the first priority, not by choice, but out of necessity. An additional consideration was that the country's economy was flourishing, including in the Galilee. The main source of income for the Galilee communities was tourism in the form of *tzimmerim*, the bed-and-breakfasts that were popping up throughout the pastoral area. Quiet along the northern border therefore became increasingly important. Prime Minister Ariel Sharon also gave other issues higher priority than Lebanon; at first he was engaged in the building of the separation fence in Judea and Samaria, and later he was busy with the disengagement from the Gaza Strip. From a philosophical point of view, it is possible that Sharon suffered from "Lebanon syndrome," for which he paid the price of his post as defense minister in 1982. There were also those who said—with an arrogance that not all of us Israelis are immune to—"Let Hezbollah collect all the iron bars they want—they'll all rust anyway!" For the record, intelligence provided an accurate picture of Hezbollah's military buildup: that is, there was no surprise.

Against this backdrop, a dynamic developed between Israel and Hezbollah, resulting in a de facto balance of fear between a guerrilla organization of several thousand fighters and the most powerful army in the Middle East.

What happened in the war itself?

Sheikh Hassan Nasrallah anticipated that the abduction of the two IDF soldiers would lead to two or three days of exchanges of fire, followed by negotiations on prisoner exchanges, as had been the case in similar situations since the withdrawal from Lebanon in 2001. This assessment was completely mistaken, as he openly admitted after the war.

Nasrallah did not appreciate that Israel had a new leadership that, while not possessing military experience, was also not captive to the conceptions of the past. This leadership decided that the balance of fear that had been building up since 2001 was no longer tolerable and had to be stopped. Of course, the force of the immediate response was also due to the fact that we'd had eight soldiers killed in the incident in addition to the two kidnapped soldiers.

For the first time since 2001, Israel challenged the balance of fear, the instigator of which was not Hezbollah, which served only as a tool, but Iran and Syria. The Israeli response also disrupted Iran's plans; Iran had built up Hezbollah in order to use it when the conditions and circumstances were convenient, and now things had blown up in their faces.

The perception in Israel at the end of the war was that we had not won. Let us analyze this assertion:

- Israeli and global public opinion is shackled by the image of Israel as winning all of its wars within a matter of days (in 1956 and 1967, it was one week, and in 1973 it was eighteen days). The Second Lebanon War, in contrast, lasted over a month. The duration of the war in itself damaged Israel's image. It must be remembered that Israel activated no more than 15 percent of the IDF's forces in this war, meaning that the war's results did not reflect the true balance of power between the two sides.

- The international media are usually against us, and this was the case here once again, from the second or third day of the war. Israel was portrayed as attacking civilians and killing children. The media coverage contained a very strong element of psychological warfare against us, which played a major role in shaping public opinion about the outcome of the war. Today, the Arab staging of fake scenes, which the major television networks fall victim to, is already a well-known phenomenon.

- This war was the most televised of all of Israel's wars, uncensored and in real time. The minimum that can be said about the Israeli media coverage is that it was unbalanced. What guides the media are ratings, so the networks competed with each other over who could be more aggressive, more negative, and more shocking. Everything negative about the war from the Israeli perspective was presented as headline news. Nothing positive received any coverage. The result was that the war was seen as a failure. I went to Kiryat Shmona and, relying on what I had seen and heard on the news, was expecting Dresden. The reality was that out of close to a thousand (!) Katyushas fired at Kiryat Shmona, there were about thirty actual hits.

- The real war took place in Lebanon. The Israeli media took this reality, molded it, distorted it, and passed on a virtual reality to the public. And this created the perception that we did not win the war.

- Asymmetric war is completely different from conventional war, in which two armies face each other and try to wear each other down until one side surrenders. A central feature of a conventional war is the conquest of territories. In a war in which a conventional army—the IDF—is facing guerrilla forces, the results are measured by the extent of the physical elimination of the guerrilla fighters and the destruction of their assets—weapons, equipment, and infrastructure.

According to this test:

- The IDF killed about a thousand Hezbollah fighters, which constituted about a third of their regular fighting force.
- We destroyed all the long-range missiles on their launchers, even before they were launched—this says something about the quality of the intelligence we had.
- We eliminated the majority of Hezbollah's medium-range missiles and launchers. Each launcher was destroyed immediately after its first launch, because of its creation of an electronic signature that enabled us to home in on it. This says something about our operational capabilities.
- We destroyed a large portion of their infrastructure (bunkers, headquarters, offices, outposts, trenches, and more).

If the objective of the war were to destroy and subjugate Hezbollah, we would have had to activate a much larger ground force than we did, occupy and hold territory, and do all of this in a week to ten days, because Israel—in the eyes of the world—does not have the luxury of long wars.

What did we not achieve in this war? We did not succeed in silencing the short-range rockets in the Galilee, which do not carry an electronic signature. We also did not bring Hezbollah to the point of raising a white flag. In this regard, one must remember what was pointed out at the beginning of this chapter—that according to Muslim belief, a victory that is not unmistakable is a defeat for the enemy and a victory for the Muslim.

There were many failures in this war, which we must investigate, draw lessons from, and correct. The media coverage blew these failures completely out of proportion, creating the image of disaster.

There were, however, some other achievements of this war, including the following:

1. The UN Security Council enacted Resolution 1701 to disarm Hezbollah. Even if it is not implemented, it greatly improves Israel's position. This is also true regarding the supply of new weapons from Syria, Iran, or any other source. Hezbollah continues to break the cease-fire agreement, and so do we, though we attack them in their territories in Lebanon and Syria.

2. For the first time, the Lebanese army was deployed along the international border between Israel and Lebanon, and the IDF was redeployed along the border fence on our side.

3. The UN international force grew and received more "teeth."

4. The two forces—the Lebanese army and the UN force—serve as a physical buffer between us and Hezbollah, which was not the case beforehand.

5. Syria's status and influence in Lebanon were weakened.

6. A bloc of moderate Arab states openly opposed to radical Muslim forces began to develop.

So what's next? In order to assess future trends, one must first examine the state of the players in the Second Lebanon War today, in 2017, the time of the writing of this book. *Iran* has signed the nuclear agreement with the United States, and the sanctions against it are gradually being lifted. Iran and the United States are cooperating, de facto, in the war against ISIS in Iraq. Iran and Syria continue to equip Hezbollah with weapons; the IDF thwarted this supply militarily in March 2017 and declared that it would continue to do so whenever conditions and intelligence allow it.

Hezbollah as a guerrilla organization has sunk deep into the Syrian swamp and is taking losses of strategic magnitude for an organization of its size. The organization's standing among the Lebanese public is at an all-time low. *Syria* has been embroiled in a civil war for several years, with ISIS having seized large parts of the country bordering Iraq, and various opposition groups threatening Bashar Assad's regime, which survives only because of the support of Putin, who has established a new reality in the region—the permanent presence of Russian air, sea, and land forces in Syria.

A few words about the current threats facing Israel. In my understanding, Hezbollah in the north and Hamas in the Gaza Strip are at the top of the IDF's priorities within Israel's inner circle of threats. ISIS threatens the Middle East and the world at large. Iran, today and in the foreseeable future, continues to constitute the biggest strategic threat to the State of Israel.

Back to the Second Lebanon War and its aftermath. In my view, the most important and significant achievement of the war was the breaking of the balance of fear that had been established between Hezbollah and the IDF along the Lebanese border, and the return of the IDF's deterrent capability. Proof of this is that, in the eleven years since the Second Lebanon War, Hezbollah has not dared disrupt the quiet along the shared border. To complete the picture of the balance of fear, one must add another aspect. Hezbollah did not stand alone against the IDF. It was supported by Iran and Syria, each of whom saw Hezbollah as its long arm against Israel, and in Iran's case, also against the US. Iran and Syria thought they were maintaining a threatening Hezbollah force along Israel's northern border that would operate only according to their directions and needs. The dynamics on the ground flew in the face of this working assumption when the July 12, 2006, incident initiated by Hezbollah spun out of its control and developed into a war that lasted more than a month.

About a year after the war, the renowned commentator Tom Friedman wrote his own balance sheet of this war. It is fitting for our purposes to quote a few words from his commentary:

On July 12, 2006, Hezbollah fighters directed by Mr. Nasrallah abducted two Israeli soldiers and killed eight others in an unprovoked attack across the Lebanon-Israel border, on the pretext of seeking a prisoner exchange. This triggered a war that killed about 1,200 Lebanese. . . . Mr. Nasrallah [is] guilty of a serious failure of judgment. . . . Mr. Nasrallah demonstrated a total failure to anticipate Israel's response to his raid. He assumed Israel would carry out the same limited retaliation it had with previous raids. Wrong. He failed to take into account the changed circumstances in Israel. The kidnapping of an Israeli soldier in Gaza a few weeks earlier, plus the fact that a new chief of staff of the Israeli Army, a new prime minister and a new defense minister had just taken office and all felt they were being tested, triggered an enormous Israeli response. Some 1,200 Lebanese died because of this gross error in judgment. . . . In unilaterally launching a war against Israel, without a vote of the Lebanese cabinet—of which Hezbollah is a member—the militia did grievous harm to Lebanon's fragile democracy and democratization in the Arab world. All the fears that if you let an Islamist party into government it will not respect the rules of the game were fulfilled by Hezbollah.[5]

Friedman's article was targeted toward the American reader, for whom any violation of democracy is an offense of the highest order. When Iran and Syria supplied Hezbollah with huge amounts of rockets, their aim was to create deterrence against Israel. They saw Hezbollah as their long arm that would pressure Israel to agree to political compromises and threaten it if it attacked them. The use of these weapons by Hezbollah, in circumstances that did not serve the objectives mentioned above, diminished the capabilities of all three players. In this respect, Nasrallah achieved nothing from this war. Until the war broke out, Hezbollah was sitting on the border and enjoying full freedom of action against Israel. Following the war, Hezbollah was pushed back, far away from the border fence, with a UN force of ten thousand troops positioned as a physical barrier between Hezbollah and the border, and with the IDF having returned to the border. According to Friedman, this was a huge strategic loss for Hezbollah.

In the years leading up to the war, Israel, because of a change in its priorities, degraded and even neglected its ground forces. The Second Lebanon War was a warning signal to Israel, which led the IDF to buckle down and upgrade its ground forces and their level of preparedness. This is another respect in which Israel benefited from the war. Israel's response to the July 12, 2006, incident cost Hezbollah and Lebanon billions of dollars' worth of damage to infrastructure, homes, and roads. In order to rebuild itself, Lebanon had to rely on the charity of the Arab states and Iran. Israel, on the other hand, entered an era of unprecedented economic growth after the war, due in large part to increased foreign investment in its high-tech industry. Friedman concluded his article by saying that if there had been a proper commission of inquiry into Nasrallah's instigation of the war, he would have been forced to resign.

I hope that I have succeeded in providing a picture of the Second Lebanon War and its results that is more balanced and, above all, more reflective of reality.

APPENDIX

IN MEMORIAM

The role of the head of the Mossad involves, inter alia, the sad obligation of delivering eulogies. In my case, I continued to fulfill this duty even after my retirement. I do apologize to all of the family members whose loved ones' eulogies I have not published here, and of these there are many. The selection of the eulogies to be included in this book was somewhat random, though I did apply two general rules: one relates to the extent of my personal closeness to the person, and the other has to do with the contents of the eulogy itself. One more apology: there were two obituaries that I wanted to publish but that, for one reason or another, got lost over time.

The eulogies, which appear in the chronological order of the dates on which they were delivered, recognize key people or those who have become symbols and role models and who dealt with the core functions of the Mossad.

The centrality of the profession of HUMINT is embodied in the eulogy for Meki Evron.

The definition of operational leadership is discussed in the eulogy for Moshe Levin ("Kokla").

Dave Kimche was the ultimate intelligence man, whose abilities crossed the boundaries of the Mossad's various disciplines.

The eulogy for Sylvia, one of the "immortal" combatants of the "Caesarea" unit, provides a small peek into the profession of running combatants.

The spouses of the Mossad's employees and combatants live in the shadow of their partners. The eulogy for Leika, Kokla's wife, reveals a touch of the world of the Mossad employees' wives.

Shlomo Gal was the ultimate operations man, who began his life in Israel as a child refugee of the Holocaust and grew up to command the Mossad's top operational unit.

I also include in this chapter remarks (not a eulogy) that I delivered on the occasion of Yitzhak Shamir's ninety-fifth birthday, in which I spoke, inter alia, about the nature of the relations between the head of the Mossad and the prime minister. I also deal with this issue in chapter 4's section on the negotiations for a peace treaty with Jordan, which were led by the late Yitzhak Rabin.

Meki Evron (Israel Intelligence Heritage and Commemoration Center, February 18, 2004)

The time line of his life passed through Ben-Shemen, the British army, the Palmach, the IDF, and the intelligence community. Meki's is a breed that is disappearing into the pages of the history of the Land of Israel. The members of this breed were role models for my generation. We saw them as the fulfillers of the Zionist dream, the new Israelis, who cast off Diaspora characteristics and became the spearhead of a new species—tall and proud, courageous, reverent toward manual labor, facing down every challenge, breaking conventions, devoting their lives to the people and the state. A species of groundbreakers.

These are people who lived and operated in an environment that was not yet regulated. They were the parents of all beginnings. They set the benchmarks, the precedents, the points of reference, and the standards. They were entrepreneurs, and entrepreneurial traits are individualism, nonconformity, the breaking of rules, the cutting of corners, the finding of shortcuts, and the utilization of the "Jewish genius" to achieve inconceivable feats.

In intelligence, Meki belonged to the school of HUMINT, human intelligence. HUMINT is the aircraft carrier of the art of intelligence. The centrality and stature of HUMINT began with the story of the biblical spies and will always retain its importance. HUMINT is a one-on-one contest between the hunter and his prey. The hunter, in order to succeed, must be endowed with an almost impossible combination of traits; he must understand the cultural environment of his prey; knowledge of his language is a great advantage; he must pick apart information about his prey, separating the wheat from the chaff; he must observe him, learn his personality, his qualities, his weaknesses; he must choose the best way to approach him and establish contact with him; he must develop a personal bond with him, create a dependence, and corrupt him. Finally, he must lead his prey to betray his people, his country, and his family, without damaging his dependence on the hunter. Meki, throughout his entire intelligence career, lived and breathed HUMINT and contributed immensely to this profession in which Israeli intelligence has excelled.

Today we have come full circle. We have developed SIGINT, COMINT, ELINT, and VISINT. We have invested billions in all these, and today we find ourselves in a hopeless situation. The "Queen of Battle" of the intelligence profession, which is also the cheapest, really no money in comparison with the other disciplines, has closed shop. Saddam Hussein was captured only because of HUMINT. Bin Laden has not been found yet because of a lack of HUMINT. All types of technical intelligence failed to provide an accurate intelligence picture of Saddam Hussein's nonconventional capabilities. One top source—if only there were one—would do for free what billions of dollars' worth of technology could not do.

In my memory, Meki was one of the few who cautioned about the deterioration of HUMINT. "Bikta," the Tzomet division's branch in Iran, was a HUMINT factory during the time that Meki was its director. This branch's consumption of "Minox" film was greater than that of the entire intelligence community put together. The branch's main intelligence products were not field reports from a source about something he heard from a second source, who had heard it from a third source. The main intelligence products were hundreds of thousands of pages photographed by—yes—agents. The IDF's successful operational responses to the Arab armies during the Six-Day War and the Yom Kippur War were made possible mainly by the regular flow of huge quantities of intelligence over a period of years from the Mossad's branch in Iran.

This is also the place to correct what in my opinion was a historical injustice done to Meki. The operation of the bringing of the Iraqi MiG 21 to Israel has long been recognized as one of the finest feathers in the cap of Israeli intelligence. Who did not bask in the glory of this success? Among the roar of the pyrotechnics and festivities, the role of Meki, who contributed greatly to the HUMINT portion of the operation, especially in its early stages, was never mentioned.

In Ben-Gurion's geostrategic doctrine, Iran played a central role in his "triangles" theory, which argued that Israel had to develop tripartite regional alliances, such as Israel-Turkey-Iran or Israel-Ethiopia-Morocco. Meki served two terms in Iran, the first in the early 1950s and the second in the 1960s. He saw as his main task the supplying of intelligence to respond to the Israeli EEI, but his presence and his work in Iran gave important added value to the realization of the concept of tripartite alliances. Meki taught the Iranians what intelligence was and why a country that has enemies needs it. He piqued their curiosity and their desire to learn and thus developed their dependence on us, which enabled our freedom of action in this country for decades.

Meki was not an easy man. He stuck by his opinions, and as far as the intelligence profession was concerned he fought tooth and nail for what he believed in; when he was convinced of his position, opinion, recommendation, or decision, he was impossible to budge. Meki, who was a classic HUMINT man, witnessed the development of the new intelligence disciplines such as SIGINT, COMINT and VISINT, and it was hard for him to get used to the changing world. He also feared that these new professions would replace HUMINT, which he referred to not as a profession but as an art.

Yael and I served under quite a few commanders in our thirty-two years in the Mossad. Meki and Ruthie were our first commanders on our first mission abroad as a newlywed couple. Luckily for us, they liked us. The way they treated us and took care of us—Yael arrived in Tehran at the beginning of her first pregnancy—served me throughout my entire career in the Mossad as the model of how a superior should treat his subordinates in all aspects of the mission abroad, which cannot be separated from the work itself.

Thank you, Ruthie, and thank you—albeit belatedly—to Meki.

May his memory be a blessing.

Moshe Levin ("Kokla") (October 19, 2009)

Fifteen years have passed since Kokla left us. The eulogy at the funeral was full of emotion. It expressed the helpless feeling that the happier the time, the sooner it passes.

Kokla left us when he was at the peak of his life in terms of his own self-realization. My words today will not be a eulogy but will rather express thoughts and meditations, more logic and less sentiment. Fifteen years have gone by, we have all aged, and thoughts arise in our minds about the concept of time—for example, the notion that when you are young the days are short and the years are long, and when you are old the days are long and the years are short—just as it seems that it was only yesterday that we lost Kokla.

The concept of friendship also transforms over the years. It goes from a sense of loss the moment that a friend is taken from you, because true friendship is tested most of all when you are in distress and in need of help and support, to a feeling of profound longing, for it is good for a person to have one friend whom he trusts and to whom he can reveal everything that is in his heart. And when that friend is gone, you have no one to open your heart to. Friendships are more valuable than blood ties. An old proverb says, "Who will you love more—your brother or your friend? I will not love my brother until he is my friend."

I thought a lot about what I would say this evening that would be fitting for this event and for those in attendance, some of whom knew Kokla and some who did not. In the end I decided that I should say a few things about leadership. Not necessarily everything I am going to say was embodied in Kokla's personality, but a considerable part certainly was.

If I had to define the attributes required of a leader, I would mention the following three:

1. The leader should have a *charismatic* personality. Charisma is an innate quality of leadership and personal charm, which fosters a great degree of loyalty. This quality is expressed in the idea of "I will follow him through fire and water."
2. The leader should be *smart*. In our context, the meaning of being smart is having good judgment. It is the ability to distinguish between the essential and the trivial; to decide on the right order of priorities; to decide to do something, and even more so, to decide not to; and to decide what the limits of your capabilities are, and when being brave crosses the line into stupidity.
3. The leader should be a *good person*. He or she should project integrity and lead by personal example. The leader should be sensitive to the problems of his subordinates and act as a teacher, not only as a commander or supervisor.

The three qualities I describe here are derived from our anatomy and beyond it, for the attribute of being a good person comes from the heart, the attribute of being smart comes from the head, and charisma is bestowed upon a leader from a higher external source.

The leader must be faithful to the principle of *overall responsibility*, be it overall responsibility for realizing an idea and vision, for people, or for carrying out a mission. This overall responsibility is derived from the authority in the hands of the leader. The authority of the leader is comprehensive in its essence, and therefore the leader cannot shake off overall responsibility. And to complete the equation, we must mention the element of the sanction, that is, if you have been granted authority and you have failed, the responsibility is entirely yours, and you have to bear the consequences, for better or for worse.

We use the titles of *manager*, *head*, and *commander* for a person who stands at the top of a pyramid of people. Each of these may or may not be a leader. What is the difference? (This comparison is based on an American academic article.)

- The manager administers; the leader innovates.
- The manager is a copy; the leader is an original.
- The manager maintains; the leader develops.
- The manager focuses on systems and structure; the leader focuses on people.
- The manager relies on control; the leader inspires trust.
- The manager has a short-range view; the leader has a long-range perspective.
- The manager asks how and when; the leader asks what and why.
- The manager does things right; the leader does the right thing.
- The manager uses delegated responsibility; the leader seeks to expand responsibility.

Kokla was first and foremost a commander with many leadership qualities. He imparted to his people the insight that the first guiding principle should be to carry out the mission at any cost. The second principle is to carry it out exacting the lowest cost possible.

Kokla believed that a commander's place should be at the inter-section at which he could make the most significant contribution to the carrying out of the mission. There is always the temptation to be at the tip of the spear, but as a commander he always knew how to assess the situation and, throughout a mission, to put himself in other places as well.

A true commander does not rest on the laurels of the glory of op-erations past and does not preserve himself for the great missions of the future. He focuses on the mission at hand.

Detailed planning, caution, and hard work were his guiding prin-ciples, and they proved to be a recipe for success. People say that God is in the details. Kokla proved that the small details are what make the difference between good and great.

Kokla believed that in every command there was still room for maneuver and discretion, which often caused me headaches and the feeling that I needed to remind him that even when he was convinced that he must stray from the command he had to take into account that there was still information that he didn't know and if he was wrong, then . . . and here he would finish my sentence, saying: "Yes, if I am wrong, the responsibility is entirely mine."

In crisis situations, or when one's back was up against the wall, Kokla would express his belief that there were no desperate situ-ations, only desperate people, and that he as the commander had to enrapture, raise morale, and find a way out of the muddle.

This was Kokla. We loved him, we trusted him, and sometimes we were angry with him. His professional contribution to the two opera-tional units in which he served, one of which he commanded, proved to be groundbreaking. And so we will remember him.

Dave Kimche (March 10, 2010)

The ultimate intelligence man has left us.

Born and educated in England, Dave pursued Middle Eastern studies in Israel, right up to and including a doctorate. The wonderful combination of these achievements, skills, and abilities created a multilingual man with extensive and profound experience in a number of Western cultures, along with his entrenched Israeliness, with the virtues and shortcomings that go along with that. He was an intellectual with a formal education and a deep understanding of the world in general and the Middle East and Africa in particular.

His immigration to Israel at the age of eighteen was out of Zionist motivations, and his affinity with Israel was immediate, absolute, and uncompromising; he shed all signs of his past affinities and later reintroduced them as tools with which to serve the State of Israel and its people. Dave was an amiable and gregarious man, and very brave, "a British gentleman," comfortable in the intellectual environment of "understatement" and "cautious optimism." With such a toolbox there wasn't an intelligence role that Dave could not fulfill with the proficiency of a virtuoso.

Dave started his intelligence career in the Mossad on the "aircraft carrier" of intelligence—HUMINT. In this profession, he learned how to get to know the enemy by the "whites of their eyes." With his ability to borrow identities, connect with people, and smooth-talk, he succeeded expertly in leading the source through the entire path of recruitment, from the establishment of contact, through the stage of "corruption," to the referral to the recruiter (usually for a foreign intelligence service) to operation, intelligence interrogation, and briefings—the production of intelligence. Dave's comprehensive operational abilities enabled him to deal successfully with the highest-level sources, and with those considered to be the most difficult to crack.

Dave was one of the founders and developers of the discipline of interservice relationships with friendly—and less friendly—intelligence services around the world. From the 1950s to the 1970s, the Mossad's responsibility for relations with countries that did not have diplomatic relations with the State of Israel was crucial to Israel's standing in the world. During the period in which Dave was responsible for this department, he was a regular visitor in the parlors of many a head of state and became accustomed to traveling alone around the globe, less with an Israeli passport and more with foreign passports, delivering Israel's messages to countries that did not want open relations with it. He maintained intelligence contacts with these countries and devised complex equations of direct and indirect interests with third parties.

One of Dave's favorite things was working with national minorities throughout the Middle East and Africa. In his family photo album, as well as that of the Mossad, one can find countless photographs of Dave, dressed in the traditional garb of the ethnic minority, with whom he formed relations on behalf of the state. In this endeavor, a great degree of solidarity was felt between the long-suffering Jewish people, who had already achieved their political independence, and the oppressed minorities who were struggling for their own self-determination or independence.

One of Dave's specialties was psychological warfare, in particular because it takes place on the intellectual battlefield in which the weapons are the human mind, and its essence is to foster ideas that can be used to create Archimedean leverage and influence that can change the world order. It was no surprise that Dave was partial to the sharp analysis involved in psychological warfare—after all, he was a descendent of the "RaDak," the biblical commentator and philosopher Rabbi David Kimche. Psychological warfare is a particularly challenging task, for every idea is a double-edged sword—if you do not succeed in controlling it and steering it toward your goal, you are liable to find yourself in a desperate situation.

Reliable sources say that Dave was, among other things, the father of the idea of defining the Pakistani nuclear effort as an attempt to create an "Islamic bomb." The rationale behind this definition was that it would help mobilize the non-Muslim world against this effort.

When Dave was the Mossad's "number two" I was still on the bottom third of the ladder, and there, around the water cooler, people talked about Dave and his exploits with reverence and looked up to him as a role model. I had a very deep appreciation for Dave, and throughout my career in the Mossad and before making any important decision I would ask for his advice.

Dave was an intellectual, a top spy, a statesman, and an operations man, one of the best the Mossad has ever known. He definitely belongs to the small club of people who have done so much for the country and who deserve the gratitude of the people of Israel, if they only knew whom to thank.

To Ruthie and the children—Dave is no longer suffering. May you know no more sorrow. We, his friends, will remember him forever.

Sylvia Raphael (September 1, 2010)

I got to know Sylvia only superficially, in her last years, and I was among those who escorted her on her last journey on Kibbutz Ramat Hakovesh. When I got to the unit in which she served, they were already talking about Sylvia as a veteran combatant the likes of which have rarely been seen. But I was involved in a defining moment that was connected to her. This was the moment when the office of the head of the Mossad first got wind about the mishap in Lillehammer, which hit everyone like a bolt of lightning. It was this affair that robbed Sylvia of her anonymity, and her love story with the Norwegian lawyer who defended her turned her personal story into a drama that even the best scriptwriters in Hollywood would have had trouble coming up with.

The things I am going to talk about tonight relate to all of the Mossad's combatants, past and present, with whom Sylvia's spirit lives on.

In the terminology of the Mossad, the term *combatant* was used exclusively for the combatants in Sylvia's unit. These were, in general, Israeli Jews operating in target countries, that is, enemy countries. There have been occasional exceptions to this rule over the years, combatants who were not Jews or Israelis but whose connection to Israel, loyalty, and personal skills qualified them to serve as combatants.

In the 1990s, members of an additional unit began to adopt the definition of themselves as combatants, though they did not work in target countries. Previously, they had been simply called Mossad employees, but because they wanted to differentiate themselves by the special operational character of their work, they adopted the title of "combatants." I did not object to this development, as I saw in it the aspiration of one group of employees to emulate another. In terms of risk, the combatants in the unit in which Sylvia served face matters of life and death. The others risk "only" long prison terms. Members of both of these units are the "tip of the spear"—they are at the forefront of the Mossad's operational activities.

The expectations, qualities, and skills demanded of Mossad combatants are the highest on any given scale of any occupation, profession, or job.

In the world of HUMINT, there is a dividing line that is never crossed between the *katza* (field intelligence officer) and the agent. The former is Israeli and Jewish, the latter is not. The former is motivated by a belief in the ideal and justness of Zionism in the Land of Israel, as well as the desire to make a contribution in the course of self-realization. The latter is driven by material motives, despair, or a desire to avenge his homeland and/or the people who wronged him.

The first thing to be derived from this comparison is the degree of trust the system has in the combatant and the agent. Trust in the combatant is unreserved, unconditional, absolute, and final. Trust in the agent is based on the principle of "respecting him while suspecting him."

A few words about operating combatants.

Over many years of operational activity, the Mossad, like other serious Western intelligence services, developed a doctrine of individual operation, that is, a runner and a combatant. The strictest among us were careful to maintain the ratio of one runner for one combatant. Others, sometimes because of financial considerations, put one runner in charge of a small number of combatants operating within the same undercover infrastructure. This doctrine did not come out of nowhere or as a result of the whim of one commander or another. Behind it stood a profound ideology and substantial considerations.

The threshold requirements of combatants are an array of qualities and skills, the most demanding of any profession or occupation one can think of. Their training period is much longer than any other in the field of intelligence. Their "need to know" level is the most constrained. The personal risks they take upon themselves are the highest we can conceive of in human society in general. The (classic) combatants work alone in a target country, and their "personal weapons" are their passport and cover story. For any error, they are liable to pay with their lives. Therefore, the responsibility of the person who sends them on their missions is also higher than in any other field, including in the case of military commanders sending their soldiers into battle. In order to maintain the combatant's personal security and to extract his or her full potential, a doctrine developed regarding the operating of combatants, relieving him or her of all daily worries. The unit takes care of all of the family's needs and releases the combatant from all administrative affairs; it provides him or her with the ultimate professional team, consisting of an intelligence officer, an operations officer, a communications officer, a weapons and technology officer, and the expert in charge of the cover story. All of these roles are the domain of the runner, who is the combatant's go-to person twenty-four hours a day, 365 days a year. The runner represents the unit's collective wisdom. He is the combatant's friend and confidant, his or her supporter and consoler, the briefer and the questioner, the admirer and the critic. If you will, the runner is the link between the combatant's authentic life and his or her operational life.

Some will say, perhaps with a hint of cynicism, that the things I am saying belong to the romantic period of the unit and that today the circumstances are different and needs are different and capabilities are different. My response to this is that so-called romanticism is an eternal value, and one that must be preserved, because this is the only way to maintain the ultimate balance of security and cost/ benefit over time, with the emphasis being on the phrase "over time."

A word about combatants with families.

First of all, it would be impossible to exist without them, because it is inconceivable that the unit be operated only by single people. Therefore, the unit, and especially the system that operates it, must create the maximum balance between the demands of the job and the duty of the combatant toward his or her family. On the basis of past experience, I would like to state that whenever there is any question about the calculations involved in maintaining this balance, then there is no doubt that family comes first. Bad decisions on this subject cause damage—sometimes serious damage—that ultimately affect the viability of an operation.

When the number of women fighting for gender equality in the State of Israel was negligible, and the term *gender* was not yet in common use, the Mossad in general and the unit in particular implemented equality between the sexes on a practical level. Female employees and combatants of the Mossad have always filled the entire range of operational roles, including senior management positions and command of operations, with male subordinates working underneath them.

An issue that comes up as part of this discussion is what the required model of behavior should be between a male combatant and a female combatant when they work as part of the same team. There are those who say not to interfere. However, I believe that it is useful to set out certain guidelines, mainly because of one particular risk. If and when the relationship between two combatants becomes romantic or sentimental, there is a danger that their decisions, or that of the commander between the two, will no longer be the result of cold and clear judgment, and when this happens, mishaps occur.

I am not sure if I have fully succeeded in laying out the principles of compartmentalization that I believe in, but the cumulative sum of what I have said should provide a sketch of the figure of the combatant and make clear that what is required of her and what she does makes her someone of much higher caliber than the average person. Such was Sylvia, and so we will remember her. In her spirit we will train the next generations of combatants.

May her memory be a blessing.

For Leika, 30 Days after Her Passing, and for Moshe Levin ("Kokla") on the Seventeenth Anniversary of His Passing (September 19, 2011)

My last meeting with Leika was on a Friday afternoon, August 12, in the tiny room in the intensive care unit of Ichilov hospital's neurosurgical department. I have had quite a few difficult meetings in my life. This was one of the most difficult.

Leika lay in her bed, which took up most of the tiny room, and her expression was calm. Her speech was quiet and slow, but clear and razor-sharp. There were another three or four friends in the room. The atmosphere, like the air, was heavy. In the intensive care unit of the neurosurgery department, the angel of death roams the halls. And in these surroundings Leika spoke of death, not only as someone who had understood and accepted it, but as someone who had already experienced it.

I sat crouched on the chair at the foot of her bed, my tongue clinging to the roof of my mouth, listening to her words, and not having the faintest idea what I should be saying in such a situation. But Leika did not wait for me to say anything, to ask anything, or to respond to her words. She continued to talk about love, about friends, about Tali and the grandchildren, about saying goodbye, about Kokla, about things that were still left to do—and all of this quietly, almost in a whisper, with a monotonous tone of acceptance, as I shrank further and further into the corner.

I stand here next to her fresh grave and talk about her and to her with the feeling that, with regard to the Shavit family and the relationship between us, she left this world without any doubts.

You were born a princess and grew up to be a queen, and that is how you parted from us, leaving us orphans. We'll miss your one-line reply, "That's me!" whenever anyone dared to comment on your principles or style. Your astuteness was based on rich life experience rather than on a formal education. You had an opinion on every matter, a contribution to make to every conversation, and you knew how to navigate your way through any debate or argument.

In the first twenty years of your life you already had the chance to see the world. You got to know it from the decks of merchant ships that crossed the oceans, as a woman newly married to a seafarer, and as a young mother raising Tali aboard these ships. Already then you were exposed to new landscapes, cultures, and people that expanded your horizons and enriched your life. In those days, we were simple and provincial people whose world more or less finished in Cyprus.

You reached the peak of your self-fulfillment when you tied your life with Kokla's. He opened to you—the young woman of the "high society parlors"—a door to a world that you found fascinating, magical, intoxicating. Paratroopers, Sayeret Matkal, the Mossad, Arik Sharon, Avraham Arnan, heads of the Mossad. A world full of secrets and riddles. Conventional wars, clandestine wars, secret missions. During your time in Paris you also got a taste of the exhilarating feeling of sharing not only in the knowledge but also in the action of protecting Israel's security. You connected to this world with your entire self, and with every stage of Kokla's successful career your happiness grew.

Today is the seventeenth anniversary of the day that Kokla left us. The two of you, Kokla and Leika, left us seventeen years apart, both after suffering the agony of the hopeless confrontation with that cursed disease.

Kokla, my brother and soulmate, you were a groundbreaking fighter who formulated new combat doctrines, never gave up on pushing the envelope when it came to taking on risks and operations, and produced generations of daring fighters who adopted the slogan "Only the bold win." If only you knew how many of your trainees now hold the highest positions in the Mossad, you would be so happy. The respect that they feel for you as their commander brings them to visit your grave every year on this day in order to pay their respects. Leika, who was dedicated to you until the day she died, continued to be the link between you and those who were under your command. Her frequent meetings with them became a regular ritual, and they regarded her as one of their own.

Our Leika—you and Kokla and Yael and I walked a long, long way together. After Kokla left us we continued to walk as a trio. We did things together; we saw the world together; we raised children and grandchildren together; we laughed, we cried, we fought, we made up, and today we are unveiling your tombstone. Please, when you meet Kokla somewhere in the fields of eternity, tell him that we did our best to look after you. Please also tell him that seventeen years have not dulled the pain and that from now on it is only doubled.

Your memory will forever be with us.

Shlomo Gal (October 2009)

I met Shlomo for the first time when he was serving as the operations director of the "Caesarea" unit (the Mossad's operations unit). By the time I met him, Shlomo carried with him a rich history of achievements, both in his military service (he received the Chief of General Staff's Citation in Qalqilya) and in the unit, first as a combatant and later as an instructor for other combatants, a director of training, and an operations commander, all the while taking part in operations in target countries and at the base, even when he was already a staff officer.

Looking back, as someone who served in the unit, commanded it, and for all his sins ended up as the head of the Mossad, from my observations I can determine that from the 1960s until his death Shlomo embodied the history of the unit in his personality, his character, and his intellectual and operational abilities. He was also one of the few whose contributions to the unit turned it into what it is—a unit that has been engaged all these years in searching for a way to fully realize its incredible potential, a unit that excels in its creativity and imagination in the face of continuous threats.

The unit's combat doctrine has undergone major changes over time: from a single permanent combatant to a team of fighters, to the joining of forces with the IDF in order to realize the potential of the combined unique abilities of each partner, the result of which was a force multiplier that produced ingenious operations with outstanding results.

Shlomo, who advanced to become the deputy commander of the unit and later its commander, also contributed to the formulation of its combat doctrine and the development of its capabilities, at the base and at the target, to thwart terrorism and the buildup of non-conventional weapons in target countries. The doctrine included both operations that the unit carried out independently and those that it carried out in cooperation with the IDF.

I mentioned earlier that one of the main things that characterized Caesarea was its search for a way to realize its potential. "Caesarea—Quo Vadis?" was the name we gave to a regular ritual, usually carried out following a stinging failure or a severe blow. The ritual accompanied a period of suspension of activity, a gathering inward, and a long and arduous series of brainstorming sessions by the unit's best people in order to seek and redefine its purposes and goals. Shlomo was a central figure in this activity, from the preparation of platforms for discussion, through the writing of conclusions, to the formulation of the documents outlining the unit's next chapter.

Caesarea was a unit that "dwelled alone" for historical reasons, as well as reasons of compartmentalization and information security, derived from the activities of Israeli combatants in target countries. The result of this isolation was that the unit did not participate as an integral part of the Mossad's system of directing intelligence collection. It acted as an independent satellite that sustained the entire intelligence cycle within itself, as both a supplier and a consumer. It developed operational capabilities based on its understanding of the threat and sought buyers for its goods. Sometimes it succeeded and sometimes it didn't.

For example, there was a platform that was maintained for years without a single IDF buyer and that finally closed down. And then, according to Murphy's Law, an operation was planned. The unit played a significant role in the operation, particularly on the intelligence side. However, had the platform, which no longer existed, been a partner in the operational branch's part in the mission, there is no doubt that the operation would have taken on a completely different character, at least in terms of its fingerprints, and would certainly have served as a precedent for a breakthrough in the innovative combat doctrine of operational branch missions.

Operations are born in one of two ways: either they are assigned as a task by a superior, or they are ideas that grow from the bottom up, usually from intelligence officers who bring it up for discussion with the head of operations. The unit's intelligence officer for many years was Rumi, may he rest in peace, who was one of the founders of the IDF's information security and of the unit's field intelligence. There is no doubt that he had a significant influence on the nature of the unit's operations, especially those that dealt with the thwarting of attacks in base and target countries. Shlomo, as a combat fighter in the IDF and in the unit, shared a common language with Rumi from the moment they met, a language that contributed greatly to the development of the unit's combat doctrine and to the character of its operations.

The relationship between the Mossad and the IDF, especially MI (Military Intelligence Directorate of the IDF), had its ups and downs but was for the most part characterized by negative competition, alongside cooperation that was practically forced upon the commanders. It was in the 1970s when the two sides, Caesarea and MI, identified a discipline whose realization could be made possible only through cooperation that would make optimal use of each party's uniqueness, when Caesarea defined for itself a long-term strategic goal, which became the unit's "pillar of fire."

Shlomo played a crucial role throughout the teething problems and transformation processes involved in this change. The young soldiers had great respect for Shlomo, who had been honored with an IDF citation that he never spoke about, from the days before they were born. Their admiration for him also stemmed from their knowledge that when Shlomo spoke about a target he was speaking about a place that he had personally experienced.

"Trees die standing tall," as the song goes. We have lost, within a short time of each other, two of the unit's greatest commanders, Shlomo and Kokla. Both of them were killed by the same cursed disease. The metaphor expressed in the song expresses the battle they both waged against the disease. They commanded their units until their final breath. This has been a great loss to the Mossad. May their souls be bound up in the bond of eternal life.

Remarks in Honor of Yitzhak Shamir's Ninety-Fifth Birthday

Dear family members, ministers, members of the Knesset, and comrades in arms from the period before the state was founded, and from the political struggles in the period following the establishment of the state:[1]

This evening is different from others, in that the guest of honor is with us in spirit but not in body. There is both joy and sadness in this. I searched the scriptures for a suitable blessing but came up empty. Nevertheless, Groucho Marx said that "anyone can get old. All you have to do is live long enough." There is no doubt that Yitzhak did this with the same determination with which he did everything throughout his drama-filled life.

And here is a passage from a poem by Leah Goldberg:

Now with the days, you have whitened and aged
your days numbered and tenfold dearer,
and you know: Every day is the last under the sun,
and you know: Every day is new under the sun.

How much wisdom these four lines contain! This evening seemed to be an appropriate event in which to recite them.

I worked with Prime Minister Shamir for three and a half intensive years, and we developed a close relationship despite our large age gap. On his ninety-fifth birthday, and the eve of my seventy-first, it is only natural to reminisce about the memories that we shared, and some that we didn't share, which I cherish and will continue to cherish all my life.

And so: it was late 1988, early 1989. Israel had a national unity government headed by Yitzhak Shamir, with Yitzhak Rabin as its defense minister. The director of the Mossad at the time, Nahum Admoni, agreed with the prime minister that he would be completing his tenure and recommended that I be the one to replace him. I had only really met the prime minister during the last year of Admoni's term, but because neither of us is a man of many words I feared that his impression of me was only superficial. Defense Minister Yitzhak Rabin's candidate for the job was the head of Military Intelligence, Amnon Lipkin-Shahak, a decorated general with vast experience and many achievements under his belt.

A few days before the prime minister was to decide which of the candidates to choose, I was in Germany in the midst of an operation to thwart an attack by the PFLP against an American air base in Germany. The warning of the attack had been conveyed to us from Mossad sources, and the Germans therefore agreed that the operation would be managed by the Mossad in coordination with them. Because the target of the attack was American, the Americans were also brought into the picture, but to their chagrin, neither we nor the Germans agreed to hand the operation over to them, and they remained in the background.

After considerable deliberation, I called Nahum Admoni in Israel and asked him to arrange a meeting for me with the prime minister, to which I would arrive directly from Germany only to immediately return there in less than twenty-four hours. Nahum agreed. My meeting with the prime minister was short and to the point; I presented him with the reasons I thought I deserved to be appointed to the job. Toward the end of the meeting, as an aside, I told him that if I was not chosen I planned on retiring. I certainly did not intend this as a threat, heaven forbid; I meant only to draw his attention to the fact that in such a case he would have to appoint both a new director and a new deputy director of the Mossad.

The prime minister appointed me to the post. Some time later I heard from one of his associates that after my meeting with him he had said something along the lines of "Who is this Shavit and who the hell does he think he is?" This, of course, was related to my comment about retiring were I not chosen for the job. Still, this episode did not have any effect on the prime minister's practical judgment or on the relationship that developed between us later on.

These days, in which our leaders publicly blame each other for decisions they deem inappropriate or for unsuitable appointments to the most senior positions in the defense establishment, it is right to acknowledge the entire set of Yitzhak Shamir's practical considerations when it came to appointing a new head of the Mossad. I was told at the time, albeit not by him, but by a close associate of his whose words I have no reason to doubt, that the prime minister, in explaining his reasons for not appointing Amnon Lipkin-Shahak, said that had he appointed him as head of the Mossad, he as prime minister and the State of Israel in general would be losing a worthy candidate to be the IDF's next chief of staff. Of course, Amnon was indeed appointed as the next chief of staff, and this was a blessing for Israel.

Leaders tend to be suspicious people. Suspicion is a necessary trait in politics. I know this from the experience of working with three prime ministers. But as far as my relationship with Yitzhak Shamir was concerned, I quickly gained his trust and enjoyed every minute of working with him. The most important element in the head of the Mossad's relationship with the prime minister is mutual trust, and the support given by the prime minister to the Mossad director. A lot of sweat, and sometimes blood, goes into building this trust and support. Bad decisions and mistakes in execution can bring about colossal damage, diplomatic and otherwise. A Mossad head who feels that he is receiving only limited backing from his prime minister will hesitate to take risks, and this will have an immediate effect on the quality of the achievements and results of the intelligence effort. In my working relationship with Prime Minister Shamir, I was absolutely certain that if and when I needed him or his support, in successes as well as in failures, he would have my back. He was always there!

In April 1987, Shimon Peres, then foreign minister in the unity government, reached what was known as the London Agreement with King Hussein. Peres, who advocated the idea of an international conference to advance the peace process between us, Jordan, and the Palestinians, concocted a plan for such a conference, purportedly initiated and to be sponsored by the United States. When Peres returned from London and presented the agreement to Prime Minister Shamir, the latter completely rejected it. The rationale behind such a conference stood in stark contrast to Shamir's political outlook at the time.

Only three months after the London Agreement, the prime minister gradually began to change his mind about King Hussein and Jordan. While the London Agreement contained the possibility of returning the West Bank, an independent dialogue with Hussein opened the strategic option of removing the threat of a front east of Israel's borders.

In July 1987, the first meeting between Prime Minister Shamir and the king took place. This meeting shaped the future relationship between the two, which was characterized by genuine chemistry and mutual trust, despite differences of opinion on core issues.

In March 1990, a technical meeting was held between Efraim, the deputy director of the Mossad, and his Jordanian counterpart in

London, which developed into a meeting with the king. This meeting marked the beginning of a new chapter in the relations between the two countries—that of the First Gulf War. As you will remember, King Hussein sided with Saddam Hussein. In the meetings that took place on the eve of Saddam's invasion of Kuwait, we warned the king not to allow Saddam to use Jordanian territory. This led to the next meeting between him and Prime Minister Shamir, which took place in the first week of January 1991, about a week before the outbreak of the First Gulf War. This meeting also took place in London. Ehud Barak, then-IDF deputy chief of staff, joined the group as well. During the conversation, the king promised not to allow the Iraqi air force to use Jordanian airspace to attack Israel and not to allow Iraqi ground forces to use Jordanian territory. In return, Shamir pledged to the king that Israel would respect Jordan's sovereignty and territorial integrity.

The Gulf War left King Hussein on his throne and the Kingdom of Jordan unharmed. Hussein saw this as a great achievement.

The cabinet meetings during the First Gulf War were held in the Templar building on the base of the General Staff. Meetings were held daily, sometimes even twice a day. In addition to the ministers, the entire top echelon of the security forces was present at the meetings. I remember—how could I forget—the tremendous pressure exerted by the top brass on the prime minister to take a decision regarding the IDF's intervention in the war, and the steadfast and uncompromising stance that the prime minister took, sometimes alone, against their recommendation. Among the thoughts that went through my mind at that time was that the decision not to do something is sometimes much harder than the decision to do something! On a humorous note, I remember also thinking that only the spine of steel of a small man like Shamir could stand up to the pressures that were exerted on him! The test of time shows that Shamir was certainly right in opposing the IDF's intervention in the war.

In 1955, Isser Harel recruited Yitzhak Shamir to the Mossad. Isser, with Prime Minister Ben-Gurion's approval, decided to recruit the best of the underground movements' members to the Mossad. I think that there are three reasons that can explain the rationale behind this decision:

1. To heal the wounds of the political and social rifts that existed on the eve of the establishment of the state and its early years
2. To make use of human resources with knowledge, experience and many successes in clandestine activity in the years prior to the establishment of the state
3. To integrate these good people into the state systems rather than to leave them outside the state as rejects

In the Mossad, Yitzhak commanded a special unit of Jewish combatants operating completely undercover in target countries. The Intelligence Corps operated a parallel unit at the time. Meir Amit, who replaced Isser as head of the Mossad, brought the unit from MI to the Mossad and united it with the Mossad unit under Shamir's command. The unification of the two units was not a simple process, and it is doubtful whether the scars from it ever healed completely. Regrettably, Shamir retired from the Mossad in 1965 as a result of this process.

Isser and Shamir had a very close relationship. After all, they spoke to one another at eye level! The military culture that prevailed in the Mossad after Isser's departure did not suit Shamir.

I used to meet with Shamir even after his retirement. He was always busy, in his infinite enthusiasm, with the need—which he defined as existential—to bring another million Jews, and another million, to Israel. I believe that today as well, the Israeli government should make this a high priority on the national agenda.

In conclusion, I can only quote from the book of Job, chapter 12, verse 12: "With aged men is wisdom, and in length of days understanding."

NOTES

Introduction

1. "Secret King Hussein-Shamir Gulf War Pact Revealed," *J: The Jewish News of Northern California*, September 29, 1995.

Chapter 1. Intelligence

1. Over the years, several details have been published about the secret ties between Israel and Morocco. See Shmuel Segev's *The Moroccan Connection: The Secret Relationship between Israel and Morocco* (Tel Aviv: Matar Books, 2008) and Amos Gilboa and Ephraim Lapid's *Israel's Silent Defender: An Inside Look at Sixty Years of Israeli Intelligence* [in Hebrew] (Jerusalem: Gefen, 2012).

2. See the Israel Intelligence Heritage and Commemoration Center website at http://bit.ly/2APOcYV.

3. See Gilboa and Lapid, *Israel's Silent Defender*: "The Syrians were particularly aware of the possibility of the existence of Israeli warning devices in their communications systems, as they had uncovered some over the years. On December 8, 1954, the Syrians captured five IDF soldiers who were on a mission to service a warning device on the Syrian Golan Heights. In previous years, the Syrians had discovered electronic systems designed to intercept

linear communication between important headquarters within the country. The Syrians were very aware over the years of the possibility that their wireless and wired systems were being tapped" (247–46; my translation).

4. Alexis C. Madrigal, "Stuxnet Is the Hiroshima of the Cyber War," *Atlantic*, March 4, 2011, http://bit.ly/2A3FFUV.

5. CORDIS, "China to Launch World's First Quantum Communication Network," August 4, 2017, http://bit.ly/2v4JBQ1.

6. See Charlie Savage, "NSA Said to Search Content of Messages to and from US," *New York Times*, August 8, 2013, http://bit.ly/2AL9TIB; Patrick Chappatte, "The NSA and Cyberweapons," *New York Times*, July 17, 2017, http://bit.ly/2A2eb25.

7. See, for example, *"Wall Street Journal*: US Spied on Netanyahu during Iran Deal Talks" (*Haaretz*, December 30, 2015, http://bit.ly/2z71pSs): "The journal's investigation also revealed how Israel's military intelligence Unit 8200 and the NSA, described as its counterpart, shared information and technology, but also spied on one another."

Chapter 2.   Intelligence and the International Arena

1. Vipin Narang, "Posturing for Peace? Pakistan's Nuclear Postures and South Asian Stability," *International Security* 34, no. 3 (Winter 2009–10): 38–78.

2. Yossi Alpher, "When Would Israel Attack Iran?," *Forward*, September 1, 2010, http://bit.ly/2yM7Qna; Robert C. Koons, "Just War and the Iran Crisis," *Public Discourse: Journal of the Witherspoon Institute*, March 7, 2012, http://bit.ly/2hxMJ13; Tamar Meisels, "Preemptive Strikes: Israel and Iran," *Canadian Journal of Law and Jurisprudence* 25, no. 2 (July 2012): 447–63, http://bit.ly/2yOiNEz.

Chapter 3.   Intelligence and National Security

1. I originally wrote this section as a lecture for the first annual memorial day of Ya'akov Karoz's passing (July 1994). I have expanded and updated it for this book.

2. "New York Times v. United States (1971): Mr. Justice Stewart, with Whom Mr. Justice White Joins, Concurring," C-Span, Landmark Cases, http://landmarkcases.c-span.org/pdf/New%20York%20Times%20v.%20 Unites%20States%20-%20Justice%20Stewart%20concurring.pdf.

3. Gadi Taub, "American Failure: Between Elections and Democracy" [in Hebrew], *Yediot Aharonot*, February 8, 2011.

4. Assaf Sagiv, "Who's Afraid of Egyptian Democracy?" [in Hebrew], *Azure*, no. 43 (Spring 2011).

Chapter 4. A Diplomatic Perspective

1. Nahum Barnea, *Yedioth Ahronoth*, Simchat Torah holiday supplement, October 4, 2015.

2. Itamar Rabinovich, *Yedioth Ahronoth*, Simchat Torah holiday supplement, October 4, 2015.

3. Samuel Huntington, *The Clash of Civilizations and the Remaking of World Order* (New York: Touchstone, 1996), 43, 47.

4. The full text of the Arab Peace Initiative, published in March 2002 in Beirut, Lebanon, at the annual Arab League Summit.

5. On this topic, I recommend reviewing the November 24, 2015, article by John Bolton in the international edition of the *New York Times*, entitled "To Defeat ISIS, Create a Sunni State."

6. Benny Morris, *The Birth of the Palestinian Refugee Problem, 1947–1949* (Cambridge: Cambridge University Press, 1989).

Chapter 5. Wars

1. Hagai Tsoref, "The 27 Days That Changed the Status of the Mossad and Its Director" [in Hebrew], *Mabat Malam* 74 (April 2016): 20–24.

2. Tsoref, "27 Days," 22.

3. Ibid., 23.

4. Ibid., 24.

5. Thomas L. Friedman, "The Arab Commission," *New York Times*, May 9, 2007.

Appendix

1. These remarks were made at an event marking Yitzhak Shamir's ninety-fifth birthday at the Menachem Begin Heritage Center in Jerusalem on November 15, 2010. For health reasons, Shamir was not able to be present that evening. The recording and transcription of these remarks are preserved in the Jabotinsky Archives.

INDEX

The letter *t* following a page number denotes a table.

Belgium, 76

Ben-Aharon, Yossi, 315

Ben-Gurion, David: on the Gaza issue, 256–61; leadership style, 256; national security doctrine of, 42, 86, 129–30, 334; and the refugee problem, 237, 242, 244–45, 247, 248–49, 251, 271; role in establishment of the state, 133–34, 237; during the Sinai Campaign (1956), 253–61, 272; structuring Israeli intelligence hierarchies, 133–34, 301; during the War of Independence, 237, 242, 244–45

Bentov, Mordechai, 266

Berlin Wall, xiii, xviii, 312

Bernadotte, Count Folke, 245–46, 250, 271

bin Laden, Osama, xvii, 62, 63, 64–65, 71, 73, 200, 202, 333

biological weapons: developed by Iran, xiv, 106–8, 123–24; developed by Iraq, 304–5; threat of, 3, 71; variables in, 56t. See also nonconventional weapons

bipolar world: changing to multipolar, xix, 4, 11, 23–24, 53; instability following end of, xix, 53–54, 204; intelligence during, 22, 24–25. See also Cold War

Birth of the Palestinian Refugee Problem, 1947–1949, The (Morris), 239–41

"Black September" (1970), 185

Boko Haram (Nigerian terrorist group), xvii, 70

Bolton, John, 122

Brazil, 47

Brezhnev, Leonid, 282, 284, 293

Britain: in the Baghdad Pact, 94; "Five Eyes" intelligence alliance, 61; Iranian nuclear agreement, 120; and Israeli-Jordanian peace talks,

179–80; MI6-Mossad relations, 23, 314–15; and the refugee problem, 245, 249, 250; and the Sinai Campaign (1956), 252, 257, 271–72; support of Arab states, 23, 270; support of Jordan, 225; during the Yom Kippur War, 294

British Mandate: Gaza in, 262; Jewish secret militias operating under, 128–29; population statistics, 239; Shai wiretapping, 52; termination of, 238, 241, 243

Brzezinski, Zbigniew, 122, 219

Buenos Aires terror attacks, 46, 48

Bull, Gerald, 311–12

Bush, George H. W., xv, 80, 316, 317

Bush, George W., 79, 80, 117, 201

Caesarea unit, 332, 347–50

Canada, 61

Center for Media and Public Affairs (US), 151, 152

Central Intelligence Agency (CIA). See CIA

Chagall, Marc, 236

chemical weapons: Egyptian use against Yemeni rebels, 28; Iranian development of, xiv, 106–8, 123–24; during the Iran-Iraq War, xiv, 106; Iraqi capabilities, 304–5, 310; Japanese terrorist group use of, 9; Saddam Hussein targeting Iraqi Kurds, 28; threat of, 3, 9, 71; variables in, 56t. See also nonconventional weapons

Cheney, Richard "Dick," 144, 313

Chernobyl nuclear reactor, 56

China: delegation visiting IDC Herzliya, 126; emergence as world power, 4, 191; and the Iranian nuclear threat, 119, 120; Kissinger's first visit to, 157; Obama administra-

tion focus on, 104, 214; Rabin's
visit to, 190–91; relations with
Israel, 191; relations with North
Korea, 114; and the Snowden
affair, 58; supplying nonconventional weapons, 29

Christopher, Warren, 176

CIA (Central Intelligence Agency):
anti-Semitism within, 51; during
the Cold War, 43–44; definition of
the Middle East, 8; EEI of, 43–44;
following the Cold War, 44; identity protection legislation, 155;
impact of Russian cyberattacks on,
131; and the Latin America threat,
48; levels of interagency cooperation, 45; military coups organized
by, 92–93; relations with the
Mossad, 36–37, 41–46, 48–51,
314; Shavit's meetings with,
36–37, 41, 48–49, 314; on the
Soviet bloc, 48–50; Tehran office,
37

Ciudad del Este (Paraguay), 48

Clarke, Richard, 33–34

Clash of Civilizations, The (Huntington),
200–201

Clinton, Hillary, 103–4

Clinton, William "Bill," 80, 176, 184, 207

Cold War: blocs during, xviii; cyber
capabilities during, 52–53; ending
of, vii–viii, xiii, 312; global instability following end of, xviii, 4,
53–54, 204, 213; global stability
during, xvii–xviii, 101, 125; impact
on intelligence EEI, 23–25, 43–44;
Middle East during, 87; nuclear
safeguards during, xviii, 111, 125;
secrecy during, 18–19; territory
lost by Russia following, 116;
US-Israeli intelligence cooperation
during, 22–23, 42–44

combatants, viii, 332, 341–45

COMINT (communications intelligence), 43, 129, 136, 333

Comintern (communist organization),
73–74

Common Market bloc, 4

communications: during the Cold War,
52–53; Forum 2000's predictions
regarding, 15–16; impact on
combat doctrine, 143; post–Cold
War transformations in, 53–54;
quantum communication, 57; and
secrecy, 2; used by radical Islamic
organizations, 71; wiretapping, 52,
57–61, 129, 356–57n3. See also
cyber intelligence; technology

Conciliation Commission (UN),
247–52, 264

"Condor" missile project, 311

Cotler, Irwin, 63

Cuban Missile Crisis, xviii, 111

cyber intelligence: development of,
51–54; during the Cold War,
52–53; needed improvements in,
82; NSA's capabilities, 58–61; prevention strategies in, 308; risks of,
61; Syrian Golan Heights operation, 52, 356n3; and technology
limitations, 51–52

cyber warfare: concept of deterrence in,
54–56; double-layered nature of,
53, 132; future of, 56–57; identifying actors in, 54–55, 131–32;
impact of Snowden affair on,
57–58; impact of US election
attack, 131–32; impact on strategic depth, 131; in a multipolar
world, 53–57; as a nonconventional weapon, 53–54, 56, 131;
normative dilemmas created by,
58–59; one-and-a-half-generations
principle, 132; prevention

cyber warfare (*cont.*)
    strategies in, 308; Stuxnet opera-
    tion, 56; threat of, 3, 52; variables
    in, 56t; "X-Force Experiment,"
    55–56. *See also* nonconventional
    weapons
Cyrus the Great, 90

Danin, Ezra, 254
David's Sling defense system, 131
Davis, John, 263, 264
Dayan, Moshe, 139, 179, 198, 253, 256,
    266–68, 272, 280, 299, 301
decisive victory doctrine, 130, 211, 307,
    317
democracy and democratization:
    attempts at adopting, 64–65, 162;
    compared to authoritarian
    regimes, 18; dangers of increasing
    tribalism, 223; dangers of Islamist
    parties to, 272, 329; economic
    needs prior to, 83; in the Gaza
    Strip, 272; impact of cyberattacks
    on, 132; national security–
    freedom of speech debate, 149–50,
    158–60; as necessary condition for
    peace, 9–10; revolutions attempt-
    ing to establish, 163–67; role of
    the media in, 151–54; secrecy in,
    18, 159–60
Department of Homeland Security
    (US), 76, 200
deterrence: Ariel Sharon's contributions
    to, 130; in cyberspace, 54–56;
    deterrence profiling, 110; Hezbol-
    lah in Iranian doctrine, 323;
    impact of satellites on, 130; impact
    on diplomatic negotiations, 197;
    and the Iranian threat, 111; in
    Israeli security doctrine, 127, 211,
    307, 320; Israel's capabilities, 131,
    328; nuclear deterrence, 54,
    109–10, 118; in prevention stra-

tegies, 307; Rabin's views on, 197;
    and the Second Lebanon War, 320,
    328; and second-strike capability,
    54, 133
Diamond, Operation (1966), 43, 334
diplomacy and diplomatic relations:
    addressing nuclear Iran threat,
    118–19; deterrence enabling flexi-
    bility in, 197; impact of cyber
    warfare on, 58; Mossad-Germany
    relations, 197; Mossad–Gulf States
    relations, 195–97; Mossad-
    Indonesia relations, 190–95;
    Mossad's role in, 11, 32, 189; role
    of secrecy in, 157–58, 189–95,
    197. *See also* peace initiatives
director of Mossad, office of, vii; on the
    Idan Hadash forum, 309; in the
    intelligence hierarchy, 171; Rasha
    forum of, 1–2; relations with
    prime ministers, 353; responsi-
    bilities of, 331; on the strategic
    research team, 7; symbolism of
    office arrangement, 2. *See also indi-
    vidual directors*
Doron, Shlomo, viii, 313–15, 318
Dreyfus case, 235
Dror, Yehezkel, 63

Eagleburger, Larry, 314
early warning capabilities: impact of
    satellites on, 130; in Israel's secu-
    rity doctrine, 127; MI as
    responsible for, 145; during the
    Yom Kippur War, 278–79, 285–91,
    292–94
Eban, Abba, 251, 256, 265, 272
EC (European Community) economic
    bloc, 4
economy: factor in peace, 9–10; follow-
    ing Second Lebanon War, 330; in
    the Galilee, 323; impact of cyber
    warfare on, 58; impact of Israeli-

Palestinian conflict on, 208; of
Iran, 100, 112, 119, 321; in Israeli-
Palestinian conflict resolution,
209–10, 234; and Israeli society,
14, 205; Mossad's economic EEI,
11; in the Muslim world, 63–64; of
Oman, 195; post–Cold War economic blocs, 4; projects linking
Gaza to Israel, 260–61; and the
refugee problem, 247; relation to
national security, 129, 157–58;
role in combatting terrorism, 83;
of the US, 40–41
EEI (Essential Elements of Information): of the CIA, 43–44; during
the Cold War era, 23–24, 25,
43–44; economic focus, 11; following the Cold War, xix, 23–25, 44,
45–46; fundamentalist terrorism
focus, xix, 23–25, 44, 45–46; Iraq
as priority of, 304–6, 309; MI's
responsibilities for, 134, 137–38,
276–77; of the Mossad, xix, 11,
24–25, 43–44; Mossad-MI priorities debate, 305–6; nonconventional threats focus, xix, 23–25,
45–46, 304–6; pluralism in responsibility for, 145
Egypt: "Condor" missile project, 29,
311; Forum 2000 insights on, 12;
in Israeli circles of conflict, 17; and
the Israeli-Palestinian conflict,
216–17, 224–25, 228; Israeli peace
agreement with, 31, 210, 214, 224,
304; in the Jordanian-Israeli peace
process, 186; Mossad's assessment
of, 8, 9; Muslim Brotherhood in,
xvii, 72, 166–67; population of,
224; relations with Jordan, 181,
188; relations with Saudi Arabia,
224; relations with US, 22, 42,
224; revolutions in, 93, 165–67;
Sadat appointed president, 304; in

the Sinai Campaign (1956),
252–53, 271–72; Soviet Union
expelled from, 213, 283, 292; use
of chemical weapons against
Yemeni rebels, 28; US intelligence
cooperation regarding, 42; during
War of Independence, 129, 224,
262; weapons supplied by Soviets,
283, 286, 288–89, 292–93. *See also*
Yom Kippur War (1973)
Eisenhower, Dwight D., 252, 272
Elazar, David "Dado," 139, 299, 305
ELINT (electronic signals intelligence),
20, 57–58, 333
Ellsberg, Daniel, 158, 159
EMP (electromagnetic pulse), 56
Eshkol, Levi, 179, 260, 265, 266
Espionage Act (1917; US), 155
Essebsi, Beji Caid, 164
Essential Elements of Information
(EEI). *See* EEI
Ethiopia, 28, 86, 129
Ethridge, Mark, 245, 246, 247–48, 250,
271
Etzel (militia), 129
Evron, Meki, 331, 332–35
Evron, Ruthie, 335
Export Control Laws (1976), 156
Eytan, Walter, 259

Fabius, Laurent, 217
Fahmi, Ismail, 284–85
family reunification plans, 239, 250–51
Fedayeen, 257–58
feudalism (Iran), 93–94
Fiesco (play), 165
Firdusi (Iranian poet), 91
First Gulf War: beginning of, 316;
impact on pan-Arabism, xv, 5,
318; impact on the Middle East,
xv–xvi, 4–5; impact on the
Mossad, 26; impacts on Israel,
318; intelligence sharing prior to,

First Gulf War (*cont.*)
312–15; international coalition during, xv, 4–5, 181, 225; Iraqi invasion of Kuwait, xv, 312, 315; Iraqi missiles launched into Israel during, xv, 306, 310, 317–18; Israeli nonintervention position during, xv–xvi, 316–18, 354; Jordanian support of Iraq, xv, 180, 181, 188, 225, 316, 354; media coverage of, 149, 152–53; Palestinians expelled from Kuwait following, 216; Shamir–King Hussein meeting prior to, xvi, 180, 315–16, 317, 354; steps leading to, xv; television coverage of, 153

First Intifada, xiii, 180

First Lebanon War, 304, 322–24

First World War, 69, 235–36, 302, 322

"Five Eyes" intelligence alliance, 61

Foreign Ministry (Israel): and Chinese relations, 191; establishment of research department in, 6; during the Jordanian peace negotiations, 186; roles and authority of, 31–32. *See also* diplomacy and diplomatic relations

Forum 2000 (Mossad): function of, 10–11; future trends identified by, 14–16; insights from, 11–14

Foz do Iguacu (Latin America), 47, 48

France: Iranian nuclear agreement, 120; needed participation to defeat ISIS, 230; nuclear cooperation with Iraq, 309; radical Islamic terrorist attacks in, 76; and the refugee problem, 247–48; and the Sinai Campaign (1956), 252, 257, 271–72; during the Yom Kippur War, 294

Freedom of Information Act, 154–55

freedom of speech: in democracies, 149–50; legislation addressing, 154–58; and media censorship, 152–55; questions regarding, 148; resolution of tension between security and, 160; tension between security and, 57, 149–60; in totalitarian states, 149. *See also* media

Friedman, Thomas, 167, 219–20, 328–30

fundamentalist Islamic terrorism: in the Arab-Israeli conflict, 19–20, 203; changing nature of, 19, 72; as clash of civilizations, 200–202; communist Comintern comparison, 73–74; compared to classical terrorism, 68; compared to war, 67–68, 77–78; convergence with organized crime, 25, 47–48, 54; defining, 27, 67, 78, 83; EEIs focusing on, xix, 24–25, 44, 45–46; factors driving, 83, 203–4; funding of, 81; global nature of, xvi–xvii, 24–25; goal of damaging national resilience, 75; goal of global Islamic caliphate, xvi, xvii, 62–63, 68, 69–70, 110, 111, 200; impact of the internet on, 161–62; impact on intelligence, 24–25; international cooperation in combatting, 45–46, 76–77, 82–84, 200; international norms regarding, 78; Israeli strategies countering, 76–81; in Latin America, 46–48; Mombasa attacks, 73; in a new Middle East model, 234; organizational structure in, 74, 77; parallels to the Israeli-Palestinian conflict, 203; preemption component, 45–46; religious component, xiii, 73, 77, 79–80, 82–83, 201–3; religious

intelligence agencies (foreign) (*cont.*) security measures for, 156–57; need for information sharing among, 34, 82; NSA, 57–61; third party principle, 21–23; during the Yom Kippur War, 285–91, 292–94. *See also* CIA

intelligence community (Israeli): annual intelligence assessment, 137–38; areas of operation, 23–24; changes in, 137, 140–42; cooperation within, 143–45; division of responsibilities, 134–37, 140–42, 276–78; establishment of, 133–34; handling of the Palestinian-Israeli conflict, 29–31; Idan Hadash forum, 309; impact of Agranat Commission on, 6–7, 35, 139–42, 305–6; importance of trust and support, 36; during the Jordanian peace negotiations, 186–87; limits of technology, 51–52; Mossad's liaison to other agencies in, 276; in the post–Cold War era, 23–25; power structure of, 133–34; prior to establishment of the state, 29–30; qualities of intelligence officers, 138–39; role in the Arab-Israeli conflict, 16–20; the Shai, 29–30. *See also* Military Intelligence (MI); Mossad, the; Shin Bet, the

Intelligence Identities Protection Act (1932; US), 155

Interdisciplinary Center (IDC) Herzliya, ix, 67

internet revolution, 149, 160–61, 163–67

Invention Secrecy Act, 156

Iran: 2009 elections in, 100, 102, 112; in the Baghdad Pact, 94; border with Iraq, 87–89; CIA military coups, 92–93; in "day after" scenarios, 120–23; dilemmas on courses of action against, 111–12; energy resources of, 321; following the Iran-Iraq War, 312; global Islamic caliphate goal, 96, 110–11, 124; history of, 90–96; IRGC regime, 96, 97, 99–100, 103, 106, 108–9, 112; in Israeli circles of conflict, 17; in Israel's northern triangle, 28, 86–87, 93, 304; Khomeini's revolution, 28, 91–92, 115, 162, 321; Khuzestan province, 88–89; Meki Evron's term in, 334; Mossad HUMINT branch in, 334; Muslim Arab conquest of, 90–91; national security doctrine and strategy of, 123–24; negotiation culture of, 95, 100, 123–24; in a new Middle East model, 232; nonconventional capabilities, xiv, 5, 12–13, 24, 28, 106–8, 123–24, 196; North Korea as model for, 113–14; nuclear agreement (2015), 103–6, 114, 117–18, 119–20, 123, 327; nuclear capabilities development, xiv, 8, 97, 107–8, 120, 124; nuclear threat of, xviii, 5, 12–13, 97, 98, 117, 124–25; options for addressing threats of, 118–21; postnuclear issues, 109–11; power structure in, 97, 98–101, 112; in the RCD pact, 94; regional hegemonic aspirations, 96, 107–8, 123–24; relations with Germany, 92; relations with India, 103; relations with Iraq, 108–9, 303; relations with Pakistan, 8, 49–50; relations with Russia, 115–18, 122; relations with Saudi Arabia, 223; relations with Syria, 108, 230; relations with US, 97, 101–6, 108–9, 115, 327; religion-secularism tensions in, 90–92, 93, 95; revolutionary process in, 162–63; in the Second Lebanon War, 321, 324, 329; under the shah, 93–94, 96; sharia state in, 96, 321; Shavit's post in, 37, 84–89; size and ethnic diversity of, 89–90, 99; in South America, 47–48; spiritual leadership in, 96, 114–15; supporting Hezbollah, 46–48, 321–22, 327, 328; as threat to Israel, 8, 12–13, 28, 92, 104, 115, 196, 328; US embassy hostage situation, 37; war with Iraq, xiv, 5, 106–7, 123, 312; wealth of, 321

Iran-Iraq War, xiv, 5, 106–7, 123, 312

Iraq: addressed by Forum 2000 team, 13; in the Baghdad Pact, 94; border with Iran, 87–89; during the Cold War, 87; "Condor" missile project, 311; following the Iran-Iraq War, 312; fundamentalist groups in, 66, 72; Iranian strategic influence in, 108–9; in Israeli circles of conflict, 17; Israeli strategy toward, 303–6; military coups in, 93, 94; in a new Middle East model, 232, 234; nonconventional capabilities, xiv, 13, 28–29, 144, 304–6; nuclear capabilities, 3, 28–29, 304–5, 309–12; Operation Diamond, 43, 334; Osirak nuclear reactor, 123, 309; population of, 303; potential role in Middle East peace, 189; and the refugee problem, 246, 259; relations with France, 309; revolution in (1958), 302–3; in the Second Gulf War, 80; Soviet supply of weapons to, 87; as threat to Israel, 3, 8–9, 13, 302, 303–6, 309–10;

treatment of the Kurds, 28, 303; US invasion of, 106, 110–11; in the War of Independence, 127, 129, 302; war with Iran, xiv, 5, 106–7, 123, 312; wealth and resources of, 303; during the Yom Kippur War, 294. *See also* First Gulf War; Hussein, Saddam

IRGC (Islamic Revolutionary Guard Corps), 96, 97, 99–100, 103, 106, 108–9, 112

Iron Dome defense system, 131

Iron Wall vision, xv

ISIS (terrorist organization): in Africa, 72; approaches to fighting, 229–30; development of, xvii; differences between al-Qaeda and, 69–70; elements needed to defeat, 230–31; in Iraq, 72, 230, 327; leadership structure, 203; in Sinai, 224; in Syria, 72, 328; as threat to Israel, 73–74, 328; wealth of, 66–67

Islam: benevolence of the victor concept, 65–66; differences between Western civilization and, 65–66; fundamentalists as small minority of, 201; historical development of, 69; Iranian attitudes toward, 90–92; Islamization process, 8, 12; jihad concept in, xvi, 70, 124; perpetual war until final victory concept, 269, 326; role of moderate in combating radical, 82–83, 201, 327

Islamic fundamentalism: addressed by Forum 2000 team, 12; anti-Semitic aspect of, 63; clash of civilizations, 200–203; dictatorship preferred to, 162; funding, 66–67; growth of, 5, 24–25; impact on intelligence, 24–25; on Israel's right to

media (Israeli): censorship debate, 150–57; following the Yom Kippur War, 295–96; impact on national agenda, 147; impact on national morale, 147, 320; impact on social values, 151; during the Jordanian peace process, 181, 189; during Rabin's visit to China, 190; and Rabin's visit to Indonesia, 192–93; recklessness of, 156; during the Second Lebanon War, 319, 320, 325; on the security-morality debate, 229–30; during the Yom Kippur War, 285

Meir, Golda, 139, 140, 262–65, 296–301

Menem, Carlos, 46–47

Merkel, Angela, 58–59

MI6 (British foreign intelligence service), 23, 314–15

Michelmore, Laurence, 265–66

military doctrine (Israel): building blocks of, 127–28; decisive victory doctrine, 130, 211, 307, 317; deterrence, 127, 211; early warning, 127; expansion of, 129; following War of Independence, 126–29; formation of, 126–29; impact of First Gulf War on, 317; moving the war into enemy territory, 127–28, 317; offensive defense doctrine, 128, 131; pre-Israeli state doctrine, 128–29; prevention strategy in, 308–9; "subjugate/vanquish" principle, 127. See also national security doctrine (Israel)

Military Intelligence (MI): annual intelligence assessment (January 1991), 5; areas of responsibility, 26, 134–37, 276–78, 305; "concept" theory, 296; connections to law enforcement agencies, 26; early days, 133–37; EEIs of, 7, 134–37, 276–78, 305, 306; establishment of, 133–34; HUMINT unit of, 87; in Idan Hadash forum, 309; impact of Agranat Commission, 6–7, 139, 305–6; as intelligence collection agency, 26, 355; in intelligence community hierarchies, 31, 133–34, 276–78; and the Iraqi nonconventional threat, 312–14; and the Jordanian peace agreement, 182; relationship between the Mossad and, 142–45, 349–50; research and assessments of, 6, 7, 26, 134–38, 305; responsibilities of head of, 277; during Shavit's tenure as director, 144–45; on the Varash forum, xii; weekly briefings by head of, 276; during the Yom Kippur War, 278–81, 295–96, 298, 301, 305. See also IDF

Mishcon, Victor, 179–80

missiles: "Condor" project, 29, 311; Iranian development program, 106–8, 117; in the Iran-Iraq War, 106, 312; Iraqi development program, 310–12; Iraqi use in First Gulf War, xv, 306, 310, 317–18; Israeli three-tiered defense, 131; in Mossad's long-term intelligence assessment, 9; US missile defense plan, 117. See also nonconventional weapons; weapons (conventional)

Mitla Pass, 282, 284, 291, 299

Modi, Narendra, 103

Modi'in 11, 277

Montazeri, Hossein Ali, 115

Morocco: addressed by Forum 2000 team, 12; civil society in, 65; and

Morocco (*cont.*)

Israeli-Palestinian conflict resolution, 228; in Israel's southern triangle, 28, 86; potential regime upheavals in, 12; revolutionary processes in, 167; role in advancing peace, 194

Morris, Benny, 239–41, 246, 251, 252

Morsi, Mohamed, 166–67

Mossad, the (Institute for Intelligence and Special Operations): achievements of, viii; areas of operation, xix, 23–26, 140–42, 175; areas of responsibility, 6–7, 25–26, 134–37, 140–42, 276–78; Caesarea operations unit, 347–50; capabilities and tools of, 309–10; during the Cold War, 43–44; combatants of, viii, 332, 341–45; combat doctrine, xix, 82, 143, 348; cooperation with foreign agencies, 11, 41–46, 48–51, 306–7, 312–14; cumulative database of, 15; debate on employees participating in war, 280; deputy director role, 2; division of roles and authority within, 31–32; EEIs of, xix, 11, 43–46, 309–10; establishment of, 133–34; following the Cold War, 23–25, 44, 45–46; Forum 2000 team internal analysis, 10–16; gender equality in, 344; impact of Yom Kippur War on, 6–7, 140–42, 305–6; in intelligence community structure, 25–26, 31–32, 133–34, 276–78, 301; intelligence gathering, 6–7, 10, 44, 45–46, 134–37, 276–78, 306–7; interface between law enforcement and, 25–27; during Jordanian peace process, viii, 184, 187; long-term assessment (January 1991), 5–10; memorial ceremony for Rabin, 177–79;

nonconventional proliferation counteraction, 306–7; Operations Directorate head responsibilities, 276; prevention responsibilities, 10, 17, 44, 45–46, 306–7; prior to Yom Kippur War, 276–78; and Rabin's visit to China, 190–91; relationship between MI and, 142–45, 276–78, 349–50; research and assessments, 5–7, 11, 143–45; role in secret diplomacy, 31–32, 86–87, 189, 191, 194, 195–97, 339–40; Shamir's work in, 355; Shavit's predictions regarding, 3–4; special operations, 6, 197–98, 309–10, 342; spouses of employees, 332; on the Varash forum, xii; during the Yom Kippur War, 278–81, 285–87, 289–95, 296–301. *See also* director of Mossad, office of

Mossadegh, Mohammad, 92–93, 94, 115

Mousavi, Mir-Hossein, 100

Moussa, Amr, 165

Mubarak, Hosni, 216–17, 311

Mughniyeh, Imad, 319

multipolar world: blocs in, 4, 23–24; characteristics of, 54; cyber warfare in, 53–57; following collapse of Soviet Union, 4, 11, 23–24; global instability in, xix, 213

Murrow, Ed, 253

Muslim Brotherhood movement, xvii, 72, 163, 166–67

Mutual Assured Destruction (MAD), xviii, 54

NAFTA (North American Free Trade Agreement), 4

Nahda, al- (political party), 163–64

Nansen, Fridtjof, 235–36

Nansen passport, 235–36
Nasrallah, Hassan, 319, 322, 324, 328–30
Nasser, Gamal Abdel, 93, 252, 279, 304
National Defense College lecture, 4–5
national resilience, 17, 75, 130, 133, 160, 205
national security doctrine (Israel): deterrence principle in, 127; economic supremacy element, 129, 157–58; elements of, 129–30; establishment of, 129–30; impact of cyber warfare on, 58; impact of globalism on, 14–15; legislation addressing, 155–56; and the media, 145–67; military supremacy element, 129–30; Mossad's strategic research team, 5–7; national resilience element, 130; nonconventional weapons threatening, 75; prevention strategies, 131, 308–9; secrecy necessary for, 156–60; security-morality debate, 229–30; strategic allies element, 42, 129; strategic military capabilities element, 129–30; technological supremacy element, 130; tensions between freedom of speech and, 150–60; terrorism threatening, 74–76; triangle theory in, 86–87, 129, 334. *See also* military doctrine (Israel)
NATO (North Atlantic Treaty Organization), 61, 102, 114, 230–31, 232
Nazareth (Israel), 242
Netanyahu, Benjamin, xiv, 10, 229, 270
New York Times v. United States (403 U.S. 713 [1971]), 157–58
New Zealand, 61
Nixon, Richard, 284, 300
nonconventional weapons: addressed by Forum 2000 team, 12–13; deterrence as central to, 54–56;

dilemmas concerning decision makers, 306–8; EEIs focusing on, xix, 23–25, 44, 45–46, 304–6; electromagnetic pulse (EMP), 56; in fundamentalist terrorism, 9, 71, 75; impact of technological advances on, 29; impact on the Mossad's scope, 24; intelligence cooperation in addressing, 27–28, 45–46, 306–7; Iranian development of, xiv, 106–8, 123–24; in the Iran-Iraq War, iv, 106; Iraqi development of, 28–29, 309–12; Israeli prevention doctrine, 306–8; Israeli resources used to fight, 28–29; preemption component in, 45–46; quantum communication as response to, 57; Shavit's predictions on, 3; threatening global stability, 27–28; variables in, 56t. *See also* biological weapons; chemical weapons; cyber warfare; nuclear weapons
North Africa, 17, 72
northern triangle alliance, 28, 86–87, 129, 334
North Korea, 29, 104, 113–14, 120, 214
NSA (National Security Agency), 57–61
nuclear power reactors: cyber threats to, 55–56; Operation Tamuz, 123, 308, 309
nuclear weapons: addressed by Forum 2000 team, 12–13; during the Cold War era, xviii, 125; "day after" scenarios, 122–23; deterrence, xviii, 54–56, 56t, 109–11; EEIs focusing on, 49–50; in fundamentalist terrorism, 71; Indian capabilities, xviii, 49–50; Iranian development of, 8, 106–8, 123–24; Iranian nuclear agreement (2015), 103–6, 114, 117–18, 119–20, 123, 327; Iranian threat, xviii, 8, 12–13, 104,

nuclear weapons (*cont.*)
111–12, 124–25; Iraqi capabilities,
3, 28–29, 304–5, 309–12; Israeli
red line conditions, 120–23; Mossad's role in prevention, 26;
Obama administration policy on,
97–98, 102–6, 109, 117, 123;
Operation Tamuz, 123, 308, 309;
options for addressing Iranian
threat, 118–21; Pakistani capabilities, xviii, 8, 49–50, 102–3;
postnuclear issues, 109–11;
Russian responses to, 97–98,
117–18; safeguards against use of,
xviii, 111–12; Shavit's predictions
on, 3; variables in, 56t; "X-Force
Experiment," 55–56

Obama, Barack, 163; on the 2002 Saudi
Initiative, 219; compared to
Trump, 233; and Egypt's revolution, 165; engagement strategy of,
101, 119, 122; Iranian nuclear
agreement, 103–6, 117–18, 123;
meeting with Putin, 117; Middle
East policy priorities, 101–2,
104–5, 109, 117, 119, 213–14;
response to Russian cyberattack,
132; and the Snowden affair, 60;
on technology dilemmas, 59
OECD (Organisation for Economic
Co-operation and Development),
209–10
oil and energy resources: addressed by
Forum 2000 team, 11; global consumption, 11; importance to
fundamentalism, 64–65; in Iran,
92, 94, 115, 321; in Iraq, 303; in
Oman, 195; in Saudi Arabia, 223;
the shah's reforms targeting, 94;
Soviet Union's coercive policy, 115;
US dependency on, 270; during
the Yom Kippur War, 294

Olmert, Ehud, 207, 209, 320
Oman, Sultanate of, 195–97
Operation Diamond, 43, 334
Operation Tamuz, 123, 308, 309
organized crime groups, 25, 47–48, 54
Oron, Yitzhak, 276
OSINT (open source intelligence), 30,
54, 136, 146, 161
Osirak nuclear reactor, 28–29, 123,
308, 309
Oslo Accords: failure of, 215; impact on
Jordanian peace negotiations, 176,
181, 182; between Israel and the
PLO, xiv, 5; protests over, 174;
Rabin's work toward, 174–77;
secrecy surrounding, 157, 174–75;
signing of, xiv, 176, 181. *See also*
Israeli-Palestinian conflict
Ostrovsky, Victor, 155
Ottoman Empire, 69

Pahlavi, Muhammad Reza (shah of
Iran), 92–94, 96
Pahlavi dynasty (Iran), 90, 92, 94
Pakistan: and the A. Q. Khan boys, 109;
assisting Arab states in nonconventional areas, 8, 29, 309; in the
Baghdad Pact, 94; in Israeli circles
of conflict, 17; nuclear capabilities
of, xviii, 8, 102–3, 340; in the RCD
pact, 94; relations with India, xviii,
49–50, 102–3, 111, 214; relations
with Iran, 8, 49–50; relations with
Iraq, 309; as threat to Israel, 8,
102; US focus on, 101, 102, 104
Palestine (proposed state), 232–33
Palestine Liberation Organization
(PLO): opposition to Egypt-Israel
peace agreement, 224; in the Oslo
Accords, xiv, 5, 175; receiving UN
observer status, xiii; on refugeehood claims, 269; Shavit's
predictions on, 3

return blocking resolution, 207–8, 235, 237–38, 245, 269–71, 273; stages of during War of Independence, 240–44; as subjects of the British Mandate, 238; UNRWA malpractice, 265–66; used as pawns by Arabs, 265–66; US positions on, 245–50, 265–66. *See also* Israeli-Palestinian conflict; UNRWA

research and assessment: annual intelligence assessment, 137–38; establishment of Mossad's division, 6–7, 143–45; establishment of Shin Bet's department, 6; impact of the Agranat Commission on, 6–7, 34–35, 140–44, 305–6; initial agency responsibilities for, 134–37; interagency sharing of, 44–45, 48–50; on the Jordanian-Israeli peace process, 186–87; MI's department prior to Yom Kippur War, 277–78; in the Mossad's mission, 11; Mossad's strategic team, 5–7; political net assessments, 10; prior to Yom Kippur War, 278–81, 296–301

resettlement (refugees): definition of Palestinian refugeehood opposing, 269–70; of First World War refugees, 235–36; options following Sinai Campaign, 254; as refugee solution, 246–47; of Second World War refugees, 236–37; UN responsibility for, 261–62

response-based strategies, 78–80

revolutionary processes, 160–67

Reza Shah (shah of Iran), 92, 94

"right of return" (Palestinian refugees): Arab "all or nothing" position, 207–8, 237–38, 249–50, 269–70, 271, 273–74; in Bernadotte's UN report, 245–46; Israeli concessions on, 271; as Israeli red line, 207–8; principle of, 237–39; in UN Resolution 194, 218, 220, 246, 263, 271, 273

Rosh Hashanah, 199

Rubinstein, Elyakim, 183, 315

Rudaki (Iranian poet), 91

Rushdie, Salman, 202

Rusk, Dean, 152

Russia: curbing nonconventional proliferation, 306; cyberattacks of, 132; desired recognition as world power, 97–98, 116–18, 233–34; famine following civil war, 236; fighting ISIS, 230; and the Iranian nuclear threat, 97–98, 119, 120; and the Israeli-Palestinian conflict, 216–17; Jewish immigration from, 258; in a new Middle East model, 232, 233–34; and North Korea, 114; during Obama administration, 104; relations with Iran, 115–18, 122; and the Snowden affair, 58; in Syria, 213, 230, 233–34, 328; territory lost following Cold War, 116. *See also* Soviet Union

sabotage (prevention tactic), 161, 308–9

Sadat, Anwar: appointed president, 304; assassination of, 202; expelling Soviet presence, 292; intentions of war, 18, 290–91; Marwan as aide to, 279; meetings with Brezhnev, 293; peace treaty with Israel, 304; policy planning memorandum, 283–84; pressure to carry out military action, 288; strategic goal of, 281–82, 291, 308; war preparations of, 286–88, 292–95

recruited to the Mossad, 354–55; relationship with King Hussein, xvi, 180, 315, 353–54; relationship with Shavit, xii–xiii, 351, 352–53

Shanghai, 190–91

Shapira, Haim Moshe, 254

Sharett, Moshe, 247, 250–51

sharia (Islamic law): in Algeria, 164; in the Arab-Israeli conflict, 19; and global terrorism, 19, 68; in Iran, 96, 162, 321; and the Muslim Brotherhood, xvii, 166

Sharon, Ariel, xiv, 130, 323–24

Shavit, Shabtai: achievements of, 36; appointed deputy director, 39; appointed Mossad director, vii, xi–xiii, 351–52; as CEO of Maccabi Healthcare Services, 198; as deputy director, 2, 36–37, 46; events during tenure as director, vii–viii, xiii–xix; as head of Kurdistan mission, 275; as head of the Operations Directorate, 6–7, 276, 278–81; retiring as director of the Mossad, 170–71; studying abroad in US, 39–41, 49; studying at the Hebrew University, 29; vacation to US, 37–39; as vice-director, 2; work plan of, 3

Shavit, Yael: post in Iran, 37, 86, 87; relationship with the Evrons, 335; relationship with the Rabins, 171; during Shavit's appointment ceremony, xii; in the US, 37–41; Yom Kippur War beginning, 279

Sheves, Shimon, 192

Shia (Shiite) Islam: and al-Qaeda, 69; concept of war in, 321, 326; duty of prudence (Taqiya) in, 95; fundamentalism in, xvi, 64, 201; in Iran, 91, 93, 108, 109, 162, 321; in Iraq,

108, 109; jihad concept in, xvi, 124; in Lebanon, 321–22; Shiite Crescent, 230, 322

Shihab 3 missile, 107

Shiite Crescent, 230, 322

Shiloah, Reuven, vii

Shin Bet, the: areas of responsibility, 26, 134–35; establishment of research department in, 6; hierarchy of, 133; impact of Yom Kippur War on, 6; insights on global terrorism from, 76–77; during the Jordanian peace negotiations, 186; on the Varash forum, xii

Shomron, Dan, xi

SIGINT (signals intelligence), 43, 136, 309, 333

Siman-Tov, Benjamin, 34–35

Sinai: ISIS in, 224; during the Six-Day War, 130; during the Yom Kippur War, 291

Sinai Campaign (1956), 127, 252–62; Ben-Gurion's Gaza issue proposals, 256–61; Britain in, 252, 257, 271–72; ending of, 252; France in, 252, 257, 271–72; goals of, 252; Israeli initiatives in Gaza following, 254–55; Israeli withdrawal from Sinai, 252–53; refugees created by, 252–53, 258–59, 261–62; US opposition to, 252, 271–72

Singapore, 192, 195

Sisi, Abdel Fattah el-, 166–67

Six-Day War (1967), 127; Golan Heights captured during, 130, 322; impact of intelligence, 334; impact on strategic depth, 130; refugee problem addressed following, 266–68, 272

Snowden, Edward, 57–60, 159, 160

social networks, 149, 160–61, 163–67

sources (intelligence): in the early days, 135–37; in friendly agency information sharing, 44; in the HUMINT system, 20, 333, 339; MI's assessments of, 135–37; MI's knowledge of, 277; principle of protecting identities of, 32–33, 44, 156–57; prior to the Yom Kippur War, 278–79. *See also* HUMINT (human intelligence)

South America, 46–48

southern triangle alliance, 28, 86, 129

South Korea, 114, 214

Soviet Union: during the Cold War, xvii–xviii, 18–19, 42, 52–54, 87; collapse of, vii, xiii, xvii, xviii, 4, 101, 312; cyber capabilities, 52–54; détente, 284–85; expelled from Egypt, 213, 283, 292; following World War II, xvii–xviii, 94; immigration of Jews from, xiii; impact of refugee problem on, 247; impact on global stability, xviii, 101; impending collapse of, 49; invasion of Afghanistan, 115; Mossad-CIA briefings on, 49, 50; operations security and secrecy in, 18–19; relations with Iran, 94, 115–18; relations with Iraq, 87, 302, 303, 310; relations with Israel, 42; relations with US, 42; during the Sinai Campaign, 252, 271; supplying weapons to Egypt, 283, 286, 288–89, 292–93; supplying weapons to Iraq, 87, 310; supplying weapons to Syria, 287, 289, 292–93; in Syria, 213, 230, 293, 328; during the Yom Kippur War, 282, 283–86, 288, 290, 292–94. *See also* Cold War; Russia

space and satellite era, 130

speech, freedom of. *See* freedom of speech

Stalin, Joseph, 115

"State Intelligence Assessment, The" (report), 141–42

state sponsors of terrorism, 71–72, 77, 79, 83–84, 204

Stephenson, Sir William, 150

Stewart, Potter, 157–58

Straits of Bab al-Mandeb, 294

strategic depth: in the cyber age, 131–32; impact of the Six-Day War on, 130; and moving the war into enemy territory principle, 128; relevance to deterrence, 133; in satellite era, 130

Stravinsky, Igor, 236

submarines, 107, 131, 197

Sudan: bin Laden supported by, 71; fundamentalist groups in, 66; in Israeli circles of conflict, 17; revolutionary processes in, 167; in the southern triangle, 28, 86

Suez Canal, 252, 253, 279, 282, 288, 298–300, 307

Suharto (Indonesian president), 190, 191, 193–95

suicide, xvi, 63, 70–71, 211

Sukarno (Indonesian president), 191

Sunni Islam, xvi, 72, 91, 201

"Sunnistan" (proposed state), 232, 234

Sykes-Picot Agreement (1916), 322

Syria: addressed by Forum 2000 team, 12; armistice agreement with Israel, 127, 129; "Black September" (1970), 185; civil war in, 328; during the First Gulf War, xv; following the Second Lebanon War, 327, 328; fundamentalist groups in, 66, 72, 322–23, 328; instability in, 72; Iranian presence in, 108, 320; in Israeli circles of conflict, 17; on the Israeli EEI, 304–6; Israeli Golan Heights warning device operation, 52, 356n3; mili-